Earth Observation for Water Resources Management

Earth Observation for Water Resources Management

Current Use and Future Opportunities for the Water Sector

Luis E. García
Diego J. Rodríguez
Marcus Wijnen
Inge Pakulski

Editors

CONTENTS

TABLES

FIGURES

Foreword

Water lies at the heart of economic and social development and is thus a critical factor in poverty reduction. Growing economies and populations require better water management to keep up with the demand for energy and food and to ensure access to safe water and adequate sanitation. Twenty-first-century growth requires modern tools to help countries to understand their water challenges, risks, and options.

The World Economic Forum's *2015 Global Risks* report ranks water crises as the most serious societal risk facing the world, given the impacts associated with water scarcity and overuse. If countries do not manage their endowments well—through improved water infrastructure and water management—they will not be prepared for the complex challenges of the twenty-first century, will experience less economic growth, and may lose significant development gains made over the past decades.

While there is a broad consensus about the benefits of good water management, putting that knowledge into practice is usually easier said than done. To be able to make good water decisions, countries need systematic ways to measure and monitor changes in water availability. They need an accurate account of their current resources—where, when, and how much—as well as an illustration of the potential changes caused by seasonal, natural, and climate-induced variability, from rainfall and runoff to evaporation and transpiration. In light of the harsh realities of climate change, this information is needed in larger quantities over broader areas and longer time periods than ever before.

Ground-based (in situ) observation networks are fundamental but, in some cases, provide infrequent or sparse information over small areas and at a high cost. Particularly in developing countries, such hydrometeorological networks have deteriorated over time, at present providing only limited information for managing compound problems. Undoubtedly, developing countries need innovative ways to get more information in an accurate, timely, and usable format that builds on their existing infrastructure for monitoring water resources.

To compensate for the current information gap, the World Bank Group's Water Global Practice has pulled together knowledge on innovative technologies, such as viewing water from a distance, mainly through satellite platforms, to help countries measure and monitor their water resources better. Remote sensing enables coverage over large areas and spans of time without heavy field personnel requirements, and its accessibility, reliability, and accuracy have improved dramatically in recent years. While both in situ and remote sensing measurements are subject to specific limitations, researchers have developed techniques that can combine or correlate data from both methods to benefit each other's strengths. Understanding the potential combinations of available options has been a challenge for many practitioners. For this reason, *Earth Observation for Water Resources Management: Current Use and Future Opportunities for the Water Sector* aims to shed light on the strengths and limitations of remote sensing in order to help specialists to provide decision makers with fast and reliable information.

This publication reflects experiences of more than 40 World Bank Group project leaders and more than 20 international experts representing space agencies, government organizations, and universities from Africa, Asia, Europe, South America, and the United States. It also integrates a report by the University of Arizona, Tucson, which was commissioned for this purpose, and another one co-funded with Australia's national science agency, the Commonwealth Scientific and Industrial Research Organisation. We hope that the wealth of knowledge presented in this publication will be useful for many development practitioners around the world who are seeking practical answers to challenging technical questions about water and will help them to benefit from the enormous capabilities of the new tools that are now available.

Jennifer Sara
Senior Director a.i.
Water Global Practice
The World Bank Group

Acknowledgments

This publication is the result of a collaborative effort involving the World Bank, the Commonwealth Scientific and Industrial Research Organisation (CSIRO), and the University of Arizona. The publication was edited by a core team comprising World Bank consultants and staff members Luis E. García, Diego J. Rodríguez, Marcus Wijnen, and Inge Pakulski.

The editors are especially thankful to peer reviewers Anna Burzykowska, Bekele Debele, Claire Kfouri, Xiaokai Li, and Zhongbo (Bob) Su, who provided valuable guidance and suggestions during the production stage. Special thanks go to professor Fernando Miralles-Wilhelm and Raúl Muñoz from the University of Maryland as well as to Matthijs Schuring and Macha Kemperman from the World Bank, who provided valuable guidance and suggestions.

This publication involved many experts, researchers, and practitioners from both inside and outside the World Bank. The editors and primary authors of parts I, II, and II of the book would like to thank all of them for sharing their experience and knowledge. Their collaboration is gratefully acknowledged.

The primary authors of part I are Aleix Serrat-Capdevila (University of Arizona), Danielle A. García Ramírez (World Bank), and Noosha Tayebi (World Bank). The contributors are World Bank staff Thadeu Abicalil, Sara Elizabeth Anthos, Timothy A. Bouley, Anna Burzykowska, Rita Cestti, Alisha Chaudhary, Xavier Chauvot de Beauchéne, Louise Croneborg, Bekele Debele, Erwin De Nys, Indira Ekanayake, Erick Fernández, Eric Foster-Moore, Maria Josefina Gabitan, Anju Gaur, Andrew Goodland, Nagaraja Rao Harshadeep, Valerie Hickey, Rafik Hirji, Kremena M. Ionkova, Claire Kfouri, Johannes Kiess, Andrey V. Kushlin, Christina Leb, Qun Li, Dhalia Lotayef, Katie L. McWilliams, Hrishi Patel, Claudia Sadoff, Keiko Saito, Susanne Schelerling, Ahmed Shawky, Rebeca Soares, Pieter Waalewijn, Marcus Wishart, and Winston Yu, as well as David Toll from the National Aeronautics and Space Administration (NASA).

The primary authors of part II are Juan P. Guerschman, Randall J. Donohue, Tom G. Van Niel, Luigi J. Renzullo, Arnold G. Dekker, Tim J. Malthus, and Tim R. McVicar, from CSIRO; and Albert I. J. M. Van Dijk, from

CSIRO and Australian National University. The Water Partnership Program of the Water Global Practice, World Bank Group, in collaboration with the Netherlands Space Office (NSO) and CSIRO, organized a specialist review workshop titled "Understanding Water through Space," which was held in The Hague, the Netherlands, from April 29 to May 2, 2014. In the wake of this workshop, the following international experts provided the production team with excellent feedback and suggestions: Wim Bastiaanssen (UNESCO, Institute for Water Education); Richard de Jeu (Vrije Universiteit Amsterdam); Brad Doorn (NASA); Steven Greb (Group on Earth Observations and Wisconsin Department of Natural Resources); Job Kleijn and Raimond Hafkenscheid (Directorate-General for International Cooperation, the Netherlands); Benjamin Koetz (European Space Agency); Xin Li and Wu Bingfang (Chinese Academy of Sciences); Paida Mangara (Satellite Earth Observation and Disaster Risks); Massimo Menenti (Technical University Delft); Fernando Miralles (University of Maryland); Mark Noort (HCP International); Morris Scherer-Warren (Agência Nacional de Águas); Aleix Serrat-Capdevila (University of Arizona); Soroosh Sorooshian (University of California, Irvine); Zhongbo (Bob) Su (Faculty of Geo-Information Science and Earth Observation, University of Twente); Michael van der Valk (Hydrology.nl); Jasper van Loon, Joost Carpay, and Ruud Grim (Netherlands Space Office); Niels Vlaanderen (Netherlands Ministry of Infrastructure and the Environment); and Brian Wardlow (University of Nebraska, Lincoln).

The primary authors of part III are Eleonora M. C. Demaria (University of Arizona) and Aleix Serrat-Capdevila (University of Arizona). This part of the publication is the product of a follow-up to the workshop "Understanding Water through Space." The workshop participants provided valuable and inspiring ideas that informed part III of this publication.

This publication was made possible by the financial contribution of the Water Partnership Program (see http://water.Worldbank.org/water/wpp) of the Water Global Practice, World Bank Group. The production of part II was funded jointly by the World Bank's Water Partnership Program and CSIRO. Within CSIRO, funding was provided by the Land and Water Flagship and by the Earth Observation and Informatics Future Science Platform.

This publication was produced under the direction of Jennifer Sara (senior director a.i., Water Global Practice), Junaid Kamal Ahmad (former senior director, Water Global Practice); William Rex (lead water resources specialist, Water Global Practice); Julia Bucknall (former manager, Water Anchor); and Marie-Chantall Uwanyiligira (practice manager, Water Global Practice).

This publication is a product of Water Partnership Program's Global Initiative on Remote Sensing for Water Resources Management (Water from Space).

Preface

BACKGROUND

A Global Initiative on Remote Sensing for Water Resources Management was launched in October 2013, financed by the World Bank's Water Partnership Program of the Water Global Practice. The initiative supports Bank project teams through (a) case studies and pilot projects in selected countries to serve as the basis for the development of approaches and procedures that can be replicated in other countries facing similar challenges; (b) targeted, short interventions of world-class experts aimed at advising and providing orientation on specific problems related to Bank investment operations; and (c) knowledge dissemination, as well as advocacy and capacity-building activities, in partnership with leading global and regional remote sensing and capacity-building organizations.

This publication is one product of that initiative, which seeks to improve the quality and effectiveness of water resources management, planning, and project design by developing and disseminating, in collaboration with the Bank's operational staff and task team leaders, a clear picture of the remote sensing (RS) products available today—how they are generated, what specific water problems and situations they can be applied to, their potential strengths and limitations, how better results could be obtained by using them jointly with in situ measurements, and how they can be validated and evaluated to inform the client better and enhance the Bank's water-related operations.

The use of remote sensing for hydrology and water resources operational purposes, while not new, is a fast-growing field. The term "operational" has many definitions and may be viewed from different perspectives. In this context, however, the term refers not to the degree of readiness of the system to be used, but rather to the usability of products generated by that system. In other words, the focus of attention is not the system itself or the products it generates but rather the accuracy, reliability, and validity of the system products that will be used to make a decision (or alter a past decision). This decision may be about the planning, design, and monitoring or operation of any given institutional or physical system. It could pertain, for instance, to the selection of crops, the operation of field irrigation systems, or the design of a hydraulic infrastructure such as a reservoir.

The scope of this publication is limited to the water resources sector and, within that sector, to the RS estimation of key variables that form the basis of the planning, design, and operation of all water resources programs and projects—precipitation, evapotranspiration, soil moisture, vegetation and vegetation cover, groundwater, surface water, snow cover, and water quality.

The RS field is changing rapidly, and this review cannot claim to present more than a picture of the current state of the art. Nevertheless, this picture is a much-needed tool for practitioners who have to make operational decisions.

CONTENT

In discussing the role of Earth observation (EO) in water resources management, this publication goes from the general to the particular, adding more detail at each level. (The terms "remote sensing" and "Earth observation" are used interchangeably in this publication.) As a framework highlighting *why* EO needs to be considered in water-related activities, it first gives a broad overview of the major global challenges for water resources that exist today, outlines the role that remote sensing can play in tackling these challenges, and examines the significance of water-related projects in the Bank's portfolio and the context in which remote sensing has been used to date in World Bank initiatives. To give insight into *what* EO can do to support operational decision making in water-related projects, the publication continues with a more in-depth discussion of the RS products available today—how they are generated, what specific water problems and situations they can be applied to, their potential strengths and limitations, and how they can be validated and "ground-truthed," to inform the client better and to enhance water-related operations. Finally, as a *how-to* guide, it

presents practical guidelines for determining (a) whether the use of EO products could be worthwhile in a specific situation and (b) how results could be improved by using them in combination with in situ measurements.

PART I. WATER AND EARTH OBSERVATIONS IN THE WORLD BANK

Chapter 1 looks briefly at some challenges to global water resources that are posed by population growth, urbanization, poverty, and other problems currently facing many countries. It also discusses possible solutions to these challenges, facilitated by the use of remote sensing, in combination with and in support of in situ measurements (this mix being especially significant when data are scarce).

Chapter 2 reviews some of the instruments that the World Bank uses to help its client countries cope with these water challenges: the Bank's water policy and strategy, its Water Global Practice, and the characteristics of its lending and technical assistance portfolios.

Chapter 3 provides an overview of the present use of RS in the Bank's water-related activities, including existing programs that Bank staff can tap to obtain specialized assistance for RS applications and products. Chapter 4 discusses ground measurements and RS observations, their respective strengths and limitations, and the current state and future of operational hydrology.

PART II. EARTH OBSERVATION FOR WATER RESOURCES MANAGEMENT

Chapter 5 takes the results reported in part I and summarizes the main global water issues addressed by the World Bank—as reflected in its portfolio—and connects them to a particular set of topics and subtopics defined by the Water Partnership Program, which is part of the Bank's Water Global Practice. This facilitates the identification of EO sensors to use, often in combination with field measurement and modeling.

Chapter 6 describes eight (hydrometeorological) variables of key relevance to water resources management that can be estimated with remote sensing: precipitation, evapotranspiration, soil moisture, vegetation and land use and land cover, groundwater, surface water, snow and ice cover, and water quality, as previously stated. It also includes a brief summary of the theoretical basis for estimating these variables through Earth observation, a list of the current and near-future sensors that can provide such information, and, where appropriate, a description of existing data products that are generated on a regular basis.

Chapter 7 provides a series of guidelines that project team leaders can use to decide whether EO may be useful and, if so, which data sources are the most suitable to consider. It also provides a simple decision-making framework that helps to determine, for a given problem, how EO products might best be used to generate the required information and how the EO data products with the most appropriate specifications should be selected. Moreover, for each water resources application, information is presented about accuracy, availability, maturity, complexity, and reliability.

PART III. VALIDATION OF REMOTE SENSING–ESTIMATED HYDROMETEOROLOGICAL VARIABLES

Part III complements part II and is structured around four chapters. Chapter 8 discusses the challenges inherent in the validation of RS estimations of hydrometeorological variables and explains the methodological approach followed for the validation exercise. Chapter 9 reports the results of a literature review of validations of estimated precipitation, evapotranspiration, soil moisture, snow cover, and

surface water. Chapter 10 reviews the validation of streamflow outputs from models using RS data as inputs. Chapter 11 summarizes the results of this review.

PART IV. CONCLUDING REMARKS

Part IV summarizes the main conclusions and recommendations regarding the role of water in development and the great potential of RS for improving water resources management, the main challenges faced when applying it in this field, and a word of caution for its sensible use. It also reviews the main elements to consider when deciding whether to use RS in water-related operations and briefly explains how the use of RS in water resources management could be enhanced through international cooperation, ultimately benefiting developing countries.

Appendix A provides two examples of the use of EO applications in World Bank projects. Appendix B provides some notable examples of systems that use Earth observation, typically in combination with ground data and modeling, to produce information on water resources.

AUDIENCE

The audience for this book includes the client countries' national water resources organizations, policy makers, and institutions dealing with the water resources sector, as well as World Bank country directors, sector managers, and task team leaders. This publication will not be equally relevant to all of its readers and some may prefer to skip certain parts. For example, policy makers in client countries or at the Bank may be interested primarily in the discussion about the potential value of using RS for key water-related issues and its importance and relevance for the Bank portfolio. Task team leaders may be interested primarily in existing programs that they can tap to obtain specialized assistance for RS applications and products, which are described in part I. Technically oriented professionals may be especially interested in the technical explanation of how RS data products relevant to water resources monitoring are derived from images obtained by satellite platforms, which is provided in part II. At the operational level, task team leaders as well as other practitioners may be interested in the decision framework presented in chapter 7 to help them to determine, for a given problem, how to use EO products to generate the required information and how to select the most suitable EO data products for their needs.

Everybody may be interested in perusing the examples and references presented throughout the publication and in the discussion of the validity of satellite-derived values for key hydrometeorological variables (presented in part III). A big effort has been made to integrate the publication's technical and operational content in a coherent way, in the hope that this approach will offer every reader something useful in their daily work.

About the Editors and Authors

EDITORS

Luis E. García is a senior hydrology and water resources consultant in the Global Water Practice of the World Bank Group. He participates in the Water Partnership Program initiatives for the operational use of remote sensing (RS) products in water projects and in the Water Expert Team. He is a civil engineer from San Carlos University in Guatemala, with an MS in hydrology and water quality from the University of California, Berkeley, and a PhD in hydrology and water resources planning from Colorado State University, Fort Collins. He has more than 30 years of experience working in water resources and watershed management, hydrology, water quality, and applied remote sensing. Prior to consulting for the Bank, he worked for 15 years at the Inter-American Development Bank (IDB) in 26 Latin American and Caribbean countries. He was principal water resources specialist at the IDB and team leader for development of the IDB's integrated water resources management strategy. He has consulted for CONAGUA (Mexico); Panama Canal Authority, Ministry of Environment and Energy of Costa Rica; Pan American Health Organization; World Health Organization; U.S. Agency for International Development (USAID); United Nations Educational, Scientific, and Cultural Organization (UNESCO); World Meteorological Organization; United Nations Environment Programme (UNEP); United Nations Development Programme; and IDB; as well as for firms from Denmark, Germany, Guatemala, Switzerland, and the United States.

Diego J. Rodríguez is a senior economist at the Water Global Practice of the World Bank Group. He is the task team leader of World Bank initiatives that quantify the trade-offs of the energy-water nexus (Thirsty Energy), the decision tree framework for confronting uncertainty in water resources planning, and the implementation of integrated urban water management. He is also program manager of the Water Partnership Program, where he provides support to operational teams on the use of economic analysis in large water infrastructure investments. Prior to joining the World Bank, he worked at the Danish Hydraulic Institute and the IDB. He has more than 20 years of experience in sectoral, operational, policy, and strategy development in water supply, sanitation, and water resources management. He holds a BS in economics from the University of Maryland, an MA in applied economics from Virginia Tech, and a PhD in economics (water) from University of Groningen.

Marcus Wijnen is a senior water resources management specialist in the Water Global Practice of the World Bank Group. He is the task team leader of the Water Expert Team, which provides high-level technical support to World Bank operational teams in the water sector. He provides a focal point on groundwater for the Water Global Practice and provides technical support to operational teams working on strategic groundwater engagements. Prior to joining the World Bank, he was a project leader for international consultancies and regional manager for Asia and the Middle East at the French Geological Survey (Bureau de Recherches Géologiques et Minières). For more than 25 years, he has worked across the globe on water resources management challenges at the local, national, and transboundary scale, employing a wide range of Earth observation methodologies in the areas of surface water quality monitoring, hydrogeological exploration, urban water use planning, and assessment of agricultural water use.

Inge Pakulski is an economist and senior editor specializing in development economics and environmental studies. In her early career, she worked for private- and public-sector entities in the Netherlands in the field of development cooperation and information technology. In recent years, she has worked almost exclusively as an editor, and mainly on development issues—water resources management, carbon emissions trading, public sector policies, and transport. She has edited numerous reports and studies for the World Bank, the IDB, and development nongovernmental organizations. She is a Dutch national and edits texts in Dutch, English, and Spanish. She also speaks French, Polish, and Portuguese. She holds an MA in economics from Erasmus University Rotterdam.

AUTHORS, PARTS I AND III

Aleix Serrat-Capdevila is a research associate professor at the Department of Hydrology and Water Resources, University of Arizona. He is also a member of the International Center for Integrated Water Resources Management (ICIWaRM), UNESCO, and of the National Aeronautics and Space Administration (NASA) and USAID SERVIR Applied Sciences Team. Before obtaining his MA and PhD at the University of Arizona, he worked in Africa, Southeast Asia, and Spain across public, private, and nongovernmental organization sectors, including for a year as a water and sanitation engineer in refugee camps and neighboring villages in Guinea-Conakry (West Africa). His work focuses on bridging the gap between scientific research and the transfer of new findings and applications toward real-world water management challenges. His main interests include participatory planning and management approaches; the impacts of climate change on regional water budgets and adaptation strategies; how to handle uncertainty and inform human adaptation; water policy; and the use of satellite precipitation products and other RS data for water monitoring and forecasting in poorly gauged basins. His main projects focus on the use of RS data for hydrologic applications to support water-related decision making, mostly in African basins. In addition to the World Bank, he also collaborates with organizations such as the Institute of Water Resources (U.S. Army Corps of Engineers), the G-WADI Program (UNESCO), the Southwest Climate Science Center (U.S. Geological Survey), the National Science Foundation, and the Alliance for Global Water Adaptation. He recently received the Commander's Award for Civilian Service for his "key role in helping ICIWaRM fulfill its mission in service of UNESCO and the United States (2009–2014)."

Danielle A. García Ramírez is a program analyst at the Global Programs Unit in the Water Global Practice of the World Bank. She has more than five years of experience working on water and sustainable development at the international level. In the past four years, she has been a member of the core program management team of the World Bank's Water Partnership Program (WPP), a multidonor trust fund that aims to improve water resources management and climate resilience in Bank operations. She also supports the WPP-funded initiatives Water from Space and Resilient Water Decisions. She holds an MSc in political economy from the University of Essex (U.K.) and specializes in quantitative methods, international development, and water management policy.

Noosha Tayebi is an RS and disaster risk management specialist for the World Bank's Water Global Practice. Her main expertise is in translating projects' operational and information requirements into technical specifications for customized Earth observation products. Prior to joining the World Bank, she worked for five years in research and development for the government of Canada on RS and geospatial applications using satellite data at Defence Research and Development Canada and in a private firm providing software engineering services to the Department of National Defence on advanced sensor integration and data visualization. She holds a BS in electrical engineering and an MS in systems science and operational research from the University of Ottawa, Canada.

Eleonora Demaria is a research hydrologist-meteorologist at the U.S. Department of Agriculture's Agricultural Research Service and a research associate at the University of Arizona, both in Tucson. An Earth scientist, she studies the interactions between land surface and atmosphere to assess the vulnerability of human and natural systems to weather and climate events. Her main research interests are the impacts of climate change on extreme precipitation and streamflow events, the role of atmospheric rivers on flooding events, and how to improve the usefulness of satellite-estimated precipitation for hydrologic purposes in developing countries. She has a BS in water resources engineering from the Universidad Nacional del Litoral in Argentina, an MS in meteorology from the University of Utah, and a PhD in hydrology from the University of Arizona. She specializes in improving hydrologic forecasting and monitoring systems using satellite precipitation estimates in flood-prone regions of South America and Africa where ground observations are sparse. She has worked at the Centro de Cambio Global at the Pontificia Universidad Católica de Chile as a research associate, where she studied the impacts of climate change on Alpine basins, and as a fellow at the Northeast Climate Science Center of the University of Massachusetts, where she focused on understanding how streamflow extremes and snow cover in the northeastern and upper midwestern United States are affected by projected climatic changes. She has also worked with the UNEP to empower Kenyan women by harvesting rainwater for their water supply.

AUTHORS, PART II

Juan Pablo Guerschman is a senior research scientist with Commonwealth Scientific and Industrial Research Organisation (CSIRO) Land and Water. He joined CSIRO in 2005, after receiving a PhD in agricultural sciences from the University of Buenos Aires (Argentina). In his first years at CSIRO, his research focused on the calibration and application of a regional carbon cycle model and the integration of remote sensing and ground-based observations through model-data assimilation for the analysis of carbon dynamics of tropical savannas. From 2007 onward, he has been a project researcher and then research scientist with the Model-Data Integration Team of the Environmental Earth Observation Program. He has played a leading role in developing and evaluating methods for using satellite observations in hydrological and land management applications. Between 2009 and 2012, he led part of the research portfolio of the Water Information Research and Development Alliance between the Bureau of Meteorology and CSIRO Water for a Healthy Country Flagship dealing with RS of land cover and landscape water and using this information to inform the Australian Water Resources and Assessment System. He has been developing algorithms for estimating vegetation cover from remotely sensed data across rangelands and croplands and applying these estimates to deliver timely information for better management of these environments.

Randall J. Donohue is a research scientist with CSIRO in the areas of ecohydrology, RS, and environmental physics, focusing on the dynamics of vegetation function under a changing climate. He has a joint PhD from Australian National University and CSIRO. His research focuses on understanding the changing interactions between vegetation, climate, carbon, and water, using RS as a primary input. He has developed frameworks for examining the role of vegetation dynamics in catchment hydrology and landscape carbon dynamics and for better understanding the impacts of elevated carbon dioxide on vegetation functioning.

Tom G. Van Niel is a scientist with CSIRO interested in spatial and temporal modeling of vegetation, water, climate, and surface radiation and heat processes. Recently he has been modeling evaporation over all of Australia based on meteorological data and thermal RS observations. He focuses on (a) improving the spatial and temporal representation of surface interactions, such as vegetation and water, through statistical and mathematical modeling; (b) spatiotemporal analysis of climate variability; and (c) improved estimation of surface radiation budget and water-heat balance through terrain analysis.

Luigi J. Renzullo is a senior research scientist with CSIRO. He received his PhD in applied physics from Curtin University (Perth, Western Australia) and possesses extensive experience in (bio)physical modeling and RS data analysis. His research explores the role that Earth observations can play as inputs and constraints on biophysical models through techniques of model-data fusion and data assimilation. He directs current research efforts to develop satellite soil moisture information products that are better suited to agricultural production modeling than satellite-derived products alone. To this end, he works with university collaborators on methods to downscale coarse-resolution data and the observation operator for assimilating data into pasture growth models.

Arnold G. Dekker is a research scientist with CSIRO and director of the CSIRO Earth Observation and Informatics Future Science Platform. He holds a PhD in hyperspectral remote sensing of inland water quality from Vrjie Universiteit in Amsterdam. Before joining CSIRO, he developed innovative methods and applications using Earth observation for inland coastal water quality detection, monitoring, and management in Europe. At CSIRO, his scientific work focuses on physical processes at an aquatic ecosystem scale, suited for resource management or for integration into predictive and hindcasting models. He is an international and national leader in defining methods for operationalizing Earth observation of aquatic ecosystems. He has led major national and international research projects. He holds a dozen international positions influencing science, implementation, and operationalization of Earth observation for tackling societal benefit areas. He holds an adjunct professorship at the University of Queensland and is a member of the Australian Marine Science Association, the Australian Government Space Coordination Committee, and the Australian Earth Observation Coordinating Group. He co-represents Australia and CSIRO as part of the International Space Agencies' Committee on Earth Observation Satellites 2016 Chair Team and in water resources–related activities of the Group on Earth Observations. He is active in several United Nations task teams that are considering how to use Earth observation for the 2030 Sustainable Development Goals agenda.

Tim J. Malthus is research group leader of the Coastal Modelling and Sensing Group in the Coastal Management and Development Program of CSIRO's Oceans and Atmosphere Business Unit. He has a BS in zoology from the University of Otago (Dunedin, New Zealand) and more than 25 years of research experience in the remote sensing of inland water quality, underwater optics, field measurement, and algorithm development. He combines skills in calibration, validation, and field spectroscopy with analysis of airborne and satellite RS data to monitor environmental change and better inform wider environmental policies. He has a background in aquatic ecology, specifically in water quality of inland and coastal waters.

Tim R. McVicar is a research scientist at CSIRO with training in biophysical modeling, remote sensing, ecohydrology, and hydroclimatology, and holds a PhD in environmental science and remote sensing from the Australian National University. He is interested in developing parsimonious modeling frameworks that capitalize on the availability of long-term temporal data to understand retrospective processes, with a view to making prospective projections—based on enhanced

system understanding—and in the nexus of vegetation dynamics, catchment water balance, and climate change. He has led several international and national projects and currently serves as editor-in-chief of the *Journal of Hydrology* and associate editor of *Remote Sensing of Environment*. He seeks to understand processes and feedbacks, to rank them from primary to tertiary importance, and to identify those where landscape management can influence the process (directly or indirectly). He is committed to parsimonious biophysical modeling and analytical frameworks and occasionally quotes Dr. Frank Westheimer's (1912–2007) Law: "A few months in the laboratory can save a few hours in the library."

Albert I. J. M. Van Dijk is professor of water science and management at the Fenner School of Environment and Society in the Australian National University and adjunct science leader with CSIRO Land and Water. With a PhD from Vrije Universiteit, he has expertise in catchment hydrology, basin water management, drought processes, water resources monitoring and forecasting, and the combination of Earth observation, ground observation, and hydrological modeling. He led development of the Australian Water Resources Assessment system, a large observing and modeling system used operationally by Australia's Bureau of Meteorology. He has authored more than 130 articles in international journals.

Abbreviations

AAA	analytical and advisory activity
AASTR	Advanced Along Track Scanning Thermal Radiometer
ALOS	Advanced Land Observation Satellite
AMSR	Advanced Microwave Scanning Radiometer
ASACT	Advanced Scatterometer
ASAR	Advanced Synthetic Aperture Radar
ASIMUTH	Applied Simulation and Integrated Modelling for the Understanding of Toxic and Harmful Algal Blooms
AVHRR	Advanced Very High Resolution Radiometer
AWAP	Australian Water Availability Project
AwiFS	Advanced Wide Field Sensor
AWRA	Australian Water Resources Assessment
BEAM	Basin Economic Allocation Model
BGC	biogeochemical global climate
CC	correlation coefficient
CILSS	Permanent Inter-State Committee for Drought Control in the Sahel
CMAP	Climate Prediction Center Merged Analysis of Precipitation
CMORPH	Climate Prediction Center MORPHing technique
CNES	Centre National d'Etudes Spatiales
CSC	Climate Services Center
CSIRO	Commonwealth Scientific and Industrial Research Organisation
CV	coefficient of variation
DEM	digital elevation model
EMS	electromagnetic spectrum
ENTRO	Eastern Nile Technical Regional Office
EO	Earth observation
ERS	European Remote Sensing Satellite

ESA	European Space Agency
ET	evapotranspiration
EUMETSAT	European Organisation for the Exploitation of Meteorological Satellites
EVI	enhanced vegetation index
FAO	Food and Agriculture Organization of the United Nations
fPAR	fraction of absorbed photosynthetically active radiation
GCM	global climate model
GEMS	Global Environmental Monitoring System
GEO	Group on Earth Observations
GIS	geographic information system
GLDAS	Global Land Data Assimilation Systems
GNIP	Global Network of Isotopes in Precipitation
GOES	geostationary operational environmental satellite
GPCC	Global Precipitation Climatological Center
GPM	Global Precipitation Measurement
GRACE	Gravity Recovery and Climate Experiment
GRDC	Global Runoff Data Center
GSMaP	Global Satellite Mapping of Precipitation
GTN-H	Global Terrestrial Network–Hydrology
GW	groundwater
HEC-Ras	Hydrologic Engineering Centers River Analysis System
HH	horizontal transmit and horizontal receive
HIRS	High Resolution Infrared Radiation Sounder
HV	horizontal transmit and vertical receive
IBRD	International Bank for Reconstruction and Development
ICIWaRM	International Center for Integrated Water Resources Management
ICPAC	Climate Prediction and Application Centre
IDA	International Development Association
IGAD	Intergovernmental Authority on Development
IGRAC	International Groundwater Resources Assessment Center
IMERG	Integrated Multisatellite Retrievals for GPM [Global Precipitation Measurement]
IPWG	International Precipitation Working Group
ISMN	International Soil Moisture Network
JAXA	Japan Aerospace Exploration Agency
JERS-1	Japanese Earth Resources Satellite 1
KGE	Kling-Gupta efficiency
LAI	leaf area index
LiDAR	Laser Imaging, Detection, and Ranging
LSWI	land surface water index
MERIS	Medium Resolution Imaging Spectrometer
MODIS	Moderate Resolution Imaging Spectrometer
MRE	Micronet-relative efficiency
NASA	National Aeronautics and Space Administration
NBI	Nile Basin Initiative
NCORE	Nile Cooperation for Results Project

NDMC	National Drought Mitigation Center
NDSI	normalized difference snow index
NDVI	normalized difference vegetation index
NIR	near infrared
NLDAS	North American Land Data Assimilation Systems
NOAA	National Oceanic and Atmospheric Administration
NOHRSC	National Operational Hydrologic Remote Sensing Center
NSE	Nash-Sutcliffe efficiency
NSIDC	National Snow and Ice Data Center
PERSIANN	Precipitation Estimation from Remotely Sensed Information Using Artificial Neural Networks
PM	Penman-Monteith
PMW	passive microwave
POES	polar-orbiting operational environmental satellite
REBM	resistance energy balance model
RIMES	Regional Integrated Multi-Hazard Early Warning System for Africa and Asia
RMSE	root mean squared error
RS	remote sensing
SADC	Southern Africa Development Community
SAR	synthetic aperture radar
SEBAL	Surface Energy Balance Algorithm for Land
SEBS	Surface Energy Balance System
SERVIR	Regional Visualization and Monitoring System
S & I	snow and ice
SMAP	Soil Moisture Active Passive
SMMR	Scanning Multichannel Microwave Radiometer
SMOS	Soil Moisture and Ocean Salinity Sensor
SPOT	Satellite for Earth Observation
SPP	satellite precipitation product
SSM/I	Special Sensor Microwave Imager
SVAT	soil-vegetation-atmosphere transfer
SW	surface water
SWIR	short-wave infrared
TIR	thermal infrared
TMI	TRMM Microwave Imager
TMPA	TRMM Multisatellite Precipitation Analysis
TOA	top of atmosphere
TRMM	Tropical Rainfall Measuring Mission
UNESCO	United National Educational, Scientific, and Cultural Organization
USAID	U.S. Agency for International Development
USDA	U.S. Department of Agriculture
UTC	Coordinated Universal Time
VIIRS	Visible/Infrared Imager Radiometer Suite
V and LC	vegetation and land cover
VIS	visible infrared
WGMS	World Glacier Monitoring Service

WIRADA	Water Information Research and Development Alliance
WISP	Water Information System Platform
WISP-3	Water Insight Spectrometer (with three radiometers)
WOIS	Water Observation and Information System
WQ	water quality
WRM	water resources management
WRSI	water requirement satisfaction index
W3RA	World-Wide Water Resources Assessment

EXECUTIVE SUMMARY

Water contributes to all aspects of economic and social development. Especially in developing countries, water supply, sanitation, and a healthy environment form the basis of successful poverty reduction and shared-growth strategies. The use of remote sensing (RS) for operational purposes in hydrology and water resources, while not new, is a fast-growing field. The term "operational," as used here, pertains not to the readiness of RS products themselves, but to the actual *use* of these products when making decisions—a decision about the planning, design, and monitoring or operation of any given institutional or physical system. It could concern, for instance, the selection of crops, the operation of field irrigation systems, or the design of hydraulic infrastructure such as a reservoir.

A Global Initiative on Remote Sensing for Water Resources Management was launched in October 2013, financed by the World Bank's Water Partnership Program of the Water Global Practice. It aims, among other things, to put together and disseminate, in collaboration with the Bank's operational staff and task team leaders as well as external partners, a clear picture of the potential role of Earth observation (EO)[1] in addressing particular water-related issues. This publication is a product of that initiative and aims to illustrate the *why*, *what*, and *how* of using EO data.

THE WHY: WATER AND EARTH OBSERVATIONS IN THE WORLD BANK

Development organizations confront many challenges in a rapidly changing world. These challenges include, among others, water scarcity as a result of growing demands for water, climatic variability and change, causes of environmental and hydrologic change other than climate, the occurrence of extreme events (floods and droughts), complex issues related to the conjunctive use of surface water and groundwater, food and energy dynamics, growth and environmental problems, as well as governance and transboundary issues.

The successful tackling of issues such as these lays the foundation for sustainable development and poverty reduction strategies that organizations such as the World Bank help client countries to develop. A review of the Bank's water-related projects shows that, over the last five years, the share of these kinds of projects in the total portfolio has almost doubled—reaching about 18 percent. Nearly 800 projects with water-related themes were approved between fiscal year 2002 and fiscal year 2012. Of these, the majority dealt with water supply and sanitation or with flood protection. Projects on irrigation and drainage and on hydropower ranked second and third, respectively.

These and other water-related projects, at some point and in one way or another, undoubtedly needed data on precipitation, temperature, evapotranspiration, normalized difference vegetation index, streamflow, soil moisture, wind speed, groundwater recharge, groundwater level, surface water level, snow or ice cover, snow or ice water equivalent, pumping and groundwater change, land subsidence evaluations, water surface elevation, and water quality. Traditionally, ground observations have provided these kinds of data. However, the number of ground hydrometeorological observations has been in decline globally since the 1980s. Among the many reasons for this decline is that, particularly in developing regions, real-time, ground-based measurements have been marked by relative scarcity, poor accessibility, deficient quality control, and lack of availability and sharing options.

Remote sensing plays an increasingly important role in providing the information needed to confront key water challenges. In poorly gauged basins, at time intervals of several days, real-time satellite estimates of precipitation and derived streamflow forecasts can help managers to allocate water among users and to operate reservoirs more efficiently. In large rivers, data on river and lake surface elevation can be used to estimate flow in the upper parts of the basin and to predict flow downstream. Soil moisture observations may give insight into how much irrigation is needed, as well as help to forecast and monitor drought conditions. Water managers in snow-dominated areas can use estimates of snow cover and snow water equivalent to assess how much water is in storage and determine what watersheds it is stored in.

Remote sensing also enables the monitoring of many parameters of surface water quality to assess the repercussions of river basin management policies, land use practices, and non-point-source pollution as well as the likelihood of algal blooms and other threats to the quality of water supply systems.

In situations involving the food-water-energy nexus, governance and adaptive management, or transboundary settings, remote sensing may help decision makers to adjust past policies or facilitate early warnings by providing information from parts of a basin lying outside a nation's borders.

In collaboration with space agencies in Europe, Japan, and the United States, the World Bank has increasingly been using RS data, as summarized in box ES.1.

Despite the growing demand for RS data, the percentage of projects in the portfolio that have

---

BOX ES.1

Remote Sensing in World Bank Water-Related Projects

In World Bank water-related projects, the following sectors and themes have been the highest users of remote sensing:

- *Flood protection* and *general water, sanitation, and flood protection* (more than 50 percent of projects using RS)
- *Irrigation and drainage* (25 percent)
- *Climate change related* (12 percent)
- *Natural disaster management* (17 percent)

In projects with a large *water resources management* component (55 percent), remote sensing has been used primarily in lending operations (46 percent) and less frequently in advisory and analytical support (9 percent of projects using RS).

Note: Sectors and themes are not mutually exclusive.

used these technologies is still low. There is great potential for their use in operations related to climate variability and change, agricultural systems, and water systems planning and management. Actual or planned uses of RS products vary from the evaluation of a project's impact on agricultural water management, agricultural water-saving measures, and support services to the provision of input for modern, basin-wide water resources information systems; feasibility studies; basin planning, monitoring, and forecasting; transboundary options for mitigating flood risks; investment planning and basin decision support systems; and institutional or community planning frameworks for addressing environmental and social issues.

The huge potential of RS applications has created the need for an easily accessible compilation of available products and their suitability for various water resource management needs as well as for guidelines to support decisions regarding when and how to use them more effectively for operational purposes.

THE WHAT: EARTH OBSERVATION FOR WATER RESOURCES MANAGEMENT

Some key variables are usually involved in these activities and, given the present state-of-the-art technology, may be estimated using remote sensing. These variables are precipitation, evapotranspiration, soil moisture, vegetation and vegetation cover, groundwater, level and extent of surface water,[2] snow cover, and optical water quality. This publication first identifies the minimum spatial and temporal resolution requirements for these types of variables and subsequently links them to relevant water activities.

Precipitation is the process by which water returns from the atmosphere to the Earth's surface in liquid form (rain), in solid form (snow or hail), or in combined form (sleet).

Because of its fine-scale spatial and temporal variability, monitoring precipitation in large areas challenges field-based measurement networks. Gauge density is not the only factor affecting when and where satellite data are expected to improve the rainfall estimation; other factors include the type of topography and rainfall. However, in large parts of the globe, rain gauge networks are sparse, and available evidence increasingly suggests that satellite-derived precipitation, together with weather model reanalysis estimates, can provide highly valuable rainfall estimates and narrow the information gap.

Evapotranspiration involves two processes—evaporation and transpiration—that occur simultaneously and are therefore difficult to distinguish one from the other. Evaporation is the change from a liquid to a gas. It may occur from the Earth's surface (for example, the soil, a water body, or other type of surface), through plant leaves (transpiration), and from rainfall on the surface of the leaves (interception). *Actual evapotranspiration* is difficult to measure, let alone estimate accurately, both spatially and temporally over large areas. This is not the case of *potential evapotranspiration*, which can be readily calculated using commonly measured hydrometeorological variables.

Actual evapotranspiration can be estimated through three methods: (a) empirical methods, (b) energy balance methods, and (c) the Penman-Monteith method. Each has specific strengths and weaknesses. These methods form the starting point of numerous EO-based implementation models. While it is unlikely that any single approach will be best suited to estimating actual evapotranspiration in every situation, a common issue is having a system in place for robust and repeatable assessment of the models. While EO-based models of actual evapotranspiration may still be used for places where no ground measurements exist, if their reliability (probability of errors) cannot be assessed, their suitability for management purposes may not be known with certainty.

Soil moisture is defined as the amount of water in the uppermost layers of the soil column, where the definition of "uppermost" varies with sensing technology or modeling application and can vary from the top 1 centimeter to the first 1 meter of soil or more. The monitoring of soil moisture has advanced considerably over the last decade, with innovative ground- and satellite-based technologies for monitoring large areas. Global monitoring of soil moisture is only achievable with satellite Earth observation in conjunction with field-based soil moisture monitoring networks. Satellite soil moisture sensing technology is based on either radiometric measurements of emissions from the soil (*passive microwave approach*) or radar technology that transmits a pulse of electromagnetic radiation to the Earth's surface and measures the backscattered signal (*active approach*). Objective assessments comparing the accuracy of satellite estimates of soil moisture with the accuracy of surface measurements are necessary to gain the user community's acceptance of the products and often involve evaluations against field-based soil moisture measurements.

Vegetation is the collective term for the coverage of plants across land areas, vegetation attributes, and processes related to the properties and functioning of those plants when considered at the landscape scale. Vegetation plays an important role in the hydrologic cycle—partitioning precipitation between evaporation and runoff. A large percentage of terrestrial evaporation is transpired by vegetation. It can be characterized *quantitatively*, using measures of height, canopy and stem density, leaf area, and the like, or *qualitatively*, as classes of vegetation or types of cover, such as forest, croplands, and tundra. Classes of vegetation cover are identified using combinations of remotely sensed variables—often combined with ancillary data such as climate and land use maps—and field observations. RS estimates of vegetation height and biomass help in distinguishing between structurally distinct types of vegetation.

Groundwater is the water contained in the saturated zone—the subsurface volume below the water table—where water fills the cracks and pores of rock, sediment, and soil. Groundwater is a critical source of water for human consumption and agriculture, especially where surface water is scarce or polluted. It also moderates streamflow, producing the longer-term base flow component of total flows, which decouples flows somewhat from the variability inherent in the climatic drivers of streamflow. As groundwater lies below the land surface, there are currently no techniques for using Earth observation to determine the groundwater level directly, so the use of remote sensing here is inferential and has limitations. The main *indirect* techniques used are satellite gravity field mapping (gravimetry) and radar interferometry.

Surface water, as treated here, refers to natural or man-made reservoirs, very wide rivers, and water accumulation caused by flooding, which can range from small overbank floods near water streams to very large floods covering hundreds of square kilometers. Measuring surface water elevation using EO technology can provide estimates of changes in total water volume in reservoirs and wetlands and also be used to estimate river discharge, although this is currently only possible in wide rivers (that is, rivers several hundreds of meters wide). A large number of algorithms exist for mapping surface water areas. One major disadvantage of using *optical imagery* is that the images are subject to cloud contamination. Radar and passive *microwave imagery* is not affected by clouds or water vapor and therefore can provide useful information on surface water under clouds.

Snow cover exists where snow accumulation is sufficient for the land surface to have a reasonably continuous layer of snow. As snow contains freshwater, meltwater from snow cover is an important source of water for consumption, irrigation, and power generation in many parts of the globe. In the visible wavelengths, snow is generally highly reflective (that is, characterized by a high albedo), which makes it relatively easy to detect, as it contrasts with the surrounding landscape. The areal extent of snow cover can be detected using optical, near infrared, and microwave sensors or a combination of these. Active and passive microwave sensors are the primary means of detecting snow depth, snow water equivalent, and snow wetness.

Water quality refers to the physical, chemical, and biological content of water and may vary geographically and seasonally, irrespective of the presence of specific pollution sources. Earth observation can only *directly* assess water quality parameters—including many chemical compounds, such as nutrients—if they have a direct expression in the optical response of the water body. Only a subset of these variables, often referred to as *optical water quality variables*, can be assessed *directly* through Earth observation (box ES.2).

In some cases, *nonoptical* products may be estimated through inference, proxy relationships, or data assimilation with remotely sensed optical properties of products such as nitrogen, phosphate, organic and inorganic micropollutants, and dissolved oxygen. However, these relationships are stochastic, may not be causal, and may have a limited range of validity. By making use of the combined information in directly measurable optical properties, it is possible to derive information about eutrophication, environmental flows, and carbon and primary productivity.

Detailed information about the various sensors is summarized in tables in the main text. These tables provide an overview of EO capabilities regarding estimation of the eight variables of interest previously mentioned. The satellite sensors are described in terms of their spectral, radiometric, and temporal characteristics. For each pertinent water resource management activity, the relevant variables that

---

BOX ES.2

Six Optical Water Quality Variables That Can Be Derived from EO Data

Directly assessed:

- Chlorophyll
- Cyanobacterial pigments
- Colored dissolved organic matter
- Total suspended matter

Indirectly assessed:

- Vertical attenuation of light coefficient
- Turbidity/Secchi disk transparency

---

can be obtained through Earth observation are classified according to their potential usefulness. In addition, the most appropriate spatial and temporal resolutions for each variable are listed.

THE HOW: PRACTICAL GUIDELINES FOR DECIDING ON THE USE OF EO PRODUCTS

For many potential applications, the use of EO data products will immediately and obviously be useful for improving water resource management and water monitoring. Yet in other cases, guidance may be needed to decide whether Earth observation could be useful and, if so, which data sources would be the most suitable to consider. For those cases, a simple decision framework is included to help to determine, for a given issue, (a) the optimum use of EO products, that is, those that generate the required information, and (b) the optimum selection method, that is, the one that ensures the EO data products with the most appropriate specifications are chosen. For the application to each specific area of water resources management, the issues of accuracy, availability, maturity, complexity, and reliability should

Questions to Aid in Deciding Whether to Use Earth Observation for Water Resources Management

1. *Define the nature of the water resource management problem.*
   - What questions need to be answered?
   - What policies or regulations drive these questions?
   - Who are the stakeholders and beneficiaries of a solution to the problem?

2. *Explore the capacity of sustaining and maintaining decision support and monitoring programs.*
   - Is local capability available and adequate?
   - Is training needed?
   - Are local and international resources required?

3. *Define the status of existing data and observation networks.*
   - What metering is currently available?
   - What is the condition of the data networks?
   - Are there any impediments to sharing, collating, and archiving the data (for example, transboundary issues)?
   - What, if anything, has been done in the past to address the issues at hand?
   - Has any monitoring or modeling been conducted?

4. *Evaluate the adequacy of field observations.*
   - Are the observations well defined?
   - Are the spatial density, frequency, continuity, and period of interest detailed?
   - Are observations accurate and available?

be duly considered. The main questions to ask are presented in box ES.3.

Information that helps to answer these questions—as a basis for determining whether specific EO products meet the data requirements of the water resources management problem under consideration—is provided in tables in the main text. The step-by-step procedure is shown in the simplified diagram in figure ES.1.

The validity or ground truth[3] of EO products is also an important characteristic to be taken into account when considering their use. Yet, while numerous reports and publications on hydrologic applications of remote sensing discuss available tools (products and models),

few include validation of the results of those tools. Still, some reports on validation efforts can be found in the literature.

It is presently believed that the *combined* use of EO and field data generally provides the best information outcomes, based on a review of the literature on the validation of EO-estimated hydrometeorological variables and the following considerations: (a) overall satellite estimations are well correlated with ground observations; (b) despite these strong correlations, satellite estimates are relatively uncertain; (c) despite the uncertainties inherent in in situ measurements, it is believed that the measurements of an EO data product will rarely be as accurate as those of an equivalent field measurement; and (d) despite the generally lower accuracy, EO products still are an important alternative data source because EO imagery can provide information with greater spatial extent, spatial density, and temporal frequency than most field-based (point-based) observation networks.

CONCLUDING REMARKS

Good water resources management and planning are essential to sustain economic and human development. Especially in developing nations, there is a need to bridge the gap between existing technologies and operational applications in support of the planning, design, operation, and management of water resources. There is great potential for space-based Earth observation to enhance the capability to monitor the Earth's vital water resources, especially in data-sparse regions of the globe. Despite this potential, EO data products are currently underused in water resources management.

Practitioners, especially in developing countries, would benefit from efforts to bridge the gap between scientific-academic and real-world uses of RS technology. Factors to consider are the cost of implementation, financial support, technical orientation, and definition of clear procedures and criteria to assess the usability of RS products for decision making and planning conditioned by uncertainty (error estimates), accuracy (characterization of errors), precision (spatial and temporal resolution), timeliness, and validity of the data. A good understanding of the potential and limitations of in situ measurements and EO-derived data can inform the design of special tools for specific purposes. Thus communication between scientists, researchers, and practitioners should be a two-way street.

NOTES

1. The terms "remote sensing" and "Earth observation" are used interchangeably in this publication.
2. *Surface water*, as used in this publication, refers to water that is on the Earth's surface, such as in a stream, river, lake, reservoir, wetland, or flooded area.
3. In remote sensing, *ground truth* refers to information collected on location. Ground truth allows image data to be related to real features and materials on the ground. The collection of ground-truth data enables calibration of RS data and aids in the interpretation and analysis of what is being sensed.

Figure ES.1 Summary of Guidelines for Determining Whether to Use EO Products

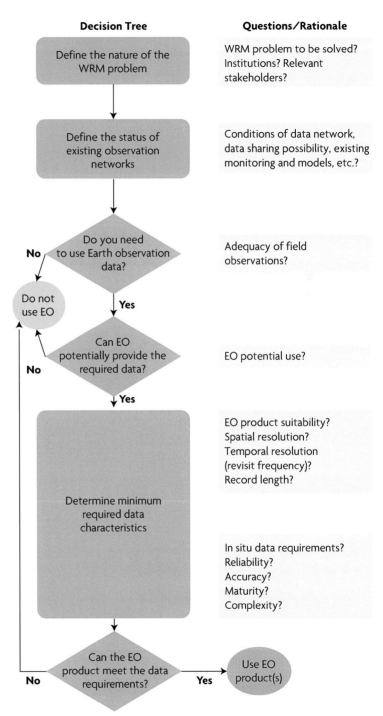

Note: WRM = water resources management; EO = Earth observation.

PART I

Water and Earth Observations in the World Bank

Aleix Serrat-Capdevila, Danielle A. García Ramírez, and Noosha Tayebi

OVERVIEW

Water is a key driver of economic and social development as well as of poverty reduction. Growing economies and populations need more water resources to sustain economic activity and provide greater access to drinking water and improved sanitation, generate renewable energy, or increase sustainable food production. While water can be catalytic for economic growth and development, too much or too little water can also be a constraint if countries are unable to prepare for climate-related hazards.

As water is present in most parts of the economy, better water management is critical to helping people, economies, and ecosystems to thrive, reduce poverty, and sustain prosperity. Better water resources management also requires institutional capacity and enabling environments in which stakeholders participate in finding integrated solutions

for development. Water thus is a fundamental input for sustainable economic growth.

While the World Bank has maintained its mission of reducing global poverty through economic development, the nature of the work it undertakes to fulfill that mission has changed over the decades of its existence. The scope of the problems that the Bank has to grapple with has expanded significantly, particularly in the realm of sustainable development, and today includes challenges related to climate change, resource depletion, natural disasters, and urbanization. These challenges require the collection and processing of data of much larger orders of magnitude than the poverty challenge alone requires. Under these circumstances, the Bank has started tapping into remote sensing techniques as a means of acquiring the extensive data needed to advance its goals.

CHAPTER 1

Key Global Water Challenges and the Role of Remote Sensing

INTRODUCTION

Over the past century, water resources management has increased in complexity as technological advances of the Industrial Revolution have allowed humans to intervene in and modify the hydrologic cycle in unprecedented ways. In many cases, this has been done without acknowledging the environmental and social costs, without a long-term vision for planning and management, and without any regulation or oversight. In addition, a good physical understanding of the impact of human intervention has often been lacking. Population and economic growth, as well as changes in land use and global dynamics, have pushed the use of water resources beyond the limits of long-term sustainability in many regions of the world. Several water resources problems and challenges have taken or are taking center stage in the sustainable management arena.

The analysis of the World Bank project portfolio has identified several water-related challenges to sustainable development. These challenges have been grouped under representative themes deemed especially relevant to reducing poverty and promoting shared growth—the overarching issues deserving attention. They are the scarcity and quality of water; the impacts of climate change and variability as well as changes not related to climate; the management of floods and droughts; the management of the conjunctive use of surface water and groundwater; the complex links between water, energy, and food production; the need for alternative models of economic growth (such as green growth); financial challenges in the provision of water and sanitation services; the need for better governance; and improved cooperation in the management of transboundary waters.

This chapter summarizes the key challenges that undermine the optimal design, use, and management of water and the socio-ecological systems that provide hydrologic services beneficial to humans. These challenges are all related to the rational use of water resources and the goals of environmental sustainability, economic efficiency, and social equity. Each section deals with a specific challenge, reviewing the role of remote sensing (RS) observations in addressing that challenge and discussing possible approaches and ways to address it.

WATER SCARCITY

Water scarcity is a human-centered concept resulting when overall demand for water exceeds supply. It often is a problem not only of supply, but also of demand; it affects the Sahel and Bangladesh, but also the Colorado River basin. Water scarcity arises when water supply and demand are out of balance:

- *Limited supply.* The supply of water can be low due to either low hydrologic availability (in arid and semiarid areas) or the lack of integrated systems to buffer seasonal or interannual variability (lack of access to water in reservoirs or aquifers or lack of sustainable and reliable mechanisms to extract it). The overreliance on a single source of water may increase the vulnerability of supply systems. In the Indus and Ganges basins, overreliance on a single source can be caused by the lack of proper management of conjunctive use, leading to a decline in aquifer levels, and by the struggle of poor rural households to access water when pumping costs rise or deeper wells are needed. The notion of water quality should also be considered, as polluted water is not a usable resource.

- *Unlimited demand.* In most instances, water scarcity is due to (a) low agricultural efficiencies, as well as municipal, industrial, and conveyance inefficiencies; (b) no or lack of enforcement of limits on water allocations or regulations on groundwater pumping or the allocation of resources (to prevent overallocation); (c) lack of proper pricing of costs associated with water use; (d) subsidies on energy costs (the main

subsidies being given to groundwater-irrigated agriculture); (e) lack of institutional frameworks and enforcement and low priority and visibility in political agendas; (f) lack of information and proper education regarding the impacts of unsustainable use and poor management practices; or (g) a combination of all of the above. Effective management of demand can often significantly reduce water scarcity through improved technology and improved efficiency of water systems. At the same time, very efficient water use and overallocation of existing water resources may lead to brittle or nonresilient systems.

Water scarcity is sometimes so severe that there is not even enough water to satisfy basic human and animal needs, as is the case in some parts of the Sahel, where it often results in widespread hunger. In places where famine is tied directly to local food production through the availability of rainfall and water in small water bodies (springs, holes, watercourses), real-time monitoring of rainfall and hydrology is essential to prepare mitigation measures for the most exposed and vulnerable populations.

Population growth, irrigation, and urbanization are by far the most significant stressors on water management. Urban centers in developing nations are among the fastest-growing areas (Africa has an annual growth rate of 3.9 percent—the highest rate of urban population growth in the world). Growing demands for water, changing land use cover and availability of water resources, as well as deteriorating water quality (due to new economic activities and poor sanitation) are becoming major challenges for sustainable water resources management and, hence, for sustainable economic growth.

A good physical understanding of resource dynamics through time and space and good near-real-time monitoring of hydrologic balances are essential to the proper management of water as a scarce resource. This understanding forms the basis for addressing all of the water resource challenges described in this chapter. Coping with climate and water variability requires good monitoring and accounting tools, to help users to prioritize and curb demand ahead of time in dry years and to consume more wisely in wet years. A better quantification of hydrologic fluxes and storages will help to enhance water security—and thus the health and well-being of populations—by providing more reliable information on water availability and use. Remote sensing—also called Earth observation (EO)—allows the measurement of many hydrometeorological and environmental variables as well as the identification of many types of land use cover. Some of the relevant variables are precipitation, soil moisture, terrestrial water storage (including vadose zone water and groundwater), evapotranspiration (ET), normalized difference vegetation index (NDVI), surface water elevation, and some water quality variables. Good monitoring of hydrometeorological fluxes and their partitioning will enable integrated, flexible water management approaches that take advantage of diverse water resources and potential feedbacks between system components.

Remote sensing can provide spatially distributed and timely observations that may allow better forecasting and more efficient use of water. For instance,

- Operational managers in snow-dominated areas can use estimates of snow cover[1] and snow water equivalent to know how much water is in storage and in what watersheds it is stored.

- In poorly gauged basins with times of concentration of many days, real-time satellite estimates of precipitation and derived streamflow forecasts can help managers to allocate water among users and to operate reservoirs more efficiently, taking into account how much water the river is expected to bring in the following days.

- In large rivers, altimeter data of river surfaces can be used to estimate flow in the upper parts of the basin and to predict downstream flows, issue flood warnings, and manage water allocation and operations (see Hossain et al. 2014).

- Soil moisture observations may provide insights into how much irrigation is needed as well as help to correct missed events or false detections of satellite precipitation products and to assess flood risk.

- ET estimates may help water managers to understand the dynamics of groundwater pumping in agricultural areas and the impact of water policies implemented and changes made in energy subsidies for pumping. More generally, they can be used in combination with ground data to understand efficiencies in water use, aimed at decreasing the rate of nonbeneficial and increasing the productivity of beneficial evapotranspiration (Wu et al. 2013).

- The Satellite Water Monitoring and Flow Forecasting System for the Yellow River—a Sino-Dutch cooperation project—is a good example of integrated efforts using RS data (from hourly visual and thermal infrared bands) to support river basin management, including energy and water balance, drought monitoring and early warning, and flow and flood forecasting (Rosema et al. 2008).

WATER QUALITY

Water quality issues are broad and differ widely, depending on the specific context and setting. Water quality issues in surface and groundwater can originate from (a) the lack of or poor-quality water supply and sanitation services, (b) land use practices, (c) industrial activities, and (d) management issues involving natural contaminants. The deteriorating quality of rivers and aquifers worldwide can also result from a combination of these factors.

In many regions of the world, urban and periurban aquifers are polluted due to the combination of inadequate treatment of sanitation and wastewater and a range of economic activities. Such contamination exacerbates the lack of access to clean water, which is itself a direct cause of poor health and malnutrition (diarrhea is one of the main causes of malnutrition). Lack of access to drinking water also has an impact on education (as children have to help their parents collect water) and poverty. Thus water supply and sanitation are essential components of integrated approaches to reducing malnutrition and poverty.

Land use practices such as deforestation and farming can severely affect the quality of surface water and groundwater. While the disruption of vegetation cover and soil practices can have an impact on total dissolved solids and turbidity, the use of fertilizers for agriculture can lead to eutrophication and hypoxia in surface water systems as well as to severely polluted aquifers. The use of chemical pesticides can also cause imbalances in natural trophic chains.

Industrial activities are a common source of contamination, especially in countries that do not have well-established regulatory and enforcement mechanisms. Polluting activities may include mining and metallurgy, processing and manufacturing industries, and the like.

Water quality issues can also stem from overexploitation and lack of management of water bodies with different natural characteristics, sometimes bringing about saline intrusion in coastal aquifers or upconing of saline groundwater below freshwater aquifers. These water quality issues, in turn, lead to water scarcity and may compromise human health. For instance, they are responsible for the naturally occurring high concentrations of arsenic in the groundwater of floodplains and deltas or other "geogenic" elements such as fluoride or uranium. While this kind of pollution has a natural origin, it is human induced. Poor or deficient management can contaminate large groundwater reservoirs by drawing in naturally occurring pollutants, including salt, fluoride, arsenic, and radioactivity.

Pharmaceuticals originating in wastewater are becoming one of the main challenges in developed countries. However, this issue is not receiving much attention in developing countries. Those contaminants are difficult to detect and expensive to quantify; moreover, their effect is not easily neutralized through special treatment. There is still only limited understanding of their impact on human and environmental health, although significant hormonal changes in some aquatic species have been observed, among other effects.

In addition to monitoring fluxes and storage levels of water, remote sensing also offers the possibility of monitoring many parameters of water quality. This makes it possible to follow water quality in time and space across vast regions, significantly complementing costly and limited field-point measurements. The water quality variables that can be assessed with remote sensing are temperature, chlorophyll (an indicator of phytoplankton biomass, trophic, and nutrient status and the most widely used index of water quality and nutrient status globally), cyano-phycocyanin and cyano-phycoerythrin (indicators of cyanobacterial biomass, which are common in harmful and toxic algal blooms), colored dissolved organic matter (the optically measurable component of dissolved organic matter in the water column, sometimes used as an indicator of organic matter and aquatic carbon), and total suspended matter and non-algal particulate matter (important for assessing the quality of drinking water and controlling the light in aquatic environments).

Direct applications of remote sensing for management include the following:

• Monitoring water quality to assess the impacts of river basin management policies and land use practices on the environment and surface water. The spatial dimension of this monitoring capability is important.

- Monitoring the likelihood of algal blooms and other water quality threats to water supply systems.

Dekker and Hestir (2012) provide a good overview of the state of the art, reporting that the main impediment to making RS monitoring operational is the lack of bio-optical information for parameterizing and validating remotely sensed information on water quality.

IMPACTS OF GLOBAL CHANGE

While it is important to understand the underlying causes and future projections of climate variability and change, many of the impacts of climate change on hydrology and climate variability may be difficult to distinguish from normal climate variability. The signal of anthropogenic climate change is expected to increase gradually, as is its impact, but its distribution across the globe will be uneven and will depend on latitude and geography.

Global climate models (GCMs), also known as general circulation models, project changes in precipitation and temperature. Beyond a research exercise, in what ways can impact studies of climate variability and change inform management and planning decisions? What is the take-home message for decision makers? Leaving aside the debate on how GCM data should be used, studies of the impact of climate change on water resources can potentially be applied to two realms: (a) planning and design efforts to cope with extreme events in the upper end of the spectrum (taking into account their return periods) and (b) management aspects depending on average water availability over the next decades.

Even when aggregated over spatial scales, GCM results contain a lot of uncertainty at the monthly and annual levels (Anagnostopoulos et al. 2010), and consequent hydrologic simulations alone are not fit for planning and design purposes and likewise unsuitable for forecasts and reservoir operations (Kundzewicz and Stakhiv 2010; Stakhiv 2010). However, GCMs are designed and intended to project future changes in climate and not to predict the weather, two different tasks whose boundaries are often blurred in debates regarding GCM accuracy.

Should an attempt be made to use GCM results to derive new flood frequencies at an hourly rate for specific basins? In the Southwestern United States, several studies have found that, while *average* precipitation will decrease, precipitation *extremes* will increase (Domínguez et al. 2012; Emori and Brown 2005; Meehl et al. 2007). While GCMs and regional climate models may provide useful projections of changes in the frequency and magnitude of extreme events, the uncertainties may be too large to inform design investments.

At the same time, climate impact studies have a more straightforward benefit for management and planning that is related to changes in averages (for which climate model projections seem to be less uncertain) and the long-term availability of water. Consequently, if changes in meteorological variables affect the mean states of hydrologic variables, efforts should be directed at quantifying these average changes (using GCMs) and the envelope of uncertainty that contains them (using traditional and new approaches), so that water managers and decision makers can adapt to changes in water availability (Serrat-Capdevila and Mishra 2012).

While precipitation projections are uncertain and sometimes contradictory, there is little disagreement over the fact that the Earth's atmosphere is warming and that temperatures will continue to rise. One can easily expect that in glacier-dominated regimes, flows could increase in the short term, which is associated with a period of progressive glacier melting. In the longer term, flows are expected to decrease drastically and become highly variable, having lost the regulating influence of a snowpack and thus being subject to the vagaries of liquid precipitation.

The change in hydrologic regimes can be caused by changes in climate (global or local), changes in land cover and use, and direct human intervention in the hydrologic cycle (dams, pumping). While climate change impacts on hydrology have a low signal-to-noise ratio, changes in land cover and use can severely affect the partitioning of rainfall into the different components of the hydrologic cycle. Changes in the amount and partitioning of precipitation into evapotranspiration, infiltration, and runoff are the main source of changes in hydrologic regimes.

Land cover change usually has an immediate impact on hydrologic responses. Villarini et al. (2009) show that changes in land use–related cover can have a significant influence on the hydrologic response of a basin. During the urbanization of their study basin, the 1,000-year flood became the 10-year flood in a period of 50 years. This illustrates the fact that nonclimatic, anthropogenic changes often stress water management more in the short term, with regard to the design of flood parameters. Nevertheless, changes in climate and climate-induced vegetation are also likely to be a significant factor in regional water balances.

Salas et al. (2012) broadly review scientific efforts to characterize natural and anthropogenic sources of change and provide a picture of the combination of processes affecting the water cycle. In addition to the ones mentioned above, these include volcanic explosions and large forest fires, which both influence the balance and composition of atmospheric energy as well as ground cover. The El Niño Southern Oscillation, the Pacific Decadal Oscillation, the Atlantic Multidecadal Oscillation, the Arctic Oscillation, and others influence climate at interannual and multidecadal intervals, and their effect on the magnitude and frequency of

floods, mean flows, and droughts is widely recognized. Dissecting the various contributions to hydrologic change from natural climatic drivers, as well as from land use change, vegetation cover change, and anthropogenic increases in atmospheric concentrations of carbon dioxide, is very challenging.

Nonclimatic drivers of change in socioecological systems such as the global economy, combined with natural climatic variability, can change social vulnerabilities and power relationships. Edwards (2006) argues that globalization has accentuated, rather than reduced, national and regional differences. Sub-Saharan Africa, in particular, has become increasingly marginalized in terms of benefiting from the global economy (O'Brien and Leichenko 2000). Population growth, rural to urban migration, and land and ecosystem degradation and deforestation in developing regions are all sources of change in hydrologic and water demand.

Given the extent of human-induced global environmental change, current climate projections, and the expected impacts on hydrology, water resources, glaciers, and snow and land cover, Earth observations are sorely needed to monitor the dynamics of change. Land use often changes in response to land and water management practices, which, in turn, are influenced by global economic forces.

Monitoring hydrometeorological and environmental variables will help to document the effects of global change. Observing, identifying, documenting, and understanding the dynamics of change should be the foundation for the design and implementation of adaptation measures. As trends and changes in variables caused by global changes will likely manifest themselves unevenly in space and time, remote sensing is essential to complement limited ground observations.

Good monitoring allows (a) identifying changes in meteorological variables and attributing causes, (b) assessing the impacts on hydrologic variables and dynamics, and

(c) understanding observed changes in regional water budgets and water resources availability.

Changes in seasonal and annual snow cover, evolution in the length of glaciers, as well as changes in vegetation, cloud cover, rainfall rates, soil moisture content, evapotranspiration, and other hydrologic variables of interest can best be quantified and spatially monitored with Earth observation. The combination of RS observations and climate impact studies using land surface and hydrologic models offers a vantage point for informing adaptation to climate and global change.

One of the main challenges in the analysis of climatic variability and trends is to reconcile modern RS observations with long historical ground records. Most historical data sets of gauge precipitation that span a significant time period are not updated continually with near-real-time observations. An example in this context is the Climate Research Unit time-series gauge precipitation data set, which provides a century-long record of monthly precipitation from 1901 to 2009. While such data sets can be used for climatologic analysis of the historical period, they usually cannot be used for near-real-time drought monitoring, as they are not updated continually. However, near-real-time, quasi-global precipitation products span a decade and a half at most. This mismatch between long-term historical data sets and near-real-time observations poses a challenge for assessing the impacts of climate variability and change as well as for spatial monitoring of drought.

Remote sensing can be combined with ground observations and socioeconomic analysis of water use to provide insights that are useful for planning, policy, and management; Hartfield et al. (2014) provides a good illustration. In a collaborative initiative with scholars and water management practitioners, they analyze the dynamics of water supply and sanitation infrastructure and urban growth using RS observations and information from water utilities. Using advanced classification techniques, they created a multitemporal (1984–2010) view of land cover change along the rapidly growing Tucson-Phoenix urban corridor. These classifications created multitemporal maps of changing urban residential, urban commercial-industrial, agricultural, roads, bare ground, natural desert cover, riparian, and water areas. These data were subsequently integrated into an ongoing analysis of urban and water policy and water allocation within the region, making it easier to evaluate the correlation of water availability and use, socioeconomic drivers, and direction and magnitude of changes in land use or cover.

EXTREME EVENTS: FLOODS AND DROUGHTS

Floods and droughts entail great economic costs and loss of lives worldwide every year. The magnitude and frequency of extreme events are expected to increase with intensification of the hydrologic cycle due to global warming (IPCC 2007, 2014)[2] and its regional hydrologic impacts (Domínguez et al. 2012; Serrat-Capdevila et al. 2013). Coping with variability requires different approaches to accommodate events from different sides of the spectrum.

A report by the American Water Resources Association, *Proactive Flood and Drought Management* (Dennis 2013), presents some lessons learned regarding how to manage extreme events. The report recommends developing management strategies based on existing hydrologic observations, data, and continued monitoring, taking into account the spatial analysis of exposure and vulnerability to floods and droughts. "Soft" ecosystem-based solutions are also recommended, promoting ecosystem services and functions as part of comprehensive approaches, both for flood-plain reconnection (flood attenuation) and for enhanced recharge purposes (drought risk reduction through conjunctive use).

The report highlights the importance of "planning for the unexpected" by anticipating extreme events of magnitudes not yet seen. While this recommendation is difficult to translate into design investments, special methodologies such as the decision scaling approach have been developed (Brown et al. 2012) and reported (García et al. 2014) to provide a cost-efficient way of adapting to changing risks. These methodologies also highlight the need to involve all stakeholders—politicians, decision makers, the private sector, agencies, and competing interest groups—in an equitable and thoughtful process, to ensure a coordinated and comprehensive, multiscale approach. The shared vision planning approach originated with the necessity to cope with drought and was developed by planning practitioners who had to address water scarcity issues and planning challenges in their professional capacity. More about the shared vision planning approach can be found in Cardwell, Langsdale, and Stephenson (2009).

With intensification of the hydrologic cycle, extreme events are expected to become more intense and more frequent, although estimates of future intensities and frequencies are fraught with large uncertainties. Diversifying resources and approaches, building flexibility into the system, as well as conserving unused buffers[3] may be the key to ensuring resilience to extreme events and to minimizing their economic costs. Full allocation and maximal use of water resources, without considering buffers and redundancies in the system, could, in the short term, lead to optimal but "brittle" solutions in the event of shocks to the system. Monitoring current trends and hydrologic conditions is essential to choosing appropriate management actions in time and to being able to share key information with users and stakeholders. RS measurements can be very useful in this context.

Several approaches use RS data to monitor the physical dimensions of drought, as illustrated by the following examples:

- The Surface Hydrology Group at Princeton University operates the experimental Africa Drought Monitor (Sheffield et al. 2014). It provides Africa-wide maps of precipitation, temperature, wind speed, and hydrologic variables, as simulated by the variable infiltration capacity model over the entire continent at a 0.25° resolution.[4] The HyDros Lab from the University of Oklahoma also provides global maps of near-real-time streamflow and soil moisture estimates from their Coupled Routing and Excess STorage model (Wang et al. 2011).[5] Both of these applications use the multisatellite precipitation analysis product of the Tropical Rainfall Measuring Mission as input on precipitation.

- Going from the global to the basin scale, the Hydrology and Water Resources Department of the University of Arizona, in partnership with the National Aeronautics and Space Administration (NASA) SERVIR Program and the International Center for Integrated Water Resources Management of the United Nations Educational, Scientific, and Cultural Organization (UNESCO), has been developing experimental monitors and 7- to 10-day streamflow forecasts in watersheds of four international African basins: the Mara (Kenya, Tanzania), the Upper Zambezi (Angola, Namibia, Zambia), the Tekeze (Eritrea, Ethiopia), and the Senegal (Guinea, Mali, Mauritania, Senegal). These efforts represent a multimodel and multiproduct approach using state-of-the-art climate projections to develop streamflow forecasts and assess climate change impacts on water availability for the current century.[6]

- Satellite rainfall estimates can also be used to derive a grid cell-level water requirement satisfaction index (WRSI)—the percentage ratio of actual crop evapotranspiration over a reference-crop evapotranspiration (non-water limited). The WRSI can be a good indicator of yield reduction due to water limitation. The Famine Early Warning System Network of the U.S. Agency for International Development (USAID) combines monitoring of rainfall, using the rainfall estimation algorithm version 2 (RFE 2.0) of the National Oceanic and Atmospheric Administration (NOAA), and crop production, using the WRSI, with socioeconomic variables (for example, prices) and a livelihoods approach to understand the strategies that people use to meet their basic needs. This provides insights into which population groups are most vulnerable to food insecurity, how long they remain vulnerable, and what the best mitigation approaches are (Verdin et al. 2005).

- Earth observation can be used to monitor small water holes, which are especially relevant to rural livelihoods, pastoralists and their herds, and wildlife migrations. A NASA-funded project uses a water-balance approach to model water levels of pools in closed basins.[7] The European Space Agency's TIGER program uses Landsat visual imagery at 30-meter resolution to monitor changes in the size of "small" water bodies.

- Estimates of the NDVI can also be used to derive the vegetation health index, which Yan et al. (2014) find to be a more accurate detector of agricultural droughts for irrigated areas than the standard precipitation index.

The use of satellite estimates for flood forecasting applications and flood alert systems is perhaps the most complex, with regard to the rainfall-runoff transformations involved (magnifying the rainfall errors in peak flow), the hydrodynamic modeling that will determine flood levels at specific locations, and the level of precision and accuracy that will be needed for the application to be beneficial. Flood warning and alert systems focus on the magnitude of peak flows. Accurately forecasting peak flows at an acceptable level of precision requires rainfall estimates of a relatively high spatial and temporal resolution (Li et al. 2008). As the extent of damage and loss of life depend on the performance of a flood warning system, the levels of acceptable uncertainty are much lower than in other applications, such as reservoir operations (which are mostly concerned with water volumes).

A forecast system has two types of prediction errors: type I (missed predictions) and type II (false alerts). While type I errors have a short-term impact (flood damage or loss of life), type II errors reduce the credibility of the forecast. The fraction of the target population that will respond to a flood warning or alert depends on a system's past performance. Thus if an RS system generates too many false alarms, an alarm from a correct prediction would likely be ignored, with potentially catastrophic effects.

RS products can be used in different applications aimed at informing flood warnings. For example,

- In the face of significant uncertainties in globally available near-real-time satellite rainfall products, the reliability of satellite-based forecasts of rainfall-runoff floods may vary with the setting, product, and season and may not always be, at present, sufficient for real-world flood warning and alert systems (Serrat-Capdevila, Valdes, and Stakhiv 2013). The need for information on changes in rainfall-runoff to provide streamflow forecasts adds an additional layer of uncertainty and can magnify errors in estimating the peak magnitude of the flood (Nikopoulos et al. 2010). The Hydro-Estimator of Central America Flash Flood Guidance produces a flash flood threat index using the "excess amount of rainfall for a three-hour period over what is needed to cause bank-full flows in small streams."[8]

- Soil moisture estimates can also be useful for predicting floods, as they provide information on the "wetness" of a basin and thus the partitioning of rainwater between infiltration and runoff, depending on the saturation level of the headwaters of the watershed. In addition, soil moisture can help to correct for errors produced using satellite precipitation products such as false detections and missed events.

- An effective and innovative approach to flood prediction in large rivers is the use of surface altimeter measurements. Tennessee Technological University, in collaboration with the Institute of Water Modeling (Bangladesh), the NASA-USAID SERVIR Program, and the International Centre for Integrated Mountain Development (Nepal), developed an 8-day flood forecasting system using river surface altimeter measurements from the Jason-2 satellite in the Ganges-Brahmaputra-Meghna system, which drains the Himalayas through Bangladesh (Hossain et al. 2014). Measurements of river surface levels upstream and a hydrodynamic model (HEC-Ras) are used to predict how the observed water levels upstream will propagate to areas downstream. Forecast validation efforts have shown a root mean square error of 0.7 meter, with lead times up to 10 days at the India-Bangladesh border (with errors ranging up to 0.5 meter and exceptionally even over 1 meter). Given the much larger changes in river levels and the fact that there is currently no alternative for an 8-day lead time forecast in Bangladesh, these errors are considered acceptable given that only RS data are used for the forecasts. Efforts are under way to improve the forecasts by using additional altimeter measurements from other satellite sensors (F. Hossain, personal communication).[9]

Regarding the role of international organizations, ongoing activities related to the World Meteorological Organization include the flood forecasting Distributed Model Intercomparison Project, the development of a framework for assessing the efficiency of flood forecasting services, and the establishment of regional flash flood guidance systems using integrated observations and model outputs. In a collaborative effort of the World Meteorological Organization, NOAA, USAID, and the Hydrologic Research Centre, integrated satellite observations, in situ observations, and models are used to implement flash flood guidance systems in streams in many regions and transboundary basins. Several satellite-based flood prediction and monitoring systems are reported to be almost operational (Lawford 2014), such as the Integrated Flood Analysis System, provided by UNESCO's International Centre for Water Hazard and Risk Management, the Global Flood Alert System, provided by the International Flood Network, and Global Flood and Landslide Monitoring, provided by NASA and the Goddard Space Flight Center (Lawford 2014).

For these systems to be truly useful for water managers and decision makers, future research and applications will have to consider the reliability of flood warning systems in addition to the estimated uncertainty in streamflow forecasts. Reflecting these complexities, Central America Flash Flood Guidance labels its flash flood threat index as "experimental" and "not for operational use." Because of the short time of concentration and the latency of rainfall products, the window for early warning action is limited in small watersheds.

CONJUNCTIVE USE OF SURFACE WATER AND GROUNDWATER

The adoption of pumps and rural electrification in the mid-twentieth century made it possible to tap vast groundwater resources, opening up a domain that institutions had not governed before. This led to a challenging issue regarding the management of surface water and groundwater, which has not yet been fully resolved. The social organization—that is, the institutions involved in managing the conjunctive use of surface water and groundwater—is still seeking ways to regulate the use of this technological innovation.

Efficient conjunctive use of surface water and groundwater provides an opportunity to handle variable surface flows and work toward sustainability in regions with severely overexploited aquifers, balancing water withdrawals with managed recharge. It requires local research on recharge processes and the potential for managed aquifer recharge,[10] storage, and recovery. Research is also needed on locally adapted policies and approaches to managing the system and achieving a sustainable pumping yield, supported by a conjunctive use strategy and implementation planning. The robustness of integrated conjunctive use water management plans can then be tested with a range of climate variability and climate change scenarios to account for uncertainty.

Examples exist in Western and Southern India, where, faced with dropping groundwater levels and aquifer mining, local communities and governments are building water harvesting and recharge structures aimed at increasing groundwater recharge during the rainy season, when surface water is abundant. These measures not only represent a successful flood mitigation strategy, but also improve water security for human and agricultural consumption, protecting and stabilizing rural livelihoods against drought and decreasing groundwater levels (Shah 2003).

In conjunctive use management, the concept of capture is important: pumping water from an aquifer system that is hydraulically connected to a surface water system will eventually deplete the surface water system. Such depletion is a form of surface water capture. It is essential that water managers understand the concept of capture and estimate its effects on the water supply, something usually based on models. Studies of capture through modeling are documented in the Colorado River delta (Maddock, Serrat-Capdevila, and Valdes 2010) and the San Pedro basin in Arizona-Sonora (Leake, Pool, and Leenhouts 2008). Capture maps display the impact that pumping in any given area would have on a specific water body, such as a nearby river. By showing in a spatially explicit manner the degree to which pumping will intercept water that would otherwise contribute to baseflows in the river, capture maps can help managers to choose pumping locations that minimize the impact of groundwater abstractions or to determine feasible pumping rates for a particular fixed location.

Taking a river basin perspective, investments in managing conjunctive use should aim to reshape infrastructure at all scales to promote groundwater recharge and to build management capacity (monitoring systems, institutional adaptations, best practices, and greater incentive compatibility) around improved groundwater governance frameworks and participatory approaches (Shah, Darghouth, and Dinar 2006; Wijnen et al. 2012). Aquifer management organizations are needed, perhaps embedded or working closely with basin councils and gathering representatives from all relevant decision-making and user organizations. Governance- and incentive-based approaches to overcome policy challenges are summarized later in this chapter.

To achieve sustainable management in conjunctive use of water, several objectives must be pursued simultaneously: introducing managed aquifer recharge, improving efficiency in water use, and adopting water demand–curbing measures to conserve water. The need for integrated approaches is illustrated by case studies in Peru's Pacific Coast valleys such as Ica, where agribusiness export companies use high-efficiency drip irrigation—farming a larger area than before with the same amount of water and eliminating return flows to the aquifer—without reducing their demand for water from the acquifer (Garduño and Foster 2010). This issue is common in many other settings such as the Hai basin in China (Wijnen et al. 2012), where a monitoring system was developed to understand the consumptive use of water using satellite-based ET estimates. It is also important to consider water quality issues in conjunctive use management schemes, in order to minimize potential threats, such as recharging contaminant loads over time via infiltration from agriculture, poor onsite sanitation, upconing of saline groundwater into the freshwater aquifer, or other management-induced water quality issues (arsenic, fluoride, and radioactive contamination).

Good monitoring of aquifer dynamics and water use patterns will facilitate the development of solutions for sustainable management. By combining groundwater monitoring with capacity building of local communities (for example, participatory monitoring approaches in India), farmers and other users can learn how to manage their groundwater resources. The sharing of collective measurements can also serve as a platform for transparency, outreach, and discussion.

Conjunctive water use management would benefit from RS applications such as the following:

- Estimation of evapotranspiration can help to quantify irrigated extensions and the consumptive use of water, making it easier to maintain an accurate inventory of the number of water users and the volume of water used. Similarly, it can contribute to an understanding of water use patterns in time and space. Evapotranspiration can provide information about irrigated and nonirrigated areas. In the United States, it is monitored so that insurance claims filed for failed harvests purportedly caused by lack of access to irrigation water may be verified.

- Estimates of evapotranspiration can be used to quantify crop water productivity—the amount of marketable crops (for example, kilograms of grain) produced per cubic meter of water consumed to grow that crop.

- The impacts of irrigation policies, energy subsidies, and other policies on agricultural water use can also be monitored through ET observations.

- Estimates of soil moisture and evapotranspiration can be used to inform both farmers and irrigation managers of the state of their fields when water conservation is urgent. While satellite-derived ET estimates make it possible to calculate the net loss of water to the atmosphere, remotely sensed soil moisture provides information about the water content of the upper 1 to 5 centimeters of soil.

- Finally, while RS measurements of changes in the gravity field—due to changes in terrestrial water content—have a very large footprint (the Gravity Recovery and Climate Experiment, GRACE, has a 300-kilometer footprint), regional aquifer-level estimates may be used to constrain regional groundwater models. In this way, GRACE data on aquifer levels can be reconciled with local (ground) well measurements to provide insight into what areas would benefit most from managed aquifer recharge.

- In large river systems with significant agriculture, such as the Indo-Gangetic plains, altimeter data on river levels upstream can help managers and operators to maximize artificial recharge efforts and optimize the allocation of water among uses and rechargeable aquifers.

THE FOOD-WATER-ENERGY NEXUS

Integrated assessments of resource use are often lacking, and analysis frameworks are rarely multidisciplinary. How can well-informed, cross-sector, and integrated decisions be made when academic research on integrated assessments is still in progress, relatively recent, or even lacking? Food requires water for agriculture and energy for growth and transportation. Water requires energy to be accessed, treated, conveyed, and delivered. In addition, energy prices significantly affect the cost of building and maintaining water infrastructure, partly through the production and delivery cost of inputs (Rodríguez, van den Berg, and McMahon 2012). In some cases, such as reverse osmosis desalination, energy prices directly influence production costs because of the high energy requirements of operation.

Water is often used to generate energy, and it is expected that renewable energy sources (biofuels) will demand even more water. Extractive fossil fuel activities in the energy sector can severely compromise water quality. Biofuel production competes with food production for water and space, raising the price of staple foods. Subsidies in the energy sector meant to lower the cost of food production often undermine the sustainability of groundwater use. In contrast, rising global energy prices (due to economic and population growth) and continued water scarcity will lead to higher food prices, which may push more people below the poverty line. Taking into account current practices and technology and a global population of 9 billion by 2050, Hanjra and Qureshi (2010) estimate a current water gap for food production of 3,300 cubic kilometers per year.

Without returning to the Malthusian versus Cornucopian debate regarding the role that technology and markets may play in solving the sustainability challenge of our time, it is clear that investments targeting improvements in irrigation infrastructure and water productivity can help to meet the demand for water for food production (Falkenmark and Molden 2008). In addition, projected increases in temperature and changes in precipitation patterns, due to climate change, will lead to changes in water availability, energy demand, as well as production, which will ripple through the system in ways that are difficult to predict (adapted from Rodríguez, van den Berg, and McMahon 2012). At the regional and local levels, the ensuing changes in resource use, economic activities, and land use will be shaped by global economic forces (energy prices, market demands), water availability, and climate change impacts. O'Brien and Leichenko (2000) dub the combined effects of globalization and local manifestations of climate change impacts "double exposure."

At a higher level, integrated assessments are essential to understanding coupled dynamics. The analysis of social metabolism takes a multidisciplinary look at how society combines water, energy, and other resources to produce goods or promote social well-being, as well as how it grows and maintains itself. Such integrative, quantitative assessments are useful for comparing competing future scenarios and comprehensive multisector plans for a region.

Near-real-time monitoring of hydrometeorological variables with remote sensing can help to inform short-term decisions on water for food security and crop production, as well as for hydropower generation. The Famine Early Warning System described earlier illustrates the use of a satellite precipitation product to monitor food security and so does the CropWatch System in China (appendix B)—a global crop monitoring system using a wide array of RS data for applications such as crop condition monitoring, drought monitoring, crop acreage estimation, crop yield estimation, grain production estimation, and cropping index monitoring (Wu et al. 2014).

The Food Early Solutions for Africa Micro-Insurance Project of the Netherlands Ministry of Development Cooperation uses visual and thermal infrared Meteosat imagery to monitor water balance, focusing on precipitation and relative evapotranspiration. Having found that the water balance (precipitation minus relative evapotranspiration) fits well with reported discharges and that the relative evapotranspiration is more closely related and proportional to reported crop yields in pilot areas, two Meteosat-based insurance indexes have been proposed: the "dekad relative evapotranspiration" (an agricultural drought index) and the "dekad cold cloud duration" (an excessive precipitation index). Numerous pilot projects with insurance companies in Africa have shown that these two indexes provide an excellent alternative to precipitation-based approaches, performing "as good as or even better" (Rosema et al. 2014).

Remote sensing of evapotranspiration can provide valuable information on the impacts that changes in energy subsidies or prices have on water use and could even inform allocation decisions in situations of energy scarcity due to competing needs for water.

An issue that could be explored further is the use of satellite-derived measures of evapotranspiration and soil moisture to identify regional soil and water management practices that have certain desirable characteristics or build on positive feedbacks, thereby promoting sustainable farming livelihoods.

GREEN GROWTH AND THE ENVIRONMENT

Models of economic growth have often ignored the role of natural capital as a factor of production and limited the assessment of economic growth to physical capital (infrastructure, machinery, buildings, hardware), labor (population, education, health), and productivity (technology, efficiency). Yet unsustainable management of the environment ultimately results in the destruction and full depreciation of natural capital, with negative repercussions for output in the short or medium term. If natural capital *is* considered a factor of production, environmental policies are a beneficial investment. While China has grown at an annual rate of 10 percent in recent years and become the second-largest economy in the world, it is estimated that the costs of environmental impacts represent about 9 percent of its gross domestic product. This fact threatens both its competitiveness and its welfare.

Green growth is an approach to economic growth that incorporates the following elements: sustainable natural resources management; more resilient communities, based on the adoption of eco-friendly practices (permaculture, soil and water conservation) and designs (comprehensive planning); investments in environmentally integrated infrastructure, green technologies, and innovation; and the gradual introduction of new pricing schemes for resource use that fully account for externalities.

Investing in environmentally sustainable growth is good for long-term economic prospects because it increases natural capital (through better management of scarce resources); raises labor productivity by improving health; increases physical capital by better managing natural risks (ecosystems provide regulatory and protective services, including flood protection, coastal storm protection, and infiltration and soil aquifer storage); increases the efficiency of resource use; stimulates the economy in the short term (through green investments); accelerates the development and dissemination of innovation; and creates knowledge spillovers.

Infrastructure is a central issue in developing countries, first because their infrastructure needs are acute and second because infrastructure policies are central to supporting green growth and alleviating water scarcity. Since infrastructure decisions have a high potential for "regret" (as they are long-lived), the current infrastructure gap offers developing countries the opportunity to "build right."

Remote sensing can help to improve the quality and effectiveness of water infrastructure planning and project design by complementing information provided by in situ measurements with available satellite-derived products. Remote sensing can be particularly valuable considering the importance of monitoring the dynamics of a complex and fast-changing world and evaluating the impact of human interventions, new infrastructure, policies, and regulations on the environment:

- Monitoring changes in land use cover after implementing green growth projects or adopting certain policies as well as monitoring changes in hydrologic variables (such as soil moisture and evapotranspiration in the wake of soil conservation interventions, for example) can provide insights into the extent to which project objectives have been met.

- Similarly, remote sensing can provide valuable information for spatial planning purposes.

FINANCIAL ISSUES

Water infrastructure that ensures a reliable water supply and well-functioning sanitation and irrigation services is a cornerstone of sustainable development and poverty alleviation, providing food and livelihood security in addition to healthy living conditions. The infrastructure gap is the difference between current levels of spending in water-related infrastructure and service provision and the spending levels required to meet the development targets. This gap has widened since the 1990s, because of the financial crisis, population growth, and deficits in the operational budget for water provisioning services in most developing countries. International financial institutions have attempted to offset these deficits through development assistance to the water sector. The World Bank Group committed more than US$100 billion in 2009 to maintain and expand existing infrastructure in countries that had cut their service budgets during previous crises.

Nevertheless, assistance fell 3 percent across all water sectors in 2011, the largest drop since 1997 (Rodríguez, van den Berg, and McMahon 2012).[11]

Estimates of investment needs vary widely— from US$103 billion per year for all developing countries until 2015 (Yepes 2008) to US$22 billion per year just for Africa, to ensure that the continent can reach the Millennium Development Goal by the year 2020 (Foster and Briceño-Garmendia 2010). Funding sources for developing countries include (a) public contributions in the form of official development assistance (grants, low-interest loans, technical assistance from donors and international financial institutions) and contributions from local governments funded by tax revenues; (b) private contributions, which have been halved during the last two decades (as the financial crisis lowered the tolerance for risky investments and a paradigm shift occurred toward more investment money but smaller investments); and (c) household contributions (toilets, septic tanks), which are not well documented but are estimated to contribute one-third of total water sector investments in Sub-Saharan Africa.

Various factors hamper the effectiveness of investments, such as the fluctuation of overseas development assistance from year to year, inadequate execution of or failure to execute budgeted funds by local governments, decentralization of responsibilities coupled with inadequate follow-up of decentralized funding and capabilities, and strong urban-rural disparities in the focus of investments. In addition, reported risks and ratings of water provisioning utilities often do not reflect the sustainability of the water supply or future hydrologic variability. For example, utility ratings in the United States are based on the volume of water sales (short-term revenues), even if groundwater is currently being mined beyond sustainable levels. Climate risks and uncertainty should be factored into long-term adaptation plans, allowing for adequate financing and pricing of services.

The main financial issues in the water sector relate to infrastructure for water provisioning and sanitation. To help to close the funding gap, Rodríguez, van den Berg, and McMahon (2012) propose a "reform cycle" with five circular and iterative components, incorporating the needs of all stakeholders. They suggest the following five components: (a) service providers deliver services more efficiently (by reducing nonrevenue water services, improving billing and collections, and carefully choosing technology for water services); (b) pricing of water is based on sound cost-recovery models (by covering the full financial cost of the services provided to guarantee their sustainability, providing incentives to use water more efficiently, giving financial compensation for ecosystem services, and introducing tariff reforms); (c) governments improve public expenditure (by clarifying who pays for what costs, strengthening the commitment to the water sector, and subsidizing users and service providers cautiously); (d) all stakeholders develop sound sector governance (by achieving political stability, the rule of law, government effectiveness, regulatory quality, public accountability, and a clear definition of the mandate of the main actors—policy, management, infrastructure development, service provision, financing, and regulation); and (e) governments and donors leverage resources to attract private investment (which demands solvent utilities, sound governance structures, and local capacity to plan and execute budgets).

Good monitoring capability can facilitate the communication with users and stakeholders, for instance, when making the case for compensating ecosystem services and covering the costs of environmental degradation rather than leaving the tab for future generations. Better governance also requires more transparent information and monitoring. Very large amounts of RS data that may be useful in this context are freely available and open to the public; only the processing and interpretation of data require some funding. In general, a good observational system should ensure proper monitoring and reporting of impacts on water resources and the environment from specific investments, measures, policies, and initiatives. This should be reflected in better, more sustainable management and provide a credibility asset for securing investment from public and private entities. Moreover, investments in capacity building (for in-house expertise of government agencies) usually provide a high return on investment.

INSTITUTIONAL FRAMEWORKS AND GOVERNANCE ISSUES

As new technologies progressively shape the way in which humans interact with the environment, new socioeconomic structures and arrangements emerge and evolve in response to the need to manage and regulate those interactions. The observed management disconnect between surface water and groundwater is a good example of how institutional frameworks have struggled to keep pace with technological advances. Since the adoption of groundwater pumping, the institutional organization regarding management of the conjunctive use of surface water and groundwater has yet to be resolved. Society still needs to regulate the use of this technological innovation in an integrated manner. Transparent, adaptive management techniques are ideal under current circumstances, as they allow people the flexibility to react to changes. However, successfully integrating existing and new policies is not easy.

Attempts to introduce sustainable policies are often hampered by the trade-off between the short-term benefits of (over)exploitation and the long-term benefits of environmentally sound policies, the unequal distribution of power and influence among various user groups, the relatively short terms of political office (four to five years), and the political disadvantage inherent in defending long-term issues (requiring regulation, demand management, and water use and service charges) versus addressing short-term needs with limited budgets and capacity.

Flexibility is an important aspect of a good, adaptive management practice. Institutions should be able to change past policies based on their observed impacts on the system. In this feedback loop linking the latest observations with the next decision-making steps, close collaboration is vital between those who monitor, study, and interpret the behavior of the system and those who ultimately make the decisions. Traditionally, these two groups have worked for different institutions, and communication between them has not necessarily been fluid. That is why an adaptive management mechanism is needed that will foster the development of new organisms and institutional strategies capable of putting new knowledge to practical use. For management to be truly adaptive, both the policies and the institutions must be flexible (Serrat-Capdevila et al. 2009, 2014).

Especially with Earth observations, there is insufficient capacity to close the feedback loop between system monitoring, modeling and scientific analysis, stakeholder participation, and decision making. Democratic societies are striving toward open and transparent water governance systems, supported by participatory mechanisms. The best approaches are those that manage to integrate structured public participation, planning and management processes, and strong scientific input, thereby contributing to science-based decision making. Thus both public and private institutions, as well as the general public, should be involved. National hydrometeorological agencies should, among other things, be responsible for analyzing and interpreting up-to-date observational records that are linked directly to water management decision-making needs.

While decision makers should spell out their criteria for making specific climate- and water-sensitive decisions as well as the information they need to make those decisions, hydrometeorological agencies should explain how their monitoring, forecasts, and assessments can be operationalized in the decision-making process. The climate adaptation strategies and plans to be developed and their exact characteristics will depend on past and current observations of water and environmental systems. These strategies and plans will have to reconcile development goals with specific interventions. Sustainable societies are those that reinvest in knowledge and understanding; capacity building and training should always be a central focus of water security (Serrat-Capdevila and Mishra 2012).

Understanding the dynamics of power in a governance system—and the interactions between political and economic processes that shape such dynamics—is essential to the design and implementation of development strategies and policies (World Bank 2009). Political economy can be defined in practical terms as "the way in which different stakeholders influence policy, governance, and resource allocation and thereby influence outcomes" (Wijnen et al. 2012). In the management of common-pool resources where abstractions by one user benefit the individual but diminish the pool available to others, monitoring and information transparency, to a large extent made possible by Earth observation, are essential to enabling both top-down (government control, privatization) and bottom-up (collective management of common-pool resources) management approaches (Hardin 1968; Ostrom et al. 1999). A good understanding of the power relations between users, user groups, agencies from multiple sectors, politicians, and the voting public should steer the design of policy and governance approaches that are likely to work best in a specific setting.

Remote sensing can support governance and institutional frameworks. For example,

- RS data can shed light on issues of data transparency and information control, preventing the pursuit of hidden agendas and informing other political economy challenges.

- RS data may help financiers and donors to determine whether specific decisions are based on sound science and information or guided by other interests. Even if the latter is true, building capabilities to use and interpret RS data is likely to be beneficial in the long term, as the political economy context may evolve (see the example in Wijnen et al. 2012).

TRANSBOUNDARY ISSUES

Transboundary basins cover more than half of the world's land surface, and their management can give rise to conflicts. A good characterization of a resource is the basis of international agreements on its use as a shared resource, more specifically, whether the sharing of surface water or groundwater is addressed. Transboundary agreements on surface water usually revolve around the delivery or release of streamflows at particular border locations (where watercourses cross borders) over a period of time. International coordination of transboundary groundwater management is more recent and perhaps more complex. International water treaties after World War II began to include uses not related to navigation, such as flood control, hydropower development, water quality management, and water allocation. Historically, the most challenging element of a deal has been getting countries to agree on the allocation of water quantities between the appropriate co-basins.

In addition to transboundary water issues involving sovereign nations, open conflicts, disputed territories, and other geopolitical issues often have a significant water dimension. Examples of this are the conflict between the West Bank and Gaza and Israel and the conflict between Sudan and South Sudan. Any serious attempt to resolve conflicts in these contexts must give due consideration to the access to and allocation of water resources.

The challenges of transboundary basins are often conditioned by a lack of data sharing and thus a lack of reliable information for all the riparian countries regarding the hydrologic state of the basin as a whole, beyond its borders. In addition, the parties involved may dispute the veracity of the data and information shared.

Subramanian, Brown, and Wolf (2012) review five case studies of transboundary collaboration from the perspective of country decision makers, providing a better understanding of the political economy of cooperation. They classify *perceived* risk in five categories and propose seven risk-reduction approaches, the first of which is to expand information, knowledge, and skills. This approach should also involve observation and analysis to meet gaps in knowledge, as well as training and capacity building.

Remote sensing is a tool for indirectly measuring hydrologic states in a (transboundary) basin beyond a nation's borders and for verifying shared information. For example,

- Remote sensing can help all parties to understand the resource dynamics (rivers and aquifer systems) because data sharing and proper monitoring are the basis for successful collaborative agreements and management efforts. Satellite-derived products can address the need of transboundary agreements for periodic monitoring and data sharing.

- Remote sensing can also be used to predict flows because it provides information from parts of the basin that lie outside a nation's borders. The Institute of Water Modeling's flood forecasts in Bangladesh using altimeter data is a perfect example. Altimeter measurements from satellite Jason-2 provide surface water levels from river reaches in India that are 600 kilometers upstream from the Bangladeshi borders.

This allows extending the lead time from a scarce three days (if observations were done at the border, as in the past) to eight days (Hossain et al. 2014). Many other RS applications can also be useful in transboundary settings.

NOTES

1. Throughout this publication, the terms "snow cover" and "snow depth" are used interchangeably.

2. Although the Intergovernmental Panel on Climate Change seemed less sure about this in 2014 than in 2007, the overall meaning still holds true: "Recent detection of increasing trends in extreme precipitation and discharge in some catchments implies greater risks of flooding at regional scale (medium confidence)" (IPCC 2014, 8), and "It is very likely that heat waves will occur more often and last longer and that extreme precipitation events will become more intense and frequent in many regions" (IPCC 2014, 10).

3. Buffers can help to cope with variability and change by building redundancy in systems. For example, in times of drought, unused water resources can be tapped that are not fully utilized during periods of no drought; the consumption of water for some uses can be decreased if needed or can be shut off for a certain period of time; and the users of reclaimed water can be changed in times of drought. In addition, because droughts are likely to have different impacts on different types of water resources, the ability to switch the system from one set of tapped resources to another builds resilience. In the case of floods, the existence of floodable areas, storage pools, soil and water conservation practices, as well as recharge infrastructures will help to slow down water flows, increase recharge, and lower the magnitude of flood peaks.

4. This interactive application can be found at http://hydrology.princeton.edu/monitor/.

5. See http://hydro/ou.edu/.

6. The near-real-time forecasts can be found at http://www.swaat.arizona.edu.

7. See http://watermon.tamu.edu/.

8. See http://www.hrc-lab.org/right_nav_widgets/realtime_caffg/index.php.

9. The forecasts are generated and publicly displayed on the Institute of Water Modeling website (http://apps.iwmbd.com/satfor/#).

10. Managed aquifer recharge involves building infrastructure or modifying the landscape to enhance groundwater recharge.

11. Rodríguez, van den Berg, and McMahon (2012) describe the current state of water financing and propose a set of approaches to improve efficiency in financing and reach development targets.

REFERENCES

Anagnostopoulos, G. G., D. Koutsoyiannis, A. Christofides, A. Efstratiadis, and N. Mamassis. 2010. "A Comparison of Local and Aggregated Climate Model Outputs with Observed Data." *Hydrological Sciences Journal* 55 (7): 1094–10.

Brown, C., Y. Ghile, M. Laverty, and K. Li. 2012. "Decision Scaling: Linking Bottom-Up Vulnerability Analysis with Climate Projections in the Water Sector." *Water Resources Research* 48 (9): W09537.

Cardwell, H., S. Langsdale, and K. Stephenson. 2009. "The Shared Vision Planning Primer: How to Incorporate Computer Aided Dispute Resolution in Water Resources Planning." Shared Vision Planning, Institute for Water Resources, U.S. Army Corps of Engineers. http://www.sharedvisionplanning.us/resReference.cfm.

Dekker, A. G., and E. L. Hestir. 2012. *Evaluating the Feasibility of Systematic Inland Water Quality Monitoring with Satellite Remote Sensing.* Water for a Healthy Country National Research Flagship. Victoria: Commonwealth Scientific and Industrial Research Organisation.

Dennis, L. 2013. *Proactive Flood and Drought Management: A Selection of Applied Strategies and Lessons Learned from around the United States,* edited by B. Bateman, W. Wright, and D. Duke. Middleburg, VA: American Water Resources Association Policy Committee.

Domínguez, F., E. Rivera, D. P. Lettenmaier, and C. L. Castro. 2012. "Changes in Winter Precipitation Extremes for the Western United States under a Warmer Climate as Simulated by Regional Climate Models." Paper submitted to Proceedings of the National Academy of Sciences of the United States of America.

Edwards, P. 2006. "Examining Inequality: Who Really Benefits from Global Growth?" *World Development* 34 (10): 1667–95.

Emori, S., and S. Brown. 2005. "Dynamic and Thermodynamic Changes in Mean and Extreme Precipitation under Changed Climate." *Geophysical Research Letters* 32 (17): L17706.

Falkenmark, M., and D. Molden. 2008. "Wake Up to Realities of River Basin Closure." *Water Resources Development* 24 (2): 201–15.

Foster, V. and C. Briceño-Garmendia, eds. 2010. *Africa's Infrastructure: A Time for Transformation.* Washington, DC: World Bank.

García, L. E., J. H. Matthews, D. J. Rodríguez, M. Wijnen, K. N. DiFrancesco, and P. Ray. 2014. *Beyond Downscaling: A Bottom-Up Approach to Climate Adaptation for Water Resources Management.* AGWA Report 01. Washington, DC: World Bank Group.

Garduño, H., and S. Foster. 2010. *Sustainable Groundwater Irrigation: Approaches to Reconciling Demand with Resources.* Strategic Overview 4. Washington, DC: World Bank.

Hanjra, M. A., and M. E. Qureshi. 2010. "Global Water Crisis and Future Food Security in an Era of Climate Change." *Food Policy* 35 (5): 365–77.

Hardin, G. 1968. "The Tragedy of the Commons." *Science* 162 (3859): 1243–48.

Hartfield, K., G. Schneier-Madanes, S. Marsh, and E. Curley. 2014. "Remote Sensing of Urban Change: Water and Urban Growth in the Sun Corridor of the U.S. Southwest." SWAN Report Working Paper, Sustainable Water Action Network, Lawrence, KS.

Hossain, F., A. H. M. Siddique-E-Akbor, W. Yigzaw, S. Shah-Newaz, M. Hossain, L. C. Mazumder, T. Ahmed, C. K. Shum, H. Lee, S. Biancamaria, F. J. Turk, and A. Limaye. 2014. "Crossing the Valley of Death: Lessons Learned from Implementing an Operational Satellite-Based Flood Forecasting System." *Bulletin of the American Meteorological Society* 95 (8): 1201–07.

IPCC (Intergovernmental Panel on Climate Change). 2007. *Climate Change 2007: The Physical Science Basis; Contribution of Working Group I to the Fourth Assessment Report of the Intergovernmental Panel on Climate Change,* edited by S. Solomon, D. Qin, M. Manning, Z. Chen, M. Marquis, K. B. Averyt, M. Tignor, and H. Miller. Cambridge, U.K.: Cambridge University Press.

——. 2014. "Climate Change 2014 Synthesis Report: Summary for Policymakers." IPCC, Geneva.

Kundzewicz, Z. W., and E. Z. Stakhiv. 2010. "Are Climate Models 'Ready for Prime Time' in Water Resources Management Applications, or Is More Research Needed?" *Hydrological Sciences Journal* 55 (7): 1085–89.

Lawford, R. 2014. *The GEOSS Water Strategy: From Observations to Decisions.* Geneva: Group on Earth Observations.

Leake, S. A., D. R. Pool, and J. M. Leenhouts. 2008. "Simulated Effects of Ground-Water Withdrawals and Artificial Recharge on Discharge to Streams, Springs, and Riparian Vegetation in the Sierra Vista Subwatershed of the Upper San Pedro Basin, Southeastern: U.S. Geological Survey Scientific Investigations." Scientific Investigation Report 2008-5207, U.S. Geological Survey, Washington, DC.

Li, L., Y. Hong, J. Wang, R. F. Adler, F. S. Policelli, S. Habib, D. Irwin, T. Korme, and L. Okello. 2008. "Evaluation of the Real-Time TRMM-Based Multi-Satellite Precipitation Analysis for an Operational Flood Prediction System in Nzoia Basin, Lake Victoria, Africa." *Natural Hazards* 50 (1): 109–23.

Maddock, T. III, A. Serrat-Capdevila, and J. B. Valdes. 2010. "Modeling Surface Water Depletions Due to Groundwater Pumping in a Transboundary Basin." Paper prepared for the International Conference "Transboundary Aquifers: Challenges and New Directions (ISARM2010)," Paris, December 6–8.

Meehl, G. A., C. Tebaldi, H. Teng, and T. C. Peterson. 2007. "Current and Future U.S. Weather Extremes and El Niño." *Geophysical Research Letters* 34 (20): L20704.

Nikopoulos, E. I., E. N. Anagnostou, F. Hossain, M. Gebremichael, and M. Borga. 2010. "Understanding the Scale Relationships of Uncertainty Propagation of Satellite Rainfall through a Distributed Hydrologic Model." *Journal of Hydrometeorology* 11 (2): 520–32.

O'Brien, K. L., and R. M. Leichenko. 2000. "Double Exposure: Assessing the Impacts of Climate Change within the Context of Economic Globalization." *Global Environmental Change* 10 (3): 221–32.

Ostrom, E., J. Burger, C. B. Field, R. B. Norgaard, and D. Policansky. 1999. "Revisiting the Commons: Local Lessons, Global Challenges." *Science* 284 (5412): 278–82.

Rodríguez, D. J., C. van den Berg, and A. McMahon. 2012. "Investing in Water Infrastructure: Capital, Operations, and Maintenance." Water Paper 74051, World Bank, Washington, DC.

Rosema, A., M. De Weirdt, S. Foppes, R. Venneker, S. Maskey, Y. Gu, W. Zhao, C. Wang, X. Liu, S. Rao, D. Dai, Y. Zhang, L. Wen, D. Chen, Y. Di, S. Qiu, Q. Wang, L. Zhang, J. Liu, L. Liu, L. Xie, R. Zhang, J. Yang, Y. Zhang, M. Luo, B. Hou, L. Zhao, L. Zhu, X. Chen, T. Yang, H. Shang, S. Ren, F. Sun, Y. Sun, F. Zheng, Y. Xue, Z. Yuan, H. Pang, C. Lu, G. Liu, X. Guo, D. Du, X. He, X. Tu, W. Sun, B. Bink, and X. Wu. 2008. *Satellite Monitoring and Flow Forecasting System for the Yellow River Basin.* Scientific final report of ORET Project 02/09-CN00069. Delft: EARS, December.

Rosema, A., J. van Huystee, S. Foppes, J. van der Woerd, E. Klaassen, J. Barendse, M. van Asseldonk, M. Dubreuil, S. Régent, S. Weber, A. Karaa, G. Reusche, R. Goslinga, R. Mbaka, F. Gosselink, R. Leftley, J. Kyokunda, J. Kakweza, R. Lynch, and K. Stigter. 2014. *FESA Micro-Insurance: Crop Insurance Reaching Every Farmer in Africa.*

Scientific Final Report of Millennium Agreements Project 38. Report commissioned by the Netherlands Ministry of Foreign Affairs, Directorate Sustainable Economic Development. Delft: EARS Earth Environment Monitoring BV.

Salas, J. D., B. Rajagopalan, L. Saito, and C. Brown. 2012. "Special Section on Climate Change and Water Resources: Climate Nonstationarity and Water Resources Management, Introduction." *Journal of Water Resources Planning and Management* 138 (5): 385–88.

Serrat-Capdevila, A., and A. Mishra, eds. 2012. "Rio+20 Water Security Recommendations." Forum on Science, Technology and Innovation for Sustainable Development, International Council for Sciences, Rio de Janeiro, Brazil, June 11–15. http://www.icsu.org/rio20/science-and-technology-forum/programme/forum%20 recommendations/water-security.

Serrat-Capdevila, A., A. Browning-Aiken, K. Lansey, T. Finan, and J. B. Valdés. 2009. "Increasing Socio-Ecological Resilience by Placing Science at the Decision Table: The Role of the San Pedro Basin Decision-Support System Model (Arizona)." *Ecology and Society* 14 (1): 37. http://www.ecologyandsociety.org/vol14/iss1/art37/.

Serrat-Capdevila, A., J. B. Valdes, F. Dominguez, S. Rajgopal, and H. Gupta. 2013. "Characterizing the Droughts of the New Century in the U.S. Southwest: A Comprehensive Assessment from State-of-the-Art Climate Model Projections." *International Journal of Water Resources Development* 29 (2): 152–71.

Serrat-Capdevila, A., J. B. Valdes, H. Gupta, and G. Schneier-Madanes. 2014. "Water Governance Tools: The Role of Science, Decision Support Systems, and Stakeholder Participation." In *Globalized Water: A Question of Governance,* edited by G. Schneier-Madanes, ch. 15. Dordrecht: Springer Netherlands.

Serrat-Capdevila, A., J. B. Valdes, and E. Z. Stakhiv. 2013. "Water Management Applications for Satellite Precipitation Products: Synthesis and Recommendations." *Journal of the American Water Resources Association* 399 (1): 1–17.

Shah, T. 2003. "Decentralized Water Harvesting and Groundwater Recharge: Can These Save Saurashtra and Kutch from Desiccation?" IWMI-Tata Water Policy Program, Colombo, Sri Lanka.

Shah, T., S. Darghouth, and A. Dinar. 2006. "Conjunctive Use of Groundwater and Surface Water." Agricultural and Rural Development Notes, Water for Food Team, World Bank, Washington, DC.

Sheffield, J., E. Wood, N. Chaney, K. Guan, S. Sadri, X. Yuan, L. Olang, A. Amani, A. Ali, S. Demuth, and L. Ogallo. 2014. "A Drought Monitoring and Forecasting System for Sub-Sahara African Water Resources and Food Security." *Bulletin of the American Meteorological Society* 95 (6): 861–82.

Stakhiv, E. Z. 2010. "Practical Approaches to Water Management under Climate Change Uncertainty." In *Hydrocomplexity: New Tools for Solving Wicked Water Problems,* edited by H. H. G. Savinje, S. Demuth, and P. Hubert. IAHS Publication 338. Wallingford, U.K.: IAHS Press.

Subramanian, A., B. Brown, and A. Wolf. 2012. "Reaching across the Waters: Facing the Risks of Cooperation in International Waters." Water Paper, World Bank, Washington, DC.

Verdin, J., C. Funk, G. Senay, and R. Choularton. 2005. "Climate Science and Famine Early Warning." *Philosophical Transactions of the Royal Society B* 360 (1463): 2155–68.

Villarini, G., J. A. Smith, F. Serinaldi, J. Bales, P. D. Bates, and W. F. Krajewski. 2009. "Flood Frequency Analysis for Nonstationary Annual Peak Records in an Urban Drainage Basin." *Advances in Water Resources* 32 (8): 1255–66.

Wang, J., Y. Hong, L. Li, J. J. Gourley, S. I. Khan, K. K. Yilmaz, R. F. Adler, F. S. Policelli, S. Habib, D. Irwin, A. S. Limaye, T. Korme, and L. Okello. 2011. "The Coupled Routing and Excess Storage (CREST) Distributed Hydrological Model." *Hydrological Sciences Journal* 56 (1): 84–98.

Wijnen, M., B. Augeard, B. Hiller, C. Ward, and P. Huntjens. 2012. "Managing the Invisible: Understanding and Improving Groundwater Governance." Water Paper, World Bank, Washington, DC.

World Bank. 2009. "Implementation Completion and Results Report of the Environmental Protection and Sustainable Development of the Guarani Aquifer System Project." World Bank, Washington, DC.

Wu, B., L. Jiang, N. Yana, C. Perry, and H. Zeng. 2013. "Basin-Wide Evapotranspiration Management: Concept and Practical Application in Hai Basin, China." *Agricultural Water Management* 145 (November): 145–53.

Wu, B., J. Meng, Q. Li, N. Yan, X. Du, and M. Zhang. 2014. "Remote Sensing-Based Global Crop Monitoring: Experiences with China's Cropwatch System." *International Journal of Digital Earth* 7 (2): 113–37.

Yan, N., B. Wu, V. K. Boken, S. Chang, and L. Yang. 2014. "A Drought Monitoring Operational System for China Using Satellite Data: Design and Evaluation." *Geomatics, Natural Hazards, and Risk.* doi: 10.1080/19475705.2014.895964.

Yepes, T. 2008. "Investment Needs for Infrastructure in Developing Countries 2008–2015." Latin America and Caribbean Region, World Bank, Washington, DC.

CHAPTER 2

The World Bank Group and Water

INTRODUCTION

Providing water services while sustainably managing a scarce resource has been at the core of World Bank Group assistance in the water sector. For the Bank, "water" comprises both water resources management (WRM) and services associated with water, such as water supply and sanitation, energy generation (power plant cooling and other energy source needs besides hydropower), irrigation, drainage and flood management, as well as environmental services. Water also plays a crucial role in other areas, from public health to urban and rural development. From the discussion in chapter 1, it is clear that World Bank activities can benefit considerably from the use of remote sensing (RS) technology and, in fact, have already done so. To assess the potential value for water-related activities, this chapter summarizes the Bank's water policy, strategies, practice, and portfolio.

WATER POLICY AND STRATEGIES

Water has been one of the most important areas of World Bank lending. The *1992 World Development Report* (World Bank 1992) highlights some of the difficulties encountered in this sector, exacerbated even then by rapid population growth and urbanization in developing countries. In response, the Bank approved a policy paper presenting a framework for improving the situation (World Bank 1993) and drawing from the Dublin Statement of the International Conference on Water and the Environment (ICWE 1992) as well as *Agenda 21* (United Nations 1992).

The objectives of the Bank's WRM policy are to support countries' efforts to reduce poverty and promote equitable, efficient, and sustainable development. This is done by sustaining the water environment while providing potable water and sanitation facilities, providing drainage services and water for productive services, and protecting people and property from floods. It stresses a comprehensive framework for formulating country policies, taking into account the interdependence of water resources.

A decade later, the 2003 Water Resources Sector Strategy and the 2003 Water Supply and Sanitation Sector Business Strategy started guiding the Bank's work in the water sector.[1] Since 2003 practices have evolved to scale up the Bank's assistance in water (see table 2.1): from reengagement in high-risk, high-return infrastructure and stronger emphasis on improving the delivery of water supply and sanitation services as well as the management of water resources to a growing focus on the role of climate change, urban development, energy, agriculture, and disaster risk management.

The Bank's water strategies are still relevant frameworks for addressing today's water-related challenges. However, in order to respond to clients' increasing demand for more and better-quality water by managing a complex series of trade-offs, the Water Global Practice has adopted a more inclusive, integrated, cross-sector approach to addressing these challenges. Laid out in the Bank's 2003 Water Resources Sector Strategy, this approach describes the main global water challenges and suggests steps that the Bank could take to make water more inclusive, such as integrating water with energy, climate, agriculture, land use, and overall economic development. This was reaffirmed in the 2010 midcycle review of the 2003 strategy (World Bank 2010).

The Bank is engaged in a wide variety of activities dealing directly with water, including support for water resources management, water supply and sanitation services, flood protection, hydropower, irrigation and drainage, as well as a variety of activities partially or indirectly related to water, such as adaptation to and mitigation of climate change, urban development, agriculture, transport, energy development, and environmental protection.

Therefore, the basic strategic challenge for the Bank is finding ways to help clients to scale up the impact of their own policies, institutions, and resources, so that the Bank's resources—whether finance or knowledge—are as effective as possible in helping clients to improve their overall approaches.

THE WATER GLOBAL PRACTICE

The World Bank Group consists of five specialized institutions: the International Bank for Reconstruction and Development (IBRD), the International Development Association (IDA), the International Finance Corporation, the Multilateral Investment Guarantee Agency, and the International Centre for Settlement of Investment Disputes. IBRD and IDA are commonly known as the World Bank, which, as of July 1, 2014, has 14 Global Practices as well as 5 Cross-Cutting Solution Areas that aim to bring best-in-class knowledge and solutions to regional and country clients.

Through this new operating model, the World Bank Group aims to help countries to achieve the twin goals of (1) ending extreme poverty by 2030 and (2) promoting shared prosperity for the bottom 40 percent of the population in every developing country.

The World Bank Group has been addressing water issues globally through large-scale financial and technical assistance to countries. To meet the growing demand for investment financing driven by the best knowledge available, the World Bank Group launched a single, integrated Water Global Practice in 2014. The Water Global Practice brings together financing, implementation, and knowledge in one platform that combines the Bank's global knowledge and country investments. This model seeks to generate transformational solutions that help countries to grow sustainably into the twenty-first century.

The World Bank Group's strategy places the poor and most vulnerable people at the center

Table 2.1 Evolution of Key Principles over Time

KEY PRINCIPLE	1993 WRM POLICY PAPER	2003 WATER RESOURCES SECTOR STRATEGY	2003 WATER SUPPLY AND SANITATION SECTOR BUSINESS STRATEGY	2010 MIDCYCLE IMPLEMENTATION REPORT
Integration and water resources management	Focuses on "modern" water resources management, that is, considers independent management of water by various sectors inappropriate; selects river basins as unit of analysis.	Places water resources management at the center of sustainable growth, with emphasis on basin-wide efficiency in irrigation.	Establishes a link between sustainable water supply and sanitation services, better management of water resources, sanitation, and wastewater, and environmental protection.	Highlights climate change adaptation and mitigation as well as need for cross-sector links.
Stakeholders and institutions	Emphasizes stakeholder participation in water resources management and need to respect the principle of "subsidiarity."	Emphasizes "political economy of change."	Focuses on need to respond to local demand and complement local initiatives; promotes private participation.	Emphasizes building client capacity for results-based decision making.
Position on infrastructure	Promotes investments to improve water quality; promotes investments to increase supply only when adequate demand management is in place.	Commits to reengage with high-risk, high-reward hydraulic infrastructure.	Recognizes that infrastructure is important but insufficient for sustainability; switches focus to operator performance and service quality.	Reaffirms emphasis on infrastructure, with efforts to link quantity and quality to infrastructure investments.
Economic and financial principles	Emphasizes incentives and economic principles for improving allocation and enhancing quality.	Emphasizes need for water pricing, cost recovery, and utility reform.	Emphasizes need for clear and consistent financial policies, affordability, and centrality of cost recovery.	Emphasizes need for more efficient water supply systems and support for low-cost, onsite sanitation.

Source: World Bank 2013.

Note: WRM = water resources management.

of its work. Efforts aim to ensure that everyone has basic access to sustainable water and sanitation services and that management of water resources addresses water considerations in sectors such as agriculture, energy, disaster risk management, and health. Finally, these efforts place water at the center of adaptation strategies to help countries to cope with the effects of climate change and build a more resilient future for generations to come.

Robust solutions to complex water issues incorporate cutting-edge knowledge and innovation. New knowledge products that draw on the Bank's global experiences and partner expertise are filling the gaps in global knowledge and transforming the design of water investment projects to deliver results. Multiyear, programmatic engagements in strategic areas are designed to make dramatic economic improvements in the long term and to improve the livelihoods of millions of the world's poorest people.

THE WATER PORTFOLIO

The World Bank portfolio is a valuable source of information on the profile of Bank activities and provides a snapshot of the budget allocated to strategic goals and priority sectors. The activities are classified by sector (using 10 different codes), according to which part of the economy received support,[2] and by theme (66 in total), corresponding to the goals of Bank activities. Each sector is subdivided into subsectors or sector codes, and the themes are grouped into 11 categories.[3] Each project in the portfolio indicates which sectors and themes it has been mapped to and the corresponding share of investment. In this publication, the sectors and themes of a project that represent the largest share are denominated "primary," while those receiving smaller shares are called "secondary."

Up to July 1, 2014, a Water Sector Board was responsible for the quality of activities associated with water, sanitation, and flood protection, which included 10 sectoral codes and 1 thematic code. Water-related projects, however, were mapped not only to the water sector and theme, but also to other sectors and themes such as agriculture, rural development, and urban development.

The following sections summarize the water portfolio to gain insight into the profile of the Bank's water-related operations. For this publication, the water portfolio was divided into (a) lending and (b) analytical and advisory activities (AAAs).

Lending

The active water portfolio as of April 30, 2014, was worth US$33 billion.[4] It included 272 active projects in the following subsectors: water supply and sanitation, flood protection, irrigation, and hydropower. Water supply and sanitation was the largest subsector, accounting for 63 percent of water lending. Irrigation was the second largest (20 percent), followed by hydropower (9 percent) and flood protection (8 percent). A little less than half (43 percent) of water financing goes to projects mapped to sectors other than water. The sectors and themes with the largest share of water components are agriculture and rural development (23 percent), urban development (34 percent), and energy (10 percent). The water portfolio's total value nearly doubled over the last five years. Lending in fiscal year 2014[5] (third quarter) rose to US$6.9 billion,[6] representing about 18 percent of the Bank's portfolio.

Figures 2.1 and 2.2 show some of the subsector and geographic trends in water lending in the past six years.

Analytical and Advisory Activities

The water portfolio also includes significant dollar amounts for AAAs that support and

Figure 2.1 Historical Water Lending, by Subsector, FY 2009–14

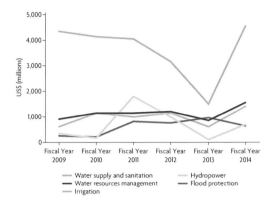

Source: Water Portfolio Monitor, FY14 Quarter 2 Update. World Bank Business Warehouse database.

Note: Data for the thematic code "water resources management" are *not* included in the total to avoid double counting, since water resources management is a cross-cutting theme.

Figure 2.2 Historical Water Lending, by Region, FY 2009–14

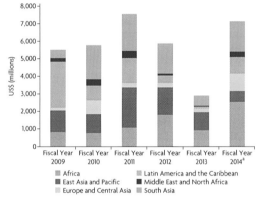

Source: Water Portfolio Monitor, FY14 Quarter 2 Update. World Bank Business Warehouse database.

a. Pipeline includes projects with a "firm" and "likely" probability of approval. Data as of January 10, 2014.

complement financing operations, primarily economic and sector work and technical assistance. Economic and sector work comprises products published by the Bank that can inform and influence the planning and design of a country strategy, lending program, or policy and that can build the client's analytical capacity. Technical assistance activities strengthen local institutions, promote knowledge exchange, and prepare clients for reform and program implementation. Technical assistance now constitutes more than two-thirds of all AAAs (72 percent). In the period covered in figures 2.1 and 2.2, Africa and East Asia and the Pacific accounted for the largest share of AAAs. In fiscal year 2014 (as of the end of the third quarter), about 70 percent of AAA was dedicated to water supply and sanitation.[7] These nonlending activities generally mirror the breakdown of investment operations.

Sector and Theme Components in the Water Portfolio

During the period analyzed (between fiscal year 2002 and fiscal year 2012), the Bank used sector and theme codes to classify projects.[8] Table 2.2 shows the total number of water projects by water sector code. A total of 179 water supply and sanitation projects and 176 general water, sanitation, and flood protection projects were identified. Together, they represent nearly half of all water-related projects. Irrigation and drainage projects represent the third largest sector, with 14.6 percent of the total number of projects. The share of both flood protection projects and hydropower projects in the total number of projects is close to 8 percent each.

Table 2.3 shows the number of projects mapped to non-water sectors that were nevertheless considered water related because water resources management was coded as a theme. Of these, the agriculture, fishing, and forestry sector is the non-water sector with the largest number of water-related projects.

Table 2.3 Water-Related Projects with Non-Water Sector Codes

NON-WATER SUBSECTOR	NUMBER OF WATER-RELATED PROJECTS
Forestry	4
General agriculture, fishing, and forestry	73
Health	6
Public administration: Agriculture, fishing, and forestry	5
Other non-water sectors with water resources management as a theme	11
Total	99

Source: Water Portfolio analysis. World Bank Business Warehouse database.

In the pool of 775 projects identified, other non-water sectors with water-related projects that did not have water resources management coded as a theme (6 in total) were also identified. The non-water sectors represented were strongly linked to climate change (1 project), environment and water resources management (3), natural disaster management (1), and land administration and management (1).

ANNEX 2A. DATA ANALYSIS METHODOLOGY OF THE SECTOR AND THEME COMPONENTS IN THE WATER PORTFOLIO

Annex 2A is available online at https:// openknowledge.worldbank.org/handle/10986 /22952.

Table 2.2 Total Water-Related Lending, by Water Subsector

WATER SUBSECTOR	TOTAL NUMBER OF WATER SECTOR PROJECTS
Flood protection	58
General water, sanitation, and flood protection	176
Hydropower	60
Irrigation and drainage	113
Ports, water, and shipping[a]	12
Public administration: Water, sanitation, and flood protection	28
Wastewater and sewerage	44
Water supply and sanitation	179
Total	670

Source: Water Portfolio analysis. World Bank Business Warehouse database.

a. Since 2011, ports, waterways, and shipping have been coded under the transport sector. Before 2011, they belonged to water. Thus only projects approved between fiscal year 2002 and fiscal year 2011 are considered as water related under this category.

NOTES

1. The Water Resources Strategy was rooted in the 1993 policy paper (World Bank 1993). Since 2003, water sector thinking has also been informed by a 2010 sector study on water and development (IEG 2010), an implementation progress report (World Bank 2010), and various other analytical work and portfolio reviews.

2. Agriculture, fishing, and forestry; public administration, law, and justice; information and communications; education; finance; health and other social services; energy and mining; transportation; water, sanitation, and flood protection; and industry and trade.

3. Economic management; public sector governance; rule of law; financial and private sector development; trade and integration; social protection and risk management; social development, gender, and inclusion; human development; urban development; rural development; and environment and natural resources management.

4. The figures in this chapter are given only as background for the process of evaluating the current and future significance of remote sensing in the Bank's water-related activities. They are also used to illustrate orders of magnitude or geographic and time-based relative comparisons. They should not be considered official Bank figures.

5. The Bank's fiscal year runs from July 1 to June 30.

6. Data as of April 4, 2014. Fiscal year 2014 commitments include projected pipeline. Data for the thematic code "water resources management" are not included in the total to avoid double counting, since water resources management is a cross-cutting theme.

7. The strategic and analytical work conducted by the Bank's Water Sanitation Program is *not* included these figures.

8. See annex 2A for a description of the methodology used in the data analysis. Annexes to this book are available online at https://openknowledge.worldbank.org/handle/10986/22952.

REFERENCES

ICWE (International Conference on Water and the Environment). 1992. "Dublin Statement on Water and Sustainable Development Adopted January 31, 1992, in Dublin, Ireland." International Conference on Water and the Environment, Dublin, January 26–31.

IEG (Independent Evaluation Group). 2010. "Water and Development: World Bank Support, 1997–2007." IEG Study Series, World Bank, Washington, DC.

United Nations. 1992. "Protection of the Quality and Supply of Freshwater Resources: Application of Integrated Approaches to the Development, Management, and Use of Water Resources." In *Agenda 21*, vol. 2, ch. 18. New York: United Nations Conference on Environment and Development.

World Bank. 1992. *World Development Report 1992: Development and the Environment*. New York: Oxford University Press.

——. 1993. "Water Resources Management." Policy Paper, World Bank, Washington, DC.

——. 2010. "Sustaining Water for All in a Changing Climate: World Bank Group Implementation Progress Report of the Water Resources Sector Strategy." World Bank, Washington, DC.

——. 2013. "Water Vision." Water Anchor Working Paper (unpublished), World Bank, Washington, DC.

CHAPTER 3

The World Bank and Remote Sensing

INTRODUCTION

This chapter presents an overview of how remote sensing (RS) has been used in the Bank to date. It begins with a summary of the internal and external programs or "windows" through which RS data have been made available for use in projects funded or managed by the World Bank, including those related to water resources management. These programs are often specific partnerships with public or private entities such as the National Aeronautics and Space Administration (NASA), the European Space Agency (ESA), or corporations selling digital imagery or software products. The nine windows identified are described briefly, and activities sponsored by these programs are summarized; most of these programs are still active.[1] The chapter then presents the results of a Bank portfolio review conducted to identify those operations that have used RS products in some way, as well as some considerations for future use derived from a limited survey of Bank staff.

INTERNAL INITIATIVES

For a long time, remote sensing was a specialized niche outside the mainstream of the Bank's work. As partnerships for remote sensing have become more commonplace and the range of available products has widened, awareness has grown among practitioners at the World Bank. In recent years, some efforts have been made to integrate initiatives and organize the use of this tool within the Bank. This process has been a learning experience, and not every application has been successful; nevertheless, capacity and experience are being built up. The following sections summarize these activities within the Bank and provide links to further resources. More details may be found in the consolidated matrix of those programs (see table 3A.1 in annex 3A, available online at https://openknowledge .worldbank.org/handle/10986/22952.

Earth Observation for Development
Earth Observation for Development is intended to be a single hub for all Earth observation

(EO) activities occurring within the Bank.[2] In combination with the GeoWB data portal,[3] it is part of a process of building internal capacity for managing geospatial data sets developed through World Bank operations.

Earth Observation for Development seeks to capture and integrate knowledge products based on RS data that had previously been developed in isolation. It aims to create a unified source for existing RS products that can also be expanded to incorporate new products as they are created. Its larger goal is to mainstream RS data and products—making them available to the broader community of development practitioners, along with best practices, lessons learned, and experiences pertaining to their use. This involves raising awareness of the role that remote sensing can play in sustainable development and of the range of existing RS products and services. It is aligned with the Bank's recent "Open Data, Open Knowledge, Open Solutions" policy reforms.

Currently, Earth Observation for Development provides access to data and products from three sources: (a) the EOWorld partnership with the European Space Agency, (b) the agreement between the World Bank and the U.S. government, involving several agencies, and (c) the agreement between the World Bank and the Japan Aerospace Exploration Agency (JAXA). Each of these is discussed briefly in the following sections.

EOWorld European Space Agency

While the partnership between the World Bank and the European Space Agency is anchored in the Bank's Urban, Rural, and Social Development Global Practice, it brings together expertise from all regions of the world and all the Global Practices of the World Bank.

The EOWorld partnership was established in two stages. In 2008, the pilot program started with 3 activities; in 2010, the partnership expanded to involve 12 activities. Those 12 activities were selected after a competitive "call for proposals." The total value of the 12 activities

was €1.3 million. In addition, ESA provided access to EO data from 15 satellite missions, for a total value of €1 million. Those satellite missions included the European Remote Sensing Satellite (ERS), Envisat, RapidEye, the Satellite for Earth Observation (SPOT), Cosmo-Skymed, TerraSAR-X, Radarsat, GeoEye, and WorldView. Five dedicated, hands-on training workshops were organized in Brazil, Indonesia, Papua New Guinea, and Zambia and at the headquarters of the Indian Ocean Commission. The ESA and the World Bank published the results of EOWorld in 2013 (European Space Agency and World Bank 2013).

Following the success of the first round of the program, ESA extended its financial and technical supervision support, launching a call for proposals for a new set of activities to produce and deliver EO information services. These activities focused on four themes: (a) urban development, (b) disaster risk management, (c) forestry, and (d) oceans (World Bank 2012).

U.S. Government and World Bank Agreement

A memorandum of understanding was signed in March 2011 between the World Bank and the U.S. government. Its goal is "supporting developing countries' effort to create a water-secure world and to fight water scarcity and poor water quality."

Under this agreement, where possible, U.S. government agencies such as NASA, the National Oceanic and Atmospheric Administration (NOAA), U.S. Geological Survey, and U.S. Department of Agriculture will provide RS data and the means necessary to interpret and employ them.

The following categories have been identified as priority areas for the use of RS data: climate variability and change, agricultural systems, and water systems planning and management. The data will support (a) sound management of water resources, (b) reliable and sustainable access to an acceptable quantity and quality of water to meet human livelihood, ecosystem, and production needs, (c) efforts to lower the risk of hydrologic events, and (d) rehabilitation of degraded watersheds. These RS tools, developed by U.S. government agencies, hold potential for developing countries to improve productivity and reduce conflict, while also increasing resilience to climate change.[4]

Under this agreement, several knowledge-exchange events have been organized to build familiarity between NASA and World Bank staff and to begin developing tools and approaches to using remote sensing for development.

Japan Aerospace Exploration Agency

JAXA and the World Bank signed an agreement in 2008 for the use of data from the Advanced Land Observation Satellite (ALOS). Developed and operated by JAXA, ALOS provided high-resolution images of the regions of Latin America and the Caribbean where severe impacts of climate change were expected.

ALOS images and data were used in support of World Bank adaptation projects in Bolivia, Colombia, Ecuador, Mexico, the Andes region of Peru, and the West Indies. These images were used to detect changes in vulnerable ecosystems regionwide, which contributed to the development of adaptation programs in the region. Images taken by ALOS of the tropical glaciers in the Andes were used to assess glacier dynamics under an adaptation project in that area. As of April 15, 2008, total investment in adaptation in Latin America, including World Bank support, totaled US$90 million. In 2011, JAXA officially terminated the operation of ALOS because of a failure of the satellite's power system. This effectively ended the collaboration.

Nile Cooperation for Results Project

The Nile Cooperation for Results Project (NCORE) is one of the latest investment projects carried out by the World Bank under the Nile Basin Initiative (box 3.1). Its development objective is "to facilitate cooperative water resources management and development in the Nile River basin. This would be achieved through the provision of targeted technical assistance to the initiative's member countries and broader stakeholders, to facilitate cooperative activities, improve integrated water resources planning and management, and identify and prepare studies of potential investments of regional significance" (World Bank 2012).

The technical assistance to be provided under NCORE will include geospatial analysis to improve the analysis of existing RS data sets on wetlands, which will facilitate the preparation of future investments. Additional efforts include improving public access to the existing database, sharing knowledge among countries and institutions, and establishing a real-time hydrometeorological portal.

BOX 3.1

The Nile Basin Initiative

The Nile Basin Initiative (NBI) is a cooperative, intergovernmental partnership among the 10 countries whose territories occupy the basin of the Nile River in Africa: Burundi, the Democratic Republic of Congo, the Arab Republic of Egypt, Ethiopia, Kenya, Rwanda, South Sudan, Sudan, Tanzania, and Uganda; Eritrea has observer status.

The NBI provides a forum for engaging dialogue on the joint management of the river and its shared watershed, sharing information, and building capacity. Notable among these efforts is the creation of a Nile Decision Support System to integrate the relevant information to assist decision makers in formulating policy for the basin. The NBI also includes some funding for common activities, plus investments in water management at the subbasin level. In the 15 years since the NBI's inception, more than a dozen projects have been completed in the Nile basin, often managed through the World Bank.

RS and geospatial data and information products are an important part of the information-sharing and capacity-building efforts of the NBI. Many of the investment projects undertaken have incorporated elements of geospatial data gathering or improved data interpretation and have built institutional capacity to create and manipulate geospatial data.

The NASA Nile Project is working with the Eastern Nile Technical Regional Office (ENTRO), which is part of the NBI. Using Tropic Rainfall Measuring Mission data, ENTRO provides flood forecasts for the Eastern Nile basin. The NASA Nile Project has also produced analyses of the water balance in the Nile basin using remote sensing data.

GeoWB, GeoCenter, and Spatial Help Desk

Facilities such as GeoWB and Spatial Help Desk provide visualization services for RS data and have created data repositories for projects across the World Bank, making RS data accessible to specific projects. GeoWB is an internal spatial data platform, managed by the World Bank's GeoCenter, that enables data sharing and map visualizations. It was launched to work on sustainable development in collaboration with Esri, the leading geographic information system (GIS) software provider. GeoCenter not only supports the GeoWB data portal, but also provides GIS and mapping services. Spatial Help Desk elaborates maps and other spatial products such as interactive files containing regular maps, three-dimensional maps, and spatial data analyses.

EXTERNAL INITIATIVES

This section briefly discusses external initiatives in which the Bank participates.

TIGER-NET

The Bank decided to participate in the TIGER Initiative, launched by ESA in March 2012, in response to growing needs for information related to integrated water resources management in Africa. TIGER-NET is a major component of the TIGER Initiative[5] and will run for three years, with a total budget of €1.5 million. TIGER-NET supports the assessment and monitoring of water resources from the watershed to the cross-border basin level aimed at (a) developing an open-source Water Observation and Information System (WOIS),[6] for monitoring, assessing, and taking stock of water resources using EO data and (b) providing capacity building and training to enable African water authorities to exploit the full capacities offered by satellites such as Sentinel and EO data. These EO products and services are used to monitor, assess, and manage water resources.

The first phase of TIGER-NET focused on consultation, review, and analysis of user needs and current technological capacity and demand for the application. During this phase it was concluded that the various institutions had very similar system requirements but that their application requirements and information needs varied according to the specific challenges posed by different water basins. In its second phase, the program will aim to extend the number of water authorities involved as host institutions for the WOIS.

More details on World Bank projects with a TIGER-NET component may be found in table 3A.2 in annex 3A (available online).

NASA SERVIR

SERVIR—the Regional Visualization and Monitoring System—was launched in 2004 as a collaborative effort of NASA, the U.S. Agency for International Development, the World Bank, and the Central American Commission for Environment and Development. It provides satellite-based EO data and science applications to help developing countries in Central America, East Africa, and the Himalayas to improve their environmental decision making with regard to the nine societal benefit areas identified by the Group on Earth Observations—disasters, ecosystems, energy, biodiversity, weather, water, climate, health, and agriculture. Other partners within the U.S. government are NOAA, U.S. Environmental Protection Agency, U.S. Forestry Service, and U.S. Geological Survey.

SERVIR facilitates decision making by government officials, managers, scientists, researchers, students, and the general public by providing Earth observations and predictive models based on data from orbiting satellites, ground-based observations, and forecast models. Since the eventual goal of SERVIR is to become self-sustaining (with host nation support), it works closely with governments and international organizations.[7] SERVIR has participated in training sessions, brown-bag lunch seminars, and presentations at Bank-organized events.

Open Landscape Partnership Program

The Open Landscape Partnership Program is a global joint initiative of satellite data providers, distributors, processors, and end users.[8] Its objective is to create a community of practice that will expand demand for open access, high-resolution satellite imagery (2-meter resolution and a 1-month frequency or better). The data could be used to further public accountability, transparency, and sustainability of natural resources management for ecologically important areas.

Subscribers to the platform's pilot phase will get free Web access to available World-View-2 satellite imagery for the stated area of interest, online mapping tools, and designated server space. They will be able to use these assets to develop and document their own crowd-mapping projects of critical landscapes and hotspots, in exchange for agreeing to contribute the documented results (including Web maps) to the platform's project library. The latter would be available, through an online forum, for review, analysis, and discussion by peer practitioners.[9]

RS APPLICATIONS IN WORLD BANK WATER–RELATED PROJECTS AND ANALYTICAL AND ADVISORY ACTIVITIES

Based on the results of the portfolio review discussed in chapter 2,[10] this section identifies the areas where RS technologies have been used in the Bank's Water Global Practice and looks at the areas where RS tools could be applied.[11] The results presented in this section provide an overview of the RS applications in Bank lending and analytical and advisory activity (AAA) related to water, aimed at identifying (a) the water challenges that the RS applications address, (b) the current operational uses of RS tools, and (c) the relationship between RS tools and specific development objective(s) of the project or AAA. Thus the analysis gives

insight into specific ways in which RS data have been used. These include filling data gaps, serving as input for modeling to evaluate a project's impact, supporting basin planning in prefeasibility studies, or helping to boost project performance or operational quality.[12]

More details on the lending and AAAs reviewed in this context may be found in table 3A.2 in annex 3A (available online). Selected examples of EO applications in Uttar Pradesh, India, and in Malawi and Zambia are presented in appendix A of this publication.

General Trends

A portfolio review identified 61 lending projects and 16 AAAs approved between July 1, 2001, and April 30, 2014, that used remote sensing (figure 3.1). The breakdown of total lending and AAA by subsector is similar to the in-depth breakdown of the portfolio (see chapter 2).[13]

The analysis indicates that the use of RS applications in lending and AAA has increased steadily over the years, especially since 2007. Yet only a small share of all the water projects identified in the period under review (about 10 percent) actually used, are using, or plan to use RS technologies or approaches in their operations or AAA.

Figure 3.1 Water-Related Lending and Analytical and Advisory Activities Using Remote Sensing, 1997–2013

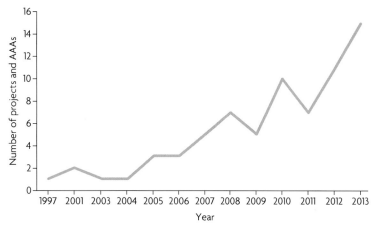

Source: RS Portfolio analysis. World Bank data.

Note: Data for 2014 have not been taken into account because this analysis only covers the first four months of 2014. AAAs = analytical and advisory activities.

About 78 percent of total lending and AAA combined are water-dedicated activities (see table 3A.2 in annex 3A (available online))—that is, activities whose investments in water or the share of water-coded subsectors represent 50 percent or more of the Bank's total commitment for that particular project or activity.

As figure 3.2 shows, Africa has the highest use of RS applications (39 percent), South Asia has the second highest (18 percent), and the Middle East and North Africa ranks third (15 percent). In Africa, RS applications have been used at the basin and subregional level. As discussed, much attention has been given to investing in RS technologies to address transboundary watershed management challenges often involving more than two countries or two or more projects. This partly explains the relatively high number of countries and projects in the Africa region using RS technologies.

Unlike the codes, which are sector specific, themes can be attached to both water and other subsectors (table 3.1). A significant share of water-related lending and AAA that have used (or planned to use) remote sensing have done so in cross-cutting areas nearly as often as they have in the area of water resources

management. Other than water resources management, climate change and natural disaster management are the two cross-sectoral themes showing the largest number of RS applications in water projects and AAA. Not only is this conclusion reflected in the project, AAA sector, and theme, but the applications themselves show that multivariate inputs from Earth observation have been considered alongside water-related variables. Thus applications in both water-dedicated and non-water-dedicated projects[14] and AAAs may also encompass non-water components.

As shown in table 3.1, the share of water resources management in water-related projects (lending) using remote sensing is 57 percent, whereas the combined share of climate change and natural disaster management themes is 26 percent. Rural services and infrastructure, although relatively small, ranks third as primary

Figure 3.2 Lending and Analytical and Advisory Activities Using Remote Sensing, by Bank Region

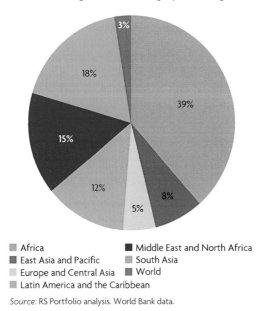

- Africa
- East Asia and Pacific
- Europe and Central Asia
- Latin America and the Caribbean
- Middle East and North Africa
- South Asia
- World

Source: RS Portfolio analysis. World Bank data.

Table 3.1 Number of Projects Using Remote Sensing in Water-Related Lending and Analytical and Advisory Activities, by Primary Theme

PRIMARY THEME	LENDING	AAA
Other than water resources management		
Climate change	6	3
Environmental policies and institutions	0	1
Infrastructure services for private sector development	0	1
Land administration and management	2	0
Natural disaster management	10	3
Pollution management and environmental health	1	0
Rural policies and institutions	1	0
Rural services and infrastructure	5	0
Urban services and housing for the poor	1	1
Water resources management	35	7
Total	61	16

Source: RS Portfolio analysis. World Bank data.

Note: AAA = analytical and advisory activity.

non-water theme. Among the AAAs, climate change and natural disaster management combined share 38 percent of all water-related activities, while water resources management takes the lead with 44 percent.

Results by Subsector

Table 3A.2 in annex 3A (available online) lists the entire sample of World Bank water-related projects and AAAs that have used (or planned to use) remote sensing; it also includes a brief description of the RS applications used in each project. Table 3.2 summarizes that table. Additional information about the relevant sectors is presented in annex 3A, which highlights the attributes related to the use of remote sensing, their characteristics, and any trends, by subsector.

World Bank Potential Demand for RS Applications

As discussed at the beginning of this chapter, several windows provide water-related RS assistance and products within the World Bank. At present, the nature of both actual and planned uses of RS applications varies widely within the Water Global Practice:

- *Evaluation of project impact on agricultural water management.* Integrated landscape management and agricultural intensification, climate-smart agriculture, and agricultural value chains

- *Agricultural water-saving measures and support services.* Irrigation planning and monitoring; reduction of nonbeneficial evapotranspiration; farm-level resilience to climate change, raising farm income by increasing farm yields and output value; planning and training tools at microwatershed levels; maps and climate information for use by farmers in decision making; agroclimatic advisory risk systems; improved Web-based information on markets, postharvesting, and value addition; farm participatory field trials and demonstrations for specific technologies; and research management to strengthen the institutional arrangements for longer-term, needs-based research identification, technology transfer, research quality assurance, and coordination of rain-fed agriculture and watershed management research

Table 3.2 Use of Remote Sensing in World Bank Lending and Analytical and Advisory Activities, by Water Subsector

CATEGORY	SECTOR	NUMBER OF PROJECTS			NUMBER OF AAAs			TOTAL (PROJECTS + AAA)	TOTAL (%)
		PRIMARY	SECONDARY	TOTAL	PRIMARY	SECONDARY	TOTAL		
1	Flood protection	9	0	9	2	0	2	11	14
2	General water, sanitation, and flood protection	19	3	22	10	3	13	35	45
3	Irrigation and drainage	16	3	19	0	0	0	19	25
4	Public administration: water, sanitation, and flood protection	3	0	3	0	0	0	3	4
5	Renewable energy and hydropower	3	0	3	0	0	0	3	4
6	Wastewater and sewerage	1	0	1	0	0	0	1	1
7	Water supply and sanitation	2	1	3	1	0	1	4	5
*	General agriculture, fishing, and forestry	1	0	1	0	0	0	1	1
	Total			61			16	77	100

Note: AAA = analytical and advisory activity.

* Not a water subsector per se, but has water resources management as a theme.

- *Use of modern, basin-wide water resources information systems.* Water information system platforms

- *Feasibility studies.* Irrigation projects, hydropower stations, and use of digital elevation models for reservoir inundation models and site identification

- *Basin planning, monitoring, and forecasting.* Watershed planning and monitoring

- *Transboundary options for flood risk mitigation.* Pilot nonstructural flood preparedness and emergency response activities; regional flood forecasting, warning, and communication systems; regional data sharing on flood operation mechanisms; urban mapping of buildings and infrastructure; urban growth monitoring; regional assessment of water resources management on shared regional aquifers

- *Investment planning and basin decision support systems.* Systematic information base and tools for water investments in systems contexts; identification of different types of infrastructure considered in the calculation of water balance

- *Institutional and community planning frameworks for addressing environmental and social issues.* Basin-wide planning (capacity building and coordination of government institutions in decision making for the sustainable use and conservation of water resources) and conservation of habitats and biodiversity.

However, a survey of task team leaders indicated that remote sensing could also be useful in the following categories and operational areas:[15]

- *Climate variability and change.* As the climate and its variability change, remote sensing could be useful for countries seeking to improve their capabilities in (a) managing droughts and floods, (b) reducing other forms of disaster risk, and (c) mitigating the impact of climate change. Against this background, remote sensing could be used for forecasting and early warning systems as well as for disaster preparedness, disaster management, and disaster response. Additionally, it could be used to improve resilience to climate variability and change.

- *Agricultural systems.* The agriculture sector in developing countries is particularly vulnerable to climate change and can benefit greatly from RS assistance, particularly toward (a) mapping evapotranspiration for use in estimating water losses and monitoring irrigation water use and (b) monitoring the performance of cropping systems for use in improving the management of both irrigated and rain-fed systems.

- *Water systems planning and management.* Comprehensive planning of water systems requires the ability to estimate surface water and groundwater fluxes in river basins. Existing RS systems can provide new tools to monitor or estimate various elements of the hydrologic cycle, including precipitation, evapotranspiration, flows, changes in available surface water and groundwater, water storage, aquifer recharge, and inundation. These data will also facilitate basin planning, inflow forecasting, systems operations, and water infrastructure management.

ANNEX 3A. WORLD BANK REMOTE SENSING PROGRAMS

Annex 3A is available online at https://openknowledge.worldbank.org/handle/10986/22952.

ANNEX 3B. METHODOLOGY AND RESULTS OF THE USE OF EARTH OBSERVATION APPLICATIONS BY WATER SUBSECTOR

Annex 3B is available online at https://openknowledge.worldbank.org/handle/10986/22952.

NOTES

1. However, a complete compilation of the data used in these activities, with a view to making all data available to World Bank staff and the public, lies in the domain of the Earth Observation for Development and GeoWB initiatives, which are described later. It is outside the scope of this publication.

2. The term "Earth observation" is sometimes used in a broad sense to include both in situ and RS observations. However, this report uses Earth observation and remote sensing interchangeably, the former being more common in Europe and the latter more common in North America.

3. GeoWB is an internal spatial data platform, managed by the Bank's GeoCenter, that enables data sharing and map visualizations.

4. For the media note prepared and presented by the U.S. Department of State on this collaboration, see http://www.state.gov/r/pa/prs/ps/2011/03/158835.htm. For the memorandum of understanding, see http://www.state.gov/e/oes/158770.htm. For a fact sheet on the agreement, see http://www.state.gov/r/pa/prs/ps/2011/03/158774.htm.

5. ESA launched the TIGER Initiative in 2002 in response to the urgent need for action highlighted by the Johannesburg World Summit on Sustainable Development and in the context of the Committee on Earth Observation Satellites. The overall objective of the initiative is to help African countries to overcome the problems they face in the collection, analysis, and use of water-related geo-information by exploiting the advantages of EO technology. For more information on the TIGER Initiative, see http://www.tiger.esa.int.

6. A WOIS is a multipurpose system consisting of a storage container for geodata, EO data-processing facilities for extracting and processing data, modeling tools for hydrologic modules, and visualization and analysis tools. Open-source software components like GRASS GIS, BEAM and NEST, Orfeo Toolbox, SWAT, PostGIS, and R scripts have been integrated so that all functionalities can be accessed as part of step-by-step, fully automated scripts. The system architecture allows customization by users and system adaption and scalability. More information about WOIS can be found in European Space Agency (2014).

7. More information can be obtained from Open Government at NASA Open (http://www.nasa.gov/open) and from the NASA fact sheet, "SERVIR: Connecting Space to Village" (http://www.nasa.gov/sites/default/files/638969main_SERVIR.pdf).

8. The Open Landscape Partnership Program is a joint initiative of Scanex Research and Development Center, Transparent World, and DigitalGlobe, Inc.—the platform's founding partners—in collaboration with NASA, OpenStreetMap, University Geoportals Consortium, the World Bank, the World Resources Institute, the World Wide Fund for Nature, Yandex, and various participants of the Critical Ecosystems Partnership Fund, the Global Forest Watch 2.0, the Global TIGER Initiative, the Global Snow Leopard Initiative, and the Save Our Species program. See http://www.openlandscape.info.

9. For information on the platform, see http://www.openlandscape.info/index.php?option=com_content&view=article&id=18&Itemid=2.

10. Updated to fiscal year 2014.

11. For more details on the methodological approach used and the data analyzed, see annex 3B (available online at https://openknowledge.worldbank.org/handle/10986/22952.

12. This "narrow" review fails to specify (a) the quality and quantity of data generated to fill information gaps, (b) whether the information gathered has been validated or the models have been calibrated, (c) the resolutions used, and (d) the extent to which RS applications significantly influenced a project's performance or the decisions about it. The limitation of this review precludes an in-depth analysis of the effectiveness of each RS application.

13. See chapter 2 for the total number of projects per subsector. However, unlike the results of the portfolio analysis, where the water supply and sanitation subsector represents a major share of the whole portfolio, in this chapter this subsector represents one of the smallest portfolio shares using remote sensing.

14. A water-dedicated project or activity is a project or activity whose share of lending commitment for water-related activities is greater than or equal to 50 percent; a non-water-dedicated project or activity is a project or activity whose share of lending commitment for water-related activities is less than 50 percent.

15. These categories are derived from a small survey conducted among Bank task team leaders active in the water sector to get a sense of their potential demand for RS applications. Given the very limited nature of the survey, the results are only indicative.

REFERENCES

European Space Agency. 2014. *Satellite Observations Supporting Integrated Water Resources*

Management in Africa. Paris: European Space Agency. http://www.tiger-net.org.

European Space Agency and World Bank. 2013. *Earth Observation for Sustainable Development*. Partnership Report. Paris: European Space Agency; Washington, DC: World Bank. http://esamultimedia.esa.int/multimedia/publications/ESA_WB_Partnership_Report_2013_complete/.

World Bank. 2012. "European Space Agency (ESA): World Bank Collaboration Earth Observation for Development." World Bank, Washington, DC. http://go.worldbank.org/IBJTNEU2U0.

CHAPTER 4

Key Data Needs for Good Water Management

INTRODUCTION

Given the challenges discussed in chapter 1 and the World Bank water-related activities annotated in chapter 2, this chapter turns to the data requirements and characteristics of a range of water resources activities. It identifies the hydrometeorological data that each specific kind of activity could use or benefit from if those data were available and links those activities to water-related sectors and subsectors of World Bank projects. Other types of data such as land cover, land subsidence, and topography are included in this characterization, as they are relevant to hydrologic applications as well. For simplicity's sake, this chapter refers to all of these variables as hydrometeorological variables.

Tables 4A.1 and 4A.2 in annex 4A (available online at https://openknowledge.worldbank.org/handle/10986/22952) give a detailed characterization of the key hydrometeorological variables that are necessary for various water resources activities, ranging from policy and planning to design, operations, and disaster management.

This chapter enumerates the variables included in this assessment and discusses how each one is relevant to specific types of water resources activities within World Bank sectors and themes. Next it addresses the issue of data availability. Lastly, the changing character of operational hydrology is briefly reviewed, concluding with a look ahead.

KEY DATA

Table 4A.1 in annex 4A (available online) presents the hydrometeorological variables deemed crucial for a specific water resources activity. The 17 variables considered in this analysis are precipitation, temperature, evapotranspiration (ET), normalized difference vegetation index (NDVI), streamflow, soil moisture, wind speed, groundwater recharge, groundwater level, surface water level, snow or ice cover, snow or ice water equivalent, land cover change, pumping and groundwater change, land subsidence, elevation, and water quality. The annex gives a brief description of these variables and explains how to read table 4A.1. The variables that can be estimated using Earth observation (EO)—precipitation, evapotranspiration, soil moisture, vegetation cover, groundwater, surface water, snow, and water quality—are described in more detail in part II.

Water Resources Activities, Sectors, and Themes

"Water resources activities" are defined as the key efforts or tasks related to the planning, design, operation, management, administration, and governance of water resources. These activities can be relevant to the water sectors, subsectors, or themes considered by the Bank in its operations. In the absence of readily available information on the specific hydrometeorological variables used in these projects,[1] the listed activities constitute an implicit link between the key data in table 4A.1 and the water-related Bank portfolio review presented in chapter 2.

The following activities are considered in this publication. They are based on information derived from the portfolio review described in chapter 2.

- *Comprehensive spatial planning and land management.* Plan how to use land resources to accommodate current and future societal needs; design infrastructure and allocate land to satisfy the need for habitation, recreation, environment, industry, water, and energy transport

- *Design environment.* Develop designs that allow the preservation of natural ecosystems in human-intervened systems

- *Design flood control.* Develop designs that contain floods up to a certain magnitude and associated probability of occurrence; use available data to calculate maximum probable precipitation and maximum probable flood; design hydrograph and infrastructure accordingly—by safely routing and dampening the event

- *Design hydropower.* Design hydropower production facilities adapted to the hydropower potential of available water resources

- *Design irrigation.* Design water extraction and efficient distribution through an irrigated area to satisfy crop water needs; topography, soil moisture, and evapotranspiration are important variables in this design process

- *Design wastewater.* Design systems that will efficiently collect gray and black waters from the point of use and treat them to the desired standard of quality before reusing or releasing them into the environment

- *Design water supply systems.* Design systems that will efficiently supply water of the desired quality for drinking and other uses in a specific area

- *Disaster management.* Mitigate the risk and impact of disasters and manage disasters when they occur

- *Energy (other than hydropower).* Develop a mix of energy sources, including eolic (wind), solar (equipment production and electricity generation), biofuel (irrigation), nuclear (refrigeration), and thermal energy

- *Food security and crop monitoring.* Monitor food production and availability, reduce human vulnerability, and operate in a framework that makes it possible to issue alerts and adopt mitigation measures in case of food insecurity or famine

- *Forest management.* Manage for aesthetics, fish, recreation, urban values, water, wilderness, wildlife, wood products, forest genetic resources, and other purposes (timber extraction, planting and replanting of various species, cutting roads and pathways through forests, and preventing fire)

- *Health issues.* Plan, monitor, and manage vector-control issues, water quality, pollution sources, and others

- *Marine and estuarine environments.* Maintain ecosystem services (storm protection, wildlife and biodiversity preservation, water treatment, fisheries, recreation, and other purposes)

- *Operations environment.* Manage to allow the preservation of natural ecosystems in human-intervened systems

- *Operations flood control.* Operate reservoir systems to regulate and dampen flood peaks and route them safely through the system

- *Operations hydropower.* Maximize hydropower production, while accounting for other constraints

- *Operations irrigation.* Extract and distribute water efficiently through irrigated areas to satisfy crop water needs

- *Operations wastewater.* Treat gray and black water flows being produced in the system, reuse treated water, and dispose of residues in an efficient way

- *Operations water supply systems.* Operate and ensure water supply to a specific level of reliability

- *Terrestrial and freshwater ecosystems.* Maintain ecosystem services (flood protection, wildlife and biodiversity preservation, water treatment, recreation, and other purposes)

- *Transboundary issues.* Understand the dynamics of use of transboundary water bodies, rivers, and aquifers, as well as the impacts of different uses on other regions and nations; use that knowledge and understanding in designing agreements and managing allocations to implement them coherently

- *Water resources administration.* Assign water rights and implement court rulings on disputes, pumping quotas, water fee collection, insurance plans, and the like

- *Water resources planning.* Develop future plans for managing water resources and necessary infrastructure, practices, and regulations

- *Water resources policy.* Assess the dynamics of water budget and resource availability in order to issue policies to guide sustainable management

- *Water resources management.* Satisfy the demands for water and balance water demand and supply by implementing existing policies

- *Water resources strategy.* Translate the principles of policy and politics into specific actions, recognizing that strategy lies between policy and planning

- *Watershed management.* Manage soil and water conservation practices and manage land use and land cover to ensure continuing ecosystem services and resource availability

- *Weather monitoring.* Use current-state variables and continuity and other equations to predict future-state variables and future weather

- *Urban design and management.* Design in a way similar to comprehensive planning but within a city.

Hydrometeorological Variables

The 17 variables selected are important for understanding the hydrologic cycle in a specific basin or region, for quantifying the availability of water resources in space and through seasons and years, and for understanding the effects of human extraction and use. Water allocation, water permits, and water use—related to both surface water and groundwater—should be based on an understanding of regional water availability as well as the requirements of ecological flows and aquifer levels. Sustainability is achieved when water uses do not jeopardize either the ability to maintain the same level of use in the long term or the functionality of ecosystems to continue offering the same level of ecosystem services. Understanding the hydrologic cycle and the dynamics of water availability in space and time is essential to making such assessments.

The variables considered in this publication were selected on the basis of their relevance for a range of water resources activities in World Bank water-related sectors, subsectors, and themes. The selected variables were compared with other classifications of EO variables deemed relevant to water management. For example, the Group on Earth Observations carried out an extensive review of user requirements for critical water cycle observations (Friedl and Unninayar 2010; Friedl and Zell 2010; see also Lawford 2014).[2] All users in that assessment ranked precipitation and soil moisture observations as, respectively, the first and second most important variables across societal benefit areas.

The selected variables include all of the 15 variables of perceived priority at the global level, although slight differences exist between the scope of the variables in Lawford (2014) and in this publication—for example, Lawford (2014) distinguishes between evapotranspiration in lakes and wetlands as separate from other kinds of evapotranspiration, between streamflow and river discharge to oceans, and between snow cover and glaciers. For practical purposes, and given its utilitarian nature, this publication does *not* distinguish between different types of evapotranspiration or streamflow or between ice or snow cover and snow water equivalent. Consequently, the variables included in this publication coincide with almost all of the "primary" essential water variables as defined in Lawford (2014).

All of these variables are highly relevant to hydrologic assessments. As precipitation represents the water input into a basin, variables such as temperature and wind speed influence ET rates. Land cover controls the partitioning of precipitation between evapotranspiration

(given meteorological forcings and interception, that is, water intercepted by plant, leaf, and branch surfaces), direct runoff, and infiltration. Infiltrated water can recharge an aquifer or subsurface flow, remain in the soil as moisture, or return to the atmosphere via evapotranspiration. Vegetation cover (measured with NDVI) is a very significant factor for transpiring soil moisture back into the atmosphere and influencing infiltration in times of rainfall.

Direct runoff and subsurface flow may all contribute to river streamflows, as well as baseflows, when the aquifer system is connected to the river. In these cases, groundwater levels are important because riparian areas and wetlands may depend on groundwater. Groundwater recharge determines the rate at which aquifers are replenished; in natural environments, it is determined by the sum of contributions to river baseflow, evapotranspiration from connected riparian ecosystems, and groundwater flowing down the gradient out of the region. Human pumping of groundwater captures flows that would otherwise become baseflow, riparian evapotranspiration, or groundwater outflow or deplete the aquifer storage (lowering groundwater levels and inducing land subsidence).

The extent of snow cover and snow water equivalent are also important variables, as they reduce ET losses, increase soil infiltration, and constitute a source of water storage that regulates river flows through the spring and into the dry seasons on most continents.

As the many variables that influence and govern the hydrologic cycle are spatially heterogeneous and vary in time, hydrologic models are essential to understanding the hydrologic system and identifying the main drivers of its hydrologic behavior. While ground observations provide point measurements, limited in time, which have to be generalized for large regions, remote sensing (RS) estimates provide spatial information at varying time frequencies. Thus the addition of

RS estimates benefits hydrologic modeling, both through historical analyses and real-time simulations, indirectly supporting water resources management and planning.

Relevance of Variables for Each Activity, Sector, and Theme

The variables of relevance to each activity can be derived by specifying the type of measurements of the variable—for point (ground-level) measurements and areal (RS) measurements, respectively. For example, precipitation can be measured at ground level with "rain gauge networks" and remotely with ground-based "radar" and different kinds of "satellite" sensors.

Longer time series are always desirable, but table 4A.1 in annex 4A (available online) provides two or three values that can be understood as "minimum length required," "adequate for use," and "optimal length," with the caveat that these are approximate values. Available data lengths are almost always shorter than desired.

Finally, table 4A.2 in annex 4A (available online) provides an initial characterization of existing data for the variables of interest. This includes some insights into accessibility of records, approximate time-series lengths of potentially available records, time intervals, and an explanation of how specific variables are measured or estimated (based on RS-derived data). A detailed explanation of how values for precipitation, evapotranspiration, soil moisture, vegetation cover, groundwater, surface water, snow, and water quality are estimated with Earth observation is given in chapter 6 of this publication.

AVAILABILITY OF DATA

To be able to manage something, one must know what it is that needs to be managed. Sustainable use of resources and resilient systems need data and a thorough understanding of natural hydrologic processes as well as patterns of human water use and their coupled dynamics. Unfortunately, the availability of data for planning and management purposes is usually less than optimal. Sometimes the quality and characteristics of the data are such that they do not allow a good analysis and interpretation.

This section starts by discussing the challenges of data collection, the decline of ground observation networks, and how ground measurements stack up against satellite observations. It then provides an overview of operational hydrology to date. Finally, it discusses the future of operational hydrology and provides insights into how to bridge the gap between management practitioners, on the one hand, and RS products and applications, on the other hand.

The collection of ground-based observational records is usually the responsibility of national water resources government agencies and regional hydrometeorological services. Other agencies and institutions (ministries of energy, agriculture, health, and transportation) and sometimes even the private sector may also collect water-related data. Given the local nature of hydrometeorological observations and the fact that the collection and storage of data in central, national archives are often not systematic, data are frequently kept in a fragmented way. In addition, as data are seen as essential information on resources and, thus, a source of power, public or third-party access may be restricted or difficult to obtain. This applies especially to transboundary basins, whenever there is a conflict or tension regarding the allocation of water among the member states, as is the case of the Nile River.

As to data needs, a distinction can be made between the need for (a) long-term data records for strategic policy, planning, and design and (b) real-time data for monitoring and forecasting to serve operational management purposes as well as short- and medium-term decision making.

Some of the factors hindering the use of data from ground-based monitoring networks for water resources operations and planning are the lack of real-time data and accessibility, coupled with quality control.

Very few observation stations are equipped with telemetry systems that allow data to be transmitted in real time, resulting in a lack of available real-time data. Most recorded data only become available after several days, weeks, or months, with a lot of readings losing most of their value for operational hydrology purposes. Many new networks in developed countries are being implemented with telemetry capabilities, and crowd-sourcing efforts for hydrometeorological observations are under way. However, the situation in developing countries is direr, as the number of observation stations is being reduced and existing ones are not being properly maintained.

Data are not easily shared across agencies, much less between nations, and they are not even easily bought, as the data owners sometimes use them to gain leverage or power. While some national hydrometeorological services in developing countries may consider data a source of revenue to relieve their difficult budgetary situation, in general, data are seen as both a public good and a strategic resource.

Many data records lack quality assurance and quality control, especially in developing countries. Data records can have many flaws, often due to the absence of a systematic data-retrieval methodology (data are collected only seasonally or when judged necessary, in the rainy season for instance), operator error (missing data lead to data gaps or invented data values), and deficient archiving (readings are not properly referenced in time and space). In addition, data records from different locations may be very heterogeneous, due to the lack of systematic procedures or uniform standards.

These problems in developing countries are caused by several factors, among others, the lack of proper funding for hydrometeorological agencies, the lack of training and capacity building for collecting data and managing databases, and inaccessibility of measurement locations due to logistical problems, safety issues, and conflicts.

International organizations attempt to overcome these challenges by promoting cooperation, data sharing, and capacity building. Many initiatives have been developed for that purpose, often aimed at a specific variable or type of data. The International Groundwater Resources Assessment Centre (IGRAC), for example, aims to assess global groundwater resources and share the information through a centralized system.[3] The Global Runoff Data Centre (GRDC) is a repository of global streamflow data records and can be accessed online.[4]

A more recent initiative attempts to connect and link existing efforts and networks observing all types of hydrometeorological variables. Established in 2001, the Global Terrestrial Network–Hydrology (GTN–H) links existing networks and systems into a network of networks for integrated observations of the global water cycle (figure 4.1).[5] The GTN–H is a joint project of the Global Climate Observing System, the Climate and Water Department of the World Meteorological Organization, and the Global Terrestrial Observing System. It is the largest association of international hydrometeorological data centers and users worldwide.

In addition, the World Bank has a freely available databank, which contains records on a broad range of topics and fields related to economic development, and a Climate Change Knowledge Portal.[6] The portal contains historical data and model projections of future climate under different climate change scenarios. The historical data include temperature and precipitation records from observational stations participating in the Global Historical Climatology Network and merged station-satellite historical data records from the U.S. National Centers for Environmental Prediction.

The Food and Agriculture Organization also has a freely available online database called

Figure 4.1 Components of the Global Terrestrial Network–Hydrology, 2013

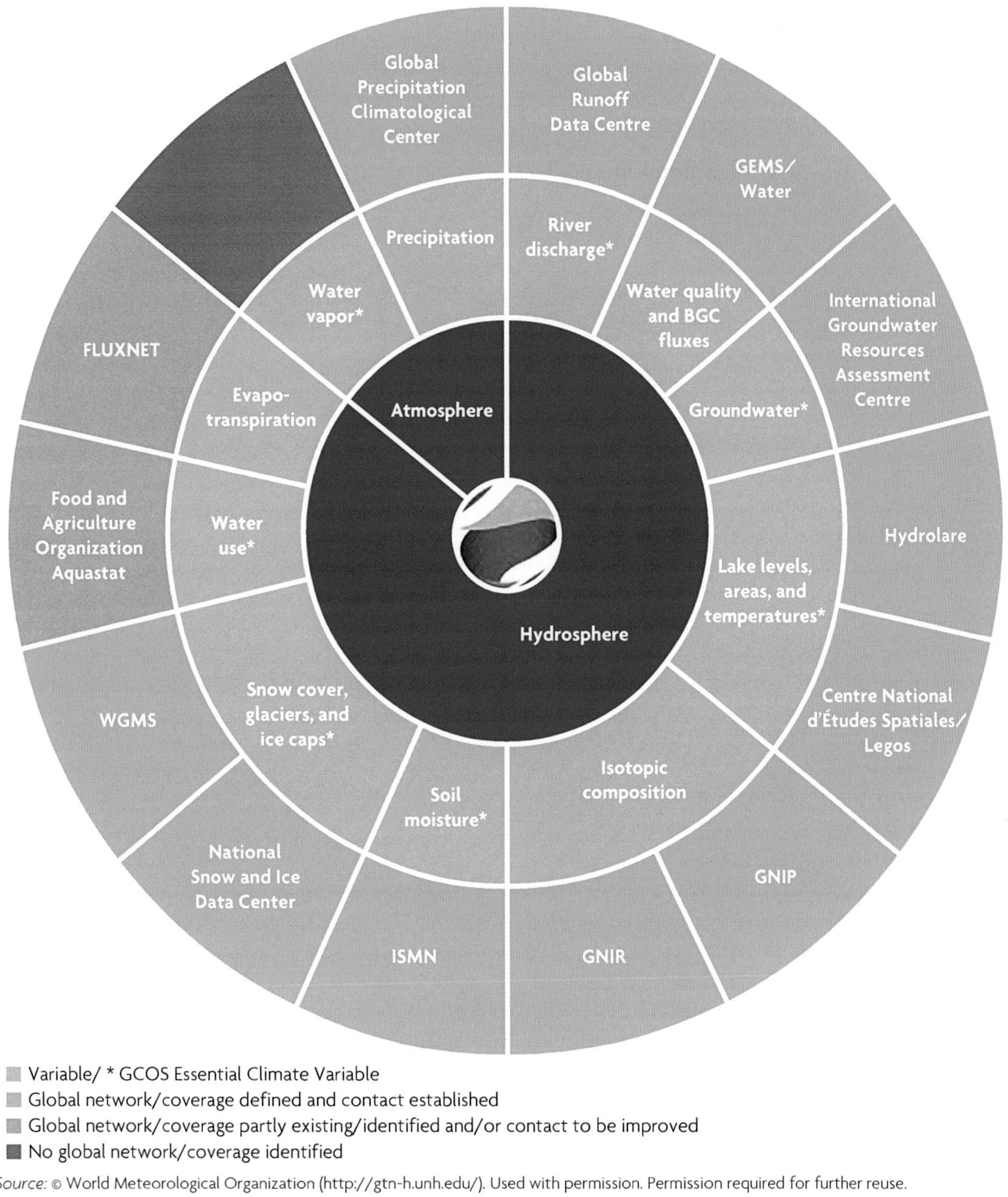

- Variable/ * GCOS Essential Climate Variable
- Global network/coverage defined and contact established
- Global network/coverage partly existing/identified and/or contact to be improved
- No global network/coverage identified

Source: © World Meteorological Organization (http://gtn-h.unh.edu/). Used with permission. Permission required for further reuse.

Note: GCOS = Global Climate Observing System; BGC = biogeochemical global climate (models); CNES = Centre National d'Études Spatiales; FAO = Food and Agriculture Organization; GEMS = Global Environmental Monitoring System; GNIP = Global Network of Isotopes in Precipitation; GNIR = Global Network of Isotopes in Rivers; GPCC = Global Precipitation Climatological Center; GRDC = Global Runoff Data Centre; IGRAC = International Groundwater Resources Assessment Centre; ISMN = International Soil Moisture Network; NSIDC = National Snow and Ice Data Center; WGMS = World Glacier Monitoring Service.

AQUASTAT, developed by the Land and Water Division.[7] The main database provides five-year averages for up to 70 variables, by country. Other databases have information on dams, institutions (by country), sediment yields in rivers, water-related investments in Africa, and irrigation investments around the world.

Decline of Ground-Based Observation Networks

The number of global, ground-based hydro-meteorological observations has gradually decreased since the 1980s (figure 4.2; Shiklomanov, Lammers, and Vorosmarty 2002; Stokstad 1999). This is due to a combination of

Figure 4.2 Availability of Historical Monthly and Daily Discharge Data in the Global Runoff Data Centre Database, 2004 and 2014

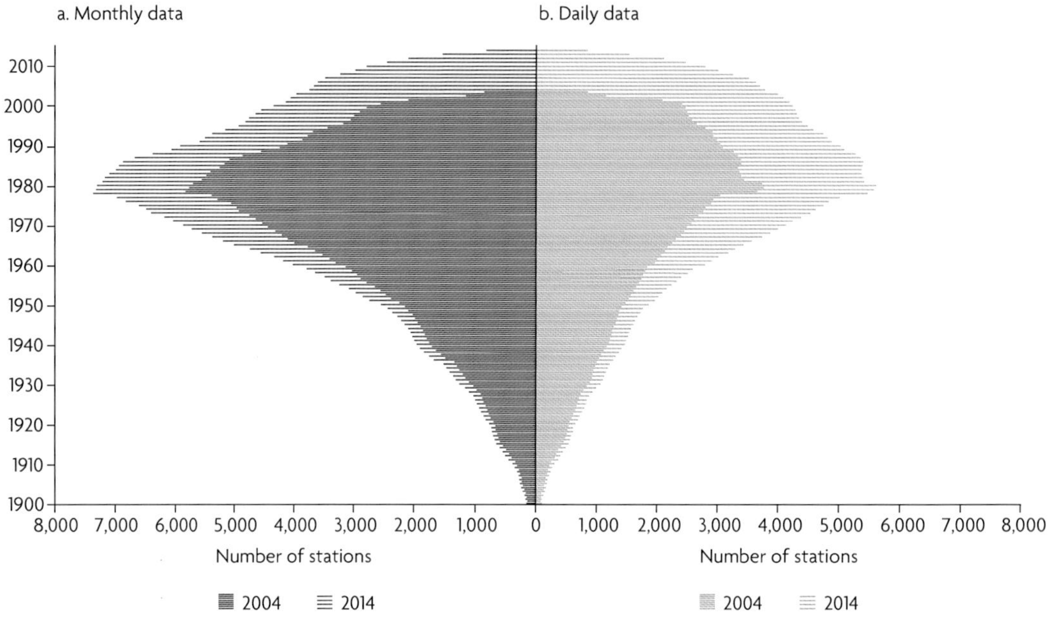

a. Monthly data

b. Daily data

Number of stations

Number of stations

≡ 2004   ≡ 2014   ≡ 2004   ≡ 2014

Source: © GRDC (Global Runoff Data Centre). Used with permission. Further permission required for reuse.

Note: While the historical size of the archive at the GRDC increased substantially between 2004 and 2014 in terms of both the number of stations and the volume of data available for the historical period, the number of available stations and data has declined since the 1980s. This decrease is due to several factors: (a) a decline in the number of monitoring stations; (b) long quality assurance process times; (c) lack of data sharing by country agencies; (d) increased operation of monitoring infrastructure by hydropower companies, which do not share the data due to its strategic value; and (e) decentralization of management and monitoring responsibilities, which multiplies the number of agencies that the GRDC has to interact with in order to obtain data updates (Ulrich Looser, GRDC head, personal communication).

factors including budget constraints and the ensuing lack of maintenance and operators as well as the existence of political turmoil and conflicts that sometimes destroy gauges, prevent readings, or halt funding altogether. Even in stable, first-world countries, spending budgets for in situ monitoring have shrunk, despite the call of the Intergovernmental Panel on Climate Change for more in situ measurements (IPCC 1991). The discontinuation of readings in stations with long time series entails the loss of "climate memory," at a time when long-term records are becoming critical to documenting and understanding climate variability and change.

Ungauged Basins

In ungauged basins, predictions are still possible through several approaches. Regionalization is a technique that attempts to fill the void of missing data by using information from

other locations to estimate variables in the basin of interest. Remote sensing can also be used to monitor ungauged basins. The Prediction in Ungauged Basins Initiative (Pomeroy, Whitfield, and Spence 2013; Seibert and Beven 2009; Sivapalan 2003; Wagener and Montanari 2011) is a good example of efforts made to overcome the problem of lack of data in ungauged or poorly gauged basins. Generally, prediction efforts for ungauged basins need data from gauged basins with similar characteristics to create analogies based on hydrologic modeling, frequency analysis, statistical correlations, parameter regionalization, and remote sensing. In general, such approaches allow for the characterization of hydrologic regimes, their variability, and tentative predictions in ungauged basins, although the latter are associated with significant levels of uncertainty due to their indirect nature.

It is difficult to predict whether the number of ground monitoring observations around the world will continue to decline or start to rise in the near future, although it is likely that large areas of the world will remain poorly gauged. The decline of existing ground-based networks in regions across the world has left satellite observations to fill this void. However, it is a fallacy to think that the latter can just substitute ground observations. Integrating and comparing measurements from the ground and from space are very necessary but complex and challenging tasks.

OPERATIONAL HYDROLOGY TODAY

Operational hydrology is the range of activities attempting to measure and understand the water balance components for use in direct practical applications of planning, design, and management of water resources. This section provides an overview of the current state-of-the-art of operational hydrology, focused specifically on developing regions, and how it is informing water management, planning, and water resources activities in general.

Ground-based observation time series have been and still are the rule for operational hydrology, and RS hydrometeorological variables are rarely, if ever, used operationally—and not merely experimentally or as relative guidance—to support decision making.

Present-day water resources planning, design, and operations of hydraulic infrastructure and management are based on and have evolved from the Harvard Water Program (1955–60). In that program, academicians and senior federal and state agency employees worked together on research and training for designing and planning water resources systems. Tools and methods were developed that, given a certain planning objective, could determine what set of structural measures, operating procedures, and water allocations

(level of development for different water uses) would best achieve the objective. Maas et al. (1962) describe the program's major accomplishments. Many of its methods for evaluating and ranking design alternatives based on economic efficiency, given a hydrologic context, are still in use today. Using ground observational records, the planning and design of infrastructure as well as management policies made use of statistical methods involving stochastic hydrology, frequency analysis, probability distributions, and extreme values.

Evolving from the narrow cost-benefit analysis through the early inclusion of environmental considerations in management and planning—that is, the principles and standards of the Water Resources Council (1983)—the principles of international water resources management are reflected in most regulatory frameworks of developed and some developing countries; the same ground observational records are being used in the same way for hydrologic and hydraulic considerations.

Data coverage and access are poor in many regions and tend to cluster around large infrastructure projects that bring in the resources for reliable monitoring networks, rather than around other, less costly initiatives in water supply and sanitation and in irrigation. With comprehensive planning and the integration of large infrastructure projects with other efforts, monitoring networks could be made better available to inform a range of water resources activities.

In developing regions of Africa, reservoirs and other infrastructure are operated with effective, traditional tools such as rule curves developed from historical records. Operations rarely incorporate real-time prediction data into the decision-making process. Regional centers focus on hydrometeorological and agricultural research, such as AGRHYMET, with 9 member states in West Africa; the Climate Services Center (CSC) of the Southern Africa Development Community (SADC), with 15 member states; the

Figure 4.3 Seasonal Forecasts Issued by Two Regional Centers in 2013

a. Seasonal rainfall forecast

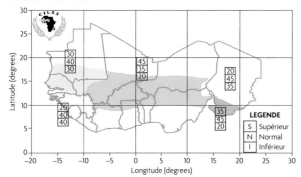

b. Seasonal streamflow forecast

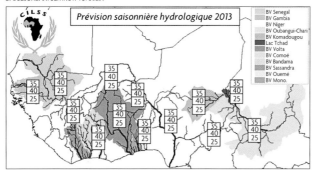

c. Seasonal rainfall forecast

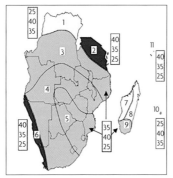

Source: AGRHYMET Regional Center 2013. Panels a and b: © AGRHYMET Regional Center. Used with permission. Further permission required for reuse. Panel c: © Southern African Development Community (SADC)–Climate Services Centre. Used with permission. Further permission required for reuse.

Note: Panels a and b show forecasts issued in 2013 by AGRHYMET-CILSS for West Africa, Chad, and Cameroon. Panel c shows a forecast issued by SADC for Southern Africa. The groups of three numbers on the panels represent probabilities in percentage of above-average (*supérieur*), average (*normal*), and below-average (*inférieur*) rainfall (a, c) or streamflow (b), respectively, for the region. The individual numbers in (c) represent areas with homogeneous rainfall.

Intergovernmental Authority on Development (IGAD) in Eastern Africa's Climate Prediction and Application Centre (ICPAC); and the Regional Center for Mapping of Resources for Development. Many of these centers could act as a repository of data, although the data are not easily shared, as they are still owned by the individual member states. One of their main research efforts is to monitor hydroclimatic conditions and drought and to prepare seasonal forecasts.

It is also fairly common for these centers to hold seasonal climate outlook forums with the participation of collaborating institutions, in which they integrate all of the climate information available and produce a seasonal forecast for the incoming rainy season for their region. For instance, AGRHYMET integrates information from Columbia University's International Research Institute for Climate and Society, the U.K. Met Office, Météo-France, the World Meteorological Organization, the African Centre of Meteorological Applications for Development, agencies from regional member states, and river basin organizations.

Forecasts are produced by assimilating different types of information based on sea surface temperatures and other climate data and are usually issued two consecutive times, as the rainy season approaches. Using a simple format, the forecasts give the probabilities of having an average, above-average, or below-average rainfall in specific regions. Two forecasts, issued in 2013 by AGRHYMET-CILSS (Permanent Inter-State Committee for Drought Control in the Sahel) and SADC, respectively, are shown in figure 4.3. Being a probabilistic forecast, whatever the volume of actual rainfall is, the forecast is never wrong, and its accuracy can only be assessed in the long term.

A key question is how these forecasts are used, or put in practice, by the member states and the practitioner community. In two workshops in Africa organized by the United Nations Educational, Scientific, and Cultural Organization with representatives from AGRHYMET, ICPAC, and SADC-CSC, the answer to this question remained elusive. The representatives of the regional centers did not know how the member states used the forecast, and neither did the representatives of the member states themselves. For several African basins, what may be lacking is an overall basin management plan with a clear decision-making process based on monitoring and observations.

Similar hydrometeorological networks exist in Central America, South America, and Asia.[8] In Central America, more than 40 climatic forums have been held to date. These forums provide climate outlooks for the next three months, and they are usually organized three times a year—in the summer of the Northern Hemisphere at the beginning of the rainy season, at the end of the rainy season, and at the end of the year when cold fronts arrive. The Central America Climate Forum is a working group directed by the Regional Committee of Water Resources of the Central American Integration System Secretariat, with the participation of national hydrometeorological services, universities, private entities, and other Central American institutions (García 2014). The climate outlooks estimate the plausible precipitation and temperature, obtained by statistical methods, compare the estimates with analogous years, and analyze results from global and regional models regarding sea surface temperatures and distributions of wind, pressure, and precipitation.

These outlooks are intended to complement the projections from the meteorological services of individual member states. Once the forecasts have been published, working groups of specialists from different sectors use them to make recommendations for their sector, to prepare for the possibility of "above-normal," "normal," or "below-normal" conditions. The sectors concerned are agriculture, fisheries and aquaculture, health and nutrition, water and sanitation, risk management, and energy. In addition, the reports suggest that each member state reissue more specific recommendations taking into account the particular contexts of each nation for each sector (SICA and OBSAN-R 2011).

In Asia, such regional climate outlook forums are much more recent, having started in 2009 for South Asia and in 2013 for Southeast Asia. Their functioning and outputs are very similar to those described above.

The Regional Integrated Multi-Hazard Early Warning System for Africa and Asia (RIMES) is hosted by the Asian Institute of Technology in Thailand and represents a consortium of 31 member states, mainly around the Indian Ocean and Central and Southeastern Asia, as well as regional international organizations and universities.[9] The governing council is composed of "heads of National Meteorological and Hydrological Services and national scientific and technical agencies generating multihazard early warning information." The key services are (a) earthquake and tsunami watch provision; (b) weather, climate, and hydrologic research and development; and (c) capacity building in end-to-end early warning.

FUTURE OF OPERATIONAL HYDROLOGY: TRANSLATING DATA INTO INFORMATION

The future of operational hydrology depends on the ability to extract relevant information from the abundance of data from different sources with different degrees of accuracy and precision and to use it for specific decision-making purposes. Given the increasing amounts of RS data available and current telecommunication capacities, it can be difficult for a manager to know what data sources to use or trust and how to combine different types of information. For any particular planning, design, or management decision, it will be essential to distill only the relevant information from all of the available data.

Chapter 7 of this publication provides a series of guidelines to help decision makers to decide whether Earth observation may be useful and, if so, to choose the most suitable EO data sources.

It is also necessary to characterize the errors and uncertainty contained in hydrometeorological estimates, as well as in data merged from different sources. Chapter 8 provides insight into the accuracy and validation of the most common EO-estimated hydrometeorological variables. The combined use of ground observations and RS estimates in an integrated manner, specifying the uncertainty bounds on final products, guarantees that the best possible use will be made of existing resources. Bayesian approaches assimilating different types of data with associated resolutions and uncertainties are appropriate for such purposes.

In addition, producing the best possible estimates by integrating different types of measurements can be tailored to specific management and decision-making purposes. What will this information be used for, beyond scientific and research purposes (which are what most space missions are currently geared toward)? In other words, managers and decision makers need to have a detailed, specific answer to the following questions: What type of information do you need to support your decision-making process? How will you change your decisions based on different forecasts or information? While these questions are two sides of the same coin, they engage different thought processes. During the Pakistan floods in 2010 (Mendoza et al. 2010), the information was there, but the mechanisms to act on it were not reliable. Other cases show that tailoring information to management purposes can also be a challenge in the developed world.

Sometimes the specific tasks required to attain the overall goals of water management agencies—or the means by which they should be developed—are poorly defined.[10] If the management tasks and specific decisions required are well defined, tools can be tailored to inform those decisions. It is logical that different models and applications will be needed for different purposes and different questions. In speaking of hydrologic models, an AGRHYMET official once acknowledged, "Everyone comes here with their own tool and they want to test it, but there is no model that will work uniformly well everywhere."

This comment illustrates the need to compare products and models. Given a specific need, what are the trade-offs between using "simple" and complex models and between using one set of input data or another? What models perform best for what purposes (flood forecasting, low flow estimation, forecasting for reservoir operations, irrigation, drought monitoring)?[11] The characteristics of an RS application for flood forecasting in a context where the main considerations are short time steps, quick response times, and accurate prediction of peak flows exceeding a certain magnitude will differ strongly from those of an application to support reservoir operations, which will be geared toward accurately predicting water volumes over longer time steps. The suitability or performance of a specific application can only be evaluated against a specific purpose.

Whether an application can be evaluated depends on whether it can be calibrated and then validated. Even in ungauged basins, biases in rainfall[12] and other variables can be corrected—based on observations from neighboring basins or regions—and these two data sets can then be compared to ensure that the estimates to be used lie within an acceptable range. The usability of RS products for decision making and planning is determined by questions revolving around the degree of uncertainty (error estimates), accuracy (the extent to which errors are characterized), precision (spatial and temporal resolution), and timeliness of the data available (for use in near real time or as historical data).

If products are used as inputs for modeling applications, it is important to know how errors are propagated through model calculations and how uncertainties are compounded through model cascades. For example, due to the nonlinearity of rainfall-to-runoff transformation and the spatial variability of rainfall over a basin, relative errors in satellite-derived precipitation estimates tend to be magnified in the value of the flood peaks (Nikopoulos et al. 2010). Thus a good understanding is needed of how a specific application propagates input errors to the output variables. Next, applications can be tested for reliability: How many times did the observations fall within the uncertainty bounds of each application's predictions?

Acknowledging the limitations of each application and being transparent and up-front about the uncertainty in its output variables form the basis of applicability. Part III of this publication presents the results of a (limited) literature review regarding the validation and accuracy of the most common EO-estimated hydrometeorological variables.

ANNEX 4A. KEY DATA FOR WATER RESOURCES MANAGEMENT

Annex 4A is available online at https://open knowledge.worldbank.org/handle/10986/22952.

NOTES

1. Which hydrometeorological variables, including those listed in table 4A.1, were considered in any particular Bank operation is not specified in the project portfolio databases.

2. The initial report (Friedl and Unninayar 2010) sought to identify the priorities for Earth observation from the user's perspective in order to inform future EO strategy. It considers user classes categorized by type and function. Major groups that use water information for decision making were identified, and then a broad range of applications was identified within each of these groups. Based on these categories, a list of EOs for the water social benefits area was generated for three spatial perspectives: global, regional, and local. Of 45 observational types of variables identified as being useful for water-related decisions, 15 variables with a perceived priority at the global level were used to identify the most critical EO priorities across all social benefits areas. Lawford (2014, table 4) displays the list of variables based on extensively reviewed user needs for water data. The final report is by Friedl and Zell (2010).

3. For information on the IGRAC, see http://www.un-igrac.org/.

4. For information on the GRDC, http://www.bafg.de/GRDC/EN/Home/homepage_node.html

5. For information on GTN–H, see http://gtn-h.unh.edu/.

6. The databank is accessible at http://data.worldbank.org/. The Climate Change Knowledge Portal is accessible at http://sdwebx.worldbank.org/climateportal/index.cfm?page=climate_data.

7. AQUASTAT is accessible at http://www.fao.org/nr/water/aquastat/main/index.stm.

8. A complete listing is available on the World Meteorological Organization's website (http://www.wmo.int/pages/prog/wcp/wcasp/clips/outlooks/climate_forecasts.html).

9. For information on RIMES, see http://www.rimes.int/.

10. An ongoing study of the Water Global Practice funded by the Water Partnership Program and the Global Facility for Disaster Reduction and Recovery, in collaboration with the World Meteorological Organization, tries to assess the current status of the national meteorological and hydrological services in different regions of the world. This study may identify needs for future support in strengthening their capabilities to include demand-driven activities in their operations.

11. The Bank's Water Partnership Program held a "Flood Model Showcase" workshop in Washington, DC, on September 23–24, 2014, to present common flood problems and various models and tools that could be used to inform decision making. The aim was to reduce exposure and vulnerability to flood-related hazards and enhance understanding of each model's "best" application, with an emphasis on the characteristics of the information each tool can provide. The report of the workshop is under preparation.

12. Most RS estimates yield consistent underestimations or overestimations of a variable with respect to its measured value on the ground. Bias correction techniques can help to remove these systematic biases. For example, satellite precipitation products consistently tend to overestimate rainfall in the tropics, as they "observe" it well above the ground surface, while some of the rainfall is likely to evaporate before reaching the ground. Bias correction helps to reconcile these estimates with direct ground measurements, as long as the biases are consistent over time.

REFERENCES

AGRHYMET Regional Center. 2013. *Bulletin spécial sur la mise à jour des prévisions des caractéristiques agro-hydro-climatiques de la campagne d'hivernage 2013 en Afrique de l'Ouest, au Tchad et au Cameroun* 23 (3, July).

Friedl, L., and S. Unninayar. 2010. "GEO Task US-09-01a: Critical Earth Observations Priorities; Water Societal Benefit Area." Final SBA Report, Group on Earth Observations, Geneva. http://sbageotask .larc.nasa.gov/Water_US0901a-FINAL .pdf.

Friedl, L., and E. Zell. 2010. "GEO Task US-09-01a: Critical Earth Observation Priorities; Final Report." Group on Earth Observations, Geneva, October. http://sbageotask.larc.nasa.gov.

García, L. E. 2014. Personal communication.

IPCC (Intergovernmental Panel on Climate Change). 1991. *The First Assessment Report of the Intergovernmental Panel on Climate Change.* Cambridge, U.K.: Cambridge University Press.

Lawford, R. 2014. *The GEOSS Water Strategy: From Observations to Decisions.* Geneva: Group on Earth Observations.

Maas, A., M. M. Hufschmidt, R. Dorfman, H. A. Thomas, S. A. Marglin, and G. Maskew Fair. 1962. *Design of Water-Resource Systems, New Techniques for Relating Economic Objectives, Engineering Analysis, and Government Planning.* Cambridge, MA: Harvard University Press.

Mendoza, G., J. Giovannettone, A. Willis, M. Wright, and E. Stakhiv. 2010. "Assessment of Pakistan's August 2010 Flood: Interim Report." Institute of Water Resources, U.S. Army Corps of Engineers, Alexandria, VA.

Nikopoulos, E. I., E. N. Anagnostou, F. Hossain, M. Gebremichael, and M. Borga. 2010. "Understanding the Scale Relationships of Uncertainty Propagation of Satellite Rainfall through a Distributed Hydrologic Model." *Journal of Hydrometeorology* 11 (2): 520–32.

Pomeroy, J. W., P. H. Whitfield, and C. Spence, eds. 2013. "Putting Prediction in Ungauged Basins into Practice." Canadian Water Resources Association, Ottawa.

Seibert, J., and K. J. Beven. 2009. "Gauging the Ungauged Basin: How Many Discharge Measurements Are Needed?" *Hydrology and Earth System Sciences* 13 (June): 883–92.

Shiklomanov, A. I., R. B. Lammers, and C. J. Vorosmarty. 2002. "Widespread Decline in Hydrological Monitoring Threatens Panarctic Research." *EOS Transactions* 83 (2): 16–17.

SICA (Sistema de Integración Centroamericana) and OBSAN-R (Observatorio Regional de Seguridad Alimentaria y Nutricional). 2011. *XIII Foro de Aplicación de los Pronósticos Climáticos a la Seguridad Alimentaria y Nutricional: Perspectivas para el período mayo-julio 2011.* Tegucigalpa, Honduras: SICA and OBSAN-R.

Sivapalan, M. 2003. "Prediction in Ungauged Basins: A Grand Challenge for Theoretical Hydrology." *Hydrological Processes* 17 (15): 3163–70.

Stokstad, E. 1999. "Scarcity of Rain, Stream Gages Threatens Forecasts." *Science* 285 (5431): 1199–200.

Wagener, T., and A. Montanari. 2011. "Convergence of Approaches toward Reducing Uncertainty in Predictions in Ungauged Basins." *Water Resources Research* 47 (6): W06301.

Water Resources Council. 1983. "Economic and Environmental Principles and Guidelines for Water and Related Land Resources Implementation Studies (Principles and Guidelines)." U.S. Water Resources Council, Washington, DC.

PART II

Earth Observation for Water Resources Management

Juan P. Guerschman, Randall J. Donohue, Tom G. Van Niel, Luigi J. Renzullo, Arnold G. Dekker, Tim J. Malthus, Tim R. McVicar, and Albert I. J. M. Van Dijk

OVERVIEW

Part II of this publication captures and expands the results reported in part I with the following aims: (a) to connect World Bank needs in water resources management (WRM) issue areas to the range of products providing Earth observation (EO) information regarding water resources; (b) to describe the current state-of-the-art of water resources–related Earth observation and provide an overview of (current and future) EO sensors as well as measured water resources variables; and (c) to provide guidance on how to decide whether Earth observation may be useful for addressing a WRM issue and approximate the likely accuracy of the variables estimated through Earth observation.

Part II may be read in two different ways, depending on the reader's background.

Persons new to monitoring and assessing WRM areas using Earth observation may want to begin with chapter 5, which provides an idea of the issues that may arise in a specific context, such as that of the World Bank. Chapter 6 discusses the state-of-the-art in those areas and provides an overview of the pertinent EO sensors with their respective specifications. Chapter 7 then provides information on whether the use of Earth observation should be considered given the specific requirements for spatiotemporal data. It provides a simple decision framework for determining how EO products might best be used to generate the required information and how to select the most suitable EO data products for a specific WRM problem. Moreover, it highlights guiding questions to ask, once EO options are deemed worth exploring for the WRM issue at hand. To make it easier to navigate the material presented in part II, chapter 7 includes a flowchart connecting all of the information.

Those who are already familiar with the material covered in chapters 5 and 6 or who have sufficient working knowledge of Earth observation may want to turn directly to the section of chapter 7 that is relevant to a specific application (or, alternatively, refer to the applications presented in appendix B). The guiding questions should help them to select the most appropriate solution to the WRM issues presented in chapter 5. If necessary, the sensor-variable tables in chapter 5 and the section of chapter 6 covering the application at hand may be of interest. Figure II.1 summarizes these two options.

Figure II.1 Schematic Showing Two Possible Ways to Read Part II

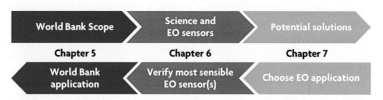

Note: Chapter 7 (green): deemed essential; chapter 6 (orange): deemed optional; chapter 5 (blue): sketches the World Bank context. EO = Earth observation.

CHAPTER 5

Earth Observations and Water Issues

INTRODUCTION

This chapter provides an overview of the issue areas related to water resources management (WRM) in a given context, such as the World Bank, and discusses the data requirements for addressing them, focusing on those variables that can be obtained or estimated through Earth observation (EO). Besides the usual surface characteristics, such as topography, land subsidence, and others mentioned in part I, Earth observation can address eight key hydrometeorological variables[1] relevant to WRM applications: precipitation; evapotranspiration; soil moisture; vegetation, land use, and land cover; groundwater; surface water; snow and ice; and water quality.

EO-RELATED WATER RESOURCES MANAGEMENT IN THE WORLD BANK CONTEXT

Part I assesses the activities funded by the World Bank to address the most challenging water-related issues in the developing world. The issues that those activities address differ widely and range from local problems, such as the provision of drinking water or sewage systems in a specific town, to larger-scale challenges, such as the likely impacts of climate change on water availability in large and often transboundary basins.

The sectors, subsectors, and themes that characterize water-related operations in the Bank's portfolio are described in part I (see also annex 2A available online at https://openknowledge .worldbank.org/handle/10986/22952). Each of these operations deals with particular water-related issues, which in some cases are common to more than one sector or subsector. Moreover, the sectoral classification identifies which part of the economy is receiving support; it is used in part I as a convenient mechanism to identify the water-related activities in the Bank's portfolio and to identify key hydrometeorological variables deemed necessary for each water resources activity. Part II focuses on issues, grouping sectors and subsectors according to the nature of the issue areas or topics they address (see box 5.1, which was adapted from the Water Partnership Program's classification).[2]

Water-Related Topics and Subtopics Considered in the World Bank Context

- Water supply for rural or urban water users
- Sanitation and hygiene
- Agricultural water management, in irrigation or in rain-fed agriculture
- Water resources management and environmental services, including aquatic ecosystems, environmental flows, invasive aquatic plants, and water and climate change
- Hydropower

Similar to the classification of sector, subsector, and theme, each of these topics deals with particular water-related issues, which, in some cases, are relevant to more than one topic. For example, flood extent mapping and flood prediction are of interest to urban water supply, environmental flows, and climate change.

FIELD MEASUREMENT, EARTH OBSERVATION, AND MODELING

Field-based or in situ measurements are generally more direct than Earth observation—that is, they measure the biophysical variable of interest using a measurement principle that has fewer uncertainties and assumptions. The measurements are, however, usually representative of a smaller area than is observed by satellite sensors. For example, a ground rain gauge takes direct measurements of the rain that falls on it, while satellite estimates can be derived indirectly from durations of cloud top temperatures or more direct measurements of rainfall between somewhere in the cloud and the ground surface.

Evapotranspiration can be measured directly using Eddy covariance methods (directly measuring relative humidity in ascending air flows) or evaporation pans (measuring water loss to evapotranspiration), while remotely sensed estimates of evapotranspiration are inferred

from measurements of thermal bands of the spectrum.

Soil moisture can be measured by sampling: weighing a sample of extracted soil, drying it, and weighing it again. The difference in weight is the evaporated soil moisture. This approach is the most direct method of measuring soil moisture and has the least uncertainty, even though the sampling procedure and drying method can introduce errors. However, it is also very labor-intensive. Less direct methods of field measurement—for instance, using time-domain reflectometers—can increase the efficiency of soil moisture measurement but require calibration and are more prone to uncertainties (among other things, due to salt concentration and turbidity, as in this example). Both field-based techniques only measure the conditions in a very small section of the sample or around the sensor.

Except for the measurement of one-dimensional flows, such as river discharge, one of the main challenges of ground observation networks is to capture the spatial variability of the variable being measured. A rain gauge measures the rainfall over a few square centimeters. Usually, observations from a few rain gauges are used, assuming that they are representative of rainfall over the entire basin. These observations may be more or less accurate, depending on the extent of the storms, topography, and other factors. Current satellite precipitation products have resolutions usually ranging from 0.25° with an average value of rainfall for a cell area of roughly 625 square kilometers to 0.04° with an average value of rainfall for a cell area of roughly 16 square kilometers. The spatial footprints of the two types of observations (ground versus satellite) are several orders of magnitude different, making direct comparisons difficult.

Earth observations by satellite-based sensors, or satellite remote sensing (RS),[3] can overcome the problem of spatial representativeness and generally also provide continuous measurements in time. However, they often rely on indirect methods to derive the value of the biophysical variable of interest. For the example of soil moisture, surface brightness temperature measured by passive microwave sensors is influenced by the soil moisture conditions and can be used to estimate this important soil property. Yet using passive microwave sensors has some drawbacks: the spatial resolution is coarse (depending on the sensor, about 12–50 kilometers), only moisture in the very top layer of soil (1–2 centimeters) affects brightness temperature, and vegetation and surface water can confound the measurement. The latter also facilitates its use for observing vegetation biomass and surface water, respectively (see chapter 6).

Thus observations from space need to be analyzed, validated, and used in accordance with their limitations, as they can contain several types or errors. Sampling and measurement errors can occur due to the measurement of a variable in the wrong place (for example, rainfall at the cloud base instead of at the ground surface) and due to indirect estimations and biases in measurement sensors, resulting in errors in the magnitude of the rate being measured. These errors will be different, depending on the specific geographic and atmospheric setting. Satellite precipitation products have performed differently, depending on the type of rainfall mechanisms, topography, and geography involved. Soil moisture estimates are influenced by the type of vegetation and cloud cover and can contain large errors. Thus case-by-case validation efforts are essential before applying them in real-world situations.

Something similar applies to the observation of other variables. False alarms and missed events are two other types of errors that are difficult to correct without ground measurements or without complementary RS observations. Even if new missions such as the Global Precipitation Measurement (GPM), launched on February 27, 2014, or the Soil Moisture Active Passive (SMAP), launched on January 29, 2015, start providing new, more accurate estimates, these still need to be validated, and the reliability of new WRM applications needs to be assessed.[4]

Field measurement and Earth observation can complement each other to enhance and overcome their respective weaknesses. However, neither type of observation provides direct information on the future or the past (that is, before the observations were made). Digital satellite remote sensing was first used in the 1970s, but its use only became widespread in the mid-1980s. Furthermore, neither form of observation provides any direct information on how specific interventions or scenarios might affect a variable of interest.

RS data or data products that blend remote sensing and ground observations are difficult to read. Responding to the need for storing large amounts of gridded data over vast areas and increasing periods of time, RS estimates are made available in files with binary, ASCII, NetCDF, or other formats. These data files require programming skills (codes or software) that are not necessarily available, much less widespread, in developing countries, in addition to hardware with a minimum computational power. While visualizations and customized applications are often developed to make the reading of data more user friendly, capacity building and perhaps additional strategies are needed to facilitate access to information contained in the data sets.

Efforts to produce data sets integrating ground observational networks and RS observations attempt to capitalize on the accuracy and precision of point measurements in the ground as well as the spatial representation provided by Earth observations. Products combining all available data in a region (that is, rain gauge networks, radar, and satellite precipitation estimates) into a gridded data set are the best possible representation at a specific spatiotemporal resolution of the true rainfall over the region, although they are not devoid of errors. Measuring and representing the "ground truth" accurately are still challenging.

Given the challenges of accurately capturing spatial variability, it is very difficult to produce a spatially explicit "ground truth" reference data set against which to compare satellite estimates. Ali, Lebel, and Amani (2005) demonstrate that errors of satellite products in some settings are likely to be significantly lower when the errors in gauge "ground truth" data and the covariance between them are taken into account. An example of a data set integrating different types of data is the Global Precipitation Climatology Project's One Degree Daily. An exhaustive list of these types of data sets can be found on the website of the International Precipitation Working Group.[5]

These limitations can be overcome—to varying extents—with the aid of computer models. These models can be predictive and can also be used to estimate conditions in times when observations were not yet available or under varying scenarios, although their outputs will only be as good as the physics and assumptions underpinning them. Nevertheless, models represent our best conceptual understanding of physical processes at any given time in history and provide insight into how components of the Earth system interact.

With the growing wealth of water information available from field networks, EO systems, and computer models, much research in recent years has been devoted to developing mathematical techniques and computing infrastructure to bring the information together in ways that enhance overall accuracy and utility (figure 5.1). Appendix B gives numerous examples of experimental and operational systems that have exploited multiple data sets and information sources to improve the monitoring of key water cycle variables, including merging

Figure 5.1 Conceptual Depiction of Information-Integration Paradigm Referred to as Model-Data Fusion

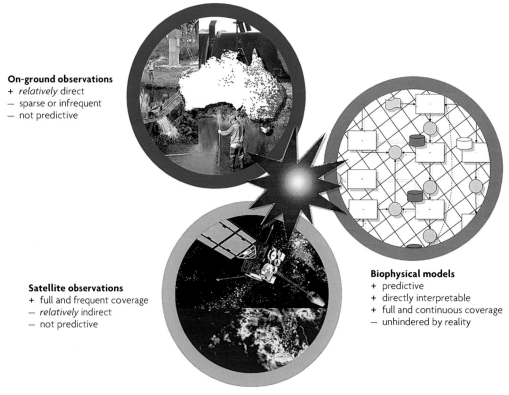

On-ground observations
+ *relatively* direct
− sparse or infrequent
− not predictive

Satellite observations
+ full and frequent coverage
− *relatively* indirect
− not predictive

Biophysical models
+ predictive
+ directly interpretable
+ full and continuous coverage
− unhindered by reality

Note: + = pros; − = cons

field measurements and RS estimates of precipitation in gauge-sparse landscapes and constraining regional water balance through multisensor calibration of a landscape hydrology model. A common thread is the increasing use of Earth observation in conjunction with models and field observation networks, where and when available, to fill the knowledge gap.

In the absence of any field observations, certain analytical frameworks that exclusively use RS data may still provide fit-for-purpose information. This is especially beneficial for countries with limited or no field observation networks. For example, drought monitoring and water quality systems can use a range of biophysical, "remotely sensed only" variables to provide useful synoptic information for decision makers and policy makers. Where field observation networks have validated such information, confidence in the use of Earth observation has increased.

RELEVANT VARIABLES PROVIDED BY EO

Among all types of information potentially useful for addressing WRM issues, many can be obtained with the aid of EO techniques. Only in very few cases does the satellite imagery (almost) measure the actual variable of interest, such as surface albedo or surface turbidity. More typically, the observations are used to infer or estimate the variable—using some modeling technique, often referred to as the retrieval algorithm or observation model.

Table 4A.1 in annex 4A (available online) compares World Bank water-related activities with the relevant variables that can be measured in situ or estimated with the aid of Earth observation. In relation to Earth observation, it is important to consider the spatial and temporal resolution that the satellite imagery must have for it to be useful for informing the issue at hand. *Spatial resolution* relates to the spatial detail that can be distinguished in the data,

much like the resolution of a photograph. Related terms are (satellite) *footprint* and *pixel size*,[6] both expressed in units of distance at the Earth's surface (although the two are not necessarily equal). *Temporal resolution* refers to the frequency with which repeat measurements are available. A related term is *revisit time*, which refers to the time period between subsequent satellite overpasses. This publication considers the general categories of spatial and temporal resolution shown in box 5.2.

The key types of variables and their minimum spatial and temporal resolution requirements can be evaluated for each WRM issue. Table 5.1 identifies the main water issues that can be addressed with the aid of Earth observation and links them to the relevant Water Partnership Program topics (and subtopics, where applicable). For each topic and subtopic, the pertinent water issues were derived from examples given on the program's website and information provided in part I of this publication.[7] The results of this analysis are discussed below and summarized in tables 5.2 and 5.3 (a rearrangement of table 5.2 that focuses on spatial and temporal resolution).

Some caveats are in order. First, the analysis undertaken sometimes makes general

---

BOX 5.2

General Categories of Resolution and Examples of Platforms Providing This Type of Data

Spatial resolution:

- S1: very fine, pixel size less than 10 meters (QuickBird, IKONOS)
- S2: fine, pixel size: 10–100 meters (Landsat, ASTER)
- S3: medium, pixel size: 100–1,000 meters (MODIS, AVHRR)
- S4: coarse, pixel size more than 1,000 meters (ASCAT, AMSR-E, GRACE)

Temporal resolution (revisit times):

- T1: near continuous, less than 3 hours (geostationary satellites)
- T2: high frequency, 3–24 hours (polar-orbiting broad-swath satellites such as MODIS, AVHRR)
- T3: medium frequency, 1–30 days (Landsat)
- T4: occasional, once only or ad hoc (SRTM, tasked radar)

Table 5.1 Relationship between Water Issues and Water Topics and Subtopics in the World Bank Water Partnership Program

ISSUE	WATER SUPPLY – RURAL	WATER SUPPLY – URBAN	SANITATION AND HYGIENE	AGRICULTURAL WATER MANAGEMENT	WRM & ENV SERVICES – AQUATIC ECOSYSTEMS	WRM & ENV SERVICES – ENVIRONMENTAL FLOWS	WRM & ENV SERVICES – INVASIVE AQUATIC PLANTS	WRM & ENV SERVICES – WATER RESOURCES AND CLIMATE CHANGE	HYDROPOWER
Identifying and monitoring water reservoirs	•	•		•		•	•		
Monitoring and predicting water quality in dams and reservoirs	•	•		•		•	•		
Mapping extent of flood	•	•	•	•	•	•		•	
Predicting extent of flood	•	•	•	•	•	•		•	
Monitoring extent of snow and glacial cover	•	•		•		•		•	•
Mapping urban and rural infrastructure	•	•	•	•					•
Assessing water use efficiency in irrigated crops	•			•					
Monitoring rates of irrigation water use	•			•					
Monitoring rates of groundwater extraction	•			•		•			
Mapping irrigated areas	•			•					
Monitoring crop production and food security	•			•				•	
Monitoring and forecasting drought		•		•		•		•	•
Monitoring water quality of coastal discharge					•				
Monitoring maritime pollution (for example, oil spills)					•				
Identifying and monitoring groundwater-dependent ecosystems						•			
Monitoring river elevation	•	•		•		•		•	•
Monitoring and controlling aquatic weeds					•	•	•		
Conducting integrated assessment of water availability under climate change scenarios								•	
Designing hydropower production facilities									•

Note: Bullet indicates where knowledge of a particular water issue is relevant to a specific water (sub)topic.

Table 5.2 Overview of Water Issues and Relevant Variables Provided by Earth Observation

ISSUES	PRECIPITATION S	PRECIPITATION T	EVAPOTRANSPIRATION S	EVAPOTRANSPIRATION T	SOIL MOISTURE S	SOIL MOISTURE T	VEGETATION AND LAND COVER S	VEGETATION AND LAND COVER T	GROUNDWATER S	GROUNDWATER T	SURFACE WATER S	SURFACE WATER T	SNOW AND ICE S	SNOW AND ICE T	WATER QUALITY S	WATER QUALITY T	OTHERS	MODELING APPROACHES
Identifying and monitoring water reservoirs																		
Monitoring and predicting water quality in dams and reservoirs															S1, S2, S3	T2, T3		Biogeochemical models
Mapping extent of flood											S2, S3	T1, T2, T3					Elevation (DEM)	Hydrodynamic models
Predicting extent of flood	S4	T1, T2			S4	T1, T2					S2, S3	T2, T3					Elevation (DEM)	
Monitoring extent of snow and glacial cover	S4	T1, T2											S2, S3, S4	T2, T3			Elevation (DEM)	
Mapping urban and rural infrastructure							S1, S2	T4										
Assessing water use efficiency	S4	T1, T2	S2, S3	T2, T3	S4	T1, T2	S2, S3	T3	S4	T2								River models
Monitoring rates of irrigation water use			S2, S3	T2, T3			S2, S3	T3										River models
Monitoring rates of groundwater extraction			S2, S3	T2, T3					S4	T2								River models
Mapping irrigated areas	S4	T1, T2	S2, S3	T2, T3	S4	T1, T2	S2, S3	T2, T3			S2, S3	T2, T3					Elevation (DEM)	
Monitoring crop production and food security	S4	T1, T2	S2, S3	T2, T3	S4	T1, T2	S2, S3	T2, T3										Crop or pasture growth models
Monitoring and forecasting drought	S4	T1, T2	S2, S3	T2, T3	S4	T1, T2	S2, S3	T3	S4	T2	S2, S3	T2, T3	S2, S3	T2, T3				Landscape water balance models
Monitoring water quality of coastal discharge															S1, S2, S3	T1, T2, T3		

(Continued)

Table 5.2 (Continued)

ISSUES	PRECIPITATION		EVAPOTRANSPIRATION		SOIL MOISTURE		VEGETATION AND LAND COVER		GROUNDWATER		SURFACE WATER		SNOW AND ICE		WATER QUALITY		OTHERS	MODELING APPROACHES
	S	T	S	T	S	T	S	T	S	T	S	T	S	T	S	T		
Monitoring maritime pollution (for example, oil spills)															S1, S2, S3	T1, T2, T3		
Identifying and monitoring groundwater-dependent ecosystems	S4	T1, T2	S2, S3	T2, T3			S2, S3	T3			S2, S3	T2, T3						
Monitoring river flow	S4	T1 T2	S2, S3	T2, T3	S4	T1, T2			S4	T2			S2, S3	T2, T3			Elevation (DEM)	Landscape water balance and river models
Monitoring and controlling aquatic weeds							S1, S2	T2, T3										
Conducting integrated assessment of water availability under climate change scenarios	S4	T1 T2	S2, S3	T2, T3	S4	T1, T2	S2, S3	T3	S4	T2	S2, S3	T2, T3	S2, S3	T2, T3				Landscape water balance and river models
Designing hydropower production facilities							S1, S2	T4									Elevation (DEM)	

Note: S = spatial; T = temporal. S1, S2, S3, and S4 refer to the spatial resolution of the data, while T1, T2, T3, and T4 refer to the temporal resolution. They are defined as follows: S1, very fine (pixel size, less than 10 meters), S2, fine (pixel size, 10–100 meters), S3, medium (pixel size, 100–1,000 meters), and S4, low (pixel size, more than 1,000 meters), T1, near continuous (revisit time, less than 3 hours), T2, high frequency (revisit time, 3–24 hours), T3, medium frequency (revisit time, 1–30 days), T4, occasional (revisit time, once only or ad hoc). Blue indicates that the data are highly valuable, green indicates that they are valuable, and white indicates that they are not relevant. For more information on these issues, see the section in chapter 6 on the type of data obtained and the section in chapter 7 on determining the minimum required data requirements; both sections are divided into subsections on each variable. DEM = digital elevation model.

Table 5.3 Overview of Water Issues and Relevant Variables Provided by Earth Observation Rearranged to Focus on Spatial and Temporal Resolution

ISSUE	SPATIAL				TEMPORAL				MODEL
	S1	S2	S3	S4	T1	T2	T3	T4	
Identifying and monitoring water reservoirs	SW	SW					SW	SW	
Monitoring and predicting water quality in dams and reservoirs	SW	SW	SW			SW	SW		Biogeochemical models
	WQ	WQ	WQ			WQ	WQ		
Mapping extent of flood		SW	SW		SW	SW	SW		
		DEM	DEM					DEM	
Predicting extent of flood				P	P	P			Hydrodynamic models
				SM	SM	SM			
		SW	SW			SW	SW		
		DEM	DEM					DEM	
Monitoring extent of snow and glacial cover				P	P	P			
		S&I	S&I	S&I		S&I	S&I		
								DEM	
Mapping urban and rural infrastructure	V&LC	V&LC						V&LC	
Assessing water use efficiency				P	P	P			River models
		ET	ET			ET	ET		
				SM	SM	SM			
		V&LC	V&LC				V&LC		
				GW		GW			
Monitoring rates of irrigation water use		ET	ET			ET	ET		River models
		V&LC	V&LC				V&LC		
Monitoring rates of groundwater extraction		ET	ET			ET	ET		River models
				GW		GW			
Mapping irrigated areas				P	P	P			
				SM	SM	SM			
		ET	ET			ET	ET		
		V&LC	V&LC			V&LC	V&LC		
		SW	SW			SW	SW		
		DEM	DEM					DEM	
Monitoring crop production and food security				P	P	P			Crop or pasture growth models
		ET	ET			ET	ET		
		V&LC	V&LC			V&LC	V&LC		
Monitoring and forecasting drought				P	P	P			Landscape water balance models
		ET	ET			ET	ET		
				SM	SM	SM			
		V&LC	V&LC				V&LC		
				GW		GW			
		SW	SW			SW	SW		
		S&I	S&I			S&I	S&I		

(Continued)

Table 5.3 (Continued)

ISSUE	SPATIAL				TEMPORAL				MODEL
	S1	S2	S3	S4	T1	T2	T3	T4	
Monitoring water quality of coastal discharge	WQ	WQ	WQ		WQ	WQ	WQ		
Monitoring maritime pollution (oil spills)	WQ	WQ	WQ		WQ	WQ	WQ		
Identifying and monitoring groundwater-dependent ecosystems				P	P	P			
		ET	ET			ET	ET		
		V&LC	V&LC				V&LC		
		SW	SW			SW	SW		
Monitoring river flow				P	P	P			Landscape water balance and river models
		ET	ET			ET	ET		
			SM		SM	SM			
			GW			GW			
		S&I	S&I			S&I	S&I		
		DEM	DEM					DEM	
Monitoring and controlling aquatic weeds	V&LC	V&LC				V&LC	V&LC		
	WQ	WQ				WQ	WQ		
Conducting integrated assessment of water availability under climate change scenarios				P	P	P			Landscape water balance and river models
		ET	ET			ET	ET		
			SM		SM	SM			
		V&LC	V&LC				V&LC		
			GW			GW			
		SW	SW			SW	SW		
		S&I	S&I			S&I	S&I		
Designing hydropower production facilities	V&LC	V&LC						V&LC	
	DEM	DEM						DEM	

Note: S1, S2, S3, and S4 refer to the spatial resolution of the data, while T1, T2, T3, and T4 refer to the temporal resolution. They are defined as follows: S1, very fine (pixel size, less than 10 meters), S2, fine (pixel size, 10–100 meters), S3, medium (pixel size, 100–1,000 meters), and S4, low (pixel size, more than 1,000 meters), T1, near continuous (revisit time, less than 3 hours), T2, high frequency (revisit time, 3–24 hours), T3, medium frequency (revisit time, 1–30 days), T4, occasional (revisit time, once only or ad hoc). Blue indicates that the data are highly valuable, green indicates that they are valuable, and white indicates that they are not relevant. DEM = digital elevation model; ET = evapotranspiration; GW = groundwater; P = precipitation; S&I = snow and ice; SM = soil moisture; SW = surface water; V&LC = vegetation and land cover; WQ = water quality.

assumptions about natural water systems, water supply and use, and the infrastructure built to support the latter. Given the importance of issues related to water for agriculture, this is particularly relevant where the characteristics of the information that can be derived in any specific application need to be compared very carefully with the characteristics of the farming systems involved. For example, farm dams are typically comparatively small structures (often less than 100 meters across). However, notable exceptions do exist—for instance, on Australia's large-scale, flood-harvesting private cotton farms, where water storage containers can measure kilometers across.

Second, it is difficult to assess data requirements without considering the current state of EO technology and methods of analysis; that is, even where EO applications have only been conceived in a theoretical sense, such ideas are usually constrained by the assumed limits to the technology.[8] This introduces a degree of circularity in the analysis, particularly when considering the lowest spatial and temporal resolution that might still be useful. For example, if satellite observation of soil moisture or water level were possible at a scale of meters and minutes, it is likely that entirely new applications would be conceived and developed and that data requirements would be modified accordingly.

Tables 5.2 and 5.3 cross-reference the issues addressed under the topic areas with relevant variables that can be measured or estimated with the aid of Earth observation. The two tables present the same information, but arranged in different ways to facilitate interpretation. For each issue, the relevant variables that can be obtained from Earth observation are listed. Each variable is classified according to its usefulness: green when considered "valuable," meaning that it is likely to be useful in addressing the issue at hand, blue when considered "highly valuable," meaning that using EO may significantly improve the ability to address the issue, and white when deemed not relevant. In addition, the most appropriate spatial and temporal resolutions are listed.

As an example, consider the efficiency of water use in crops, an important issue for agricultural water management. Earth observation can provide information on evapotranspiration[9] to estimate water use by crops and can also identify the location of the irrigated crops—both types of data may well be essential. These data can be obtained at fine and medium spatial resolution and with high and medium frequency (temporal resolution); the preferable combination will depend on the nature of the application. Furthermore, Earth observation can be used to estimate rainfall, which is particularly useful where the field rainfall measurement network is inadequate. Precipitation data from Earth observation are only available at coarse spatial resolution, but with high or even near-continuous frequency. Finally, Earth observation can provide potentially relevant information on the amount of moisture in the top layer of soil and on the volume of groundwater, but again, only at coarse resolution.

Table 5.3 may be used as a guide for determining the data needs and availability for each water issue. Chapter 6 explains each variable, detailing its relevance, the theoretical basis for its estimation with Earth observation, and the current and future technologies available for its measurement.

The following list explains the information conveyed schematically in tables 5.2 and 5.3:

- *Identifying and monitoring water reservoirs.* Applications could include identifying water reservoirs for monitoring compliance or observing water storage as part of a drought warning system. They may also be used to observe water resources and climate change as well as hydropower. Depending on the size of the reservoirs, high spatial resolution may be required (S1, S2). Generally, slow water dynamics mean that a moderate frequency is likely to be required (T3, T4).

- *Monitoring and predicting water quality in dams and reservoirs.* In addition to the need to locate these water bodies (through remote sensing or other sources), Earth observation can be used at similar spatial resolutions and temporal revisit times (S1, S2, S3, T2, T3) to quantify water quality. This is particularly relevant for assessing the health risks to human and animal populations who depend on these water bodies. It may also be related to water resources, climate change, and hydropower.

- *Mapping flood extent.* Floods are a hazard to both rural and urban populations because they can affect the provision of potable water. Flood extent can be monitored with Earth observation; normally, high to medium spatial resolution is required, depending on the extent of the flood and the physical characteristics of the terrain. In large floodplains, medium resolution (S3) may suffice, but high resolution (S2) may be required in many other cases. Normally, high-frequency imagery (T2) is desired, but opportunistic acquisition of medium-frequency imagery (T3) can also be useful. Digital elevation models (DEMs) can help to identify flooded areas.

- *Predicting flood extent.* Besides mapping flood extent when flooding occurs, predicting flood extent is highly relevant to urban water supply and, of course, to disaster management. DEMs are critical in this context; in addition to weather forecasts, antecedent rainfall and soil moisture conditions can be very useful. Flood extent can be predicted by considering previously flooded areas and estimating the associated recurrence times. It may be combined with hydrodynamic models to simulate water flows and flood extent during high-rainfall events upstream.

- *Monitoring extent of snow and glacial cover.* Many regions of the world obtain part of their water supply from melting snow and ice. This is the case in high-latitude regions, in mountainous regions, and in valleys at the foothills of high mountains. Measuring the area and water equivalent of snow and ice can help to estimate the volume of water runoff to be expected during spring and summer. Snow and ice can be measured with Earth observation at high, medium, and coarse spatial resolution (S2, S3, S4); high as well as medium frequency (T2, T3) are required and possible. In addition to the direct mapping of snow and ice areas, Earth observation of precipitation can improve water equivalent estimates, and DEMs can also indicate where snow is likely to fall and persist.

- *Mapping urban and rural infrastructure.* Applications include the identification of existing facilities and land cover mapping before construction. Generally, very high or high spatial resolution imagery (S1, S2) is needed, either from satellites or from airborne imagery on occasion (T4).

- *Assessing water use efficiency in irrigated crops.* Water use efficiency is the ratio of agricultural produce to the amount of water

used by the crop. Efficient agricultural management ensures the sustainable use of water. The key variable to monitor is evapotranspiration, which can be done at high and medium spatial resolutions (S2, S3) and also at high- and medium-frequency revisit times (T2, T3), depending on the application. Other useful variables are land cover, at the same spatial resolution and at least once during the growing cycle (T3), and precipitation and soil moisture, typically at coarse spatial resolution (S4), but perhaps daily or more frequently (T1, T2).

- *Monitoring rates of irrigation water use.* Similar to assessing water use efficiency, monitoring irrigation water use requires estimating crop ET rates. Information on the location and size (land cover mapping) of irrigated crops is useful. It is also important in relation to water resources and climate change.

- *Monitoring rates of groundwater extraction.* Water volumes extracted from groundwater cannot be estimated directly with Earth observation. Gravimetric measurements can provide coarse resolution (S4) estimates of groundwater, which can inform basin-wide changes in groundwater levels. In local studies, a combination of river models and satellite ET estimates may help to constrain groundwater extraction estimates, which are also of importance for urban water supply.

- *Mapping irrigated areas.* The location of crops can be determined by using land cover classification techniques at high or medium spatial resolution (S2, S3) and revisit times (T2, T3). Whether specific crops have been irrigated cannot be established directly with Earth observation, unless water remains in the surface for long periods, as is the case of paddy rice. However, it may be determined with ancillary information, such as the connectedness to surface water reservoirs or rivers, or with information regarding the estimated water balance deficit (that is, the difference between precipitation and evapotranspiration) during the growing season, which can be obtained with Earth observation.

- *Monitoring crop production and food security.* Earth observation can be used to estimate crop production via vegetation indexes, normally at high and medium spatial (S2, S3) and temporal (T2, T3) resolutions. Remotely sensed precipitation and evapotranspiration can be useful too. Crop growth models or pasture growth models (in the case of livestock production) can also be useful and may be parameterized with EO data.

- *Monitoring and forecasting drought.* Drought monitoring typically uses vegetation index[10] anomalies and precipitation data. However, remotely sensed total water storage, surface soil moisture, and rainfall are increasingly being incorporated into drought monitoring systems. Forecasting drought requires landscape water balance models that can be forced (up to the forecast date) or calibrated with additional EO information on rainfall, evapotranspiration, soil moisture, groundwater, and snow and ice, where relevant.

- *Monitoring water quality of coastal discharge.* Water quality in rivers can affect marine ecosystems by discharging excessive levels of sediments and nutrients. These discharges can be monitored with Earth observation either in rivers or estuaries themselves or in coastal waters. The effects of the discharge, such as algal blooms, can also be detected. While inland water bodies may require high or very high spatial resolution (S1, S2), coastal environments typically require medium spatial (S3) and high temporal (T2) resolution.

- *Monitoring maritime pollution (for example, oil spills).* Coastal pollution can be monitored with Earth observation using methods similar to those described under the previous item.

- *Identifying and monitoring groundwater-dependent ecosystems.* Groundwater-dependent ecosystems require access to groundwater to meet some or all of their water requirements. Their survival can be threatened by consumptive use of water for agriculture, mining, and other purposes. These systems typically need to be identified at high or medium spatial resolution (S2, S3) and can be supported by EO-based land cover mapping and estimates of water balance deficit. Mapping of open water can help to distinguish ecosystems dependent on groundwater from those dependent on surface water inflows.

- *Monitoring river streamflow.* River streamflow can be monitored directly with Earth observation using radar altimetry, but currently only for comparatively broad rivers and at a limited number of locations. Flows can also be modeled with landscape and river models, which can be informed (forced or calibrated) with EO estimates of precipitation, soil moisture, evapotranspiration, snow and ice extent (where relevant), and groundwater.

- *Monitoring and controlling aquatic weeds.* Aquatic weeds can be a challenging problem affecting navigation, water supply, and habitats. They may be detected and mapped with land cover classification techniques and tend to be related to water quality. This kind of monitoring is normally done, and necessarily so, at very high or high spatial resolution (S1, S2).

- *Conducting integrated assessment of water availability under climate change scenarios.* Proper characterization and understanding of the water balance and its drivers in the past and present are necessary to predict the availability of water over large regions under climate change scenarios. Almost all of the variables mentioned here can be useful. Landscape and river models are important for integrating the various observations and creating scenarios of future conditions.

- *Designing hydropower production facilities.* Designing hydropower facilities requires the availability of accurate DEMs, which can be obtained from airborne or satellite imagery. It may also benefit from mapping of land cover, including existing buildings and vegetation types, at very high or high resolution (S1, S2).

NOTES

1. As in part I, for simplicity's sake, other types of data relevant to hydrologic applications—such as land cover, land subsidence, and topography—are also referred to as hydrometeorological variables.

2. The Water Partnership Program sometimes changes its classification slightly (see http://water .worldbank.org/wpp). As of February 15, 2015, the subtopics are water supply, sanitation, irrigation and drainage, hydropower, and water resources management. The program's "thematic highlights" are water resources management, climate change, food security, energy security, water for environment, water supply and sanitation, integrated urban water management, remote sensing, and disaster risk management. For practical purposes, part II uses the categories listed as topics, combined with the program's action areas.

3. Although some define Earth observation as consisting of remote sensing *and* in situ measurements, this publication uses the terms Earth observation and remote sensing interchangeably.

4. For the GPM, see http://www.nasa.gov/mission_ pages/GPM/launch/. For the SMAP, see https:// smap.jpl.nasa.gov/.

5. For information on these types of data sets, see http://www.isac.cnr.it/~ipwg/data/datasets1.html.

6. *Spatial resolution* is defined as the size of the smallest individual component or dot (called a *pixel*) from which the image is constituted. For instance, if a satellite's resolution is stated as "5 meters," each pixel in the imagery has a size of 5 meters by 5 meters. The *footprint* is the area of the Earth covered by the microwave radiation from a satellite dish (transponder). The size of the footprint depends on the location of the satellite in its orbit, the shape and size of the beam produced by its transponder, and the distance from the Earth.

7. Therefore, this list is not exhaustive. For example, monitoring water reservoirs and water quality in dams and reservoirs may also relate to water resources and climate change and to hydropower, monitoring rates of irrigation water use may also relate to water resources and climate change, monitoring groundwater extraction may also relate to urban water supply, and so on.

8. Henry Ford supposedly said about his cars, "If I had asked people what they wanted, they would have said faster horses."

9. *Evapotranspiration* is the process by which water is transferred from the land to the atmosphere by evaporation from the soil and other surfaces and by transpiration from plants.

10. A *vegetation index* describes the greenness—the relative density and health of vegetation—for each pixel in a satellite image.

REFERENCE

Ali, A., T. Lebel, and A. Amani. 2005. "Rainfall Estimation in the Sahel. Part I: Error Function." *Journal of Applied Meteorology* 44 (11): 1691–706.

CHAPTER 6

Earth Observations for Monitoring Water Resources

INTRODUCTION

This chapter provides an overview of the main variables that can be derived from satellite Earth observation (EO) and are relevant to the water issues presented in chapter 5. Most EO instruments obtain an image of radiation intensity in specific portions of the electromagnetic spectrum (EMS). The radiation is reflected from the sun by the Earth's surface, called *optical* remote sensing (RS); emitted by the Earth's surface itself, called *passive* remote sensing; or first emitted by the instrument and then reflected from the surface, called *active* remote sensing, such as radar. Exceptions to EMS imagers are satellite altimeters and the Gravity Recovery and Climate Experiment (GRACE) gravimetry mission, whose primary measurements are distance to the Earth's surface and between the two satellites, respectively.

CHARACTERISTICS OF SENSORS

Fundamental to the design of any EMS sensor are its characteristics in the spectral, radiometric,

and temporal domains. EMS sensors are defined by the extent, resolution, and density in each of those domains (table 6.1) plus the spatial domain (Emelyanova et al. 2012).

This data framework provides a means to assess the likely utility of different types of RS data to estimate key biophysical variables in particular applications. Because of the limits on measurement and telecommunication technology, there is typically a trade-off between the performance that a sensor can achieve in each of these dimensions. For example, imagery obtained by the Moderate Resolution Imaging Spectroradiometer (MODIS) sensors has a temporal, spectral, and radiometric resolution that is about an order of magnitude higher than that obtained by Landsat, but its spatial resolution is an order of magnitude lower (figure 6.1, panel a).

This framework only considers observational characteristics, although important operational considerations often also exist, such as the following:

- Data availability and the cost of purchase, if any

Table 6.1 Data Framework Comprising Domain-Characteristic Elements

DOMAIN	EXTENT	RESOLUTION	DENSITY
Spectral	Portion(s) of the EMS being sampled	Bandwidth(s)[a]	Number of bands in a particular portion of the EMS[b]
Radiometric	Dynamic range of radiances (minimum and maximum radiance per band)	Change in radiance due to change by one digital number	Number of bits used across the dynamic range of radiances
Temporal	Recording period over which the data are available[c]	Period of data acquisition[d]	Satellite repeat characteristics[e]

Source: Modified from McVicar and Jupp 2002.

Note: EMS = electromagnetic spectrum.

    a. The narrower the bandwidth, the higher the spectral resolution.

    b. For example, hyperspectral sensors (Hyperion) have higher spectral density than broadband instruments (Landsat TM/ETM+), although they sample similar EMS ranges.

    c. For some remotely sensed systems (AVHRR and Landsat TM), data have been recorded near-continuously for about 30 years.

    d. For remotely sensed images, this is a matter of seconds, which contrasts with meteorological data such as the daily rainfall totals.

    e. For some applications using optical (that is, reflective and thermal) data, the availability of cloud-free images is an important consideration. Whereas the satellite's repeat characteristics do not change, cloud cover will change the effective temporal density of a site over time.

Figure 6.1 Characteristics of MODIS and Landsat TM Data Domain

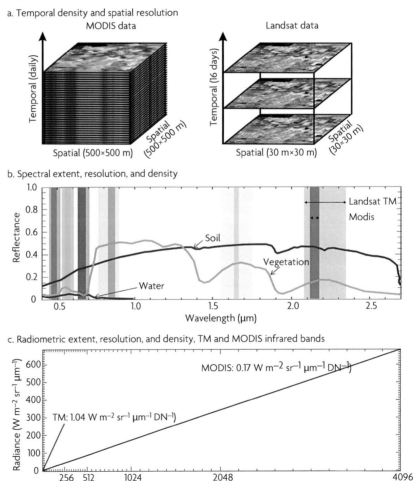

a. Temporal density and spatial resolution

b. Spectral extent, resolution, and density

c. Radiometric extent, resolution, and density, TM and MODIS infrared bands

Source: Emelyanova et al. n.d. © Commonwealth Scientific and Industrial Research Organisation (CSIRO). Used with permission. Further permission required for reuse.

Note: Panel a shows temporal density and spatial resolution. Panel b shows spectral extent, resolution, and density (darker colors represent the MODIS bands, while the lighter colors represent the Landsat TM bands). Panel c shows radiometric extent, resolution, and density for the TM and MODIS infrared bands. MODIS = Moderate Resolution Imaging Spectroradiometer; TM = thematic mapper.

- Data latency (the time that passes between the actual observation and the moment the data are made available)

- Reliability (any guarantees with regard to future availability and latency, stability of the data characteristics, and the like)

- Data format (size of the data files, requirements for specialized skills, software, or hardware)

- Degree of validation and acceptance (whether stakeholders will accept the data being used or the quality of the data compared with data from alternative sources)

- Interpretability and uncertainty (how unambiguous is the interpretation of the data in the context of a specific application)

This list is not meant to be exhaustive.

TYPES OF DATA OBTAINED FROM EARTH OBSERVATION

This publication has adopted the definitions given in table 6.2. The remainder of this chapter explains how the main data products relevant to water resources monitoring are obtained from raw or processed data. Appendix B provides a list of notable examples of information products.

Precipitation
Definition
Precipitation is the process by which water returns from the atmosphere to the Earth's surface in liquid form (rain), solid form (snow or hail), or a combined form (sleet). The ability to quantify precipitation distributions in space and time is critical to establishing infrastructure to capture and store water resources for an ever-growing population. Due to its fine-scale spatial and temporal variability, monitoring large-area precipitation challenges field-based measurement networks. A rain gauge can provide an accurate estimate of precipitation at a point in the landscape, but there is uncertainty about whether this estimate is representative of rainfall at some distance away from the gauge location. This problem is especially pronounced for particular rainfall regimes, such as convective storms (figure 6.2). Space-based methods of estimating precipitation offer ways to fill the information "gap" either by merging with existing surface measurement networks—to constrain estimation between gauges—or by providing direct estimates when and where no other information is available.

Estimating Space-Based Precipitation
Satellite-based estimation of precipitation began in the 1970s with the advent of weather satellites. Multichannel radiometers aboard geostationary satellite platforms provide visible infrared (VIS) and thermal infrared (TIR) imagery of the Earth's surface at medium (S3), about 1-kilometer, spatial resolution and very high (T1) temporal resolution. These satellite data were used to generate the first set of precipitation estimates for large areas of the globe,

Table 6.2 Types of Data Obtained from Earth Observation

DATA TYPE	DESCRIPTION
Raw data	Sensor measurements as received directly from the satellite, formatted as "digital counts"
Processed data	*Top of atmosphere (TOA) signal.* Raw data processed to TOA data: conversion to real-world units, such as radiance (watt per steradian per square meter per nanometer [$W{\cdot}sr^{-1}{\cdot}m^{-2}{\cdot}nm^{-1}$]) or reflectance (%); signal calibration
	Surface signal. TOA data processed to surface-equivalent data: corrections applied to remove atmospheric and solar-sensor viewing-angle effects; scene stitching; geolocation and reprojection
Data products	Conversion of processed data into products that describe real-world (usually biophysical) variables such as chlorophyll concentration, leaf area, rainfall rate, surface temperature, and soil moisture mass
Information products	Conversion of data products into management-relevant information for decision support, for example, eutrophication state of Cobalt Lake, flood risk of the Emerald River delta, and sustainable irrigation rates in the Crimson basin

Note: TOA = top of atmosphere.

Figure 6.2 Space-Based Precipitation Measurements from TRMM Satellite

a. Rainfall off the coast of Madagascar

b. Rainfall over southeastern United States

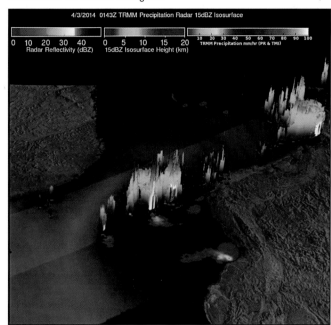

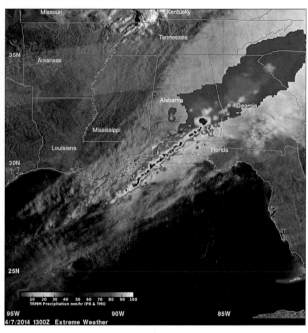

Source: NASA (http://pmm.nasa.gov/mission-updates/trmm-news/trmm-sees-severe-weather).

Note: (a) Large convective rainfall storm off the northwest coast of Madagascar as detected by Tropical Rainfall Measuring Mission (TRMM) Satellite's precipitation radar on April 3, 2014, at 01:43 UTC (Coordinated Universal Time); (b) a frontal rainfall system developing into a line of intense storms over southeast United States at 13:00 UTC on April 7, 2013.

based on a relationship between cloud top temperatures and precipitation rate (roughly, the lower the temperatures, the higher the rate of precipitation). However, Arkin and Meisner (1987) show that TIR-based estimates of precipitation are relatively poor, as the relationship between the cloud top temperature and precipitation rate break down for resolutions in time shorter than one day and resolutions in space lower than 2.5° in latitude and longitude.

The next advance in satellite-based estimation of precipitation occurred in the 1980s with the deployment of passive microwave sensors aboard polar-orbiting satellites. In contrast to the weak relationship underpinning TIR-based precipitation, the scattering and emission of passive microwave radiation by ice particles or rain droplets in clouds is better understood and modeled (Kummerow et al. 2001). Satellite-based, passive microwave brightness temperatures between 10–200 gigahertz have stronger relationships with precipitation, and the retrievals derived from

these data are generally considered superior to those obtained from TIR observations.

Both microwave and thermal approaches to estimating satellite-based precipitation have strengths and weaknesses. For example, TIR-based estimates from geostationary satellites have full-disk (global) coverage at near continuous (T1) temporal resolution of one-six to 1 hour and a coarse to medium spatial resolution of less than 5 kilometers (S3 or S4), but result in poor precipitation estimates at the high resolution. Conversely, passive microwave estimates from polar-orbiting satellites are more accurate but cover less of the globe, have coarser spatial resolution of about 10–100 kilometers (S4), and have less frequent repeat coverage (T4) for any given sensor.

The mid-1990s ushered in a new era of deriving multisatellite precipitation estimates, as algorithms were developed that exploited the high spatial and temporal coverage of the geostationary TIR estimates with the more accurate passive microwave-based estimates, making the best of both approaches (Huffman et al. 1997; Joyce et al. 2004; Kubota et al. 2007; Sorooshian et al. 2000).

Table 6.3 summarizes the characteristics of some of the more commonly used satellite precipitation products (SPPs). A common feature of these products is that they all use both microwave and thermal EO data to generate precipitation estimates.

The launch of the Tropical Rainfall Measuring Mission (TRMM) satellite in 1997 placed the world's first precipitation radar in orbit. Precipitation radar provides detailed information on the vertical structure (250-meter resolution) of rainfall and offers the most accurate precipitation estimates from space (Kummerow et al. 2001). At a satellite orbit of 350 kilometers in altitude, swath width of 215 kilometers, and orbital inclination limiting its coverage to ±35° latitude, the data provided by precipitation radar are far from global. However, the quality of the precipitation estimates makes precipitation radar a valuable source of information for calibrating both passive microwave and TIR instrumentation across multiple satellite platforms, thus extending the potential coverage of precipitation estimation. This is the basis for the TRMM Multisatellite Precipitation Analysis (TMPA) system, which generates quasi-global precipitation estimates going back as far as January 1, 1998 (Huffman et al. 2007).

The TMPA system sets the standard for the operational production of global satellite-derived precipitation estimates. While peer systems (that is, rainfall analysis systems based primarily on satellite observations) may have higher resolution in space and time than some of the TMPA products (table 6.3), agencies throughout the world have used TMPA's (quasi-) operational status to feed into their rainfall analysis systems (Mitra et al. 2009; Rozante et al. 2010) and to inform current and planned global flood and drought monitoring systems (Pozzi et al. 2013; Wu et al. 2012). The suite of precipitation products from the TMPA system (including precipitation radar only, microwave only, and merged microwave-TIR products) is available in real time and in post–real time (known as research grade products). In 2012, the system underwent a major transition from v6 (version 6) to v7 in which all products from the start of production in December 1997 were reprocessed. Studies have demonstrated the superiority of TMPA v7 to its predecessor (Chen et al. 2013).

On February 27, 2014, an H-IIA rocket from the Japan Aerospace Exploration Agency (JAXA) launched into orbit the first satellite of the core observatory of the Global Precipitation Measurement (GPM) mission, building on and continuing the long history of space-based estimation of precipitation. GPM will provide a multisatellite view of global precipitation at unparalleled spatial and temporal coverage. Many of the techniques for estimating precipitation from space and for blending results from multiple satellite sensors have been honed over decades—from the early, cloud top temperature methods of geostationary thermal Earth observation to the recent constellation of polar-orbiting microwave imagers of the TMPA system. The GPM mission continues this legacy of space-based monitoring of precipitation (Hou et al. 2013).

The core observatory of the GPM mission has a design life of three years, with battery life of at least five years and extended mission life until 2021 (Hou et al. 2013). Global precipitation products will be generated at three-hourly intervals, with a latency of three to four hours every day, by combining data from a "constellation" of current and planned microwave sensors through the Integrated Multisatellite Retrievals for GPM (IMERG) system (Huffman et al. 2013).

Satellite-Derived Precipitation Products

Table 6.3 lists the characteristics of some of the better-known global precipitation products that are derived from multiple satellite sensors. The International Precipitation Working Group provides a more comprehensive list of SPPs, including single-source products, model reanalyses (weather model–derived precipitation products), and gauge-only gridded estimates.[1]

Table 6.3 Overview of Main Characteristics of Some Widely Used Global Satellite-Derived Precipitation Estimates

NAME	PRIMARY SATELLITE(S) OR SENSOR(S)	SPATIAL RESOLUTION[c]	TEMPORAL FREQUENCY	DATA LATENCY	MAIN REFERENCE (NUMBER OF CITATIONS)	ACCESS
TMPA[a] – 3B40RT	Combined TMI, SSM/I, AMSU, and AMSR-E data	0.25°	3 hours	6–7 hours	Huffman et al. 2007 (967)	Anonymous ftp site: ftp://trmmopen.gsfc.nasa.gov/pub/merged/3B40RT
TMPA – 3B41RT	Infrared brightness temperatures (geostationary) spatially aggregated and calibrated to microwave rain rates	0.25°	3 hours	6–7 hours	Huffman et al. 2007	Anonymous ftp site: ftp://trmmopen.gsfc.nasa.gov/pub/merged/3B41RT
TMPA – 3B42RT	Thermal infrared (TIR)-rainfall calibrated with precipitation radar and merged with TMI and whatever other passive microwave data are available	0.25°	3 hours	6–7 hours	Huffman et al. 2007	Anonymous ftp site: ftp://trmmopen.gsfc.nasa.gov/pub/merged/3B42RT
TMPA – 3B42	TIR-rainfall calibrated with precipitation radar and merged with TMI, SSM/I, AMSU, and AMSR-E data; monthly aggregates adjusted with rain gauge measurements	0.25°	3 hours	1–2 months	Huffman et al. 2007	Links from http://disc.sci.gsfc.nasa.gov/
TMPA – 3B42 daily	Same as TMPA-3B42, but aggregated to daily rainfall totals	0.25°	Daily	3–4 months	Huffman et al. 2007	Links from http://disc.sci.gsfc.nasa.gov/
CMORPH – 30 minutes	Passive microwave, including TMI, SSM/I, AMSU, AMSR-E (TIR used for motion vectors)	0.07°	30 minutes	18–24 hours	Joyce et al. 2004 (473)	ftp://ftp.cpc.ncep.noaa.gov
CMORPH – 3-hourly		0.25°	3 hours	2–3 days	Joyce et al. 2004	
CMORPH – daily		0.25°	Daily	2–3 days	Joyce et al. 2004	
QMORPH – 30 minutes		0.07°	30 minutes	3–4 hours	Joyce et al. 2004	
QMORPH – daily		0.25°	30 minutes	3–4 hours	Joyce et al. 2004	
PERSIANN	TIR, passive microwave, including TMI, SSM/I, and AMSU	0.25°	1 hour	About 2 days	Sorooshian et al. 2000 (252); Hsu et al. 1997	http://chrs.web.uci.edu/persiann/data.html
PERSIANN – CCS	TIR data, geostationary	0.04°	1 hour	About 1 hour	Hong et al. 2004	http://hydis.eng.uci.edu/gawdi/
PERSIANN – CDR	GridSat-B1 CDR TIR window (near 11 microns)	0.25°	Daily	About 3 months	Ashouri et al. 2014	http://www.ncdc.noaa.gov/cdr/operationalcdrs.html (requires user registration)
PERSIANN – CONNECT (precipitation objects[b])	TIR, passive microwave	0.25°	1 hour		Sellars et al. 2013	http://chrs.web.uci.edu/research/voxel/index.html
GSMaP	Passive microwave, including TMI, SSM/I, and AMSU	0.1°			Kubota et al. 2007 (84)	http://sharaku.eorc.jaxa.jp/GSMaP/index.htm

Note: Data latency refers to the minimum time period between satellite data acquisition and product available for download. — = not available; AMSR = Advanced Microwave Sounding Unit; CCS = cloud classification system; CDR = climate data record; CMORPH = Climate Prediction Center MORPHing technique; GSMaP = Global Satellite Mapping of Precipitation; PERSIANN = Precipitation Estimation from Remotely Sensed Information Using Artificial Neural Networks; QMORPH = variation of CMORPH; SSM = Special Sensor Microwave; SSM/I = Special Sensor Microwave Imager; TIR = thermal infrared; TMI = TRMM Microwave Imager; TMPA = TRMM Multisatellite Precipitation Analysis; TRMM = Tropical Rainfall Measuring Mission.

a. Many TMPA-derived products provide monthly average rain rate and profile information at 0.5°–5° resolution. These products can be found at http://disc.sci.gsfc.nasa.gov/precipitation.

b. Precipitation object is a four-dimensional data construct comprising geographic latitude and longitude, precipitation intensity, and time. This system applies a connectivity algorithm to precipitation objects through time, which allows identification of individual precipitation events from the PERSIANN precipitation product archive.

c. National Aeronautics and Space Administration missions that produce data parameters with a coarse spatial resolution typically report the resolution in geographic degrees or fractions of degrees. The size of a degree (or fraction of a degree) depends on how close the measured area is to the equator and the poles.

However, the verification statistics are reported at an aggregate scale (for example, national average), while performance of these products is spatially variable at the local scale. For example, regions with orographic rainfall pose a challenge to satellite retrieval of rainfall (due to the light intensity of orographic rainfall), and rainfall in those regions is typically underestimated or missed in the satellite products.

Known Issues

Satellite-derived precipitation estimates have the potential to improve spatially distributed hydrologic model estimation and prediction (Gebremichael and Hossain 2010; Pan, Li, and Wood 2010). Unlike the isolated point measurements provided by rain gauges, satellite-based precipitation estimates offer greater spatial coverage of rainfall estimation with higher temporal frequency than many of the current gauging networks. Radar rainfall offers high-resolution (about 1 kilometer), high-frequency (about 10 minutes) precipitation estimates for areas within about a 150- to 300-kilometer radius of the radar location. However, the estimates are known to be affected by beam blockage and greater uncertainty moving away from the radar. For these reasons, as Gourley et al. (2010) and other studies have shown, they can give poorer estimates compared with some SPPs. Nevertheless, where radar data are available and well calibrated, radar rainfall can be useful for small-scale hydrologic prediction. However, much of the global land area is "unobserved" by ground-based rainfall radar systems, which limits their use in large-area (especially continental or global scale) water resources assessment.

The coarse spatial resolution of many of the SPPs currently available is considered one of the impediments to their widespread adoption by the hydrologic modeling community and water resources managers. Moreover, the fact that the precipitation products are retrievals derived from brightness temperature observations makes them less desirable or credible to some potential users than the direct measurements made by rain gauges.

Precipitation estimates from microwave-based satellite observations are known to underestimate light rainfall rates, typical of precipitation resulting from orographic lift[2] and cold fronts, for example. This is due to the reduced contrast in brightness temperatures from the land surface and scattering layer for low clouds. This can be a further impediment to the adoption of SPPs, particularly in mountainous areas of the Earth's surface.

Geostationary SPPs are based on cloud top temperatures. The underlying assumption here is that a weak relationship exists between the observed temperature of clouds and rain rate, the idea being that lower temperatures indicate clouds extending higher up into the atmosphere than their surroundings. While this relationship may hold for strongly convective systems, with cumulonimbus clouds extending into the stratosphere, the relationship is less solid for rain-producing clouds (for example, stratiform) in the lower to middle parts of the troposphere. Furthermore, the well-known misregistration between the location of the cloud top and the rain front further compounds the lack of reliability of geostationary-based rainfall estimation.

Observation frequency is another issue with SPPs, especially for the detection of extreme rainfall events (for example, AghaKouchak et al. 2011). Most modern SPPs are derived primarily through passive microwave sensors aboard polar-orbiting satellites, each with a repeat frequency of typically more than one day. Satellite constellations mitigate the issue somewhat by potentially providing many snapshots of an area from multiple polar-orbiting platforms. For example, the TMPA product 3B42RT (table 6.3) uses data from any available passive microwave sensor within a 90-minute window on either side of the synoptic time (which is at three-hour intervals over a day). However, given the typically short duration and very localized nature of extreme convective rainfall events, the event could pass undetected or be underrepresented in the derived products.

Studies evaluating SPPs and precipitation forecast from numerical weather prediction models have shown that SPPs do comparatively well at detecting "summer" rainfall, characterized by convective weather systems, whereas weather model forecasts are better for "winter" rain, which is largely stratiform (Ebert, Janowiak, and Kidd 2007; Sapiano et al. 2010). The complementarity of the satellite- and model-derived precipitation has spurred some researchers to consider combining the two sources of information, for example, as a simple ensemble mean of the data sets (Peña-Arancibia et al. 2013) or through more statistics-based merging approaches (Sapiano, Smith, and Arkin 2008). For instance, the Asia-Pacific Water Monitor of the Commonwealth Scientific and Industrial Research Organisation (CSIRO) uses a blending method that emphasizes precipitation estimates from the TRMM satellite product for areas closer to the equator and weather model precipitation estimates from the European Centre for Medium-Range Weather Forecasts for areas toward the poles.[3]

Blended Satellite- and Gauge-Based Precipitation Analyses

Rain gauge measurements are typically not used to retrieve rainfall data from satellite-based platforms (either geostationary or polar orbiting) or to conduct numerical weather prediction (reanalysis), except by some products to correct retrospective bias in the rainfall estimates. Blending multiple precipitation data sets has been the practice for many years among researchers in rainfall radar (for example, gauge-corrected reflectivity; Krajewski 1987) and satellite-derived precipitation (for example, merged passive microwave and TIR imagery; Huffman et al. 1997).

By exploiting the accuracy of station-level rain gauge measurements and the spatial coverage of gridded rainfall products, the blending of these two sources of information mitigates the shortcomings of the respective data sets to produce improved precipitation estimates. The statistical blending of satellite-derived precipitation products and rain gauge measurements has only been explored relatively recently to generate high-resolution rainfall estimates at continental scales (Chappell et al. 2013; Mitra et al. 2009; Renzullo et al. 2011; Rozante et al. 2010; Vila et al. 2009; Xiong et al. 2008). When further combined with reanalyses, the results are often a great deal improved (Sheffield, Goteti, and Wood 2006).

Renzullo et al. (2011) explore the role of satellite precipitation to enhance gauge-based analysis in Australia (figure 6.3). They examine several statistical methods for blending a TMPA near-real-time product (3B42RT) with gauge measurements from approximately 2,000 stations distributed across Australia reporting daily (that is, 24-hour accumulated) rainfall in real time. The blending of satellite estimates with gauge data resulted in a clear improvement over the use of satellite data alone, and the satellite data imparted more realistic patterns of rainfall distribution in the blended product than in "smoother," gauge-only analyses. However, the quantitative evaluation of the blended satellite-gauge rainfall product using the independent set of post-real-time rain gauge observation revealed that the estimates were no better than the gauge-only analyses. Subsequent investigation (reported in the supplementary material of Chappell et al. 2013) shows that the result was due largely to the fact that the evaluation occurred predominantly in well-gauged parts of the continent, where the gauge analysis has lower error. The satellite-derived product was only likely to improve estimation for parts of the country with fewer than four gauges per 10,000 square kilometers (equivalent to a 1° x 1° cell; figure 6.4).

Figure 6.3 Daily Rainfall Estimates for March 1, 2010, in Australia

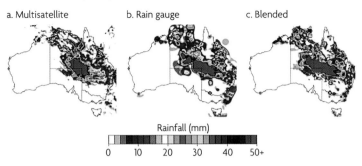

a. Multisatellite   b. Rain gauge   c. Blended

Rainfall (mm)

0   10   20   30   40   50+

Source: CSIRO 2011. © CSIRO. Used with permission. Further permission required for reuse.

Note: Panel a is from a National Aeronautics and Space Administration multisatellite rainfall product. Panel b is from analysis of rain gauges. Panel c is from combining the gauge and satellite rainfall estimates. The rain front shown led to widespread flooding in southern Queensland and northern New South Wales.

Figure 6.4 Distribution of Real-Time Rain Gauges and Areas Where Satellite-Derived Precipitation Is Likely to Improve Accuracy of Rainfall Estimation in Australia

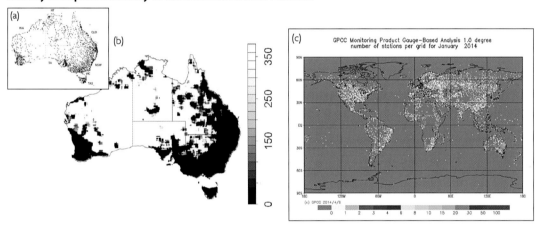

Sources: Renzullo et al. 2011 (panels a and b); Global Precipitation Climatological Center (http://gpcc.dwd.de) (panel c). © Water Information Research and Development Alliance (WIRADA) (panels a and b). Used with permission. Further permission required for reuse. Note: Panel a shows the location of the approximately 2,000 rain gauges reporting 24-hour accumulated rainfall in real time (the distribution is typical for any given day of the year). Panel b depicts the number of days in a year where the density of rain gauges is less than four gauges per 1° x 1° (satellite-derived precipitation is likely to improve rainfall estimates in the white regions). Panel c shows the number of gauges per 1° x 1° grid cell from the Global Precipitation Climatological Center.

The factors affecting when and where satellite data are expected to produce better rainfall estimation include type of topography and rainfall in addition to gauge density. However, in large parts of the globe, rain gauge networks are sparse (figure 6.4, panel c) and there is growing evidence to suggest that satellite-derived precipitation, together with weather model reanalysis estimates, can provide highly valuable rainfall estimates and narrow the information gap.

SPPs can enhance global precipitation estimation when the data are used in conjunction with multiple sources of precipitation data (for example, gauge, radar, and forecasts). Sheffield, Goteti, and Wood (2006) use global, 1° x 1° daily precipitation data, derived from the Global Precipitation Climatology Project's Special Sensor Microwave Imager (SSM/I) and gauge observations, to correct modeled daily rainfall reanalysis from the National Center for Environmental Prediction and the National Center for Atmospheric Research.[4] Furthermore, they use the three-hourly TMPA 3B42RT rain rates to disaggregate the daily data temporally into three-hourly rainfall estimates globally. The result is a precipitation data set with improved accuracy compared with model prediction and, in some instances, satellite products alone.

Evapotranspiration

Definition

Evaporation is the phase change from a liquid to gas. Evapotranspiration (ET) may occur from the Earth's surface (the soil, a water body, or other type of surface), through plant leaves (termed *transpiration*), and from rainfall on the surface of leaves (termed *interception*). While the term evapotranspiration covers these three components, interception is not explicitly used in the compound word. Evaporation, like precipitation, has the dimensions of depth per time, and common units are millimeters per hour, per day, or per year. When spatially integrated over an area such as a paddock, catchment, basin, or country, the dimensions become volume per time, and common units are cubic meters per day.

Actual evapotranspiration is difficult to measure at a single location (Leuning et al. 2012), let alone to estimate accurately both spatially and temporally over large areas. This is different than potential evapotranspiration, which can be readily calculated using commonly measured meteorological variables (Donohue, McVicar, and Roderick 2010) or instrumental equivalents of potential ET such as pan evaporation, which can be readily measured (Roderick, Hobbins, and Farquhar 2009a, 2009b).

The distinction between actual evapotranspiration, potential evapotranspiration, and pan evaporation is important (McMahon et al. 2013). Potential ET and pan evaporation are estimates and measurements, respectively, of atmospheric evaporative demand under environmental conditions with limitless access to water, so they are not representative of actual evapotranspiration when and where the surface is not saturated. Actual ET can be conceptualized as a two-stage process. In the first stage, following sufficient precipitation or irrigation, water is freely available, and actual ET is energy limited. In the second stage, water is limiting, and as the soil dries and plants close their stomata, actual ET declines. The water-limited part of the actual ET process is complex, depending on both biology (where there is vegetation) and meteorology. However, when water is not limiting, energy-limited actual ET is determined primarily by four principal meteorological drivers: net radiation, air temperature, relative humidity, and wind (McVicar et al., "Global Review and Synthesis," 2012a; McVicar et al., "Less Bluster Ahead?" 2012b).

Relevance

Actual evapotranspiration connects many of the Earth's hydrologic and related environmental processes at local, regional, and global scales. For example, actual ET links the water balance to the energy balance, vegetation to hydrology, and hydrology to climate. Actual evapotranspiration is both a matter of environmental physics and biology, as it is governed by the conditions of the physical environment at the surface and in the atmosphere, but also by photosynthesizing vegetation, which transpires water to assimilate carbon (described later in this section). Through vegetation, actual evapotranspiration is the primary hydrologic "lever" by which man can either inadvertently alter or actively manage the water cycle. As such, it is relevant to water management in agriculture, environmental services, climate change, and hydropower (see tables 5.2 and 5.3). For models of actual ET to be relevant to water management, they ideally should have the following characteristics:

- Have coverage that is suited to the purpose

- Be spatially and temporally dynamic at moderate to high resolution

- Accurately close the energy and mass balance (as a means of quality control).

For the first two characteristics, optical EO data are often used for spatial modeling of actual evapotranspiration. Closing the energy and mass balance from Earth observation is generally problematic, however, because it requires estimating 24-hour latent heat flux from as few as a single measurement made at a specific time of the day (Kalma, McVicar, and McCabe 2008; Van Niel et al. 2012).

Theoretical Basis of Remote Sensing of Actual Evapotranspiration

Empirical methods of estimating actual ET take advantage of the numerous links that it has to the energy balance, the water balance, and vegetation, which allow for various functional relationships to be established. For well-vegetated surfaces, the largest component of actual ET is usually transpiration. This means that a good estimate of actual ET can sometimes be made using simple statistical relationships with remotely sensed vegetation indexes that reflect the dynamics of vegetation greenness. For example, Nagler et al. (2007, 2009) and Yebra et al. (2013) find that the enhanced vegetation index (EVI) scales actual ET well. Although this simple relationship is likely to work well in many places, it is not useful everywhere. For instance, actual ET over a water body might be very high, but this would be missed when relating actual evapotranspiration to EVI. As actual ET is also part of the water balance, it should, at least for certain times and places, have a strong relationship to remotely sensed moisture indexes. In particular, areas of the world that are water limited might be well modeled with a simple relationship to a metric of moisture availability. For example, to estimate actual ET over arid Australia, Guerschman et al. (2009b) use both the EVI and the global vegetation moisture index with monthly precipitation to define a coefficient useful for scaling potential ET. They find that this method performs well compared to a variety of other methods, most of which are much more complicated to implement (King et al. 2011). Figure 6.5 illustrates the effects of basing ET estimates primarily on vegetation.

Empirical methods have also been developed to estimate actual ET from surface temperature derived from thermal EO data and a vegetation index (traditionally the normalized difference vegetation index or NDVI). This method has been called the "triangle" or "trapezoid" method, describing the general shape of the surface temperature versus NDVI data space (Lambin and Ehrlich 1996). The extremes of the surface temperature axis of this data space form the "cool edge" and "warm edge," representing more or less actual ET, respectively. The NDVI axis represents the amount of green vegetation cover. The end members of the data space, then, represent the maximum and minimum evaporation and the maximum and minimum transpiration. This method provides a linearization of the ratio of actual to potential ET (see Van Niel and McVicar 2004 for a detailed description). The triangle method is suited for estimating relative amounts of actual ET over local to regional areas, but is less adept at modeling absolute amounts of actual ET over large basins or continents or comparing actual ET from one region to another.

The main advantage of empirical methods is their simplicity; their main disadvantages are their reliance on ground measurements of

Figure 6.5 Examples of Actual Evapotranspiration Estimates for Region in Western Queensland, Australia, during Flow Event in February 2004

a. CMRSET model

b. PML model

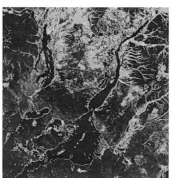
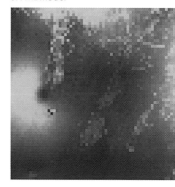

Source: Reproduced with permission from King et al. 2011. © WIRADA. Used with permission. Further permission required for reuse.

Note: The CMRSET model (Guerschman et al. 2009b) uses remotely sensed vegetation and moisture indexes. The PML model (Zhang et al. 2008) is based primarily on vegetation dynamics. The color scale is the same for the two images (blue-red = 0–5 millimeters per day). The location of the region shown is 139E-142E, 23S-26S.

actual ET and, generally, the inability to be improved via better process understanding. That is, once more or better ground data become available, it will probably be possible to improve these types of models by optimizing the fit, but they are mostly statistical in nature so they have limited capacity to inform process understanding. They also generally do not allow for better estimation based on improved understanding of the system. Nonetheless, empirical approaches can be a practical way to estimate actual ET.

Energy Balance Methods

The Earth's surface is heated by solar radiation and loses this heat through long-wave radiation, sensible heat flux (that is, heating the air), and latent heat flux (that is, using energy to evaporate water). Surface temperature can be used to estimate sensible heat flux. If net radiation (that is, incoming minus outgoing radiation) and changes in heat storage can be estimated as well (Zhu et al. 2014), latent heat flux can be calculated as the difference between all of these terms because of the requirement for energy balance (that is, the law of conservation of energy).

Most energy balance methods for estimating actual ET use satellite-derived radiometric or "skin" temperature data. Some of these models explicitly recognize that surface temperature measured by satellite is sometimes insufficient to solve the energy balance accurately by modeling two separate "layers," one in the vegetation canopy and one at ground surface, generally called two-layer models. They approximate a set of simultaneous equations that estimate an equal number of unknowns (Friedl 1995; Jupp et al. 1998), one of them being the effective surface temperature that is required in the energy balance equation. Energy balance methods require modeling of available energy and aerodynamic resistance, which are potential sources of uncertainty.

Various implementations of the energy balance method have been developed (Anderson et al. 2007, 2011; Bastiaanssen et al. 1998; Jupp et al. 1998; Menenti and Choudhury 1993; Norman et al. 2003; Su 2002). The energy balance approach, and in particular the two-layer model, has the inherent risk of being overparameterized compared to the data likely to be available for modeling, especially over large basins or continents. Therefore, many attempts have been made to make the model parsimonious with the data available for modeling large areas (Roerink, Su, and Menenti 2000; Sobrino et al. 2005).

Energy balance methods often first estimate relative evaporation (that is, the evaporative fraction) by defining "hot" and "cold" pixels from the image (for example, SEBAL, the Surface Energy Balance Algorithm for Land; Bastiaanssen et al. 1998) or by defining hypothetical "dry" and "wet" conditions determining the theoretical limits to evaporation (for example, SEBS, the Surface Energy Balance System; Su 2002). For an algorithm like SEBAL, for example, identifying appropriate "hot" or "cold" pixels is paramount, making it sometimes suited to use in agricultural areas with adjacent dryland and irrigated types of land cover. In other environments with less hydrologic contrast or when the area of interest is too large (covering drastically different climate zones), however, representative "hot" or "cold" pixels may not be readily found, making SEBAL less suitable. Furthermore, energy balance methods usually do not explicitly consider evaporation due to interception, even though interception can represent more than 20 percent of precipitation for certain types of vegetation (Miralles et al. 2010).

Most common applications of energy balance methods have used data from polar-orbiting platforms such as AVHRR (Advanced Very High Resolution Radiometer), MODIS, and Landsat (table 6.4). Resultant values represent an "instantaneous" flux, which requires scaling to actual ET integrated over a longer time period (for example, a day or a month) to be relevant to hydrology. Subsequent scaling of latent heat to daily or monthly actual ET is a source of considerable

Table 6.4 Overview of Sensors Most Suitable for Estimating Actual Evapotranspiration from EO Data

ORBIT AND SATELLITE SENSOR SYSTEM	PIXEL SIZE (METERS)	SPECTRAL BANDS	REVISIT CYCLE	RAW DATA COST PER SQUARE KILOMETER (US$)	DATE LAUNCHED (END) OR PLANNED LAUNCH	EMPIRICAL	PM LAI	REBM
Polar orbiting								
MODIS	250–1,000	29	2 times a day	Free	2000	①	①	①
VIIRS and JPSS	375–750	14	2 times a day	Free	2012	①	①	①
AVHRR	1,000	4	Daily	Free	1981	②	①	①
Landsat 5 TM	30–90	7	16 days	Free	1985 (2012)	①	①	①
Landsat 7 ETM+	30–60	8	16 days	Free	2000	①	②	②
Landsat 8	30–100	11	16 days	Free	2013	①	①	①
Geostationary								
GOES (2nd and 3rd generation)	1,000–4,000	4	15 minutes	Free	1994	②	①	①
Meteosat (2nd generation)	1,000–3,000	7	15 minutes	Free	2002	①	①	①
Himawari-8	500–2,000	10	15 minutes	Free	2014	①	①	①

Note: The suitability of each sensor to provide data useful for the three classes of models is shown with numbers and colors, as follows: ① highly suitable, ② suitable. AVHRR = Advanced Very High Resolution Radiometer; ETM+ = Enhanced Thematic Mapper Plus; GOES = geostationary operational environmental satellite; JPSS = Joint Polar Satellite System; MODIS = Moderate Resolution Imaging Spectrometer; PM LAI = Penman-Monteith leaf area index; REBM = resistance energy balance model; TM = Thematic Mapper; VIIRS = Visible/Infrared Imager Radiometer Suite.

uncertainty (McVicar and Jupp 2002; Van Niel et al. 2011, 2012). However, because the energy balance approach makes use of "instantaneous" surface temperature, it is directly suited to the use of geostationary data. For example, the algorithm disALEXI uses geostationary data over North America to observe the change in surface temperature during the morning (Anderson et al. 2011), making it suitable for modeling flux, which is closer to the theoretical nature of the phenomena being estimated. The advantage of the energy balance method is that it counters the main disadvantage of the empirical approaches: energy balance methods are eminently suited to inform and be improved by better process understanding.

Penman-Monteith Methods

One of the main obstacles to calculating actual evapotranspiration from an energy balance perspective is the need to derive the effective surface temperature of an area. This is particularly problematic when the area of interest (that is, a pixel) is heterogeneous (for example, partly vegetated and partly bare soil). Thermal

EO data are not a pure solution to this problem due to issues regarding specific time-of-day acquisition, cloud cover, and differences between the radiometric "skin" temperature received at the sensor and the effective surface temperature that solves the energy balance at ground level. In days prior to operational EO-based land surface temperature products, the so-called Penman-Monteith "combination equation" was derived, eliminating the need to estimate surface temperature (Monteith 1965, 1981; Penman 1948).

The Penman-Monteith equation combines the aerodynamic formulation of actual evapotranspiration and the energy balance with an approximation of the saturation vapor pressure calculated at surface temperature. The problem with using the Penman-Monteith equation, however, is that, although the need to know surface temperature was eliminated, it was replaced by a different unknown parameter—the surface (or canopy) conductance (sometimes written in the form of resistance, in which case it would be the surface or canopy resistance). While the number of unknown parameters remains unchanged, one advantage is that this model allows for the unknown parameter to be addressed in a different way: through conductance. Conductance is a parameter associated with transpiration and carbon assimilation in the process of photosynthesis, so it allows estimation of actual ET through vegetation characteristics.

The Penman-Monteith equation is a process-based model, so it is in a different category than the empirical relationships primarily using statistically fitted relationships between actual ET and vegetation indexes. It is based, to a large degree, on the energy balance, but as surface conductance is commonly modeled through remotely sensed vegetation products like a vegetation index or a leaf area index (LAI), it is also considered to be in a different category than the energy balance methods discussed above. However, the three types of methods sometimes overlap, making their distinction less clear.

For example, surface conductance is an unknown, and only empirical methods are available to estimate it. Yebra et al. (2013) compares fully empirical approaches with Penman-Monteith approaches, including approaches based on the MODIS leaf area index and on the Guerschman et al. (2009b) crop factor approach. They conclude that, among these, the best approach to modeling actual ET is through the use of an empirical relationship to estimate surface conductance from vegetation indexes, where each of the three indexes tested (enhanced vegetation index [EVI], normalized difference vegetation index [NDVI], and the Guerschman Kc index) has specific strengths and weaknesses.

Alternatively, surface conductance can be modeled using estimates derived from field measurements, whether by upscaling leaf-level measurements of stomatal conductance (Kelliher et al. 1995) or by using field-level estimates of surface conductance derived from lysimeters or other water balance methods, or, more commonly in recent years, by using micrometeorological methods and flux tower Eddy covariance measurements, in particular.

Furthermore, the so-called FAO-56 method (Allen et al. 2007) can be seen as an intermediate method in that it calculates a hypothetical evapotranspiration for an idealized crop and then applies an empirical method to scale this hypothetical ET factor. The satellite-based method developed by Guerschman et al. (2009b) is akin to the FAO-56 approach. Since it is suitable for use with higher-spatial-resolution sensors like Landsat ETM+, it (and methods like it) can be used for estimating actual evapotranspiration at the level of an irrigation scheme, farm, or even a field (figure 6.6).

Because there are various global EO-based vegetation data sets, the Penman-Monteith equation is commonly used to estimate actual ET. However, just as is the case for purely empirical relationships, the Penman-Monteith approach will not necessarily perform well where actual ET is not driven primarily by transpiration. To implement the approach over vast areas, it also relies on a model of available energy and aerodynamic conductance, which may add considerable error or uncertainty to the estimation. The Penman-Monteith approach models actual ET through the link between vegetation and energy balance; thus the main impediment to its implementation is the need to determine surface conductance. However, due to the reliance of the Penman-Monteith method on vegetation dynamics and stomatal conductance, the relationship between this actual ET estimate and crop growth or gross primary production modeling is closer.

Methods have been developed that use satellite LAI products to estimate surface conductance from an assumed (or optimized) leaf-level stomatal conductance value. Some readily available global vegetation LAI products from Earth observation have promoted the development of LAI-scaled global ET estimates (Mu, Zhao, and Running 2011; Zhang et al. 2012).

Past, Present, and Future Sensor Availability for Mapping Actual Evapotranspiration

Table 6.4 lists some existing and planned sensors that can provide estimates of actual ET.

Figure 6.6 Mapping of Actual Evapotranspiration Using High-Resolution Satellite Images for Part of Lower Gwydir Region in New South Wales, Australia

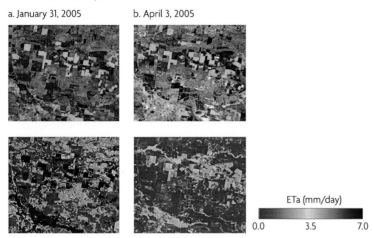

a. January 31, 2005   b. April 3, 2005

ETa (mm/day)

0.0   3.5   7.0

Source: Emelyanova et al. 2012. © CSIRO. Used with permission. Further permission required for reuse.

Note: The top row shows false color composites of the original Landsat TM (thematic mapper) imagery; the bottom row shows estimated actual evapotranspiration rates. The colors in the top row correspond to vigorous vegetation (green), open water (black-blue), and dry land (purple).

Most optical sensors can be used for mapping actual ET for at least one of the three general categories. Those sensors that include bands in the visible (VIS) and near-infrared (NIR) spectrum are generally suited to empirical methods using vegetation indexes and to the Penman-Monteith approach (which also requires meteorological data). Sensors having short-wave infrared (SWIR) bands in addition to VIS-NIR bands allow for determining empirical relationships with moisture indexes and for estimating actual ET from surfaces with no vegetation, including water bodies. Many of the optical sensors also record thermal data, making them suitable for both empirical and energy balance approaches that use surface temperature. MODIS, Landsat, and VIIRS (Visible/Infrared Imager Radiometer Suite) are examples of sensors that acquire the data useful for all three categories of models. Sensors like AVHRR do not have SWIR bands, but are useful in the vegetative index and surface temperature-based approaches.

Existing RS-Based Data Products and Services for Actual Evapotranspiration

There are numerous EO-based implementations of the three categories of actual ET models just described. Examples of these three categories, with relevant references, are provided in table 6.5. As discussed above, each approach has strengths and weaknesses. The simplicity of the empirical approach is offset by its inability to inform and be informed by process understanding. The ability of the Penman-Monteith approach to estimate actual ET better through vegetation dynamics is offset by its inability to model water bodies or soil evaporation. The ability of the energy balance approach to inform process understanding and use geostationary thermal data is offset by difficulties in scaling instantaneous observations to longer time periods and relative ET to absolute ET as well as by model complexity. Furthermore, while the approaches have been classified into three categories, specific implementations may sometimes blur these distinctions.

While it is unlikely that any single approach will be best suited to estimate actual ET for all situations, a common relevant issue is having a system in place for robust and repeatable assessment of ET models. For instance, the ET intercomparison and evaluation framework within Australia was designed to assess eight continental models of actual ET to help to inform the Australian Water Resources Assessment

Table 6.5 Examples of Studies Using the Three General Classes of Actual ET Models

TYPE OF MODEL AND EO ALGORITHM	REFERENCES
Empirical	
CMRSET	Guerschman et al. 2009b
Surface temperature versus NDVI	Lambin and Ehrlich 1996
Actual ET versus EVI	Nagler et al. 2007, 2009
Penman-Monteith	
Unnamed	Yebra et al. 2013
Unnamed	Cleugh et al. 2007
PML	Leuning et al. 2012; Zhang et al. 2008
MODIS ET	Mu, Zhao, and Running 2011
Energy balance	
SEBAL	Bastiaanssen et al. 1998
SEBS	Su 2002
ETWatch	Wu et al. 2012
S-SEBI	Roerink, Su, and Menenti 2000; Sobrino et al. 2005
dis(ALEXI)	Anderson et al. 2007; Norman et al. 2003
NDTI	Jupp et al. 1998; McVicar and Jupp 2002

Note: ALEXI = Atmosphere-Land Exchange Inverse; CMRSET = CSIRO MODIS Reflectance-based Scaling ET; EO = Earth observation; ET = evapotranspiration; EVI = enhanced vegetation index; MODIS ET = Moderate Resolution Imaging Spectrometer evapotranspiration; NDTI = normalized difference temperature index; NDVI = normalized difference vegetation index; PML = Penman-Monteith-Leuning; SEBAL = Surface Energy Balance Algorithm for Land; SEBS = Surface Energy Balance System; S-SEBI = Simplified Surface Energy Balance index.

(AWRA; see appendix B). Key to this type of assessment framework is some form of field measurement, which can be used in the ET model itself (for empirical methods) and for validation of all types of models. So-called Eddy covariance flux data are often used for these purposes.[5]

For places where no ground measurements exist, EO-based models of actual ET can still be used, but in the absence of error assessment, their suitability for management purposes may not be known with certainty. Figure 6.7 illustrates the accuracy that might be expected for a forested site, where actual ET is not overly challenging to estimate. Typically, at moderate to low resolution (about 5 kilometers, monthly time step), actual ET can be estimated to within 1 millimeter per day or better. Of course, this will depend on site, algorithm, and data characteristics. Other important considerations are reliability, maturity, and complexity of the system required to produce the estimate of actual ET.

Soil Moisture
Definition
Soil moisture is defined as the amount of water in the uppermost layers of the soil column, where the definition of "uppermost" varies depending on sensing technology or modeling application and can vary from the top 1 centimeter to the first 1 meter of soil or more. Soil moisture is highly variable in space and time, and its importance to water resources is apparent via the link between key water balance terms and hydrologic processes in the soil column. As a measure of catchment antecedent moisture[6] condition, soil moisture affects the amount of evaporation from soil, transpiration by vegetation, and partitioning of rainfall into infiltration and surface runoff. Soil moisture has had a role in characterizing hydroclimate and monitoring the effects of climate change (for example, drought monitoring; Bolten et al. 2010) for more than 20 years, but this role has been "formalized" only relatively recently by its listing among the World Meteorological

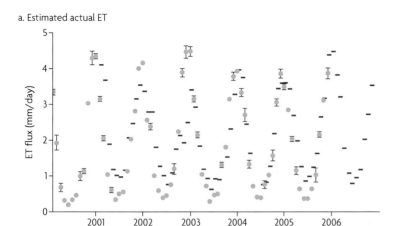

a. Estimated actual ET

b. Measured actual ET

Mean: −0.2126 SD: 0.6692

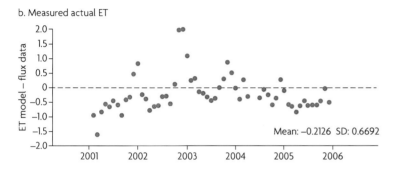

Figure 6.7 Comparison of Actual ET Estimates Derived from the NDTI Model with Actual ET Measurements from the Tumbarumba, NSW, Flux Tower

Source: Reproduced from King et al. 2011. © WIRADA. Used with permission. Further permission required for reuse.

Note: In the top panel, the blue dots represent actual ET estimates from the normalized difference temperature index model (Jupp et al. 1998; McVicar and Jupp 2002), which are compared to actual ET measurements from the Tumbarumba, NSW, flux tower (black dashes). The red dots in the bottom panel show the differences between model estimates and the flux tower measurements (in units of millimeters per day). ET = evapotranspiration; NDTI = normalized difference temperature index.

Organization's Global Climate Observing System essential climate variables (Bojinski et al. 2014).

Soil moisture monitoring has advanced considerably over the last decade, with burgeoning innovative ground- and satellite-based technologies for large-area monitoring (for a comprehensive summary, see Ochsner et al. 2013). These technologies include coordinated global networks of field-based sensors (Dorigo et al. 2013; Smith et al. 2012) and a novel proximal sensing technique based on cosmic ray detectors (Desilets, Zreda, and Ferré 2010; Zreda et al. 2012).

While field-based detectors can measure moisture very accurately at various depths for a point in the landscape, cosmic ray probes provide an integrated root-zone moisture measurement for an area of about 600 meters in diameter (Desilets and Zreda 2013)—an area suitable for many agricultural and land management applications. Cosmic ray probes have been applied beyond root-zone soil moisture sensing, including estimating aboveground biomass (Franz et al. 2013) and constraining land surface models

through calibration and data assimilation (Zreda et al. 2012). Both field-based and proximal sensing are valuable information sources in their own right, and they provide essential data for the evaluation and calibration of satellite-derived and modeled soil moisture products, helping to build confidence in their accuracy.

Global monitoring of soil moisture is only achievable with satellite Earth observation in conjunction with field-based soil moisture monitoring networks. Satellite soil moisture products have been derived from a contiguous series of space-borne sensors spanning 30 years (Liu et al. 2012). However, the first dedicated soil moisture monitoring mission from space was not launched until 2009 (Kerr et al. 2012). Time series of satellite soil moisture have been used in climate studies (Jung et al. 2010; Liu et al. 2009; Seneviratne et al. 2010) and have refined our understanding of rainfall generation processes (Taylor et al. 2012).

The assimilation of satellite soil moisture into land surface models has been shown to improve soil water representation in the models (Draper et al. 2012; Renzullo et al. 2014) and led to improvements in estimated evaporative fluxes, drainage, and discharge (Brocca et al. 2012; Dharssi et al. 2011; Draper et al. 2011; Pipunic et al. 2013; Reichle and Koster 2005). It is through integration with landscape hydrology models and field-based monitoring networks (via calibration and data assimilation) that the satellite soil moisture products offer greatest potential for monitoring large-area water resources, particularly as a constraint for parts of the Earth where traditional ground observation networks have sparse, intermittent, or no coverage at all.

Brief Summary of Soil Moisture Sensing from Space

The dielectric properties of soil are greatly altered by the amount of liquid water present in the soil. The relationship between moisture in the soil and emitted radiation (about 1–20 gigahertz or a 1.5–30-centimeter region of the electromagnetic spectrum) has been conceptually understood since the 1970s and encapsulated in various physical models (Dobson et al. 1985; Wang and Schmugge 1980). The potential for Earth observation to measure soil moisture on a small scale was demonstrated shortly thereafter with several field experiments involving tower-mounted and airborne microwave radiometers (Jackson and Schmugge 1989). Until that point, the primary use of microwave instruments on satellites had been communications, monitoring of snow and sea ice extent, and atmospheric soundings of temperature and moisture. It was only in the early 2000s that these space-based microwave sensors started being used to estimate soil moisture, with the first global satellite soil moisture products available in 2002 (de Jeu and Owe 2003; Wagner et al. 2003; figure 6.8).

Satellite soil moisture sensing technology is based on either radiometric measurements of emissions from the soil (the so-called passive microwave approach) or radar technology transmitting pulse of electromagnetic radiation to the Earth's surface and measuring the backscattered signal (the so-called active approach). One of the defining characteristics separating active and passive sensors is their contrasting spatial resolution: passive sensors require large integrating areas for adequate signal-to-noise (ratios)[7] so the instantaneous field-of-view (pixel) has a resolution of 30–120 kilometers, whereas the resolution of active systems, for a given frequency, is a function of beam width, pulse duration, and satellite antenna length. This means that the resolution required to sustain a good signal-to-noise ranges from about 10 meters to 10 kilometers. Examples of active and passive satellite EO systems used in the production of global soil moisture products are listed and defined in table 6.6. They include SSM/I, TMI (TRMM Microwave Imager), AMSR-E (Advanced Microwave Scanning Radiometer for EOS), AMSR2 (Advanced Microwave Scanning Radiometer2), and SMOS (Soil Moisture and Ocean Salinity Sensor) for passive radiometry and ERS (European Remote Sensing Satellite), ASAR (Advanced Synthetic Aperture Radar), and ASACT (Advanced Scatterometer) for active scatterometry.

Until recently, satellite soil moisture products were typically derived from X- and C-band

Figure 6.8 Remote Sensing–Based Soil Moisture Monitoring

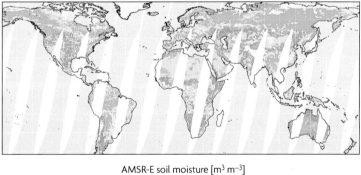

AMSR-E soil moisture [m³ m⁻³]

0   0.1   0.3   0.5   0.7

Source: CSIRO, using data from Owe, de Jeu, and Holmes 2008. © CSIRO. Used with permission. Further permission required for reuse.

Note: Satellite soil moisture products for January 2, 2006, derived by applying the retrieval algorithm of Owe, de Jeu, and Holmes (2008) to the descending passes of the AMSR-E sensor aboard NASA's Aqua satellite. AMSR-E = Advanced Microwave Scanning Radiometer for EOS; NASA = National Aeronautics and Space Administration.

Table 6.6 Overview of Key Characteristics of Soil Moisture Sensors Aboard Past, Current, and Near-Future Satellite Platforms

SENSOR	SATELLITE PLATFORM	MISSION LIFE SPAN	SOIL MOISTURE PRODUCT PROVIDER	TYPE	UNITS	RESAMPLED RESOLUTION (KILOMETERS)	SWATH (KILOMETERS)	GLOBAL COVERAGE	KEY REFERENCE	DATA ACCESS
Aquarius	SAC-D	June 2010–	NSIDC	Active and passive L band	$m^3\,m^{-3}$	100	390	Daily: 7-day composite[a]	Bindlish and Jackson 2013	ftp://n5eil0lu.ecs.nsidc.org/SAN/AQUARIUS/
ASAR	Envisat	March 2002–April 2012	ESA	Active C band	%	1	100–405	3–8 days	Wagner et al. 2008	http://rs.geo.tuwien.ac.at/products/
ASCAT	MetOp (-A, -B)	October 2006–	TUW	Active C band	%	12.5	550	1.5 days	Wagner, Lemoine, and Rott 1999	Registered user: ftp.ipf.tuwien.ac.at
AMSR-E	Aqua	May 2002–October 2011	NSIDC	Passive X band	$g\,cm^{-3}$	25	1,445	Daily	Njoku et al. 2003	ftp://n4ftl0lu.ecs.nasa.gov/SAN/AMSA/
AMSR-E	Aqua	May 2002–October 2011	VUA	Passive C band	$m^3\,m^{-3}$	25	1,445	Ascending and descending	Owe, de Jeu, and Holmes 2008	Level-2 swath data: ftp://hydro1.sci.gsfc.nasa.gov/data/s4pa/WAOB/LPRM_AMSRE_SOILM2.00 2 — Level-3 ascending 0.25° gridded data: ftp://hydro1.sci.gsfc.nasa.gov/data/s4pa/WAOB/LPRM_AMSRE_A_SOILM3.002/ — Level-3 descending 0.25° gridded data: ftp://hydro1.sci.gsfc.nasa.gov/data/s4pa/WAOB/LPRM_AMSRE_D_SOILM3.002/ — Level-4 assimilated root-zone soil moisture: ftp://hydro1.sci.gsfc.nasa.gov/data/s4pa/WAOB/LPRM_AMSRE_D_RZSM3.00l/
AMSR-E	Aqua	May 2002–October 2011	NSIDC	Passive X band	$m^3\,m^{-3}$	25	1,445	Ascending and descending	Jones and Kimball 2012	ftp://sidads.colorado.edu/pub/DATASETS/nsidc0451_AMSRE_Land_Parms_v01/
AMSR2	GCOM-W1	May 2012–	JAXA	Passive C band	$m^3\,m^{-3}$	50	1,450	Ascending and descending	Koike 2013	https://gcom-w1.jaxa.jp/auth.html
AMSR2	GCOM-W1	May 2012–	VUA	Passive C band	$m^3\,m^{-3}$	10 and 25	1,450	Ascending and descending	Parinussa et al. 2014	http://globalchange.nasa.gov/

(Continued)

Table 6.6 (Continued)

SENSOR	SATELLITE PLATFORM	MISSION LIFE SPAN	SOIL MOISTURE PRODUCT PROVIDER	TYPE	UNITS	RESAMPLED RESOLUTION (KILOMETERS)	SWATH (KILOMETERS)	GLOBAL COVERAGE	KEY REFERENCE	DATA ACCESS
AMI	ERS (-1,-2)	July 1991–June 2011	TUW	Active C band	%	25	500	3 days	Wagner, Lemoine, and Rott 1999	http://rs.geo.tuwien.ac.at/products/
MIRAS	SMOS	November 2009–December 2014	ESA	Passive L band (multiple-angle)	$m^3\,m^{-3}$	50	1,000	3 days	Kerr et al. 2012	Registered users: http://www.esa.int/Our_Activities/Observing_the_Earth/The_Living_Planet_Programme/Earth_Explorers/SMOS/Overview
C-SAR	Sentinel-1a	April 2014–	ESA	Active C band	%	0.004–0.08	80–400	5 days	Unknown	Unknown
SMAP (launch 2015)	SMAP	2015–	NSIDC	Active and passive L band		11	1,000	1.5 days	Entekhabi et al. 2010	NSIDC site
SSM/I	DMSP	October 1987–	VUA	Passive K band		25	1,700	Daily	Owe, de Jeu, and Holmes 2008	Registered users: http://www.esa-soilmoisture-cci.org
SMMR	Nimbus	November 1977–December 1987	VUA	Passive C, X band		25	780	Ascending and descending	De Jeu and Owe 2003	Registered users: http://www.esa-soilmoisture-cci.org
TMI	TRMM	November 1997–	VUA	Passive X band		25	878	Equatorial daily	Owe, de Jeu, and Holmes 2008	Level-2 swath data: ftp://hydrol.sci.gsfc.nasa.gov/data/s4pa/WAOB/LPRM_TMI_SOILM2.00I/ Level-3 0.25° gridded daytime data: ftp://hydrol.sci.gsfc.nasa.gov/data/s4pa/WAOB/LPRM_TMI_DY_SOILM3.00I/ Level-3 0.25° gridded nighttime data: ftp://hydrol.sci.gsfc.nasa.gov/data/s4pa/WAOB/LPRM_TMI_NT_SOILM3.00I/
WindSat	Coriolis	January 2003–	NOAA	Passive C band		25	1,025	1.5 days	Li et al. 2010	http://www.ospo.noaa.gov/Products/land/smops/
Windsat	Coriolis	January 2003–	VUA	Passive C band		25	1,025	1.5 days	Parinussa Holmes, and de Jeu 2012	Registered users: http://www.esa-soilmoisture-cci.org

Note: Microwave bands L, C, X, and K correspond to frequency ranges 1–2, 4–8, 8–12, and 18–26 GHz, respectively. The end-of-life dates for some of the current missions are speculative. AMI = active microwave instrument; ASAR = Advanced Synthetic Aperture Radar; ASCAT = Advanced Scatterometer; AMSR-E = Advance Microwave Scanning Radiometer–Earth Observing System; C-SAR = Circular Synthetic Aperture Radar; ESA = European Space Agency; JAXA = Japan Aerospace Exploration Agency; MIRAS = Microwave Imaging Radiometer with Aperture Synthesis; NOAA = National Oceanic and Atmospheric Administration; NSDIC = National Snow and Ice Data Centre; SMAP = Soil Moisture Active Passive; SMM/I = Special Sensor Microwave Imager; SMMR = Scanning Multi-channel Microwave Radiometer; TMI =TRMM Microwave Imager; TUW = Vienna University of Technology; VUA = VU University Amsterdam; $m^3\,m^{-3}$ = cubic meter of water per cubic meter of soil; $g\,cm^{-3}$ = grams per cubic centimeter.

a. Seven-day composite is based on images collected over 7 consecutive days. The benefit is that it eliminates most cloud cover found in daily images.

microwave signals (8–12 and 4–8 gigahertz frequency range, respectively), which means that their values correspond to emissions or backscatter from the top 1–2 centimeters of soil. The launch of SMOS (Barré et al. 2008) ushered in a new era of L-band (1–2 gigahertz or 15–30 centimeters) sensing technology dedicated to monitoring soil moisture in the top 5 centimeters of soil, which will continue with the scheduled launch of Soil Moisture Active Passive (SMAP) (Entekhabi et al. 2010).

The SMAP mission of the National Aeronautics and Space Administration (NASA) launched in January 2015 is the first dedicated soil moisture sensing mission to combine both active and passive sources for high-resolution (about 10 kilometers) mapping of soil moisture for the globe on a daily basis.

Satellite Soil Moisture Products

Satellite soil moisture products are generated by different groups around the world, including government research agencies (NASA, JAXA, European Space Agency [ESA], the National Snow and Ice Data Center [NSIDC]) and universities (VU University of Amsterdam, Vienna University of Technology). Different groups have used different retrieval algorithms to derive soil moisture from brightness temperature observations by the same satellite sensors. For example, the University of Amsterdam and NSIDC derive soil moisture from C-band brightness temperature data from the AMSR-E, but they employ different retrieval schemes and radiative transfer model parameterization (detailed in Owe, de Jeu, and Holmes 2008 and Njoku et al. 2003, respectively). Different products may represent soil moisture values quite differently; for instance, values based on radiative transfer equations are typically expressed in volumetric or gravimetric units, while scatterometer-derived estimates are expressed in percentage wetness or degree of saturation (0–100 percent).

Beyond differences in resolution, there is demonstrated complementarity of satellite soil moisture retrievals from active and passive sensors due to their respective performance across different landscapes. For example, Dorigo et al. (2010) derived the error structure of the AMSR-E (passive) and ASCAT (active) soil moisture products over the globe using a statistical technique called triple collocation (Scipal et al. 2008). Examination of the error patterns showed that AMSR-E errors were largest in landscapes with a moderate to high level of tree cover, due to the influence of vegetation on the emitted signal, while ASCAT errors were largest in dry arid areas, due to the scattering properties of dry soil and undulations (dunes) in those landscapes. Others have reported similar findings; for example, Draper et al. (2012) show that assimilating ASCAT into NASA's catchment model led to significantly less accurate estimates of root-zone moisture over highly variable terrain compared to using AMSR-E.

Comparing the accuracy of satellite soil moisture estimates with surface measurements is necessary to gain acceptance of the products by the user community and often involves evaluations against field-based soil moisture measurements, such as individual soil moisture products (Albergel et al. 2011), alternative soil moisture products from the same sensor (Draper et al. 2009), or soil moisture products across sensors (Su et al. 2011, 2013). However, care must be taken to use consistent definitions when comparing soil moisture values using model and field-based measurements. Differences may be observed due to incompatibility of soil moisture units, spatial resolution (that is, from point to pixel), sampling depth (emission depth), as well as differences in the product-processing methods. Given the range of potential sources of inconsistency, drawing conclusions from observed differences poses difficulties (Leroux et al. 2013; Wagner et al. 2003).

Investigations often reveal that no one soil moisture product is "best" for all locations and applications and that it is advisable to exploit the complementarity between products (active, passive, and modeled) and to generate merged soil moisture estimates (Draper et al. 2012; Liu et al. 2012; Renzullo et al. 2014). Knowing how each source of soil moisture data should be used to produce the most suitable merged estimates requires spatially explicit quantification of the random errors of each product (see figure 6.9 for an example). This is where the triple collocation technique has gained popularity in the community of satellite soil moisture data users (Dorigo et al. 2010; Miralles et al. 2010; Scipal et al. 2008; Yilmaz and Crow 2014; Zwieback et al. 2012).

In addition to measuring moisture in the uppermost layers of the soil column, satellite microwave sensors are used to map the land surface freeze-thaw state. Like soil moisture, satellite mapping of global freeze-thaw state is achieved by exploiting the large difference in dielectric properties between frozen and thawed surfaces. The freeze-thaw state of the land surface is an important link between the hydrologic cycle and the carbon cycle via vegetation dynamics, specifically plant phenology (Kimball, McDonald, and Zhao 2006).

Global maps of the freeze-thaw state have been derived from satellite microwave sensors spanning the last 30 years at 0.25° resolution (Kim et al. 2011). The freeze-thaw products are raster maps with three discrete classes: frozen, thawed, and transitional, where the transitional class can be further divided into transitional (a.m. frozen, p.m. thaw) or inverse-transitional (a.m. thaw, p.m. frozen) using successive day-night passes. The SMAP mission aims to generate freeze-thaw coverage for the globe at 3-kilometer resolution with a two-day repeat cycle for latitudes above 50° north (McDonald, Kimball, and Kim 2010).

Considerations for Use in Water Management Applications

Although satellite technologies only provide soil moisture information for the very few top centimeters of soil, the data have been shown to be useful in climate studies (Jung et al. 2010; Taylor et al. 2012), weather forecasting (Dharssi et al. 2011), and hydrologic prediction (Brocca et al. 2010, 2012; Pauwels et al. 2002), especially in combination with land surface models by data assimilation (Draper et al. 2012; Renzullo et al. 2014). Land surface model estimates of root-zone moisture are demonstrably improved through the assimilation of satellite soil moisture. The value to water resources management (WRM) is further enhanced through the estimated constraint that the model imparts to other components of the water cycle (evapotranspiration and runoff). Root-zone soil moisture is useful for monitoring drought and modeling landscape ecology. However, the coarse spatial resolution of the data is probably an impediment to widespread adoption, especially in agricultural applications. Climate studies require long time series of harmonized soil moisture values. This has recently been achieved by Liu et al. (2012), using 30 years of soil moisture data derived from several satellites.

The complementarity of active and passive soil moisture retrievals has been recognized. It is envisaged that future application of satellite

Figure 6.9 Comparing Error Estimates for Soil Moisture Products Derived from Active and Passive Microwave Sensors Using Triple Collocation Technique

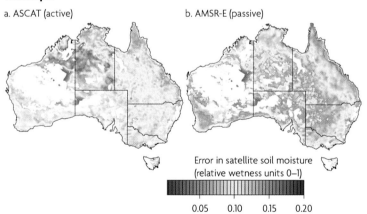

a. ASCAT (active)   b. AMSR-E (passive)

Error in satellite soil moisture (relative wetness units 0–1)

0.05   0.10   0.15   0.20

Source: Adapted from Renzullo et al. 2014.

Note: Error estimates for soil moisture products from ASCAT (active) and AMSR-E (passive) microwave sensors for Australia derived using the popular triple collocation technique. The technique requires three independent estimates of soil moisture to infer the errors in the respective data. The third product used (not displayed) was a top-layer soil moisture estimate from the Australian Water Resources Assessment (AWRA) landscape model. White spaces in the maps correspond to locations where the temporal dynamics of the three soil moisture data differed significantly and the triple collocation technique did not yield an estimate. AMSR-E = Advance Microwave Scanning Radiometer–Earth Observing System; ASCAT = Advanced Scatterometer.

soil moisture studies to climate, weather, and water resources management will be based on products that combine the typically higher accuracy but coarser resolution of passive sensors with the higher spatial resolution but noisier signal of active sensors. Indeed, this is the motivation behind the SMAP mission, which will be the first dedicated soil moisture monitoring mission carrying both active and passive sensing systems.

Vegetation and Vegetation Cover

Definition

Vegetation is the collective term for the coverage of plants across land areas. Vegetation attributes and processes relate to the emergent properties and functioning of those plants when considered at the landscape scale. Vegetation can be characterized quantitatively using measures of height, canopy and stem density, and leaf area, among others. It can also be described qualitatively, as vegetation classes or cover types, such as forest, croplands, tundra, and the like.

Relevance

The role of vegetation in the hydrologic cycle is well established (Budyko and Miller 1974; Monteith 1972; Ol'dekop 1911; Rodríguez-Iturbe et al. 2001; Specht 1972), modifying the direct role of the climate in the partitioning of precipitation between evaporation and runoff. It has been estimated that between 80 and 90 percent of terrestrial evaporation is transpired by vegetation (Jasechko et al. 2013). Besides impoundments, vegetation is the main pathway by which humans modify the terrestrial water balance. Far from being a passive factor, vegetation has a significant and highly dynamic impact on its surroundings, influencing just about all land surface processes. The ubiquitous, exposed, and temporally dynamic nature of vegetation means that Earth observation is a powerful and cost-effective means of quantifying many of the key roles that vegetation plays in the hydrologic cycle.

Earth observation can also be used to classify vegetation into distinct types of vegetation cover that describe various combinations of growth form (trees, shrubs, grasses), phenology (deciduous, nondeciduous), and sometimes climate types (temperate, arid, tropical). Data on type of vegetation cover provide a convenient, but static, means of summarizing the broad roles of different functional types of vegetation. Typical types may include forest, grassland, and cropland. When nonvegetation classes such as water, snow, urban, and bare soil are included, the categorization might better be referred to as land cover types.

One of the most important roles of vegetation in the water cycle is to modify evaporation rates. In order to photosynthesize, vegetation extracts soil water and groundwater and evaporates it into the atmosphere as transpiration. As a result, positive relationships exist between transpiration rates and leaf photosynthetic capacity and between transpiration rates and leaf area. Transpiration rates also tend to be positively related to rooting depth: the deeper the rooting system, the greater the capacity of the soil to store water for plants, which means a greater proportion of precipitation has the potential to become transpiration and a smaller proportion becomes runoff. Vegetation also affects the energy balance by changing surface albedo (that is, the reflectivity of the land surface). Albedo alters the amount of sunlight absorbed at the land surface, which can change ET rates.

In regions prone to soil water deficits, remotely sensed information may be used to assess the magnitude of the impact of such deficits on vegetation health and be interpreted in terms of ecosystem health, range productivity, and crop production, for example. This explains the direct use of vegetation EO data in some drought monitoring systems.

Vegetation can also affect pollutant mobilization and hence water quality, particularly in relation to nutrients and sediment loads. In general, for a given intensity of precipitation event, the higher the amount of bare soil, the greater the rate of soil erosion will be. So the larger the total cover—including both foliage and litter cover—the better water quality tends to be.

Since vegetation does not directly determine water supply or demand (as do precipitation, radiation, and others), but instead modifies these things, information on vegetation is typically used as one of numerous inputs into water balance models to represent the indirect effect of vegetation on the water cycle.

Some of these key vegetation attributes cannot be observed directly with remote sensors. Instead, it is common to use structural attributes of vegetation, aggregated into vegetation cover types, as surrogates. So, for example, tall vegetation with high foliage cover is typically associated with forests. Forests usually have high leaf area and deep roots and so have relatively high transpiration rates. Conversely, grasslands and pastures have low vegetation, with more variable leaf area, shallower roots, and relatively low transpiration rates. Assigning general attributes to broad types of vegetation is the basis for using data on vegetation cover class in most water cycle analyses.

Remote Sensing of Vegetation

The most important and widely used satellite-derived, vegetation-related variables are albedo, LAI, and fPAR (the fraction of sunlight absorbed by foliage). Of these, only albedo is more or less directly observed by the satellite. The remaining attributes can only be inferred using related metrics or EO-driven modeling. Generally speaking, any sensor that measures at least infrared and NIR reflectance can be used to produce these products. Leaf area is almost universally represented by the LAI (the area of leaves per unit of ground area). It is also nearly linearly related to fPAR and fractional foliage cover (the fraction of ground covered by green foliage), when leaf areas are low (that is, LAI less than 6).

LAI and fPAR are typically derived from NDVI, which is calculated from infrared and NIR reflectance values. Methods have been developed to use NDVI to produce approximate estimates of albedo, fractional foliage cover, fPAR, and LAI, if total leaf area is reasonably low. The enhanced vegetation index, which is a MODIS-derived product (Huete et al. 2002), is increasingly used. It is also highly correlated with LAI but is less sensitive to saturation (that is, the diminished ability to estimate LAI accurately in high leaf areas).

Table 6.7 outlines the most prominent sources of these core vegetation-related variables. Current sources are listed, as are expected future sources. Historical sources are also shown, as these are important for looking at the long-term dynamics in vegetation (for drought monitoring, for example). The information in table 6.7 was obtained from the Committee on Earth Observation Satellites's Earth Observation Handbook and the World Meteorological Organization's Observing Systems Capability Analysis and Review Tool, both of which are excellent resources.[8]

Numerous studies evaluate and compare some of these products within and across different satellite sensors, globally and regionally (Beck et al. 2011; Hill et al. 2006; Morisette et al. 2006; Tucker et al. 2005). Often, a product developed regionally will outperform, for that region, a product derived globally. For this reason, caution is sometimes warranted when using globally derived products in regional applications.

Other vegetation characteristics can also be of use to WRM applications. Leaf photosynthetic capacity is an important predictor of crop growth. It is not generally, and certainly not routinely, estimated using Earth observation, as it requires hyperspectral sensors. It is, however, an emerging EO product (Houborg et al. 2013; Wu et al. 2009).

Rooting depth cannot be observed with remote sensing. Yet there are methods for estimating rooting depth indirectly from water balance models (Ichii et al. 2006), which can be driven by Earth observation, often via remotely sensed evapotranspiration. These methods typically use rooting depth as a tuning parameter in either water balance or gross primary

Table 6.7 Overview of Sensors Most Suitable for Estimating Vegetation and Land Cover

DATA CURRENCY AND FUNCTIONAL TYPE OF SENSOR	MISSION INSTRUMENTS	MISSION NAME (SHORT)	SPATIAL RESOLUTION (METERS)	REVISIT PERIOD (DAYS)	ACCESSIBILITY	LAUNCH DATE	END DATE	NDVI	ALBEDO	fPAR	LAI
Archival											
Optical	TM	Landsat 5	30	16	Open	July 1982	June 2013	1	1	1	1
	MSS	Landsat 1-3	80	18	Open	July 1972	September 1983	2	2	2	2
	AVHRR/2	NOAA 7-14	1,100	1	Open	June 1981		1	2	1	4
Current											
Active microwave	X-band SAR	TanDEM-X	16	11	Open	June 2010		2	4	2	4
	X-band SAR	TerraSAR-X	16	11	Open	June 2007		2	4	2	4
	S-band SAR	HJ-1C	20	31	Open	November 2012		2	4	2	4
	SAR (RADARSAT-2)	RADARSAT-2	25	24	Constrained	December 2007		2	4	2	4
Optical	MSI	RapidEye	6.5	1	Open	August 2008		2	2	2	2
	ASTER	Terra	15	16	Open	December 1999		1	1	1	1
	OLI	Landsat-8	30	16	Open	February 2013		1	1	1	2
	ETM+	Landsat 7	30	16	Open	April 1999		1	1	2	2
	Hyperion	NMP EO-1	30	16	Open	November 2000	October 2014	1	1	1	1
	AWiFS	RESOURCESAT-2	55	26	Open	April 2011		1	1	1	1
	LISS-III (Resourcesat)	RESOURCESAT-2	55	26	Open	April 2011		1	1	2	2
	MISR	Terra	250	16	Open	December 1999		2	2	2	2
	MODIS	Aqua	250	16	Open	May 2002		1	1	1	1
	MODIS	Terra	250	16	Open	December 1999		1	1	1	1
	AVHRR/3	NOAA-18	1,100	1	Open	May 2005		1	2	1	4
	AVHRR/3	NOAA-19	1,100	1	Open	February 2009		1	2	1	4
	VEGETATION	SPOT-5	1,150	26	Unknown	May 2002	December 2014	1	2	1	2
	VIIRS	Suomi NPP	1,600	16	Open	October 2011		1	1	1	1

(Continued)

Table 6.7 (Continued)

DATA CURRENCY AND FUNCTIONAL TYPE OF SENSOR	MISSION INSTRUMENTS	MISSION NAME (SHORT)	SPATIAL RESOLUTION (METERS)	REVIST PERIOD (DAYS)	ACCESSIBILITY	LAUNCH DATE	END DATE	NDVI	ALBEDO	fPAR	LAI
Future											
Active microwave	SAR (RCM)	RADARSAT C-1	50	12	Constrained	2018		2	4	2	4
	SAR (RCM)	RADARSAT C-2	50	12	Constrained	2018		2	4	2	4
	SAR (RCM)	RADARSAT C-3	50	12	Constrained	2018		2	4	2	4
Optical	LISS-III (Resourcesat)	RESOURCESAT-2A	5.8	26	Open	2015		1	1	2	2
	MSI (Sentinel-2)	Sentinel-2 A	10	10	Open	2015		1	2	1	2
	MSI (Sentinel-2)	Sentinel-2 B	10	10	Open	2016		1	2	1	2
	MSI (Sentinel-2)	Sentinel-2 C	10	10	Open	2020		1	2	1	2
	LISS-IV	RESOURCESAT-2A	23.5	26	Open	2015		1	1	2	2
	HISUI	ALOS-3	30	60	Unknown	2016		1	1	1	1
	AWiFS	RESOURCESAT-2A	55	26	Open	2015		1	1	1	1
	OLCI	Sentinel-3 A	300	27	Open	2015/16		1	2	2	2
	OLCI	Sentinel-3 B	300	27	Open	2017		1	2	2	2
	OLCI	Sentinel-3 C	300	27	Open	2020		1	2	2	2
	VIIRS	JPSS-1	1,600	16	Open	2017		1	1	1	1

Sources: Committee on Earth Observation Satellites (CEOS) Earth Observation Handbook (http://www.eohandbook.com/) and the WMO Observing Systems Capability Analysis and Review Tool (http://www.wmo-sat.info/oscar/).

Note: NDVI = normalized difference vegetation index; fPAR = fraction of absorbed photosynthetically active radiation; LAI = leaf area index. The suitability of each sensor to provide useful data is shown with numbers and colors, as follows: 1 highly suitable, 2 suitable, 4 not suitable.

productivity models, when all other parameters are known with reasonable certainty.

Vegetation litter (that is, dead vegetation) cover can now be detected fairly routinely from most of the main land-observing satellite platforms that have at least some SWIR capacity. It is, however, best detected from hyperspectral sensors (Guerschman et al. 2009a). Observations of litter cover also enable estimates to be made of the fraction of bare soil (that is, the ground area not covered in vegetable matter).

Vegetation Cover Classes

Vegetation cover classes are identified using combinations of remotely sensed variables, often in conjunction with ancillary data such as climate and land use maps and field observations. Remotely sensed estimates of vegetation height from radar or Laser Imaging, Detection, and Ranging (LiDAR) and biomass, likewise from radar or LiDAR, are useful for distinguishing between structurally distinct types of vegetation.

The main EO method for deriving classes of vegetation cover, however, is by classifying the temporal (seasonal) dynamics in leaf area. For example, when LAI has high seasonal variability, it is reasonable to assume that this is caused by short-lived vegetation that dies back (including crops) or by deciduous woody vegetation. Many of the main satellite programs used for vegetation sensing provide these vegetation or land cover maps as precalculated information products available for off-the-shelf use (table 6.8). Among these, only the MODIS Land Cover Type product provides dynamic annual mapping.

Vegetation height can be estimated using either optical photogrammetry, satellite-borne LiDAR (Simard et al. 2011), or synthetic aperture radar (SAR; Kellndorfer et al. 2004; Wegmuller and Werner 1997).

Vegetation biomass is the mass of live plant tissue. Aboveground biomass is usually estimated from optical Earth observation, radar, LiDAR, or a combination of these, using empirical conversion functions (Goetz et al. 2009; Lucas et al. 2010). More recently, aboveground biomass has also been estimated using the vegetation optical depth index, which is a relative measure of aboveground vegetation water content derived from passive microwave remote sensing (Andela et al. 2013).

Example Applications

Earth observation of vegetation has an important role to play in providing information for meteorological and agricultural drought monitoring systems, by focusing directly on the impact of drought on vegetation using

Table 6.8 Examples of Global Vegetation Cover Maps

NAME	SENSOR	AGENCY	COVER CLASSES	SPATIAL RESOLUTION	CURRENCY	SOURCE
UMD Land Cover Classification	AVHRR	University of Maryland	14	1°, 8 kilometers, 1 kilometer	1998	Hansen et al. 2000
MODIS Land Cover Type (MCD12Q1)	MODIS Terra and Aqua	U.S. Geological Survey	17	500 meters	Yearly, 2001–12	Friedl et al. 2010
ESA-GlobCover	MERIS	European Space Agency and Catholic University of Louvain	22	300 meters	2009	
FROM-GLC	Landsat TM and ETM	Tsinghua University	11	30 meters		Gong et al. 2012

Source: CEOS 2015, OSCAR database.

Note: AVHRR = Advanced Very High Resolution Radiometer; ESA = European Space Agency; ETM = Enhanced Thematic Mapper; FROM-GLC = Finer Resolution Observation and Monitoring of Global Land Cover; MERIS = Medium Resolution Imaging Spectrometer; MODIS = Moderate Resolution Imaging Spectrometer; TM = Thematic Mapper; UMD = University of Maryland.

time-series analysis of information on vegetation "greenness," where the current anomaly in greenness is compared with the long-term mean value (or an alternative reference value, such as the same time last year). Typically, vegetation drought monitoring approaches are combined with other approaches (for an example, see Mu et al. 2012). Such analyses are useful for monitoring and predicting food shortages and for targeting investments in agricultural infrastructure. The following are some examples of current drought monitoring systems that include vegetation Earth observation:

- The U.S. government's *Global Drought Information System*, which uses AVHRR NDVI, among several other satellite-derived vegetation indexes[9]

- The European Commission's *European Drought Observatory*, which uses fPAR, derived from MERIS (Medium Resolution Imaging Spectrometer), and the

normalized difference water index, derived from MODIS (figure 6.10)[10]

- The Australian Bureau of Meteorology's *Climate Maps*, which provide AVHRR NDVI maps[11]

- Princeton University's *African Drought Monitor*, which uses MODIS NDVI[12]

- The University of Montana's *global terrestrial drought severity index*, which uses the MODIS evapotranspiration and NDVI products.[13]

Actual evaporation rates can be estimated using the Penman-Monteith model (Monteith 1981). As discussed in the section on evapotranspiration, this requires estimating a "surface conductance" parameter, which is related primarily to vegetation characteristics. Spatially explicit, temporally varying estimates of evapotranspiration can be made across large areas when the surface conductance parameter is driven by using RS information to assign "typical" values to land cover classes or by using LAI or NDVI directly (Leuning et al. 2008; Zhang et al. 2010). Yebra et al. (2013) review the suitability of alternative MODIS vegetation EO data for estimating evapotranspiration and find that NDVI and EVI produce the best predictions of canopy conductance.

The majority of spatially explicit hydrologic models need to incorporate the role of vegetation in the water cycle and do so by including some vegetation-specific parameters. As with the estimation of evapotranspiration, the information used may be fully dynamic and quantitative (continuously varying fields of LAI, rooting depths, and so forth). More typically, though, vegetation is described as types of vegetation cover (with static boundaries), assigning vegetation-specific characteristics to each type of cover. This does not require satellite observations for the period of analysis, which has obvious advantages for predicting presatellite or future conditions. These characteristics can be scalars (that is, static) or variables (that

Figure 6.10 Combined Drought Indicator for Europe, Mid-March 2014

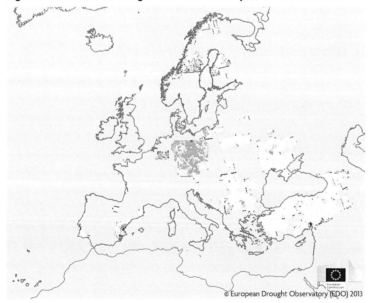

Source: © European Drought Observatory. Used with permission. Further permission required for reuse.

Note: The combined drought indicator is based on anomalies in the standard precipitation index, modeled soil moisture, and remotely sensed fPAR. Yellow is "watch," where the index is anomalously low; orange is "warning," where low rainfall translates into a soil moisture anomaly; red is "alert," when these two conditions are accompanied by an fPAR anomaly. fPAR = fraction of absorbed photosynthetically active radiation.

is, dynamic, for example, a prescribed seasonal pattern), with remotely sensed data being a prime source of information for the latter.

The AWRA system (van Dijk 2010; van Dijk and Renzullo 2011) is used by the Australian Bureau of Meteorology for water resources assessment and accounting and is one example of a spatial water balance estimation model that uses remotely sensed vegetation information. The landscape is divided into "tree" and "herbaceous" cover types (derived from AVHRR imagery), and each is assigned a fixed rooting depth but spatially and seasonally varying LAI (derived from MODIS imagery). Figure 6.11 shows an example AWRA output.

Techniques exist to use remotely sensed vegetation information for assessing the area of irrigated agriculture. Such mapping is important, as there can be a significant difference between the "irrigable area" (that is, the area that is equipped with infrastructure for irrigation) and the area actually irrigated at any given time. Techniques are based on the concept that, in semiarid and arid environments at least, regional time-series analysis of greenness (LAI, fPAR, or NDVI) can identify areas that are unusually green and contrast with the surrounding landscape. This information may be combined with crop phenological signatures (that is, timing and rates of green-up and senescence) within the greenness signal to identify the area of land that has been irrigated within a given region (Conrad et al. 2011; Ozdogan et al. 2010; Pervez and Brown 2010 for examples and more information). Figure 6.12 shows a map of an irrigated area in the Indian Krishna basin, derived from MODIS imagery.

Groundwater
Definition
Groundwater is the water contained in the saturated zone—the subsurface volume below the water table—where water fills the cracks and pores of rock, sediment, and soil. Groundwater can be recharged by rainfall, snowmelt, irrigation, and rivers. It discharges when water resurfaces through springs and wells, flows into lakes, streams, and the ocean, or is extracted by vegetation. Groundwater moves at varying speeds, depending on the storage pressure and the porosity of the storage medium, among other things. Aquifers are subsurface layers where

Figure 6.11 Map of AWRA-Derived Total Annual Landscape Water Yields in 2011–12 for Tasmania, Australia

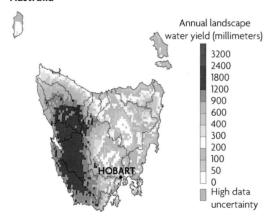

Source: Bureau of Meterology (BoM) 2012. © BoM. Used with permission. Further permission required for reuse.

Note: AWRA = Australian Water Resources Assessment.

Figure 6.12 Map of Irrigated Land Cover Types in the Krishna Basin, India

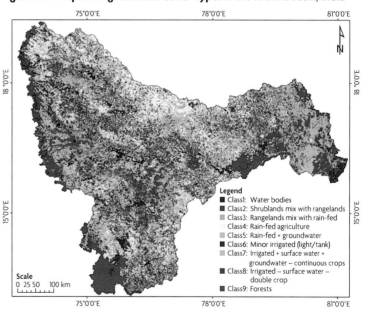

Source: Gumma, Thenkabail, and Nelson 2011.

Note: Irrigated land cover types are shown in green and red. This map is derived from Moderate Resolution Imaging Spectrometer (MODIS) imagery 2000–01.

groundwater is confined, sometimes under pressure, by adjacent rock and clay layers of low permeability.

Relevance

Groundwater is a critical source of water for human consumption and agriculture, especially where surface water is scarce or polluted. It also moderates streamflow, producing the longer-term baseflow component of total flows, which decouples flows somewhat from the variability inherent in the climatic drivers of streamflow. The two greatest risks to groundwater supplies are overextraction and pollution.

Approximately 43 percent of all irrigated agriculture depends on groundwater (Siebert et al. 2010), and this proportion is rising rapidly—often resulting in unsustainable extraction rates (Gleeson et al. 2012; Wada et al. 2010; Wada, van Beek, and Bierkens 2012). Groundwater is also a major source of drinking water, with, for example, 51 percent of the U.S. population relying on groundwater.[14] Groundwater is the primary source of water in the Middle East and Northern Africa (where fossil groundwater reserves are used) and in countries such as Denmark, Jamaica, Portugal, and Slovakia with high-yielding sources, often in limestone or "karst" aquifers (FAO 2013).

Remote Sensing of Groundwater

As groundwater lies below the land surface, there are currently no EO techniques for direct observation of groundwater level. The main indirect techniques are through satellite gravity field mapping (gravimetry) and radar interferometry (table 6.9). The former measures changes in the regional gravity field, while the latter measures changes in land surface elevation. Both techniques assume that there is a relationship between changes in gravity fields or surface elevations, respectively, and changes in groundwater storage.

In water-limited landscapes, changes in shallow groundwater may also be inferred by examining the effects on other surface processes.

When groundwater reaches the surface in an otherwise dry landscape, the additional water supply can be detected through its enhancement of surface evaporation rates and vegetation productivity. Groundwater-dependent ecosystems are tied to this process. Areas where evaporation or vegetation productivity or cover are higher than what would be expected for the given precipitation can be detected using remotely sensed evaporation or vegetation cover. Details on how these two attributes can be remotely sensed may be found in the section on evapotranspiration and ground cover, and an example of such an analysis is provided in chapter 7. An excellent resource on the use of Earth observation in groundwater applications is Meijerink et al. (2007).

Satellite gravimetry—satellites that measure gravity fields—is able to detect changes in these fields between subsequent overpasses. With suitable postprocessing to remove the effects of phenomena such as tides and tectonic movements, postglacial rebound, atmospheric composition, and changes in the mass or other features of surface water, gravimetric observations can provide information on changes in subsurface water mass. Currently there is one set of gravity measurement satellites—the GRACE mission by NASA and the German Aerospace Centre, which was launched in 2002 (Tapley et al. 2004). This satellite mission is currently operating seven years beyond its intended five-year lifetime, and the quality of its observations is slowly degrading. A follow-on GRACE mission is planned for 2017.

GRACE's coarse spatial resolution (about 400 kilometers) means that it can be used only for large, basin-scale applications. Nonetheless, its unique ability to monitor integrated changes in water storage everywhere makes it a valuable sensor. Several reviews have been conducted of the application of GRACE to assess water storage (Güntner 2008; Ramillien, Famiglietti, and Wahr 2008; Syed et al. 2008) and groundwater depletion (Leblanc et al. 2009; Rodell, Velicogna, and Famiglietti 2009).

Table 6.9 Overview of Sensors Most Suitable for Estimating Groundwater

DATA CURRENCY AND FUNCTIONAL TYPE OF SENSOR	SENSOR	PLATFORM	SPATIAL RESOLUTION (METERS)	REVISIT PERIOD (DAYS)	ACCESSIBILITY	LAUNCH DATE	GRAVITY FIELD	SURFACE HEIGHT
Current								
Active microwave	X-band SAR	TanDEM-X	1–16	11	Open	June 2010	4	2
	X-band SAR	TerraSAR-X	1–16	11	Open	June 2007	4	2
	SAR 2000	COSMO-SkyMed 1	1–100	16	Constrained	June 2007	4	2
	SAR 2000	COSMO-SkyMed 2	1–100	16	Constrained	December 2007	4	2
	SAR 2000	COSMO-SkyMed 3	1–100	16	Constrained	October 2008	4	2
	SAR 2000	COSMO-SkyMed 4	1–100	16	Constrained	November 2010	4	2
	SAR (RADARSAT-2)	RADARSAT-2	8–172	24	Constrained	December 2007	4	2
	PALSAR-2 (ALOS-2)	ALOS-2	10	14	Constrained	March 2014	4	2
Gravimetric	GRACE	GRACE	400,000	1	Open	March 2002	1	4
Future								
Active microwave	C-band SAR	Sentinel-1 B	10–50	12	Open	2015	4	2
	C-band SAR	Sentinel-1 C	11–50	12	Open	2019	4	2
	SAR (RCM)	RADARSAT C-1	8–100		Constrained	2018	4	2
	SAR (RCM)	RADARSAT C-2	8–100	24	Constrained	2018	4	2
	SAR (RCM)	RADARSAT C-3	8–100		Constrained	2018	4	2
Gravimetric	GRACE II	GRACE FO	400,000	1	Open	2017	1	4

Note: The suitability of each sensor to provide useful data is shown with numbers and colors, as follows: ① highly suitable, ② suitable, ④ not suitable.

Recently, GRACE observations were used along with ocean, lake, and river water level altimetry to constrain fully spatial estimates of the water balance for the globe at 100-kilometer resolution (van Dijk et al. 2013).

Satellite radar interferometry allows measurements of very small changes in soil surface elevation that can help to detect changes in groundwater storage. The technique relies on the change in the distance between the satellite and a given location on the Earth's surface between successive satellite overpasses. These changes can be measured very accurately (to less than 1 centimeter) using SAR instruments.

Becker (2006) and Galloway and Hoffmann (2007) provide reviews of different applications of interferometry to groundwater characterization and monitoring and demonstrate interferometry's utility for supporting groundwater management directly or by improving the ability to model groundwater. SAR can be used to monitor seasonal and long-term changes in groundwater storage, provided the relationship between vertical surface movement and groundwater storage, known as Terzhagi's Principle, can be quantified. Changes in vertical surface movement must be interpreted carefully and regionally, as there may be many context-specific considerations—such as whether the local geological materials deform at all in response to changes in groundwater mass and whether there is much interference from local vegetation.

Limitations

By its nature, groundwater cannot be observed directly using Earth observation, so the use of remote sensing here is inferential and has limitations. First, RS observations can provide information on groundwater levels or recharge and discharge rates only when combined with other sources of observations—both RS and field data. This entails the use of models, where the actual data product (levels or recharge and discharge rates) is a modeled variable derived from an array of inputs.

Second, the use of RS observations to provide management-relevant groundwater information is still in the development stage—it has not yet reached a stage of maturity, where the data products are generated routinely or operationally or where the product has been widely tested and accepted by the scientific and practitioner communities.

Lastly, while the GRACE-derived gravimetric data provide new and potentially valuable insights into groundwater-related processes, the data are of exceptionally coarse resolution and generally restricted to large, basin-scale applications of no finer than 300-kilometer resolution.

Surface Water

Definition

Because of its particular relevance for water assessment and water cycle studies, surface water is treated separately from other types of land cover. Water bodies can vary greatly in size and duration. This section focuses on the following:

- Natural or man-made reservoirs, which can range from water bodies such as small ponds of a few square meters to large lakes of several thousands of square kilometers. Generally, these water bodies change in area and volume relatively slowly in time (that is, in a matter of weeks to months).

- Surface water due to flooding, which can range from small overbank floods near water streams to very large floods covering hundreds of square kilometers. In general terms, floods are more dynamic in time than reservoirs and can change in area and volume in a matter of hours or days.

Relevance

Monitoring surface water areas is relevant to applications linked to agriculture, urban water use, and flood mitigation. Surface water may be used for irrigation as well as for human or animal consumption in both rural and urban areas. Many ecosystems, such as wetlands, depend on regular flooding, and their health can be compromised if too much surface water is diverted to other uses.

Earth observation can be used for estimating the area of such reservoirs and floods. The reservoir size that satellite sensors can measure depends on the spatial resolution and the area-to-perimeter ratio of the reservoir. Estimating the total volume of water available in reservoirs requires making assumptions about the depth of such areas, based on local bathymetry measurements, although in some cases radar or LiDAR altimetry can also be used to track water levels.

Monitoring flooding events with remote sensing involves the same physical principles as monitoring water in reservoirs. However, the main difference is that, generally, flood events are more dynamic in time and therefore require the use of imagery acquired with high temporal repetition and, even more critical, not prone to cloud obscuring.

Measuring surface water elevation can provide estimates of changes in the total volume of water in reservoirs and wetlands and river discharge, although this is currently only possible in wide rivers (that is, several hundreds of meters).

Theoretical Basis for Remote Sensing of Surface Water: Estimating Area and Water Level

There are two principal ways to estimate area: optical imaging and radar and passive microwave imaging.

The main optical characteristic of water is that it absorbs most of the incoming solar radiation in the visible and infrared regions and therefore reflects less radiation than other landscapes. This characteristic has been exploited since the mid-1970s (Rango and Anderson 1974; Rango and Salomonson 1974). In the VIS-NIR wavelengths (about 400–900 nanometers), sediments, chlorophyll, and other elements affecting water quality can modify the spectral signal and, in some cases, make the discrimination of water from soil and vegetation more problematic (although these same properties can be exploited for deriving water quality parameters, as discussed in the section on optical water quality). In the SWIR region (about 900–2,500 nanometers), water quality does not interfere, and any water body will reflect very low amounts of radiation.

One major disadvantage of using optical imagery is that the images are subject to cloud contamination. This is particularly problematic in tropical regions during the monsoon season, when cloud-free imagery may be rare. In addition, optical sensors are poorly suited to detecting water under dense canopies, such as in the Amazon or Congo basins, where much of the floodplains may be located in inundated forests (Mayaux et al. 2002; Mertes et al. 1995).

Many algorithms exist for mapping surface water areas. These include the use of simple threshold values in a spectral band (Overton 2005; Powell, Letcher, and Croke 2008), combinations of two bands such as the normalized difference water or vegetation indexes (Brakenridge and Anderson 2006; Sakamoto et al. 2007), and, in some cases, ancillary variables to improve the detection of water in the presence of topographic shading effects (Guerschman et al. 2011; Ordoyne and Friedl 2008).

Radar and passive microwave imagery are (by very good approximation) not affected by clouds or water vapor and therefore can provide useful information on surface water under clouds. In addition, radar is better suited than optical sensors for detecting water under dense canopies (Rosenqvist et al. 2002).

The backscatter coefficient[15] of smooth open water bodies is low, which allows discrimination of water from land using radar. However, SAR is susceptible to wind-induced waves, which increase scattering back to the sensor, creating difficulties for detecting surface water (Smith and Alsdorf 1998). Complications also arise when there is vegetation above the water surface. This dramatically increases backscatter and can create uncertainties in automated mapping. Interferometric coherence from multitemporal observations is another alternative to delineate surface water accurately, for example, from the ERS-1, ERS-2 tandem mission.

Water bodies have significantly lower brightness temperatures than their surroundings, and the emissivity polarization difference is generally large, which makes it feasible to detect water bodies with microwave measurements (De Jeu 2003). Possibly the greatest disadvantage of passive microwave sensors is their coarse resolution, which has hampered their adoption for environmental monitoring. Single "pixel" calibration against field discharge measurements has been used for monitoring discharge during (relatively large) flood events, however.

Several types of active sensors, including laser, profiling radar, interferometric SAR, and swath radar, are able to characterize water levels. Laser systems emit a pulse of light (normally VIS or NIR) and measure the time that the echo takes to return to the sensor. Radar altimeters work on a similar principle. Interferometric SAR uses multiple images to estimate changes in elevation (and in terrain). These techniques have been used to measure ocean levels since the early 1990s. Over land, the accuracy of the level measurements depends on the size of the water bodies being measured; over rivers, surfaces are about 10 centimeters at best and more typically about 50 centimeters. With increased averaging over large lakes (more than 100 square kilometers), accuracy improves to 3–4 centimeters (Alsdorf, Rodríguez, and Lettenmaier 2007). This makes satellite altimetry suitable for monitoring large water bodies, particularly in remote areas where field-based gauging is not available.

Sensors for Surface Water Remote Sensing

Table 6.10 provides a list of existing and planned sensors that can produce data for estimating the area and height of surface water. The classification of the suitability of each sensor for mapping water area and water height in reservoirs and floods is somewhat subjective and driven by a series of constraints. For example, for measuring water in reservoirs, spatial resolution is usually the most important factor, so high- or very high-resolution sensors—either optical or radar—are more suitable than medium-resolution sensors. As mentioned, optical sensors are subject to clouds, but current high-resolution radar needs to be tasked. For water in floods (generally larger in area than reservoirs and more rapidly changing over time), timely acquisition is more valuable, so medium-spatial-resolution optical and radar sensors may be considered more suitable.

Most optical sensors can be used to map surface water. Sensors that include bands in the SWIR are the best suited to the task, as water bodies unambiguously absorb most of the radiation on those wavelengths. Examples of such sensors include MODIS, Landsat, and VIIRS. Optical sensors with bands only in the VIS-NIR can also be used to map surface water, although they are less suitable for differentiating water from other types of land cover such as wet or dry soil, particularly when the water contains many suspended sediments or chlorophyll. Examples of such sensors include AVHRR, QuickBird, and IKONOS.

All of these sensors generally have a trade-off between spatial and temporal resolution. Landsat and MODIS, for example, have a similar spectral ability to identify surface water, but while Landsat is able to do so at high spatial resolution (30-meter pixels), MODIS does so at medium resolution (250- or 500-meter pixels, depending on the bands used; see figure 6.13). At the same time, MODIS can capture about two images of the same area per day (depending on the latitude) from the Terra and Aqua satellites, whereas Landsat revisits each site every 16 days. These differences need to be considered when assessing the ability of each sensor to monitor surface water area.

The spatial resolution and cloud-penetrating ability of radar makes it particularly useful for mapping the extent of surface water during flood events. However, such acquisitions need to be tasked, making

Table 6.10 Overview of Sensors Most Suitable for Mapping Surface Water Extent and Height

DATA CURRENCY AND FUNCTIONAL TYPE OF SENSOR	MISSION INSTRUMENTS	MISSION NAME (SHORT)	SPATIAL RESOLUTION (METERS)	REVISIT PERIOD (DAYS)	ACCESSIBILITY	LAUNCH DATE	END DATE	SURFACE WATER IN RESERVOIRS	SURFACE WATER IN FLOODS	WATER LEVEL
Archival										
Optical	TM	Landsat 5	30	16	Open	July 1982	June 2013	1	2	4
	MSS	Landsat 1–3	80	18	Open	July 1972	September 1983	2	2	4
	AVHRR/2	NOAA 7–14	1,100	1	Open	June 1981		3	3	4
Active microwave	SAR (RADARSAT-1)	RADARSAT-1	25	24	Constrained	November 1995	March 2013	2	2	4
	PALSAR	ALOS	7–44	14	Constrained	January 2006	September 2012	1	2	4
	ASAR (stripmap)	Envisat	30		Constrained	March 2002	April 2012	1	2	4
	ASAR (wide swath)	Envisat	150		Open	March 2002	April 2012	2	1	4
	AMI-SAR	ERS-1	30	35	Constrained	July 1991	March 2000	1	2	4
	AMI-SAR	ERS-2	30	35	Constrained	April 1995	July 2011	1	2	4
Radar altimetry	NRA	TOPEX/Poseidon		10	Open	January 1992	January 2005	4	4	1
	GFO-RA	GFO		17	Open	February 1998	October 2008	4	4	1
	Poseidon-2	JASON-1		10	Open	December 2001	July 2013	4	4	1
Current										
Optical	OSA	IKONOS	3.3		Constrained	September 1999		2	3	4
	GIS	GeoEye	1.6		Constrained	September 2008		2	3	4
	MSI	RapidEye	6.5	1	Open	August 2008		2	3	4
	ASTER	Terra	15	16	Open	December 1999		1	2	4
	OLI	Landsat-8	30	16	Open	February 2013		1	2	4
	ETM+	Landsat 7	30	16	Open	April 1999		1	2	4
	MODIS	Aqua	250	16	Open	May 2002		2	1	4
	MODIS	Terra	250	16	Open	December 1999		2	1	4

(Continued)

Table 6.10 (Continued)

DATA CURRENCY AND FUNCTIONAL TYPE OF SENSOR	MISSION INSTRUMENTS	MISSION NAME (SHORT)	SPATIAL RESOLUTION (METERS)	REVISIT PERIOD (DAYS)	ACCESSIBILITY	LAUNCH DATE	END DATE	SURFACE WATER IN RESERVOIRS	SURFACE WATER IN FLOODS	WATER LEVEL
Optical, cont.	AVHRR/3	NOAA-18	1,100	1	Open	May 2005		3	2	4
	AVHRR/3	NOAA-19	1,100	1	Open	February 2009		3	2	4
	VEGETATION	SPOT-5	1,150	26	Unknown	May 2002		1	2	4
	VIIRS	Suomi NPP	1,600	16	Open	October 2011		2	2	4
Active microwave	SAR (RADARSAT-2)	RADARSAT-2	25	24	Constrained	December 2007		1	2	
	PALSAR-2 (stripmap)	ALOS-2	10	14	Constrained	June 2014		1	2	4
	PALSAR-2 (ScanSAR)	ALOS-2	100	14	Open	June 2014		2	2	4
	C-SAR (stripmap)	Sentinel-1A	4x5		Constrained	April 2014		1	2	4
	C-SAR (IW)	Sentinel-1A	5x20		Constrained	April 2014		1	1	4
Radar altimetry	Poseidon-3	JASON-2			Open	June 2008		4	4	1
Future										
Optical	MSI (Sentinel-2)	Sentinel-2 A	10	10	Open	2015		1	2	4
	MSI (Sentinel-2)	Sentinel-2 B	10	10	Open	2016		1	2	4
	MSI (Sentinel-2)	Sentinel-2 C	10	10	Open	2020		1	2	4
Radar altimetry	KaRIN	SWOT			Open	2020		4	4	1
	Poseidon-3B	JASON-3			Open	2015		4	4	1

Note: The ability of each sensor to detect surface water in reservoirs or floods and water height is shown with colors and numbers as (1) highly suitable, (2) suitable, (3) potentially suitable, and (4) not suitable. The revisit cycle and pixel size indicate the size of the water bodies potentially detectable and the temporal repetition.

Figure 6.13 Example of Satellite Imagery Captured during Flood Event in Northern New South Wales, Australia

a. Landsat imagery   b. MODIS imagery

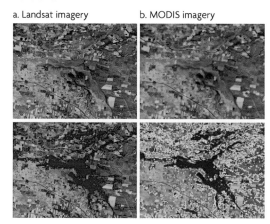

Source: Adapted from Guerschman et al. 2011; WIRADA 2012. © CSIRO. Used with permission. Further permission required for reuse. © WIRADA. Used with permission. Further permission required for reuse.

Note: On the left, Landsat imagery and, on the right, Moderate Resolution Imaging Spectrometer (MODIS) imagery. Top-row figures show the surface reflectance in false color; bottom-row figures show an object-oriented classification of surface water in red (bottom left) and the open water likelihood index as an estimate of the fraction of the pixel covered with water (bottom right).

existing radar sensors impractical for routine global monitoring at high resolution (less than 100 meters). So far, the highest resolution available for radar in routine mode for part of the globe is about 1 kilometer (ASAR global monitoring [GM]). The C-band Synthetic Aperture Radar (C-SAR) instrument on board the Recently launched Sentinel-1 mission is intended to improve that to global coverage at 5-by-20-meter resolution in the ScanSAR-Interferometric wide-swath mode.

Lake and reservoir altimetry is normally obtained using the radar altimetry instruments on the Jason (1 and 2), TOPEX (Ocean Topography Experiment)/Poseidon, and ERS-2 satellites. The Ice, Clouds, and Elevation Satellite (ICESat) provided useful LiDAR measurements with accuracies of 3 centimeters over footprints of 70 meters, but an instrument failed after launch, and the satellite is inactive. An ICESat-2 is planned for launch in 2016. A general disadvantage of altimetry is that it does not provide full coverage but instead measures along the orbit track, which means that the height of surface water level can only be measured when and where it is sufficiently covered by the tracks.

A most promising future development is the Surface Water and Ocean Topography Mission, which is scheduled for launch in 2020. It will include a radar altimeter, an interferometer (Ka-Band Radar Interferometer [KaRIN]), and a microwave radiometer (Rodríguez and Estéban-Fernández 2010).

Applications

This section highlights some notable examples of research applications. Hess (2003) uses Japanese Earth Resources Satellite 1 SAR data to map inundation in the Amazon basin during the high- and low-water seasons at 100-meter resolution. Papa et al. (2010) combine passive (SSM/I) and active (ERS) microwave with optical (AVHRR) imagery to describe the global patterns of surface water extent from 1993 to 2004. Papa et al. (2010) develop a technique to combine these disparate data sources, which overlap only partially in time, to intercalibrate the surface water estimates. They report a slight decrease in the global inundated area for the period analyzed, mainly in the tropics.

In an example application, CSIRO combined Landsat- and MODIS-based mapping with flow measurements to produce the Murray-Darling basin floodplain inundation model (Overton et al. 2011). This model provides a regional-scale model of the spatial extent of floodplain inundation under ecologically significant flood return periods. The model was developed using the flow scenarios modeled under the Murray-Darling Basin Sustainable Yields Project (see appendix B), allowing mapping under different climate and development scenarios.

Several data services provide flooding or lake and reservoir levels in near real time, including the following:

- The Dartmouth Flood Observatory[16]

- The Near-Real-Time Global MODIS Flood Mapping [17]

- Crop Explorer[18]

- LEGOS HydroWeb[19]

- The European Space Agency's River & Lake.[20]

Some of these examples are discussed further in appendix B.

Snow

Definition

Snow cover exists where the accumulation of snow is sufficient for the land surface to have a reasonably continuous layer of snow. The accumulation and melting of snow cover provide an important supply of freshwater across many mountainous and high-latitude (mainly northern hemisphere) regions. Outside of the areas permanently covered with snow, snow cover provides a supply of water only in the spring and summer. Important attributes of snow cover are its areal extent, thickness, and water content. The electromagnetic and structural properties of snow are of particular importance in this context as their unique characteristics allow for remote sensing of their extent, depth, and mass.

Since the same mass of water can take up different volumes when frozen (depending on its structure as snow or ice), it is useful to describe snow in terms of snow water equivalent—the mass or depth of water obtained when a certain volume of snow is melted. While glaciers and other terrestrial ice bodies provide important sources of freshwater, the remote sensing of ice bodies is not covered in this review. For an excellent overview of the remote sensing of both snow cover and glaciers, see Rees (2006).

Relevance

As snow contains freshwater, meltwater from snow cover provides an important source of water for consumption, irrigation, and power generation in many parts of the globe. As a source of water, it is highly seasonal, so surface impoundments are often constructed to capture and store meltwater across seasons. Snow is also a source of floodwater. Apart from the natural, seasonal cycle of flooding associated with spring snowmelt, snow can also be a source of severe flooding when unusually warm conditions occur prior to or during the normal spring melt. Both the temperature and liquid water content of snow (snow wetness) are good indicators of how close the snowpack is to melting and therefore are important for forecasting floods, along with measures of snow extent and depth or snow water equivalent.

Remote Sensing of Snow

In the visible wavelengths, snow is generally highly reflective (that is, has a high albedo), which makes it relatively easy to detect, as it contrasts with the surrounding landscape. In thermal infrared wavelengths, it also possesses easily recognizable features, often being colder than its surroundings and therefore emitting less radiation in these wavelengths. Snow cover also affects the microwave radiation emitted from the Earth. It alters the attenuation of microwaves, and analysis of the attenuation patterns can reveal important details about the depth, composition (that is, the solid and liquid fractions), and structure of the snow pack. This attenuation can be measured using passive microwave sensors, which detect microwaves emitted from the Earth's surface after passing through the overlying snow pack, or using active microwave sensors (typically SAR), which detect the backscatter of sensor-emitted microwave radiation.

The reliability of remotely sensed, snow-related information decreases as cloud cover, tree or forest cover, and terrain complexity increase. Low sun illumination angles, typical of the higher northern latitudes, reduce the quality of remotely sensed information. Frei et al. (2012) provide a useful overview of remotely sensed snow products. Table 6.11 outlines the most prominent remote sensors relevant to measuring snow (cover) extent, snow moisture, and snow water equivalent. Both current and expected future sources are listed. The

Table 6.11 Overview of Sensors Most Suitable for Mapping Snow Extent, Snow Moisture, and Snow Water Equivalent

DATA CURRENCY AND FUNCTIONAL TYPE OF SENSOR	SENSOR	PLATFORM	SPATIAL RESOLUTION (METERS)	REVISIT PERIOD (DAYS)	ACCESSIBILITY AND COST	LAUNCH DATE	END DATE	SNOW EXTENT	SNOW WATER EQUIVALENT	SNOW MOISTURE
Current										
Active microwave	SAR 2000	COSMO-SkyMed 1	1–100	16	Constrained	June 2007	June 2014	2	1	2
	SAR 2000	COSMO-SkyMed 2	1–100	16	Constrained	December 2007	December 2014	2	1	2
	SAR 2000	COSMO-SkyMed 3	1–100	16	Constrained	October 2008	October 2015	2	1	2
	SAR 2000	COSMO-SkyMed 4	1–100	16	Constrained	November 2010	November 2017	2	1	2
	X-band SAR	TanDEM-X	1–16	11	Open	June 2010	December 2015	1	1	1
	X-band SAR	TerraSAR-X	1–16	11	Open	June 2007	December 2015	1	1	1
	SAR (RADARSAT-2)	RADARSAT-2	8–172	24	Constrained	December 2007	April 2015	2	2	2
Hyperspectral	Hyperion	NMP EO-1	30	16	Open	November 2000	October 2014	1	4	4
Optical	LISS-IV	RESOURCESAT-2	5.8	26	Constrained	April 2011	April 2016	2	4	4
	MSI	RapidEye	6.5	1	Open	August 2008	August 2019	2	4	4
	ASTER	Terra	15	16	Open	December 1999	October 2015	1	4	4
	LISS-III	RESOURCESAT-2	23.5	26	Open	April 2011	April 2016	2	4	4
	LISS-III	RESOURCESAT-2A	23.5	26	Open	October 2015	October 2020	2	4	4
	ALI	NMP EO-1	30	16	Open	November 2000	October 2014	2	4	4
	ETM+	Landsat 7	30	16	Open	April 2099	January 2017	2	4	4
	OLI	Landsat 8	30	16	Open	February 2013	May 2023	2	4	4
	AWiFS	RESOURCESAT-2	55	26	Open	April 2011	April 2016	2	4	4
	AWiFS	RESOURCESAT-2A	55	26	Open	October 2015	October 2020	2	4	4

(Continued)

Table 6.11 (Continued)

DATA CURRENCY AND FUNCTIONAL TYPE OF SENSOR	SENSOR	PLATFORM	SPATIAL RESOLUTION (METERS)	REVISIT PERIOD (DAYS)	ACCESSIBILITY AND COST	LAUNCH DATE	END DATE	SNOW EXTENT	SNOW WATER EQUIVALENT	SNOW MOISTURE
Optical, cont.	OLS	DMSP F-16	560	0.5	Constrained	October 2003	October 2014	②	④	④
	OLS	DMSP F-17	560	0.5	Constrained	November 2006	June 2014	②	④	④
	OLS	DMSP F-18	560	0.5	Constrained	October 2009	April 2014	②	④	④
	OLS	DMSP F-15	560	0.5	Constrained	December 1999	May 2014	②	④	④
	AVHRR/3	NOAA-18	1,100	1	Open	May 2005	December 2015	②	④	④
	AVHRR/3	NOAA-19	1,100	1	Open	February 2009	March 2016	②	④	④
	AIRS	Aqua	13,000	16	Open	May 2002	October 2015	②	④	④
	MSU-GS	Elektro-L N1	1,000–4,000		Open	January 2011	December 2018	②	④	④
	MODIS	Aqua	250–1,000	16	Open	May 2002	October 2015	①	④	④
	MODIS	Terra	250–1,000	16	Open	December 1999	October 2015	①	④	④
	VIIRS	Suomi NPP	400–1,600	16	Open	October 2011	March 2017	①	④	④
Passive microwave	AMSU-A	Aqua	48,000	16	Open	May 2002	October 2015	①	②	④
	AMSU-A	NOAA-18	48,000	1	Open	May 2005	December 2015	①	②	④
	SSM/I	DMSP F-15	15,700–68,900	0.5	Constrained	December 1999	May 2014	②	②	④
	SSM/IS	DMSP F-16	25,000–42,000	0.5	Constrained	October 2003	October 2014	②	②	④
	SSM/IS	DMSP F-17	25,000–42,000	0.5	Constrained	November 2006	June 2014	②	②	④
	SSM/IS	DMSP F-18	25,000–42,000	0.5	Constrained	October 2009	April 2014	②	②	④
	AMSR-E	Aqua	5,000–50,000	16	Open	May 2002	October 2015	①	①	①
Thermal	TIRS	Landsat 8	100	16	Open	February 2013	May 2023	②	④	④

(Continued)

Table 6.11 (Continued)

DATA CURRENCY AND FUNCTIONAL TYPE OF SENSOR	SENSOR	PLATFORM	SPATIAL RESOLUTION (METERS)	REVISIT PERIOD (DAYS)	ACCESSIBILITY AND COST	LAUNCH DATE	END DATE	SNOW EXTENT	SNOW WATER EQUIVALENT	SNOW MOISTURE
Future										
Active microwave	PALSAR-2 (ALOS-2)	ALOS-2	10	14	Unknown	March 2014	March 2019	4	2	4
	C-band SAR	Sentinel-1 B	10–50	12	Open	December 2015	May 2023	2	1	2
	C-band SAR	Sentinel-1 C	11–50	12	Open	March 2019	June 2026	2	1	2
	SAR (RCM)	RADARSAT C-1	8–100		Constrained	July 2018	November 2025	2	2	2
	SAR (RCM)	RADARSAT C-2	8–100	24	Constrained	July 2018	November 2025	2	2	2
	SAR (RCM)	RADARSAT C-3	8–100		Constrained	July 2018	November 2025	2	2	2
	C-band SAR	Sentinel-1 A	9–50	12	Open	March 2014	January 2021	2	1	2
Optical	PRISM-2 (ALOS-3)	ALOS-3	1	60	Unknown	December 2015	December 2020	2	4	4
	LISS-IV	RESOURCESAT-2A	5.8	26	Constrained	October 2015	October 2020	2	4	4
	HYSI (Cartosat-3/3A)	CARTOSAT-3	12		Constrained	July 2017	July 2022	1	4	4
	OLS	DMSP F-19	560	0.5	Constrained	March 2014	March 2019	2	4	4
	MSU-GS	Arctica	1,000–4,000	1	Open	December 2015	December 2018	2	4	4
	MSU-GS	Elektro-L N2	1,000–4,000	—	Open	June 2014	June 2019	2	4	4
	MSU-GS	Elektro-L N3	1,000–4,000	—	Open	December 2015	December 2022	2	4	4
	VIIRS	JPSS-1	400–1,600	16	Open	January 2017	March 2024	1	4	4
Passive microwave	SSM/IS	DMSP F-19	25,000–42,000	0.5	Constrained	March 2014	March 2019	2	2	4

Sources: Committee on Earth Observation Satellites (CEOS) Earth Observation Handbook (http://www.eohandbook.com/) and the World Monitoring Organization Observing Systems Capability Analysis and Review Tool (http://www.wmo-sat.info/oscar/).

Note: The suitability of each sensor to provide useful data is shown with numbers and colors, as follows: 1 highly suitable, 2 suitable, and 4 not suitable. SWE = snow water equivalent. — = not available.

University of Utah and the University of California, Santa Barbara, have generated a MODIS-based snow cover product specifically for use in areas with complex terrain (Painter et al. 2009).

SNOW EXTENT

The areal extent of snow cover can be detected using optical, near infrared, and microwave sensors or a combination of these. Operational snow cover maps are currently produced with MODIS and AVHRR imagery using visible and infrared sensors. The strength of visible and infrared sensors is their relative abundance and ease of access. They are, however, sensitive to cloud cover, which can be common at high altitudes or in environments with significant snow cover.

Various snow extent products are available. The two most widely used infrared- and NIR-based products are the MODIS product suites and the ice mapping system (IMS). The MOD10 suite of products provides daily, eight-day, and monthly estimates of global snow cover at 500-meter and 0.05° resolutions (see Hall et al. 2002, 2010; Salomonson and Appel 2004). The National Snow and Ice Data Center produces the interactive multisensor snow and ice mapping data product. This is a daily product for the Northern Hemisphere at 4-kilometer and 24-kilometer resolutions (Helfrich et al. 2007; Ramsay 1998).

SNOW WATER EQUIVALENT

Active and passive microwave sensors are the primary means of detecting snow depth, snow water equivalent, and snow wetness. The great advantage of microwave sensors is that they are not sensitive to cloud cover and can detect more than snow extent alone. Their disadvantages are that they are sensitive to the presence of trees and, in the case of passive sensors, have relatively low spatial resolutions. Dietz et al. (2011) provide an excellent review of microwave-based methods for detecting snow.

The ESA produces the GlobSnow snow water equivalent data product, which is provided on a daily, weekly, and monthly basis for the Northern Hemisphere. This information product first became available in 1979 and still exists today (Pulliainen 2006; Takala et al. 2011). The NSIDC produces an AMSR-E-based product for the world at 25-kilometer resolution that starts in mid-2002 (Kelly et al. 2003). A snow-depth product for China has been generated by the Environmental and Ecological Science Data Center for West China. This is a 25-kilometer resolution product spanning 1978 to 2006 that is derived from passive microwave data (SMMR and SMM/I; see Che et al. 2008). More current snow depth, extent, and snow water equivalent data products have recently been developed for northern China (Dai et al. 2012).

Optical Water Quality and Macrophytes
Definition
For practical purposes, "inland waters" are defined as inland surface waters, including rivers, lakes, artificial reservoirs, and estuaries and their associated wetlands. "Water quality" refers to the physical, chemical, and biological content of water and may vary geographically and seasonally, irrespective of the presence of specific pollution sources. Many factors affect water quality. No single measure exists for good water quality. Therefore, the term "water quality" does not describe an absolute condition but rather a condition *relative* to the use or purpose of the water (for example, for drinking, irrigation, industrial, recreational, or environmental purposes). Water that is suitable for irrigation, for instance, may not meet drinking water standards. Thus "water quality" refers to the natural state of water bodies and to their response to a combination of stressors such as changes in land use; nutrient inputs; contamination from farming practices, industrial activity, and urbanization; and changes in hydrology, flow regimes, and climate.

Remote Sensing of Water Quality

Earth observation can only be used directly to assess a subset of water quality variables, often referred to as optical water quality variables, including concentrations of the following:

- Chlorophyll (milligrams per cubic meter), which is an indicator of phytoplankton biomass, trophic, and nutrient status and the most widely used index of water quality and nutrient status globally

- Cyanophycocyanin (milligrams per cubic meter) and cyanophycoerythrin (milligrams per cubic meter), which are indicators of cyanobacterial biomass common in harmful and toxic algal blooms

- Colored dissolved organic matter (per meter absorption at 440 nanometers), which is the optically measurable component of dissolved organic matter in the water column, sometimes used as an indicator of organic matter and aquatic carbon

- Total suspended matter (milligrams per cubic meter) and nonalgal particulate matter, which are important for assessing the quality of drinking water and controlling the light characteristic of aquatic environments.

Additionally, the following conditions can be estimated:

- Vertical light attenuation (per meter) and turbidity, which measure the underwater light field and are important for assessing the degree of light limitation, rates of primary production, species composition, and other ecosystem responses

- Emergent and submerged macrophytes down to depth visibility, which are important indicators of wetland and aquatic ecosystem health and function

- Bathymetry (meters), which can estimate water depth when the bottom or bottom cover of a water body reflects a measurable amount of light through the water column to above the surface.

Earth observation cannot directly assess water quality parameters that do not have a direct expression in the optical response of the water body. These parameters include many chemical compounds such as nutrients. However, in some cases, nonoptical products may be estimated through inference, proxy relationships, or data assimilation with remotely sensed optical properties of products such as nitrogen, phosphate, organic and inorganic micropollutants, and dissolved oxygen. However, these relationships are stochastic, may not be causal, and may have a limited range of validity. By making use of the combined information in directly measurable optical properties, it is possible to derive information about eutrophication, environmental flows, and carbon and primary productivity.

Relevance

Access to clean, safe drinking water is a key determinant of quality of life and is linked directly to human health. Depending on the use to which the water is put, polluted or contaminated water may not be regarded as a usable resource. Similarly, as contaminant concentration is often related to water volume and flow, water quality is ultimately linked to water quantity. Water supply and sanitation are thus essential components of any integrated approach to malnutrition and poverty reduction, and water quality is a key related challenge in sustainable development.

The quality of water is affected by stressors including urbanization, population growth, land use change, deforestation, farming, overexploitation, and contamination from extractive industries in the mining and energy sectors. As such, the relevance of water quality issues will change in different settings, and their impact will ultimately depend on the water's intended use.

Water quality monitoring is a key source of information for ensuring that both human and ecosystem health are not compromised and for determining the water's suitability for other purposes (irrigation, industry). Nation-states require information on water quality to inform key policy and legislative requirements that may include assessments against water quality guidelines and targets, national water quality management strategies, water resources assessments, state of the environment reporting, and strategies formulating adaptive responses to climate change. However, even developed countries (such as Australia and the United States) may not have any nationally coordinated water quality monitoring programs, and the authorities may instead rely on individual states to provide such information; moreover, frameworks for disseminating such information are often lacking altogether or poorly developed (Dekker and Hestir 2012).

Despite international efforts to monitor global inland water quality, existing data are scarce and declining, have poor geographic and temporal coverage, may lack quality assurance and control, and may be of questionable accuracy (Srebotnjak et al. 2012). The international coordinating group, the Group on Earth Observations (GEO), recognizes the value of Earth observation for improving understanding of global water quality, its hotspots, and trends; for ensuring food and energy security; for facilitating poverty reduction; for protecting the health of humans and ecosystems; and for maintaining biodiversity. GEO has formed the Inland and Near-Coastal Water Quality Remote Sensing Working Group to promote the development of improved optical water quality products (GEO 2011).

Through the provision of synoptic, consistent, and comparable data, Earth observation has the opportunity to overcome some of the gaps and deficiencies in current, field-based water quality monitoring efforts. Sufficient archives of EO data now exist to monitor global trends in water quality for several decades and to develop suitable reports to address specific questions raised by decision and policy makers.

Theoretical Basis for Remote Sensing of Inland Water Quality

Earth observation of the water quality parameters identified above is achieved through optical means principally in the VIS-NIR spectrum (about 400–900 nanometers). The light reaching the surface of a water body consists of direct sunlight and diffuse skylight after scattering and absorption have interacted in the atmosphere (figure 6.14). At the surface, this light is either reflected by the surface or refracted as it passes across the air-water interface. Within the water column, the water itself and different particulate and dissolved water column constituents transform the light by transmitting, absorbing, or scattering the down-welling light. Of the light that is scattered, a proportion may be backscattered in an upward direction and pass across the water-air interface at the right angle to be observed by airborne or satellite sensors once it has again passed through the atmosphere.

In the visible region (about 400–900 nanometers), the influence of sediments, chlorophyll, and colored dissolved organic matter interacts to modify the shape and amount of the spectrally reflected signal (Kirk 2011); RS water quality algorithms largely take advantage of these variations in the "shape" of spectral reflectance. In wavelengths longer than 900 nanometers, water itself is such a strong absorber that very little radiation is reflected from water bodies (figure 6.15). For this reason, the water quality variables listed above are often referred to as "optical water quality variables."

The algorithms for translating the measured spectral reflectance from a water body to water quality variables include empirical approaches (Tyler et al. 2006; Wang et al. 2009); semi-empirical approaches (Gons 1999; Härmä et al. 2001); and physics-based,

Figure 6.14 Schematic of the Light Interactions That Drive Optical EO Involving the Air, Water, and Substrate

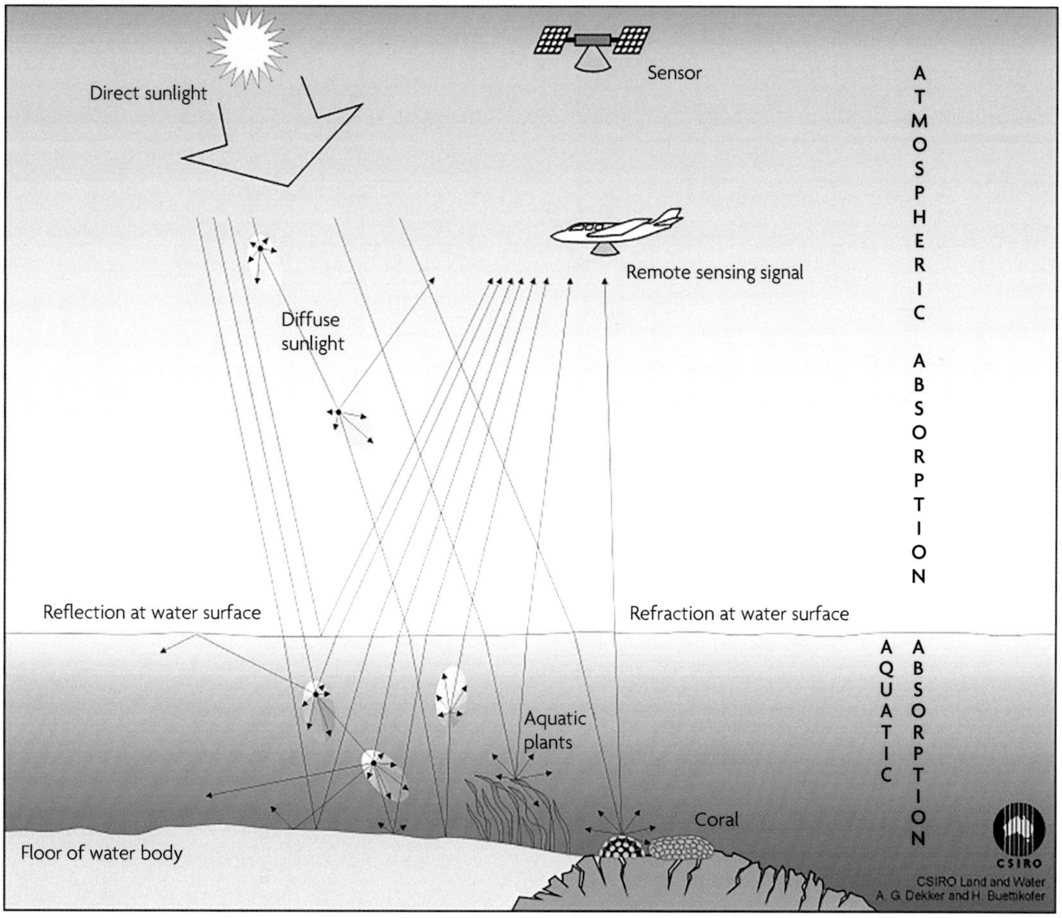

Source: CSIRO Land and Water (A. G. Dekker and H. Buettikofer).

Note: EO = Earth observation.

Figure 6.15 Typical Reflectance Spectrum from Eutrophic Inland Water Body and Regions in Which Different Water Quality Parameters Influence the Shape of That Spectrum

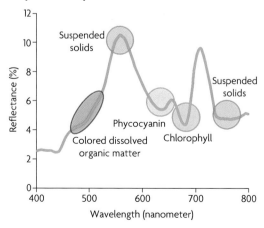

semi-analytical spectral inversion methods (Brando et al. 2012; Lee et al. 1998). These three methods are outlined below and subsequently compared with regard to their need for field measurements as well as their reliability, accuracy, maturity, and complexity (see chapter 7).

Empirical approaches statistically relate field samples of the optical water quality variables to radiance or reflectance values measured by a satellite or airborne sensor. There is no need to understand the underlying physical relationships in such algorithms (such as atmospheric and underwater light processes). However, they do require *coincident* field measurements to calibrate the relationships for specific water bodies and, as such, struggle when water column constituents lie outside the range on which the pertinent statistical relationship is based (in both space and time) and are not easily adapted to new satellite sensors. Empirical methods are also less reliable when undertaking retrospective monitoring, especially when the characteristics of lake water quality may change and end up outside the range of those on which the empirical relationship is based.

Semi-empirical algorithms improve over pure empirical approaches by choosing the most appropriate single or spectral band combination to estimate the water column constituent. They can also partly annul some of the atmospheric and water surface effects. Semi-empirical algorithms, however, also suffer from extrapolation errors beyond the range of constituents observed, the need to establish new, semi-empirical algorithms when switching sensors or water bodies, and the lack of reliability in retrospective monitoring when characteristics of lake water quality change. They are therefore less accurate than fully empirical methods.

The water quality variables retrieved using empirical and semi-empirical algorithms include total suspended matter, suspended inorganic matter, colored dissolved organic matter, turbidity, transparency, chlorophyll, and cyanophycocyanin pigments (Matthews 2011). With few exceptions (such as Minnesota lakes in the United States; Olmanson, Brezonik, and Bauer 2011), neither approach offers significant confidence for application in a national monitoring system (Dekker and Hestir 2012). The Minnesota lakes method worked because it was supported by a vast, citizens' science-based field measurement effort.

Semi-analytical inversion algorithms are built around knowledge of the underlying physics of light transfer in waters and use the inversion of predictions of light reflecting from a water body, generated by forward radiative transfer models, to estimate key water quality constituents simultaneously. Such approaches show improved accuracy for estimating water column composition (Dekker, Vos, and Peters 2001), are capable of assessing the error in the estimation of water quality constituents, are repeatable over time and space, are transferable to new water bodies and other sensors, and can be applied retrospectively to image archives (Dekker et al. 2006; Odermatt et al. 2012). This means that retrospective monitoring of changes in optical water quality is possible to assess the impacts and mitigation of various stressors to the system.

A recommended pathway for longer-term operational use is to develop a robust, semi-analytical inversion method for application globally. Semi-empirical methods can be used in the interim, as they often are reasonably robust for a category of water types and for a single EO sensor system. Empirical approaches are only useful as proof of concept. In general, they are not recommended if all optically active substances (chlorophyll, colored dissolved organic matter, total suspended solids, cyanophycocyanin, cyanophycoerythrin and the resulting physical properties of turbidity, Secchi disk depth, and vertical light attenuation) need to be determined.

Mapping Inland Aquatic Macrophytes

Table 6.12 highlights the abilities of current and future optical sensors to differentiate among the growth habits of different macrophytes. In addition to providing valuable habitat to multiple freshwater ecosystem species, emergent wetland vegetation has extremely high rates of net primary production and evapotranspiration, drives a large portion of wetland carbon formation and storage, and plays an important role in wetland sediment stability and accretion (Byrd et al. 2014; Zhou and Zhou 2009). Floating and submersed plants provide important structuring for freshwater ecosystems, influencing the physical and chemical environment and food web (Liu et al. 2013; Meerhoff et al. 2003; Santos, Anderson, and Ustin 2011; Vanderstukken et al. 2014).

Table 6.12 Existing and Near-Future Satellite Sensor Systems of Relevance for Inland and Near-Coastal Water Quality

DATA CURRENCY AND FUNCTIONAL TYPE OF SENSOR	SENSOR FUNCTIONAL TYPE (OPTICAL AND NEARBY INFRARED)	SPATIAL RESOLUTION (PIXEL SIZE)	SPECTRAL BANDS (WATER-RELEVANT SPECTRAL RANGE, 400–1,000 NANOMETERS)	REVISIT FREQUENCY CYCLE (ONCE EVERY X DAYS)	RAW DATA COST PER SQUARE KILOMETER (US$)	LAUNCH DATE	END DATE	WATER QUALITY VARIABLES						MACROPHYTES		
								CHL	CYP	TSM	CDOM	K_d	TURB SD	EMERGENT	FLOATING-LEAVED	SUBMERSED
Archival																
Ocean-coastal	MERIS	1.2 and 0.3 kilometers	15	2 days	Free	March 2002	May 2012	1	1	1	1	1	1	3	4	4
Mid-spatial resolution	LANDSAT 1 to 7	30 meters	4	16 days	Free	July 1972		3	Surface bloom	2	2	2	2	2	3	3
SAR	ERS 1	30 meters	C band, VV polarization	35 days	Free	1991 (ERS-1)	2000 (ERS-1)	4	4	4	4	4	4	3	4	4
	ERS 2	30 meters	C band, VV polarization	35 days	Free	1995 (ERS-2)	2011 (ERS-2)	4	4	4	4	4	4	3	4	4
	ALOS PALSAR	10–100 meters	L band, HH, VV, HV, VH	46 days	Commercial or R&D	2006	2011	4	4	4	4	4	4	1	4	4
Current																
Coarse spatial resolution	MODIS-A&T	1 kilometer	9	Daily	Free	December 1999		1	2	1	1	1	1	4	4	4
	MODIS-A&T	500 meters	2	Daily	Free	December 1999		4	4	2	2	2	2	4	3	3
	MODIS-A&T	250 meters	2	Daily	Free	December 1999		2	4	2	4	2	2	3	3	3
	OCM-2	300 meters	15	2–3 days	Free	September 2009		1	1	1	1	1	1	3	4	4
	Suomi-VIIRS	740 meters	7	Twice daily	Free	October 2011		1	2	1	1	1	1	4	4	4
Geostationary	SEVIRI on MSG	1 kilometer	2	96 per 24 hours	Free	2002		3	4	2	4	2	2	4	4	4
	GOCI	500 meters	8	Half hourly	Free	2010		1	3	1	2	1	1	4	4	4
	Himawari-8	500 meters–2 kilometers	4	10 minutes possible	Free	2014		3	4	1	3	2	1	4	4	4
Mid-spatial resolution	LANDSAT 8	30 meters	5	16 days	Free	September 2013		3	Surface bloom	2	2	2	2	2	2	2

(Continued)

Table 6.12 (Continued)

DATA CURRENCY AND FUNCTIONAL TYPE OF SENSOR	SENSOR FUNCTIONAL TYPE (OPTICAL AND NEARBY INFRARED)	SPATIAL RESOLUTION (PIXEL SIZE)	SPECTRAL BANDS (WATER-RELEVANT SPECTRAL RANGE, 400–1,000 NANOMETERS)	REVISIT FREQUENCY CYCLE (ONCE EVERY X DAYS)	RAW DATA COST PER SQUARE KILOMETER (US$)	LAUNCH DATE	END DATE	WATER QUALITY VARIABLES					TURB	MACROPHYTES		
								CHL	CYP	TSM	CDOM	K_d	SD	EMERGENT	FLOATING-LEAVED	SUBMERSED
High spatial resolution	IKONOS, QuickBird, SPOT-5, 6 GeoEye	2–4 meters	3 to 4	Programmable: 60 days to 2–3 days	5 to 15	October 1999–		3	Surface bloom	2	2	2	2	2	2	2
	RapidEye	6.5 meters	5	Daily	1.5	August 2008		3	Surface bloom	2	2	2	2	2	2	2
	WORLDVIEW-2	2 meters spectral– 0.5 meter in black and white	8	Programmable: 60 days to 1 day	30	October 2009		2	2	1	2	1	1	1	1	1
SAR	Radarsat 2	30 meters	C band, fully polarimetric	24 days	Commercial	2007		4	4	4	4	4	4	2	4	4
	ALOS 2	3–100 meters	L band, HH, VV, HV, VH	14 days	Commercial	May 2014		4	4	4	4	4	4	1	4	4
	Sentinel 1	5–20 meters	C band, HH, VV, HV, VH	12 days	Free	March 2014		4	4	4	4	4	4	2	4	4
Future																
High spatial resolution	Sentinel 2	10- to 60-meter bands	10	10 days per sensor; 5 days with 2 Sentinel-2 sensors	Free	2014		2	Surface bloom	1	1	1	1	2	2	2
	WORLDVIEW-3	1.24 meters spectral–0.50 meter in black and white	8	Programmable: 60 days to 1 day	30	2014		2	2	1	2	1	1	1	1	1
Ocean-coastal	Sentinel-3	300 meters	21	Daily (with 2 satellites)	Free	2015		1	1	1	1	1	1	3	4	4

(Continued)

Table 6.12 (Continued)

DATA CURRENCY AND FUNCTIONAL TYPE OF SENSOR	SENSOR FUNCTIONAL TYPE (OPTICAL AND NEARBY INFRARED)	SPATIAL RESOLUTION (PIXEL SIZE)	SPECTRAL BANDS (WATER-RELEVANT SPECTRAL RANGE, 400–1,000 NANOMETERS)	REVISIT FREQUENCY CYCLE (ONCE EVERY X DAYS)	RAW DATA COST PER SQUARE KILOMETER (US$)	LAUNCH DATE	END DATE	WATER QUALITY VARIABLES					TURB		MACROPHYTES		
								CHL	CYP	TSM	CDOM	K_d	SD	EMERGENT	FLOATING-LEAVED	SUBMERSED
Hyperspectral	EnMap	30 meters	90	Programmable (once per 4 days)	Free	2017		1	1	1	1	1	1	2	2	2
	PRISMA	20 meters spectral–2.5 meters in black and white	60	25 days	Free	2017		1	1	1	1	1	1	2	2	2
SAR	Cosmo-Skymed	5–100 meters	X band, HH, VV, HV, VH	16 days	Commercial or R&D			4	4	4	4	4	4	3	4	4
	TerraSAR-X/ Tandem-X	0.25–40 meters	X band	3 days	Commercial or R&D	2007 (2010)		4	4	4	4	4	4	3	4	4

Note: The suitability of each sensor to provide useful data is shown with numbers and colors, as follows: 1 highly suitable, 2 suitable, 3 potentially suitable, 4 not suitable. Products in development are coarse particle-size distributions and phytoplankton functional types; integrated products could be eutrophication index; water quality index, algal bloom index; carbon contents and flux; contaminant estimation. CHL = chlorophyll; CYP = cyanobacterial pigments such as cyanophycocyanin and cyanophycoerythrin; TSM = total suspended matter; CDOM = colored dissolved organic matter; K_d = vertical attenuation of light coefficient; Turb = turbidity; SD = Secchi disk transparency. R&D = research and development.

Routine mapping of the biophysical parameters of macrophytes—derived from high-resolution optical satellite or airborne imagery in lakes and shallow, lentic environments—has value for assessing cover and the effectiveness of management practices in controlling excessive aquatic plant growth. Macrophytes may be separated into three groups, based on their principal growth habits—submersed, floating-leaved, and emergent—and the mapping of species by growth habit using both airborne and satellite data can be reasonably accurate (Hunter et al. 2010; Malthus and George 1997; Tian et al. 2010). The mapping is done largely on the basis of reflectance values in NIR wavebands, which are much stronger from emergent and floating-leaved species. Hyperspectral data can differentiate several aquatic plant associations (Tian et al. 2010) and be used to detect submersed aquatic species, even in highly turbid environments (Hestir et al. 2008; Santos et al. 2012), as can the use of LiDAR and textural analysis of image data (Proctor, He, and Robinson 2013; Verrelst et al. 2009). Differentiation of species, however, currently poses a greater challenge. Because of the high spatial and phenological variability of aquatic macrophytes, high-spectral-resolution data are needed to discriminate communities adequately (Klemas 2013) and measure the biogeochemical features needed for species discrimination and physiological function (Santos et al. 2012; Ustin et al. 2004).

SAR data also have value in offering weather-independent monitoring of aquatic macrophytes and wetlands as well as flooding extent (Silva et al. 2008). Dielectric signal differences arise from the presence of water as surface water and within vegetation, thus making it possible to detect dry and flooded vegetation and, hence, to map the extent of flooding and of emergent vegetation (Costa 2004; Evans et al. 2010). The lack of penetration of microwaves into water prevents detection of submersed macrophyte species.

Common SAR wavelength bands include X (3-centimeter wavelength), C (5.6-centimeter), S (10-centimeter), L (23-centimeter), and P (75-centimeter) bands, and common SAR detectors may be set up to receive defined polarizations in the same (horizontal transmit and horizontal receive [HH] or vertical transmit and vertical receive [VV]) or cross-polarization modes (horizontal transmit and vertical receive [HV] or vertical transmit and horizontal receive [VH]). Longer microwave wavelengths (L band) penetrate further into canopies, and differences in polarization behavior may also help to detect differences in specific vegetation canopy (Martínez and Le Toan 2007).

The intensity of the radar backscatter is related directly to the roughness and, combined with volumetric scattering, wavelength, and polarization, provides specific vegetation responses and hence information on canopy characteristics (Evans et al. 2010; Kasischke and Bruhwiler 2003; Klemas 2013). Common satellite-borne SAR systems, as well as their characteristics and abilities to differentiate emergent vegetation, are highlighted in table 6.12. However, because wetlands are highly spatially heterogeneous, the large footprint provided by most SAR systems also limits their ability to discriminate wetland plant species successfully from space.

Applications

Systematic examples of truly operational monitoring of inland water quality beyond that applied to single water bodies are lacking, reflecting the challenges in applying more simple empirical and semi-empirical algorithms. Using empirical methods, Olmanson, Bauer, and Brezonik (2008) compiled a comprehensive water clarity database assembled from Landsat imagery over 1985–2005 for more than 10,500 Minnesota lakes larger than 8 hectares in surface area. This study highlighted the geographic patterns in clarity linked to land use at the level of both individual lake and eco-region.[21]

Algorithm development to allow application beyond a single inland water body is only now being addressed in some research projects targeting larger lakes with ocean color sensors (Global Lakes Sentinel Services [GLaSS] and GloboLakes). The monitoring of water quality conditions across the Great Barrier Reef World Heritage Park offers the best example of the potential to deliver water quality products derived from semi-analytical inversion algorithms. MODIS data are used to derive concentrations of key water quality constituents for the reef on a daily basis, and the data are delivered via the Australian Bureau of Meteorology's Marine Water Quality Dashboard.[22]

The following data services and research projects provide water quality products derived from Earth observation:

- Downstream services of the European Union and ESA Copernicus Programme[23]

- Marine water quality and forecasting by the European Union and ESA's Environment Monitoring Services[24]

- Monitoring of harmful algal bloom in Lake Erie by the National Oceanic and Atmospheric Administration (NOAA)[25]

- Development of a harmful algal bloom advisory and forecasting capability by the European Union's ASIMUTH (Applied Simulations and Integrated Modelling for the Understanding of Toxic and Harmful Algal Blooms) project[26]

- Global Earth observation for integrated water resource assessment by EartH2Observe.[27]

These examples are discussed further in appendix B.

Past, Present, and Future Sensor Availability for Inland Water Mapping

In many countries, field-based water quality monitoring efforts are insufficient to provide national-scale assessments of inland water quality. In improving the design of such assessments, the following are key considerations:

- *Temporal sampling* to represent the dynamics of water quality and the range of conditions that can occur over diurnal, seasonal, and annual cycles (droughts and flooding) as well as to develop a time series for trend analysis. Retrospective processing of satellite images, with archives dating back to the mid-1980s, may also reveal temporal changes, trends, and anomalies across inland water and near-coastal water systems.

- *Spatial sampling* to represent water bodies under consideration and provide understanding of system processes such as heterogeneity, environmental flows, interrelationships between water bodies, and catchment runoff effects.

End user requirements should determine the optimal spatial sampling scheme, but logistical, operational, and financial constraints usually prevent the optimal sampling scheme from being realized. Extensive distances, for instance, may make capturing the spatial distribution of measurements using field-based methods unfeasible. EO-derived water quality information, albeit for a more limited set of parameters, may be used to overcome the challenges in water quality sampling schemes based solely on field-based approaches to provide complementary oversight of water quality conditions and trends. In future, capacity building should focus on integrating EO data and field-based observations and on developing early warning tools for algal blooms.

Table 6.12 provides an overview of existing and upcoming satellite sensor systems of relevance for monitoring inland water quality internationally and their suitability for measuring optical water quality variables. While policy, legislative, environmental, and climate change drivers should steer the development of an operational system for inland water quality monitoring, the ideal satellite sensor system for inland water quality does not exist; there are trade-offs between spatial, temporal, spectral, and radiometric characteristics. Thus having satellite sensors available for detecting and monitoring retrospective, current, and future inland water quality is necessary for developing regional, national, and transboundary inland water quality monitoring systems using Earth observation.

Different satellite systems show different trade-offs between temporal frequency (once a day to once a year), spatial resolution (2-meter to 1.2-kilometer pixels), spectral resolution (and the related issue of more water quality variables at higher confidence levels), radiometric resolution (how accurate and how many levels of reflectance are measurable), and the cost of acquiring unprocessed satellite data (ranging from US$0 to about US$30 per square kilometer). This also influences their usefulness for inland water quality assessment.

Tools are needed for reporting information on water quality at a variety of scales (continental, transboundary, regional, and national). However, satisfying this need is challenging given the multiple-size scales of inland water bodies with respect to the different spatial and spectral resolutions offered by the different satellite sensors.

Spatial resolution has consequences for imaging small water bodies such as small- or medium-width river systems. In such situations, high-spatial-resolution imagery (with pixel sizes of 2 to 10 meters) may be the only option, possibly leading to significant data acquisition costs. A multiple-resolution approach is most cost-effective where coarse (but frequent) satellite imagery is used for larger lakes, reservoirs, and river sections and high-resolution imagery is acquired and processed only when necessary. Rather than imaging *all* water bodies, a "virtual station concept" approach could systematically image a *selection* of water bodies that represent the associated aquatic ecosystem (be it natural or artificial). This would be especially effective for smaller or narrow water bodies, reducing the need for high-resolution imagery and thus also reducing cost.

Spectral resolution (the number, width, and placing of spectral bands) ultimately determines the amount and accuracy of water quality variables that are discernable from a water body (table 6.12). Sensors with few bands may only be used to detect total suspended matter, vertical light attenuation, Secchi disk transparency, turbidity, and colored dissolved organic matter if a blue spectral band is available. Algal pigments such as chlorophyll may also be detected. However, at low concentrations, accuracy will be low, as broad spectral bands cannot discriminate the more narrow features of pigment spectral absorption from other absorbing and backscattering materials in the water column. As the number of narrower and more suitably positioned spectral bands increases (MODIS, MERIS, and Ocean Colour Monitor [OCM]-2), chlorophyll becomes an accurately measurable variable, and types of phytoplankton pigment such as cyanobacterial pigments may become detectable.

Radiometric resolution determines the lowest level of radiance or reflectance that the sensor can reliably detect per spectral band. As the spectral and spatial resolution increases, the useful signal relative to noise in the data decreases, but this trade-off in spectral, spatial, and radiometric resolution is countered by improvements in detector technology where, in general, more modern sensors have a higher radiometric sensitivity overall than older sensors.

NOTES

1. For more information on the data sets of the International Precipitation Working Group, see http://www.isac.cnr.it/~ipwg/data/datasets.html.

2. *Orographic lift* occurs when an air mass is forced from a low elevation to a higher elevation as it moves over rising terrain. As the air mass gains altitude, it quickly cools down adiabatically, which can raise the relative humidity to

100 percent and create clouds and, under the right conditions, precipitation.

3. For more information on the Asia-Pacific Water Monitor, see http://eos.csiro.au/apwm/.

4. For information on the Global Precipitation Climatology Project, see http://www.gewex.org/gpcp.html.

5. For information on Eddy covariance flux data, see http://www.fluxnet.ornl.gov/.

6. *Antecedent moisture* is a term from the fields of hydrology and sewage collection and disposal that describes the relative wetness or dryness of a watershed or sanitary sewershed. Antecedent moisture conditions change continuously and can have a very significant effect on the flow responses in these systems during wet weather.

7. *Signal-to-noise ratio* is the ratio of the level of the signal carrying real information to the level of the signal carrying spurious information (as a result of defects in the system).

8. For the Earth Observation Handbook database, see http://www.eohandbook.com/. For the Observing Systems Capability Analysis and Review Tool, see http://www.wmo-sat.info/oscar/.

9. For the Global Drought Information System, see www.drought.gov.

10. For the European Drought Observatory, see http://edo.jrc.ec.europa.eu/.

11. For the Climate Maps, see http://www.bom.gov.au/jsp/awap/ndvi/.

12. For the African Drought Monitor, see http://drought.icpac.net/.

13. For the global terrestrial drought severity index, see http://www.ntsg.umt.edu/project/dsi.

14. For the Groundwater Foundation, see http://www.groundwater.org/get-informed/basics/groundwater.html.

15. *Backscatter* is the portion of the outgoing radar signal that the target redirects directly back toward the radar antenna, *backscattering* is the process by which backscatter is formed, and *backscatter coefficient* is a measure of the reflective strength of a radar target.

16. For the Dartmouth Flood Observatory, see http://floodobservatory.colorado.edu/.

17. For Near-Real-Time Global MODIS Flood Mapping, see http://oas.gsfc.nasa.gov/floodmap/.

18. For Crop Explorer, see http://www.pecad.fas.usda.gov/cropexplorer/global_reservoir/.

19. For LEGOS (Laboratoire d'Etudes en Géophysique et Océanographie Spatiales) HydroWeb, see http://www.legos.obs-mip.fr/en/soa/hydrologie/hydroweb/.

20. For the European Space Agency's East Rivers & Lakes, see http://tethys.eaprs.cse.dmu.ac.uk/RiverLake/.

21. For information on the project, see http://water.umn.edu/lwc/index.html.

22. For the Marine Water Quality Dashboard, see http://www.bom.gov.au/marinewaterquality/.

23. For an overview of the EU-ESA Copernicus Programme Downstream services, see http://gmesdata.esa.int/web/gsc/core_services/downstream_services.

24. For more information on the Copernicus Programme's Environment Monitoring Services, see http://www.myocean.eu/web/26-catalogue-of-services.php.

25. For information from NOAA's Great Lakes Environmental Laboratory, see http://www.glerl.noaa.gov/res/Centers/HABS/lake_erie_hab/lake_erie_hab.html.

26. For the ASIMUTH project, see http://www.asimuth.eu/.

27. For EartH2Observe, see http://www.earth2observe.eu/.

REFERENCES

AghaKouchak, A., A. Behrangi, S. Sorooshian, K. Hsu, and E. Amitai. 2011. "Evaluation of Satellite-Retrieved Extreme Precipitation Rates across the Central United States." *Journal of Geophysical Research* 116 (January): D02115.

Albergel, C., E. Zakharova, J.-C. Calvet, M. Zribi, M. Pardé, J.-P. Wigneron, N. Novello, Y. Kerr, A. Mialon, and N. Fritz. 2011. "A First Assessment of the SMOS Data in Southwestern France Using in Situ and Airborne Soil Moisture Estimates: The CAROLS Airborne Campaign." *Remote Sensing of Environment* 115 (10): 2718–28.

Allen, R. G., M. Tasumi, A. Morse, R. Trezza, J. L. Wright, W. Bastiaanssen, W. Kramber, I. Lorite, and C. W. Robison. 2007. "Satellite-Based Energy Balance for Mapping Evapotranspiration with Internalized Calibration (METRIC) Applications." *Journal of Irrigation and Drainage Engineering* 133 (4): 395–406.

Alsdorf, D. E., E. Rodríguez, and D. P. Lettenmaier. 2007. "Measuring Surface Water from Space." *Reviews of Geophysics* 45 (2): RG2002.

Andela, N., Y. Y. Liu, A. I. J. M. van Dijk, R. A. M. de Jeu, and T. R. McVicar. 2013. "Global Changes in Dryland Vegetation Dynamics (1988 and 2008) Assessed by Satellite Remote Sensing: Comparing a New Passive Microwave Vegetation Density Record with Reflective Greenness Data." *Biogeosciences* 10 (10): 6657–76.

Anderson, M. C., W. P. Kustas, J. M. Norman, C. R. Hain, J. R. Mecikalski, L. Schultz, M. P. González-Dugo, C. Cammalleri, G. d'Urso,

A. Pimstein, and F. Gao. 2011. "Mapping Daily Evapotranspiration at Field to Continental Scales Using Geostationary and Polar Orbiting Satellite Imagery." *Hydrology and Earth System Sciences* 15 (1): 223–39.

Anderson, M. C., J. M. Norman, J. R. Mecikalski, J. A. Otkin, and W. P. Kustas. 2007. "A Climatological Study of Evapotranspiration and Moisture Stress across the Continental United States Based on Thermal Remote Sensing: 1. Model Formulation." *Journal of Geophysical Research* 112 (D10): D11112.

Arkin, P. A., and B. N. Meisner. 1987. "The Relationship between Large-Scale Convective Rainfall and Cold Cloud Cover over the Western Hemisphere during 1982–1984." *Monthly Weather Review* 115 (1): 51–74.

Ashouri, H., H.-L. Hsu, S. Sorooshian, and D. K. Braithwaite. 2014. "PERSIANN-CDR: Daily Precipitation Climate Data Record from Multi-Satellite Observations for Hydrological and Climate Studies." *Bulletin of the American Meteorological Society* 96 (1). doi:10.1175/BAMS-D-13-00068.1.

Barré, H. M. J. P., B. Duesmann, Y. H. Kerr, and S. Member. 2008. "SMOS: The Mission and the System." *IEEE Transactions on Geoscience and Remote Sensing* 46 (3): 587–93.

Bastiaanssen, W. G. M., M. Menenti, R. A. Feddes, and A. A. M. Holtslag. 1998. "A Remote Sensing Surface Energy Balance Algorithm for Land (SEBAL). 1. Formulation." *Journal of Hydrology* 212-213 (December): 198–212.

Beck, H. E., T. R. McVicar, A. I. J. M. van Dijk, J. Schellekens, R. A. M. de Jeu, and L. A. Bruijnzeel. 2011. "Global Evaluation of Four AVHRR-NDVI Data Sets: Intercomparison and Assessment Against Landsat Imagery." *Remote Sensing of Environment* 115 (10): 2547–63.

Becker, M. W. 2006. "Potential for Satellite Remote Sensing of Ground Water." *Ground Water* 44 (2): 306–18.

Bindlish, R., and T. J. Jackson. 2013. "Soil Moisture Products Using Aquarius/SAC-D Observations." Algorithm Theoretical Basis Document Version 2.0. U.S. Department of Agriculture Hydrology and Remote Sensing Lab, Beltsville, MD. http://nsidc.org/data/docs/daac/aquarius/pdfs/Aquarius_VSM_ATBD_UsersGuide.pdf.

Bojinski, S., M. Verstraete, T. C. Peterson, C. Richter, A. Simmons, and M. Zemp. 2014. "The Concept of Essential Climate Variables in Support of Climate Research, Applications, and Policy." *Bulletin of the American Meteorological Society* 95 (9): 1431–43. doi:10.1175/BAMS-D-13-00047.1.

Bolten, J. D., W. T. Crow, X. Zhan, T. J. Jackson, and C. A. Reynolds. 2010. "Evaluating the Utility of Remotely Sensed Soil Moisture Retrievals for Operational Agricultural Drought Monitoring." *IEEE Journal on Selected Topics in Applied Earth Observations and Remote Sensing* 3 (1): 57–66.

Brakenridge, R., and E. Anderson. 2006. "MODIS-Based Flood Detection, Mapping, and Measurement: The Potential for Operational Hydrological Applications." *Transboundary Floods Reducing Risks through Flood Management* 72 (1): 1–12.

Brando, V. E., A. G. Dekker, Y-Je Park, and T. Schroeder. 2012. "Adaptive Semi-Analytical Inversion of Ocean Color Radiometry in Optically Complex Waters." *Applied Optics* 51 (15): 2808.

Brocca, L., F. Melone, T. Moramarco, W. Wagner, V. Naeimi, Z. Bartalis, and S. Hasenauer. 2010. "Improving Runoff Prediction through the Assimilation of the ASCAT Soil Moisture Product." *Hydrology and Earth System Sciences* 14 (10): 1881–93.

Brocca, L., T. Moramarco, F. Melone, W. Wagner, S. Member, S. Hasenauer, and S. Hahn. 2012. "Assimilation of Surface- and Root-Zone ASCAT Soil Moisture Products into Rainfall–Runoff Modeling." *IEEE Transaction on Geoscience and Remote Sensing* 50 (7): 2542–55.

BoM (Bureau of Meteorology). 2012. "Australian Water Resources Assessment." Australian Bureau of Meteorology, Melbourne.

Budyko, M. I., and D. Miller. 1974. "Climate and Life." International Geophysics Series 18. Bondi, Australia: Geniza.

Byrd, K. B., J. L. O'Connell, S. Di Tommaso, and M. Kelly. 2014. "Evaluation of Sensor Types and Environmental Controls on Mapping Biomass of Coastal Marsh Emergent Vegetation." *Remote Sensing of Environment* 149 (June): 166–80. doi:10.1016/j.rse.2014.04.003.

Chappell, A., L. J. Renzullo, T. H. Raupach, and M. Haylock. 2013. "Evaluating Geostatistical Methods of Blending Satellite and Gauge Data to Estimate Near Real-Time Daily Rainfall for Australia." *Journal of Hydrology* 493 (June): 105–14.

CEOS (Committee on Earth Observation Satellites). 2015. The Earth Observation Handbook. http://www.eohandbook.com/.

Che, T., X. Li, R. Jin, R. Armstrong, and T. J. Zhang. 2008. "Snow Depth Derived from Passive Microwave Remote-Sensing Data in China." *Annals of Glaciology* 49 (1): 145–54.

Chen, S., Y. Hong, J. J. Gourley, G. J. Huffman, Y. Tian, Q. Cao, B. Yong, P.-E. Kirstetter, J. Hu, J. Hardy, Z. Li, S. I. Khan, and X. Xue. 2013. "Evaluation of the Successive V6 and V7 TRMM Multisatellite Precipitation Analysis over the Continental United States." *Water Resources Research* 49 (12): 1–13.

Cleugh, H. A., R. Leuning, Q. Mu, and S. W. Running. 2007. "Regional Evaporation Estimates from Flux Tower and MODIS Satellite Data." *Remote Sensing of Environment* 106 (3): 285–304.

Conrad, C., R. R. Colditz, S. Dech, D. Klein, and P. L. G. Vlek. 2011. "Temporal Segmentation of MODIS Time Series for Improving Crop Classification in Central Asian Irrigation Systems." *International Journal of Remote Sensing* 32 (23): 8763–78.

Costa, M. P. F. 2004. "Use of SAR Satellites for Mapping Zonation of Vegetation Communities in the Amazon Floodplain." *International Journal of Remote Sensing* 25 (10): 1817–35.

CSIRO (Commonwealth Scientific and Industrial Research Organization). 2011. *Water: Science and Solutions for Australia.* Canberra: CSIRO Publishing. http://www.publish.csiro.au/pid/6557.htm.

Dai, L., T. Che, J. Wang, and P. Zhang. 2012. "Snow Depth and Snow Water Equivalent Estimation from AMSR-E Data Based on a Priori Snow Characteristics in Xinjiang, China." *Remote Sensing of Environment* 127 (December): 14–29.

de Jeu, R. A. M. 2003. "Retrieval of Land Surface Parameters Using Passive Microwave Remote Sensing." Vrije Universiteit, Amsterdam.

de Jeu, R. A. M., and M. Owe. 2003. "Further Validation of a New Methodology for Surface Moisture and Vegetation Optical Depth Retrieval." *International Journal of Remote Sensing* 24 (22): 4559–78.

Dekker, A. G., V. E. Brando, J. M. Anstee, S. Fyfe, T. J. M. Malthus, and E. V. Karpouzli. 2006. "Remote Sensing of Seagrass Ecosystems: Use of Spaceborne and Airborne Sensors." In *Seagrass Biology, Ecology, and Conservation,* edited by A. Larkum, R. Orth, and C. Duarte. Heidelberg: Springer Verlag.

Dekker, A. G., and E. L. Hestir. 2012. *Evaluating the Feasibility of Systematic Inland Water Quality Monitoring with Satellite Remote Sensing.* Water for a Healthy Country National Research Flagship. Canberra: CSIRO. https://publications.csiro.au/rpr/download?pid=csiro:EP117441&dsid=DS10.

Dekker, A. G., R. J. Vos, and S. W. M. Peters. 2001. "Comparison of Remote Sensing Data, Model Results and In Situ Data for Total Suspended Matter (TSM) in the Southern Frisian Lakes." *Science of the Total Environment* 268 (1-3): 197–214.

Desilets, D., and M. Zreda. 2013. "Footprint Diameter for a Cosmic-Ray Soil Moisture Probe: Theory and Monte Carlo Simulations." *Water Resources Research* 49 (6): 3566–75.

Desilets, D., M. Zreda, and T. P. A. Ferré. 2010. "Nature's Neutron Probe: Land Surface Hydrology at an Elusive Scale with Cosmic Rays." *Water Resources Research* 46 (11): 1–7. doi:10.1029/2009WR008726.

Dharssi, I., K. Bovis, B. Macpherson, and C. Jones. 2011. "Operational Assimilation of ASCAT Surface Soil Wetness at the Met Office." *Hydrology and Earth System Sciences Discussions* 8 (2): 4313–54.

Dietz, A. J., C. Kuenzer, U. Gessner, and S. Dech. 2011. "Remote Sensing of Snow: A Review of Available Methods." *International Journal of Remote Sensing* 33 (13): 4094–134.

Dobson, M. C., F. T. Ulaby, M. T. Hallikainen, and M. A. El-Rayes. 1985. "Microwave Dielectric Behavior of Wet Soil: Part II; Dielectric Mixing Models." *IEEE Transactions on Geoscience and Remote Sensing* GE-23 (1): 35–46.

Donohue, R. J., T. R. McVicar, and M. L. Roderick. 2010. "Assessing the Ability of Potential Evaporation Formulations to Capture the Dynamics in Evaporative Demand within a Changing Climate." *Journal of Hydrology* 386 (1-4): 186–97.

Dorigo, W. A., K. Scipal, R. M. Parinussa, Y. Y. Liu, W. Wagner, R. A. M. de Jeu, and V. Naeimi. 2010. "Error Characterisation of Global Active and Passive Microwave Soil Moisture Datasets." *Hydrology and Earth System Sciences* 14 (12): 2605–16.

Dorigo, W. A., A. Xaver, M. Vreugdenhil, A. Gruber, A. Hegyiová, A. D. Sanchis-Dufau, and M. Drusch. 2013. "Global Automated Quality Control of In Situ Soil Moisture Data from the International Soil Moisture Network." *Vadose Zone Journal* 12 (3). doi: 10.2136/vzj2012.0097.

Draper, C., J.-F. Mahfouf, J.-C. Calvet, E. Martin, and W. Wagner. 2011. "Assimilation of ASCAT Near-Surface Soil Moisture into the SIM Hydrological Model over France." *Hydrology and Earth System Sciences* 15 (12): 3829–41.

Draper, C. S., R. H. Reichle, G. J. M. De Lannoy, and Q. Liu. 2012. "Assimilation of Passive and Active Microwave Soil Moisture Retrievals." *Geophysical Research Letters* 39 (4). doi:10.1029/2011GL050655.

Draper, C. S., J. P. Walker, P. J. Steinle, R. A. M. de Jeu, and T. R. H. Holmes. 2009. "An Evaluation of AMSR–E Derived Soil Moisture over Australia." *Remote Sensing of Environment* 113 (4): 703–10.

Ebert, E. E., J. E. Janowiak, and C. Kidd. 2007. "Comparison of Near-Real-Time Precipitation Estimates from Satellite Observations and Numerical Models." *Bulletin of the American Meteorological Society* 88 (1): 47–64.

Emelyanova, I. V., T. R. McVicar, T. G. Van Niel, L. T. Li, and A. I. J. M. van Dijk. 2012. "On Blending Landsat-MODIS Surface Reflectances in Two Landscapes with Contrasting Spectral, Spatial, and Temporal Dynamics." WIRADA Project 3.4: Technical Report, CSIRO Water for a Healthy Country Flagship, Australia. https://publications.csiro.au/rpr/download?pid=csiro:EP128838&dsid=DS1.

Emelyanova, I. V., T. G. Van Niel, and T. R. McVicar. n.d. "Clarifying Terminology in Multi-Sensor Data Fusion Literature: A Taxonomic Approach." CSIRO, Canberra.

Entekhabi, D., E. G. Njoku, P. O'Neill, K. H. Kellogg, W. T. Crow, W. N. Edelstein, J. K. Entin, S. D. Goodman, T. J. Jackson, J. Johnson, J. Kimball, J. R. Piepmeier, R. D. Koster, N. Martin, K. C. McDonald, M. Moghaddam, S. Moran, R. Reichle, J.-C. Shi, M. W. Spencer, S. W. Thurman, T. Leung, and J. Van Zyl. 2010. "The Soil Moisture Active Passive (SMAP) Mission." *Proceedings of the IEEE* 98 (5): 704–16.

Evans, T. L., M. P. F. Costa, K. H. Telmer, and T. S. F Silva. 2010. "Using ALOS/PALSAR and RADARSAT-2 to Map Land Cover and Seasonal Inundation in the Brazilian Pantanal." *IEEE Journal of Selected Topics in Applied Earth Observations and Remote Sensing* 3 (4): 560–75.

FAO (Food and Agriculture Organization). 2013. AQUASTAT Database. Rome: Food and Agriculture Organization of the United Nations (FAO).

Franz, T. E., M. Zreda, R. Rosolem, B. K. Hornbuckle, S. L. Irvin, H. Adams, T. E. Kolb, C. Zweck, and W. J. Shuttleworth. 2013. "Ecosystem-Scale Measurements of Biomass Water Using Cosmic Ray Neutrons." *Geophysical Research Letters* 40 (15): 3929–33.

Frei, A., M. Tedesco, S. Lee, J. Foster, D. K. Hall, R. Kelly, and D. A. Robinson. 2012. "A Review of Global Satellite-Derived Snow Products." *Advances in Space Research* 50 (8): 1007–29.

Friedl, M. A. 1995. "Modeling Land Surface Fluxes Using a Sparse Canopy Model and Radiometric Surface Temperature Measurements." *Journal of Geophysical Research* 100 (D12): 25435–46.

Friedl, M. A., D. Sulla-Menashe, B. Tan, A. Schneider, N. Ramankutty, A. Sibley, and X. Huang. 2010. "MODIS Collection 5 Global Land Cover: Algorithm Refinements and Characterization of New Datasets." *Remote Sensing of Environment* 114 (1): 168–82.

Galloway, D., and J. Hoffmann. 2007. "The Application of Satellite Differential SAR Interferometry-Derived Ground Displacements in Hydrogeology." *Hydrogeology Journal* 15 (1): 133–54.

Gebremichael, M., and F. Hossain, eds. 2010. *Satellite Rainfall Applications for Surface Hydrology*. Dordrecht: Springer Science+Business Media.

GEO (Group on Earth Observations). 2011. "Progress Report on GEO Inland and Near-Coastal Water Quality Remote Sensing Working Group." https://www.earthobservations.org/documents/sbas/wa/201101_coastal_and_inland_wq_remote_sensing_wg_progress_report.pdf

Gleeson, T., Y. Wada, M. F. P. Bierkens, and L. P. H. van Beek. 2012. "Water Balance of Global Aquifers Revealed by Groundwater Footprint." *Nature* 488 (7410): 197–200.

Goetz, S. J., A. Baccini, N. T. Laporte, T. Johns, W. Walker, J. Kellndorfer, R. A. Houghton, and M. Sun. 2009. "Mapping and Monitoring Carbon Stocks with Satellite Observations: A Comparison of Methods." *Carbon Balance and Management* 4 (1): 1–7.

Gong, P., J. Wang, L. Yu, Y. Zhao, Y. Zhao, L. Liang, Z. Niu, X. Huang, H. Fu, S. Liu, C. Li, X. Li, W. Fu, C. Liu, Y. Xu, X. Wang, Q. Cheng, L. Hu, W. Yao, H. Zhang, P. Zhu, Z. Zhao, H. Zhang, Y. Zheng, L. Ji, Y. Zhang, H. Chen, A. Yan, J. Guo, L. Yu, L. Wang, X. Liu, T. Shi, M. Zhu, Y. Chen, G. Yang, P. Tang, B. Xu, C. Giri, N. Clinton, Z. Zhu, J. Chen, and J. Chen. 2012. "Finer Resolution Observation and Monitoring of Global Land Cover: First Mapping Results with Landsat TM and ETM+ Data." *International Journal of Remote Sensing* 34 (7-7): 2607–54.

Gons, H. J. 1999. "Optical Teledetection of Chlorophyll A in Turbid Inland Waters." *Environmental Science and Technology* 33 (7): 1127–32.

Gourley, J. J., Y. Hong, Z. L. Flamig, L. Li, and J. Wang. 2010. "Intercomparison of Rainfall Estimates from Radar, Satellite, Gauge, and Combinations for a Season of Record Rainfall." *Journal of Applied Meteorology and Climatology* 49 (3): 437–52.

Guerschman, J. P., M. J. Hill, L. J. Renzullo, D. J. Barrett, A. S. Marks, and E. J. Botha. 2009a. "Estimating Fractional Cover of Photosynthetic Vegetation, Non-Photosynthetic Vegetation, and Bare Soil in the Australian Tropical Savanna Region Upscaling the EO-1 Hyperion and MODIS Sensors." *Remote Sensing of Environment* 113 (5): 928–45.

Guerschman, J. P., A. I. J. M. Van Dijk, G. Mattersdorf, J. Beringer, L. B. Hutley, R. Leuning, R. C. Pipunic, and B. S. Sherman. 2009b. "Scaling of Potential Evapotranspiration with MODIS Data Reproduces Flux Observations and Catchment Water Balance Observations across Australia." *Journal of Hydrology* 369 (1-2): 107–19.

Guerschman, J. P., G. Warren, G. Byrne, L. Lymburner, N. Mueller, and A. I. J. M. Van Dijk. 2011. *MODIS-Based Standing Water Detection for Flood and Large Reservoir Mapping: Algorithm Development and Applications for the Australian Continent.* Canberra: CSIRO.

Gumma, M. K., P. S. Thenkabail, and A. Nelson. 2011. "Mapping Irrigated Areas Using MODIS 250 Meter Time-Series Data: A Study on Krishna River Basin (India)." *Water* 3 (1): 113–31.

Güntner, A. 2008. "Improvement of Global Hydrological Models Using GRACE Data." *Surveys in Geophysics* 29 (4-5): 375–97.

Hall, D. K., G. A. Riggs, J. L. Foster, and S.V. Kumar. 2010. "Development and Evaluation of a Cloud-Gap-Filled MODIS Daily Snow-Cover Product." *Remote Sensing of Environment* 114 (3): 496–503.

Hall, D. K., G. A. Riggs, V. V. Salomonson, N. E. DiGirolamo, and K. J. Bayr. 2002. "MODIS Snow-Cover Products." *Remote Sensing of Environment* 83 (1-2): 181–94.

Hansen, M. C., R. S. DeFries, J. R. G. Townshend, and R. Sohlberg. 2000. "Global Land Cover Classification at 1 Km Spatial Resolution Using a Classification Tree Approach." *International Journal of Remote Sensing* 21 (6-7): 1331–64.

Härmä, P., J. Vepsalainen, T. Hannonen, T. Pyhalahti, J. Kamari, K. Kallio, K. Eloheimo, and S. Koponen. 2001. "Detection of Water Quality Using Simulated Satellite Data and Semi-Empirical Algorithms in Finland." *Science of the Total Environment* 268 (1-3): 107–21.

Helfrich, S. R., D. McNamara, B. H. Ramsay, T. Baldwin, and T. Kasheta. 2007. "Enhancements to, and Forthcoming Developments in, the Interactive Multisensor Snow and Ice Mapping System (IMS)." *Hydrological Processes* 21 (12): 1576–86.

Hess, L. 2003. "Dual-Season Mapping of Wetland Inundation and Vegetation for the Central Amazon Basin." *Remote Sensing of Environment* 87 (4): 404–28.

Hestir, E. L., S. Khanna, M. E. Andrew, M. J. Santos, J. H. Viers, J. A. Greenberg, S. S. Rajapakse, and S. L. Ustin. 2008. "Identification of Invasive Vegetation Using Hyperspectral Remote Sensing in the California Delta Ecosystem." *Remote Sensing of Environment* 112 (11): 4034–47. doi:10.1016/j.rsc.2008.01.022.

Hill, M. J., U. Senarath, A. Lee, M. Zeppel, J. M. Nightingale, R. J. Williams, and T. R. McVicar. 2006. "Assessment of the MODIS LAI Product for Australian Ecosystems." *Remote Sensing of Environment* 101 (4): 495–518.

Hong, Y., R. F. Adler, F. Hossain, S. Curtis, and G. J. Huffman. 2007. "A First Approach to Global Runoff Simulation Using Satellite Rainfall Estimation." *Water Resources Research* 43 (8): W08502. doi:10.1029/2006WR005739.

Hong, Y., K.-L. Hsu, S. Sorooshian, and X. Gao. 2004. "Precipitation Estimation from Remotely Sensed Imagery Using an Artificial Neural Network Cloud Classification System." *Journal of Applied Meteorology* 43 (12): 1834–52.

Hou, A.Y., R. K. Kakar, S. Neeck, A. A. Azarbarzin, C. D. Kummerow, M. Kojima, R. Oki, K. Nakamura, and T. Iguchi. 2013. "The Global Precipitation Measurement (GPM) Mission." *Bulletin of the American Meteorological Society* 95 (5): 701–22.

Houborg, R., A. Cescatti, M. Migliavacca, and W. P. Kustas. 2013. "Satellite Retrievals of Leaf Chlorophyll and Photosynthetic Capacity for Improved Modeling of GPP." *Agricultural and Forest Meteorology* 177 (1): 10–23.

Hsu, K. L., X. G. Gao, S. Sorooshian, and H. V. Gupta. 1997. "Precipitation Estimation from Remotely Sensed Information Using Artificial Neural Networks." *Journal of Applied Meteorology* 36 (9): 1176–90.

Huete, A., K. Didan, T. Miura, E. P. Rodriguez, X. Gao, and L. G. Ferreira. 2002. "Overview of the Radiometric and Biophysical Performance of the MODIS Vegetation Indices." *Remote Sensing of Environment* 83 (1-2): 195–213.

Huffman, G. J., R. F. Adler, P. Arkin, A. Chang, R. Ferraro, A. Gruber, and U. Schneider. 1997. "The Global Precipitation Climatology Project (GPCP) Combined Precipitation Dataset." *Bulletin of the American Meteorological Society* 78 (1): 5–20.

Huffman, G. J., R. F. Adler, D. T. Bolvin, G. J. Gu, E. J. Nelkin, K. P. Bowman, Y. Hong, E. F. Stocker, and D. B. Wolff. 2007. "The TRMM Multisatellite Precipitation Analysis (TMPA): Quasi-Global, Multiyear, Combined-Sensor Precipitation Estimates at Fine Scales." *Journal of Hydrometeorology* 8 (1): 38–55.

Huffman, G. J., D. T. Bolvin, D. Braithwaite, K. Hsu, R. Joyce, and P. Xie. 2013. *NASA Global Precipitation Measurement (GPM) Integrated Multi-SatellitE Retrievals for GPM (IMERG)*. Algorithm Theoretical Basis Document, Version 4.1.

Hunter, P. D., D. J. Gilvear, A. N. Tyler, N. J. Willby, and A. Kelly. 2010. "Mapping Macrophytic Vegetation in Shallow Lakes Using the Compact Airborne Spectrographic Imager (CASI)." *Aquatic Conservation: Marine and Freshwater Ecosystems* 20 (7): 717–27.

Ichii, K., H. Hashimoto, M. A. White, C. Potter, L. R. Hutyra, A. R. Huete, R. B. Myneni, and R. R. Nemani. 2006. "Constraining Rooting Depths in Tropical Rainforests Using Satellite Data and Ecosystem Modeling for Accurate Simulation of Gross Primary Production Seasonality." *Global Change Biology* 13 (1): 67–77.

Jackson, T. J., and T. J. Schmugge. 1989. "Passive Microwave Remote Sensing System for Soil Moisture: Some Supporting Research." *IEEE Transactions on Geoscience and Remote Sensing* 27 (2): 225–35.

Jasechko, S., Z. D. Sharp, J. J. Gibson, S, J. Birks, Y. Yi, and P. J. Fawcett. 2013. "Terrestrial Water Fluxes Dominated by Transpiration." *Nature* 496 (7445): 347–50.

Jones, L. A., and J. S. Kimball. 2012. "Daily Global Land Surface Parameters Derived from AMSR-E." National Aeronautics and Space Administration,

Distributed Active Archive Center, National Snow and Ice Data Center, Boulder, CO.

Joyce, R. J., J. E. Janowiak, P. A. Arkin, and P. P. Xie. 2004. "CMORPH: A Method That Produces Global Precipitation Estimates from Passive Microwave and Infrared Data at High Spatial and Temporal Resolution." *Journal of Hydrometeorology* 5 (3): 487–503.

Jung, M., M. Reichstein, P. Ciais, S. I. Seneviratne, J. Sheffield, M. L. Goulden, G. Bonan, A. Cescatti, J. Chen, R. de Jeu, A. J. Dolman, W. Eugster, D. Gerten, D. Gianelle, N. Gobron, J. Heinke, J. Kimball, B. E. Law, L. Montagnani, Q. Mu, B. Mueller, K. Oleson, D. Papale, A. D. Richardson, O. Roupsard, S. Running, E. Tomelleri, N. Viovy, U. Weber, C. Williams, E. Wood, S. Zaehle, and K. Zhang. 2010. "Recent Decline in the Global Land Evapotranspiration Trend Due to Limited Moisture Supply." *Nature* 467 (7318): 951–54.

Jupp, D. L. B., G. L. Tian, T. R. McVicar, Y. Qin, and F. Li. 1998. *Soil Moisture and Drought Monitoring Using Remote Sensing I: Theoretical Background and Methods.* Technical Report 95. Canberra: CSIRO Earth Observation Centre.

Kalma, J. D., T. R. McVicar, and M. F. McCabe. 2008. "Estimating Land Surface Evaporation: A Review of Methods Using Remotely Sensed Surface Temperature Data." *Surveys in Geophysics* 29 (4): 421–69.

Kasischke, E. S., and L. P. Bruhwiler. 2003. "Emissions of Carbon Dioxide, Carbon Monoxide, and Methane from Boreal Forest Fires in 1998." *Journal of Geophysical Research* 107 (D1): FFR 2-1–FFR 2-14.

Kelliher, F. M., R. Leuning, M. R. Raupach, and E. D. Schulze. 1995. "Maximum Conductances for Evaporation from Global Vegetation Types." *Agricultural and Forest Meteorology* 73 (1-2): 1–16.

Kellndorfer, J., W. Walker, L. Pierce, C. Dobson, J. A. Fites, C. Hunsaker, J. Vona, and M. Clutter. 2004. "Vegetation Height Estimation from Shuttle Radar Topography Mission and National Elevation Datasets." *Remote Sensing of Environment* 93 (3): 339–58.

Kelly, R. E., A. T. Chang, L. Tsang, and J. L. Foster. 2003. "A Prototype AMSR-E Global Snow Area and Snow Depth Algorithm." *IEEE Transactions on Geoscience and Remote Sensing* 41 (2): 230–42.

Kerr, Y. H., S. Member, P. Waldteufel, P. Richaume, J. P. Wigneron, S. Member, and S. Delwart. 2012. "The SMOS Soil Moisture Retrieval Algorithm." *IEEE Transactions on Geoscience and Remote Sensing* 50 (5): 1384–403.

Kim, Y., J. S. Kimball, K. C. McDonald, and J. Glassy. 2011. "Developing a Global Data Record of Daily Landscape Freeze/Thaw Status Using Satellite Passive Microwave Remote Sensing." *Geoscience and Remote Sensing* 49 (3): 949–60. doi:10.1109/TGRS.2010.2070515.

Kimball, J. S., K. C. McDonald, and M. Zhao. 2006. "Spring Thaw and Its Effect on Terrestrial Vegetation Productivity in the Western Arctic Observed from Satellite Microwave and Optical Remote Sensing." *Earth Interactions* 10 (21): 1–22.

King, E. A., T. G. Van Niel, A. I. J. M. Van Dijk, Z. Wang, M. J. Paget, T. Raupach, J. P. Guerschman, V. Haverd, T. R. McVicar, I. Miltenberg, M. R. Raupach, L. J. Renzullo, and Y. Zhang. 2011. *Actual Evapotranspiration Estimates for Australia: Intercomparison and Evaluation.* Water for a Healthy Country National Research Flagship. Canberra: Commonwealth Scientific and Industrial Research Organisation.

Kirk, J. T. O. 2011. *Light and Photosynthesis in Aquatic Ecosystems.* 3d ed. Cambridge, U.K.: Cambridge University Press.

Klemas, V. 2013. "Remote Sensing of Coastal Wetland Biomass: An Overview." *Journal of Coastal Research* 29 (5): 1016–28.

Koike, T. 2013. "Level 2 (Soil Moisture)." In *Descriptions of GCOM-W1 AMSR2 Level 1R and Level 2 Algorithms*, ch. 8. Japan Aerospace Exploration Agency Earth Observation Research Center. http://suzaku.eorc.jaxa.jp/GCOM_W/data/doc/NDX-120015A.pdf.

Krajewski, W. F. 1987. "Cokriging Radar-Rainfall and Rain Gauge Data." *Journal of Geophysical Research* 92 (D8): 9571–80.

Kubota, T., S. Shige, H. Hashizume, K. Aonashi, N. Takahashi, S. Seto, H. Masafumi, N. Yukari, T. U. Takayabu, N. Katsuhiro, I. Koyura, K. Misako, and O. Ken'ichi. 2007. "Global Precipitation Map Using Satellite-Borne Microwave Radiometers by the GSMaP Project: Production and Validation." *IEEE Transactions on Geoscience and Remote Sensing* 45 (7): 2259–75.

Kummerow, C., Y. Hong, W. S. Olson, S. Yang, R. F. Adler, J. McCollum, R. Ferraro, G. Petty, D. B. Shin, and T. T. Wilheit. 2001. "The Evolution of the Goddard Profiling Algorithm (GPROF) for Rainfall Estimation from Passive Microwave Sensors." *Journal of Applied Meteorology* 40 (11): 1801–20.

Lambin, E. F., and D. Ehrlich. 1996. "The Surface Temperature-Vegetation Index Space for Land Cover and Land-Cover Change Analysis." *International Journal of Remote Sensing* 17 (3): 463–87.

Leblanc, M. J., P. Tregoning, G. Ramillien, S. O. Tweed, and A. Fakes. 2009. "Basin-Scale, Integrated Observations of the Early 21st Century Multiyear Drought in Southeast Australia." *Water Resources Research* 45 (4): W04408.

Lee, K., L. Carder, C. D. Mobley, R. G. Steward, and J. S. Patch. 1998. "Hyperspectral Remote Sensing for Shallow Waters: I. A Semi-Analytical Model." *Applied Optics* 37 (27): 6329–38.

Leroux, D. J., Y. H. Kerr, P. Richaume, and R. Fieuzal. 2013. "Spatial Distribution and Possible Sources of SMOS Errors at the Global Scale." *Remote Sensing of Environment* 133 (June 15): 240–50. doi:10.1016/j.rse.2013.02.017.

Leuning, R., E. van Gorsel, W. J. Massman, and P. R. Isaac. 2012. "Reflections on the Surface Energy Imbalance Problem." *Agricultural and Forest Meteorology* 56 (April 15): 65–74.

Leuning, R., Y. Q. Zhang, A. Rajaud, H. Cleugh, and K. Tu. 2008. "A Simple Surface Conductance Model to Estimate Regional Evaporation Using MODIS Leaf Area Index and the Penman-Monteith Equation." *Water Resources Research* 44 (10): W10419.

Li, L., P. W. Gaiser, B.-C. Gao, R. M. Bevilacqua, T. J. Jackson, E. G. Njoku, C. Rudiger, J.-C. Calvet, and R. Bindlish. 2010. "WindSat Global Soil Moisture Retrieval and Validation." *IEEE Transactions on Geoscience and Remote Sensing* 48 (5): 2224–41. doi: 10.1109/TGRS.2009.2037749.

Liu, X., Y. Zhang, Y. Yin, M. Wang, and B. Qin. 2013. "Wind and Submerged Aquatic Vegetation Influence Bio-Optical Properties in Large Shallow Lake Taihu, China." *Journal of Geophysical Research: Biogeosciences* 118 (2): 713–27. doi:10.1002/jgrg.20054.

Liu, Y. Y., W. A. Dorigo, R. M. Parinussa, R. A. M. de Jeu, W. Wagner, M. F. McCabe, and A. I. J. M. van Dijk. 2012. "Trend-Preserving Blending of Passive and Active Microwave Soil Moisture Retrievals." *Remote Sensing of Environment* 123 (August): 280–97.

Liu, Y. Y., A. I. J. M. van Dijk, R. A. M. de Jeu, and T. R. H. Holmes. 2009. "An Analysis of Spatiotemporal Variations of Soil and Vegetation Moisture from a 29-Year Satellite-Derived Dataset over Mainland Australia." *Water Resources Research* 45 (7): 1–12.

Lucas, R., J. Armston, R. Fairfax, R. Fensham, A. Accad, J. Carreiras, J. Kelley, P. Bunting, D. Clewley, S. Bray, D. Metcalfe, J. Dwyer, M. Bowen, T. Eyre, M. Laidlaw, and M. Shimada. 2010. "An Evaluation of the ALOS PALSAR L-Band Backscatter—Above Ground Biomass Relationship Queensland, Australia: Impacts of Surface Moisture Condition and Vegetation Structure." *IEEE Journal of Selected Topics in Applied Earth Observations and Remote Sensing* 3 (4): 576–93.

Malthus, T. J., and D. G. George. 1997. "Airborne Remote Sensing of Macrophytes in Cefni Reservoir, Anglesey, UK." *Aquatic Botany* 58 (3-4): 317–32.

Martínez, J. M., and T. Le Toan. 2007. "Mapping of Flood Dynamics and Spatial Distribution of Vegetation in the Amazon Floodplain Using Multitemporal SAR Data." *Remote Sensing of Environment* 108 (3): 209–23.

Matthews, M. W. 2011. "A Current Review of Empirical Procedures of Remote Sensing in Inland and Near-Coastal Transitional Waters." *International Journal of Remote Sensing* 32 (21): 6855–99.

Mayaux, P., G. F. Rauste, Y. M. Simard, and S. Saatchi. 2002. "Large-Scale Vegetation Maps Derived from the Combined L-Band GRFM and C-Band CAMP Wide Area Radar Mosaics of Central Africa." *International Journal of Remote Sensing* 23 (7): 1261–82.

McDonald, K. C., J. S. Kimball, and Y. Kim. 2010. "The Soil Moisture Active/Passive (SMAP) Freeze/Thaw Product: Providing a Crucial Linkage between Earth's Water and Carbon Cycles." In *AGU Fall Meeting Abstracts,* vol. 1, 1219. Washington, DC: American Geophysical Union.

McMahon, T. A., M. C. Peel, L. Lowe, R. Srikanthan, and T. R. McVicar. 2013. "Estimating Actual, Potential, Reference Crop, and Pan Evaporation Using Standard Meteorological Data: A Pragmatic Synthesis." *Hydrology and Earth System Sciences* 17 (April 10): 1331–63.

McVicar, T. R., and D. L. B. Jupp. 2002. "Using Covariates to Spatially Interpolate Moisture Availability in the Murray-Darling Basin: A Novel Use of Remotely Sensed Data." *Remote Sensing of Environment* 79 (2-3): 199–212.

McVicar, T. R., M. L. Roderick, R. J. Donohue, L. T. Li, T. G. Van Niel, A. Thomas, J. Grieser, D. Jhajharia, Y. Himri, N. M. Mahowald, A. V. Mescherskaya, A. C. Kruger, S. Rehman, and Y. Dinpashoh. 2012a. "Global Review and Synthesis of Trends in Observed Terrestrial Near-Surface Wind Speeds: Implications for Evaporation." *Journal of Hydrology* 416-417 (January 24): 182–205.

McVicar, T. R., M. L. Roderick, R. J. Donohue, and T. G. Van Niel. 2012b. "Less Bluster Ahead? Ecohydrological Implications of Global Trends of Terrestrial Near-Surface Wind Speeds." *Ecohydrology* 5 (4): 381–88.

Meerhoff, M., N. Mazzeo, B. Moss, and L. Rodríguez-Gallego. 2003. "The Structuring Role of Free-Floating Versus Submerged Plants in a Subtropical Shallow Lake." *Aquatic Ecology* 37 (4): 377–91. doi:10.1023/B:AECO.0000007041.57843.0b.

Meijerink, A. M. J., D. Bannert, O. Batelaan, M. W. Lubczyński, and T. Pointet. 2007. *Remote Sensing Applications to Groundwater.* IHP-VI Series on Groundwater 16. Paris: UNESCO.

Menenti, M., and B. J. Choudhury. 1993. "Parameterization of Land Surface Evaporation by Means of Location Dependent Potential Evapora-transpiration and Surface Temperature Range." In *Exchange Processes at the Land Surface for a Range of Space and Time Scales,* edited by H.-J. Bolle, R. A. Feddes, and J. D. Kalma, 561–68. Yokohama: International Association of Hydrological Sciences.

Mertes, L. A. K., D. L. Daniel, J. M. Melack, B. Nelson, L. A. Martinelli, and B. R. Forsberg. 1995. "Spatial Patterns of Hydrology, Geomorphology, and Vegetation on the Floodplain of the Amazon River in Brazil from a Remote Sensing Perspective." *Geomorphology* 13 (1-4): 215–32.

Miralles, D. G., J. H. Gash, T. R. H. Holmes, R. A. M. de Jeu, and A. J. Dolman. 2010. "Global Canopy Interception from Satellite Observations." *Journal of Geophysical Research: Atmospheres* 115 (D16122): 8.

Mitra, A. K., A. K. Bohra, M. N. Rajeevan, and T. N. Krishnamurti. 2009. "Daily Indian Precipitation Analysis Formed from a Merge of Rain-Gauge Data with the TRMM TMPA Satellite-Derived Rainfall Estimates." *Journal of the Meteorological Society of Japan* 87A: 265–79.

Monteith, J. L. 1965. "Evaporation and Environment." *Symposia of the Society for Experimental Biology* 19 (2): 205–34.

——. 1972. "Solar Radiation and Productivity in Tropical Ecosystems." *Journal of Applied Ecology* 9 (3): 747–66.

——. 1981. "Evaporation and Surface Temperature." *Quarterly Journal of the Royal Meteorological Society* 107 (451): 1–27.

Morisette, J. T., F. Baret, J. L. Privette, R. B. Myneni, J. E. Nickeson, S. Garrigues, N. V. Shabanov, M. Weiss, R. A. Fernandes, S. G. Leblanc, M. Kalacska, G. A. Sanchez-Azofeifa, M. Chubey, B. Rivard, P. Stenberg, M. Rautiainen, P. Voipio, T. Manninen, A. N. Pilant, T. E. Lewis, J. S. Iiames, R. Colombo, M. Meroni, L. Busetto, W. B. Cohen, D. P. Turner, E. D. Warner, G. W. Petersen, G. Seufert, and R. Cook. 2006. "Validation of Global Moderate-Resolution LAI Products: A Framework Proposed within the CEOS Land Product Validation Subgroup." *IEEE Transactions on Geoscience and Remote Sensing* 44 (7): 1804–17.

Mu, Q., M. Zhao, J. S. Kimball, N. G. McDowell, and S. W. Running. 2012. "A Remotely Sensed Global Terrestrial Drought Severity Index." *Bulletin of the American Meteorological Society* 94 (1): 83–98.

Mu, Q., M. Zhao, and S. W. Running. 2011. "Improvements to a MODIS Global Terrestrial Evapotranspiration Algorithm." *Remote Sensing of Environment* 115 (8): 1781–800.

Nagler, P. L., E. P. Glenn, H. Kim, W. Emmerich, R. L. Scott, T. E. Huxman, and A. R. Huete. 2007. "Relationship between Evapotranspiration and Precipitation Pulses in a Semiarid Rangeland Estimated by Moisture Flux Towers and MODIS Vegetation Indices." *Journal of Arid Environments* 70 (3): 443–62.

Nagler, P., K. Morino, R. S. Murray, J. Osterberg, and E. Glenn. 2009. "An Empirical Algorithm for Estimating Agricultural and Riparian Evapotranspiration Using MODIS Enhanced Vegetation Index and Ground Measurements of ET. I. Description of Method." *Remote Sensing* 1 (4): 1273–97.

Njoku, E. G., T. L. Jackson, V. Lakshmi, T. Chan, and S. V. Nghiem. 2003. "Soil Moisture Retrieval from AMSR-E." *IEEE Transactions on Geoscience and Remote Sensing* 41 (2): 215–29.

Norman, J. M., M. C. Anderson, W. P. Kustas, A. N. French, J. Mecikalski, R. Torn, G. R. Diak, T. J. Schmugge, and B. C. W. Tanner. 2003. "Remote Sensing of Surface Energy Fluxes at 101-M Pixel Resolutions." *Water Resources Research* 39 (8): 1221.

Ochsner, T. E., M. H. Cosh, R. H. Cuenca, W. A. Dorigo, C. S. Draper, Y. Hagimoto, Y. H. Kerr, K. M. Larson, Eni G. Njoku, E. E. Small, and M. Zreda. 2013. "State of the Art in Large-Scale Soil Moisture Monitoring." *Soil Science Society of America Journal* 77 (6): 1888–919. doi:10.2136/sssaj2013.03.0093.

Odermatt, D., A. Gitelson, V. E. Brando, and M. Schaepman. 2012. "Review of Constituent Retrieval in Optically Deep and Complex Waters from Satellite Imagery." *Remote Sensing of Environment* 118 (3): 116–26.

Ol'dekop, E. M. 1911. "On Evaporation from the Surface of River Basins." Transactions on Meteorological Observations 4.

Olmanson, L. G., M. E. Bauer, and P. L. Brezonik. 2008. "A 20-Year Landsat Water Clarity Census of Minnesota's 10,000 Lakes." *Remote Sensing of Environment* 112 (11): 4086–97. doi:10.1016/j.rse.2007.12.013.

Olmanson, L. G., P. L. Brezonik, and M. E. Bauer. 2011. "Evaluation of Medium- to Low-Resolution Satellite Imagery for Regional Lake Water Quality Assessments." *Water Resources Research* 47 (9). doi: 10.1029/2011WR011005.

Ordoyne, C., and M. A. Friedl. 2008. "Using MODIS Data to Characterize Seasonal Inundation Patterns in the Florida Everglades." *Remote Sensing of Environment* 112 (11): 4107–19.

OSCAR (Observing Systems Capability Analysis and Review Tool) (database). World Meteorological Organization, Geneva, Switzerland. http://www.wmo-sat.info/oscar/.

Overton, I. C. 2005. "Modelling Floodplain Inundation on a Regulated River: Integrating GIS, Remote Sensing and Hydrological Models." *River Research and Applications* 21 (9): 991–1001.

Overton, I. C., T. M. Doody, D. Pollock, J. P. Guerschman, G. Warren, W. Jin, Y. Chen, and B. Wurcker. 2011. *The Murray–Darling Basin Floodplain Inundation Model (MDB-FIM)*. Technical Report. Canberra: Commonwealth Scientific and Industrial Research Organisation.

Owe, M., R. A. M. de Jeu, and T. Holmes. 2008. "Multisensor Historical Climatology of Satellite-Derived Global Land Surface Moisture." *Journal of Geophysical Research* 113 (F1): F01002.

Ozdogan, M., Y. Yang, G. Allez, and C. Cervantes. 2010. "Remote Sensing of Irrigated Agriculture: Opportunities and Challenges." *Remote Sensing* 2 (9): 2274–304.

Painter, T. H., K. Rittger, C. McKenzie, P. Slaughter, R. E. Davis, and J. Dozier. 2009. "Retrieval of Subpixel Snow Covered Area, Grain Size, and Albedo from MODIS." *Remote Sensing of Environment* 113 (4): 868–79.

Pan, M., H. Li, and E. Wood. 2010. "Assessing the Skill of Satellite-Based Precipitation Estimates in Hydrological Applications." *Water Resources Research* 46 (9): W09535.

Papa, F., C. Prigent, F. Aires, C. Jimenez, W. B. Rossow, and E. Matthews. 2010. "Interannual Variability of Surface Water Extent at the Global Scale, 1993–2004." *Journal of Geophysical Research: Atmospheres* 115 (D12): L11401.

Parinussa, R. M., T. R. H. Holmes, and R. A. M. de Jeu. 2012. "Soil Moisture Retrievals from the WindSat Spaceborne Polarimetric Microwave Radiometer." *IEEE Transactions on Geoscience and Remote Sensing* 50 (7): 2683–94. doi:10.1109/TGRS.2011.2174643.

Parinussa, R. M., G. Wang, T. R. H. Holmes, Y. Y. Liu, A. J. Dolman, R. A. M. de Jeu, T. Jiang, P. Zhang, and J. Shi. 2014. "Global Surface Soil Moisture from the Microwave Radiation Imager On Board the Fengyun-3B Satellite." *International Journal of Remote Sensing* 35 (19): 7007–29. doi:10.1080/0143 1161.2014.960622.

Pauwels, V. R. N., R. Hoeben, N. E. C. Verhoest, F. P. De Troch, and P. A. Troch. 2002. "Improvement of TOPLATS-Based Discharge Predictions through Assimilation of ERS-Based Remotely Sensed Soil Moisture Values." *Hydrological Processes* 16 (5): 995–1013.

Peña-Arancibia, J. L., A. I. J. M. Van Dijk, L. J. Renzullo, and M. Mulligan. 2013. "Evaluation of Precipitation Estimation Accuracy in Reanalyses, Satellite Products, and an Ensemble Method for Regions in Australia and South and East Asia." *Journal of Hydrometeorology* 14 (4): 1323–33.

Penman, H. L. 1948. "Natural Evaporation from Open Water, Bare Soil, and Grass." *Proceedings of the Royal Society of London. Series A, Mathematical and Physical Sciences* 193 (1032): 120–45.

Pervez, M. S., and J. F. Brown. 2010. "Mapping Irrigated Lands at 250-m Scale by Merging MODIS Data and National Agricultural Statistics." *Remote Sensing* 2 (10): 2388–412.

Pipunic, R. C., J. P. Walker, A. W. Western, and C. M. Trudinger. 2013. "Assimilation of Multiple Data Types for Improved Heat Flux Prediction: A One-Dimensional Field Study." *Remote Sensing of Environment* 136 (September): 315–29.

Powell, S. J., R. A. Letcher, and B. F. W. Croke. 2008. "Modelling Floodplain Inundation for Environmental Flows: Gwydir Wetlands, Australia." *Ecological Modelling* 211 (3–4): 350–62.

Pozzi, W., J. Sheffield, R. Stefanski, D. Cripe, R. Pulwarty, J. V. Vogt, and R. Lawford. 2013. "Toward Global Drought Early Warning Capability: Expanding International Cooperation for the Development of a Framework for Monitoring and Forecasting." *Bulletin of the American Meteorological Society* 94 (6): 776–85.

Proctor, C., J. H. He, and V. Robinson. 2013. "Texture Augmented Detection of Macrophyte Species Using Decision Trees." *ISPRS Journal of Photogrammetry and Remote Sensing* 80 (June): 10–20.

Pulliainen, J. 2006. "Mapping of Snow Water Equivalent and Snow Depth in Boreal and Sub-Arctic Zones by Assimilating Space-Borne Microwave Radiometer Data and Ground-Based Observations." *Remote Sensing of Environment* 101 (2): 257–69.

Ramillien, G., J. S. Famiglietti, and J. Wahr. 2008. "Detection of Continental Hydrology and Glaciology Signals from GRACE: A Review." *Surveys in Geophysics* 29 (4): 361–74.

Ramsay, B. H. 1998. "The Interactive Multisensor Snow and Ice Mapping System." *Hydrological Processes* 12 (10-11): 1537–46.

Rango, A., and A. T. Anderson. 1974. "Flood Hazard Studies in the Mississippi River Basin Using Remote Sensing." *Water Resources Bulletin* 10 (5): 1060–81.

Rango, A., and V. V. Salomonson. 1974. "Regional Flood Mapping from Space." *Water Resources Research* 10 (3): 473–84.

Rees, W. G. 2006. *Remote Sensing of Snow and Ice*. Boca Raton, FL: Taylor and Francis.

Reichle, R., and R. Koster. 2005. "Global Assimilation of Satellite Surface Soil Moisture Retrievals into the NASA Catchment Land Model." *Geophysical Research Letters* 32 (2): L02404.

Renzullo, L., A. Chappell, T. Raupach, P. Dyce, M. Li, and Q. Shao. 2011. *An Assessment of Blended Satellite-Gauge Precipitation Products for Australia*. Water for a Healthy Country National Research

Flagship. Canberra: Commonwealth Scientific and Industrial Research Organisation.

Renzullo, L. J., A. I. J. M. Van Dijk, J.-M. Perraud, D. Collins, B. Henderson, H. Jin, A. B. Smith, and D. L. McJannet. 2014. "Continental Satellite Soil Moisture Data Assimilation Improves Root-Zone Moisture Analysis for Water Resources Assessment." *Journal of Hydrology* 519 (D): 2747–62

Rodell, M., I. Velicogna, and J. S. Famiglietti. 2009. "Satellite-Based Estimates of Groundwater Depletion in India." *Nature* 460 (August 20): 999–1002.

Roderick, M. L., M. T. Hobbins, and G. D. Farquhar. 2009a. "Pan Evaporation Trends and the Terrestrial Water Balance. II. Energy Balance and Interpretation." *Geography Compass* 3 (2): 761–80.

—. 2009b. "Pan Evaporation Trends and the Terrestrial Water Balance. I. Principles and Observations." *Geography Compass* 3 (2): 746–60.

Rodríguez, E., and D. Estéban-Fernández. 2010. "The Surface Water and Ocean Topography Mission (SWOT): The Ka-Band Radar Interferometer (KaRIn) for Water Level Measurements at All Scales." *Proceedings of SPIE—The International Society for Optical Engineering* 7826: 782614–18.

Rodríguez-Iturbe, I., A. Porporato, F. Laio, and L. Ridolfi. 2001. "Plants in Water-Controlled Ecosystems: Active Role in Hydrologic Processes and Response to Water Stress; I. Scope and General Outline." *Advances in Water Resources* 24 (7): 695–705.

Roerink, G. J., Z. Su, and M. Menenti. 2000. "S-SEBI: A Simple Remote Sensing Algorithm to Estimate the Surface Energy Balance." *Physics and Chemistry of the Earth, Part B: Hydrology, Oceans, and Atmosphere* 25 (2): 147–57.

Rosenqvist, Å., M. Shimada, B. Chapman, L. Dutra, S. Saatchi, and O. Tanaka. 2002. "Introduction from the Guest Editors." *International Journal of Remote Sensing* 23 (7): 1215.

Rozante, J. R., D. S. Moreira, L. G. G. de Goncalves, and D. A. Vila. 2010. "Combining TRMM and Surface Observations of Precipitation: Techniques and Validation over South America." *Weather and Forecasting* 25 (3): 885–94.

Sakamoto, T., N. Van Nguyen, A. Kotera, H. Ohno, N. Ishitsuka, and M. Yokozawa. 2007. "Detecting Temporal Changes in the Extent of Annual Flooding within the Cambodia and the Vietnamese Mekong Delta from MODIS Time-Series Imagery." *Remote Sensing of Environment* 109 (3): 295–313.

Salomonson, V. V., and I. Appel. 2004. "Estimating Fractional Snow Cover from MODIS Using the Normalized Difference Snow Index." *Remote Sensing of Environment* 89 (3): 351–60.

Santos, M., L. Anderson, and S. Ustin. 2011. "Effects of Invasive Species on Plant Communities: An Example Using Submersed Aquatic Plants at the Regional Scale." *Biological Invasions* 13 (2): 443–57. doi:10.1007/s10530-010-9840-6.

Santos, M. J., E. L. Hestir, S. Khanna, and S. L. Ustin. 2012. "Image Spectroscopy and Stable Isotopes Elucidate Functional Dissimilarity between Native and Nonnative Plant Species in the Aquatic Environment." *The New Phytologist* 193 (3): 683–95. doi:10.1111/j.1469-8137.2011.03955.x.

Sapiano, M. R. P., J. E. Hanoiak, W. Shi, R. W. Higgins, and V. B. S. Silva. 2010. "Regional Evaluation through Independent Precipitation Measurements: USA." In *Satellite Rainfall Applications for Surface Hydrology*, edited by M. Gebremichael and F. Hossain, 169–204. Dordrecht: Springer Science+Business Media.

Sapiano, M. R. P., T. M. Smith, and P. A. Arkin. 2008. "A New Merged Analysis of Precipitation Utilizing Satellite and Reanalysis Data." *Journal of Geophysical Research* 113 (D22): 1–17.

Scipal, K., T. Holmes, R. A. M. de Jeu, V. Naeimi, and W. Wagner. 2008. "A Possible Solution for the Problem of Estimating the Error Structure of Global Soil Moisture Data Sets." *Geophysical Research Letters* 35 (24). DOI: 10.1029/2008GL035599.

Sellars, S., P. Nguyen, W. Chu, X. Gao, K. Hsu, and S. Sorooshian. 2013. "Computational Earth Science: Big Data Transformed into Insight." *EOS Transactions American Geophysical Union* 94 (32): 277–78.

Seneviratne, S. I., T. Corti, E. L. Davin, M. Hirschi, E. B. Jaeger, I. Lehner, B. Orlowski, and A. J. Teuling. 2010. "Investigating Soil Moisture-Climate Interactions in a Changing Climate: A Review." *Earth-Science Reviews* 99 (3-4): 125–61.

Sheffield, J., G. Goteti, and E. F. Wood. 2006. "Development of a 50-Year High-Resolution Global Dataset of Meteorological Forcings for Land Surface Modeling." *Journal of Climate* 19 (13): 3088–111.

Siebert, S., J. Burke, J. M. Faures, K. Frenken, J. Hoogeveen, P. Döll, and F. T. Portmann. 2010. "Groundwater Use for Irrigation—A Global Inventory." *Hydrology and Earth System Sciences, Discussions* 7 (3): 3977–4021.

Silva, T. F., M. F. Costa, J. Melack, and E. L. M. Novo. 2008. "Remote Sensing of Aquatic Vegetation: Theory and Applications." *Environmental Monitoring and Assessment* 140 (1-3): 131–45.

Simard, M., N. Pinto, J. B. Fisher, and A. Baccini. 2011. "Mapping Forest Canopy Height Globally with Spaceborne Lidar." *Journal of Geophysical Research* 116 (G4): 4021.

Smith, L. C., and D. E. Alsdorf. 1998. "Control on Sediment and Organic Carbon Delivery to the Arctic Ocean Revealed with Space-Borne Synthetic Aperture Radar: Ob' River, Siberia." *Geology* 26 (5): 395–98.

Smith, A. B., J. P. Walker, A. W. Western, R. I. Young, K. M. Ellett, R. C. Pipunic, R. B. Grayson, L. Siriwardena, F. H. S. Chiew, and H. Richter. 2012. "The Murrumbidgee Soil Moisture Monitoring Network Data Set." *Water Resources Research* 48 (7): 1–6. doi:10.1029/2012WR011976.

Sobrino, J. A., M. Gomez, J. C. Jimenez-Munoz, A. Olioso, and G. Chehbouni. 2005. "A Simple Algorithm to Estimate Evapotranspiration from DAIS Data: Application to the DAISEX Campaigns." *Journal of Hydrology* 315 (1-4): 117–25.

Sorooshian, S., K. L. Hsu, X. Gao, H. V. Gupta, B. Imam, and D. Braithwaite. 2000. "Evaluation of PERSIANN System Satellite-Based Estimates of Tropical Rainfall." *Bulletin of the American Meteorological Society* 81 (9): 2035–46.

Specht, R. L. 1972. "Water Use by Perennial Evergreen Plant Communities in Australia and Papua New Guinea." *Australian Journal of Botany* 20 (3): 273–99.

Srebotnjak, T., G. Carr, A. de Sherbinin, and C. Rickwood. 2012. "A Global Water Quality Index and Hot-Deck Imputation of Missing Data." *Ecological Indicators* 17 (June): 108–19.

Su, Z. 2002. "The Surface Energy Balance System (SEBS) for Estimation of Turbulent Heat Fluxes." *Hydrology and Earth System Sciences* 6 (1): 85–100.

Su, Z., P. de Rosnay, J. Wen, L. Wang, and Y. Zeng. 2013. "Evaluation of ECMWF's Soil Moisture Analyses Using Observations on the Tibetan Plateau." *Journal of Geophysical Research*: *Atmospheres* 118 (11): 5304–18.

Su, Z., J. Wen, L. Dente, R. van der Velde, L. Wang, Y. Ma, K. Yang, and Z. Hu. 2011. "The Tibetan Plateau Observatory of Plateau Scale Soil Moisture and Soil Temperature (Tibet-Obs) for Quantifying Uncertainties in Coarse Resolution Satellite and Model Products." *Hydrology and Earth System Sciences* 15 (7): 2303–316.

Syed, T. H., J. S. Famiglietti, M. Rodell, J. Chen, and C. R. Wilson. 2008. "Analysis of Terrestrial Water Storage Changes from GRACE and GLDAS." *Water Resources Research* 44 (2): W02433.

Takala, M., K. Luojus, J. Pulliainen, C. Derksen, J. Lemmetyinen, J. P. Karna, J. Koskinen, and B. Bojkov. 2011. "Estimating Northern Hemisphere Snow Water Equivalent for Climate Research through Assimilation of Space-Borne Radiometer Data and Ground-Based Measurements." *Remote Sensing of Environment* 115 (12): 3517–29.

Tapley, B. D., S. Bettadpur, J. C. Ries, P. F. Thompson, and M. M. Watkins. 2004. "GRACE Measurements of Mass Variability in the Earth System." *Science* 305 (5683): 503–05.

Taylor, C. M., R. A. A. de Jeu, F. Guichard, P. P. Harris, and W. A. Dorigo. 2012. "Afternoon Rain More Likely over Drier Soils." *Nature* 489 (7416): 423–26.

Tian, Y. Q., Q. Yu, M. J. Zimmerman, S. Flint, and M. C. Waldron. 2010. "Differentiating Aquatic Plant Communities in a Eutrophic River Using Hyperspectral and Multispectral Remote Sensing." *Freshwater Biology* 55 (8): 1658–73.

Tucker, C. J., J. E. Pinzon, M. E. Brown, D. A. Slayback, E. W. Pak, R. Mahoney, E. F. Vermote, and N. El Saleous. 2005. "An Extended AVHRR 8-Km NDVI Dataset Compatible with MODIS and SPOT Vegetation NDVI Data." *International Journal of Remote Sensing* 26 (20): 4485–98.

Tyler, A. N., E. Svab, T. Preston, M. Présing, and A. Kovács. 2006. "Remote Sensing of the Water Quality of Shallow Lakes: A Mixture Modelling Approach to Quantifying Phytoplankton in Water Characterized by High-Suspended Sediment." *International Journal of Remote Sensing* 27 (8): 152.

Ustin, S. L., D. A. Roberts, J. A. Gamon, G. P. Asner, and R. O. Green. 2004. "Using Imaging Spectroscopy to Study Ecosystem Processes and Properties." *BioScience* 54 (6): 523. doi:10.1641/0006-3568 (2004)054[0523:UISTSE]2.0.CO;2.

Vanderstukken, M., S. A. J. Declerck, E. Decaestecker, and K. Muylaert. 2014. "Long-Term Allelopathic Control of Phytoplankton by the Submerged Macrophyte Elodea Nuttallii." *Freshwater Biology* 59 (5): 930–41. doi:10.1111/fwb.12316.

Van Dijk, A. I. J. M. 2010. *The Australian Water Resources Assessment System*. Technical Report 3. Landscape Model (version 5.0) Technical Description. Water for a Healthy Country National Research Flagship. Canberra: CSIRO.

Van Dijk, A. I. J. M., and L. J. Renzullo. 2011. "Water Resource Monitoring Systems and the Role of Satellite Observations." *Hydrology and Earth System Sciences* 15: 39–55.

Van Dijk, A. I. J. M., L. J. Renzullo, Y. Wada, and P. Tregoning. 2013. "A Global Water Cycle Reanalysis (2003–2012) Reconciling Satellite Gravimetry and Altimetry Observations with a Hydrological Model Ensemble." *Hydrology and Earth System Sciences Discussions* 10: 15475–523.

Van Niel, T. G., and T. R. McVicar. 2004. "Current and Potential Uses of Optical Remote Sensing in Rice-Based Irrigation Systems: A Review." *Australian Journal of Agricultural Research* 55 (2): 155–85.

Van Niel, T. G., T. R. McVicar, M. L. Roderick, A. I. J. M. van Dijk, J. Beringer, L. B. Hutley, and

E. van Gorsel. 2012. "Upscaling Latent Heat Flux for Thermal Remote Sensing Studies: Comparison of Alternative Approaches and Correction of Bias." *Journal of Hydrology* 468-469 (October 25): 35–46.

Van Niel, T. G., T. R. McVicar, M. L. Roderick, A. I. J. M. van Dijk, L. J. Renzullo, and E. van Gorsel. 2011. "Correcting for Systematic Error in Satellite-Derived Latent Heat Flux due to Assumptions in Temporal Scaling: Assessment from Flux Tower Observations." *Journal of Hydrology* 409 (1-2): 140–48.

Verrelst, J., G. W. Geerling, K. V. Sykora, and J. G. P. W. Clevers. 2009. "Mapping of Aggregated Floodplain Plant Communities Using Image Fusion of CASI and Lidar Data." *International Journal of Applied Earth Observation and Geoinformation* 11 (1): 83–94.

Vila, D. A., L. G. G. de Gonçalves, D. L. Toll, and J. R. Rozante. 2009. "Statistical Evaluation of Combined Daily Gauge Observations and Rainfall Satellite Estimates over Continental South America." *Journal of Hydrometeorology* 10 (2): 533–43.

Wada, Y., L. P. H. van Beek, and M. F. P. Bierkens. 2012. "Nonsustainable Groundwater Sustaining Irrigation: A Global Assessment." *Water Resources Research* 48 (6): 2055.

Wada, Y., L. P. H. van Beek, C. M. van Kempen, J. W. T. M. Reckman, S. Vasak, and M. F. P. Bierkens. 2010. "Global Depletion of Groundwater Resources." *Geophysical Research Letters* 37 (20): L20402.

Wagner, W., G. Lemoine, and H. Rott. 1999. "A Method for Estimating Soil Moisture from ERS Scatterometer and Soil Data." *Remote Sensing of Environment* 70 (2): 191–207.

Wagner, W., C. Pathe, M. Doubkova, D. Sabel, A. Bartsch, S. Hasenauer, G. Blöschl, K. Scipal, J. Martínez-Fernández, and A. Löw. 2008. "Temporal Stability of Soil Moisture and Radar Backscatter Observed by the Advanced Synthetic Aperture Radar (ASAR)." *Sensors* 8 (February): 1174–97.

Wagner, W., K. Scipal, C. Pathe, D. Gerten, W. Lucht, and B. Rudolf. 2003. "Evaluation of the Agreement between the First Global Remotely Sensed Soil Moisture Data with Model and Precipitation Data." *Journal of Geophysical Research* 108 (D19): 4611.

Wang, J.-J., X. X. Lu, S. C. Liew, and Y. Zhou. 2009. "Retrieval of Suspended Sediment Concentrations in Large Turbid Rivers Using Landsat ETM+: An Example from the Yangtze River, China." *Earth Surface Processes and Landforms* 34 (8): 1082–92.

Wang, J. R., and T. J. Schmugge. 1980. "An Empirical Model for the Complex Dielectric Permittivity of Soils as a Function of Water Content." *IEEE Transactions on Geoscience and Remote Sensing* GE-18 (4): 288–95.

Wegmuller, U., and C. Werner. 1997. "Retrieval of Vegetation Parameters with SAR Interferometry." *IEEE Transactions on Geoscience and Remote Sensing* 35 (1): 18–24.

WIRADA (Water Information Research and Development Alliance). 2012. *Water Information Research and Development Alliance: Science Symposium Proceedings,* Melbourne, Australia, August 1–5, 2011. Water for a Healthy Country National Research Flagship. Canberra: CSIRO.

Wu, C., Z. Niu, Q. Tang, W. Huang, B. Rivard, and J. Feng. 2009. "Remote Estimation of Gross Primary Production in Wheat Using Chlorophyll-Related Vegetation Indices." *Agricultural and Forest Meteorology* 149 (6-7): 1015–21.

Wu, H., R. F. Adler, Y. Hong, Y. Tian, and F. Policelli. 2012. "Evaluation of Global Flood Detection Using Satellite-Based Rainfall and a Hydrologic Model." *Journal of Hydrometeorology* 13 (4): 1268–84.

Xiong, A.-Y., P.-P. Xie, J.-Y. Liang, Y. Shen, M. Chen, R. J. Joyce, J. E. Janowiak, and P. A. Arkin. 2008. "Merging Gauge Observations and Satellite Estimates of Daily Precipitation over China." In *Proceedings of the 4th Workshop of the International Precipitation Working Group (IPWG),* Beijing, China, October 13–17. Bologna: Institute of Atmospheric Sciences and Technology. http://www.isac.cnr.it/~ipwg/meetings/beijing- 2008/.

Yebra, M., A. I. J. M. Van Dijk, R. Leuning, A. R. Huete, and J. P. Guerschman. 2013. "Evaluation of Optical Remote Sensing to Estimate Actual Evapotranspiration and Canopy Conductance." *Remote Sensing of Environment* 129 (February 15): 250–61.

Yilmaz, M. T., and W. T. Crow. 2014. "Evaluation of Assumptions in Soil Moisture Triple Collocation Analysis." *Journal of Hydrometeorology* 15 (3): 1293–302. doi:10.1175/JHM-D-13-0158.1.

Zhang, K., J. S. Kimball, R. R. Nemani, and S. W. Running. 2010. "A Continuous Satellite-Derived Global Record of Land Surface Evapotranspiration from 1983 to 2006." *Water Resources Research* 46 (9): W09522.

Zhang, Y. Q., F. H. S. Chiew, L. Zhang, R. Leuning, and H. A. Cleugh. 2008. "Estimating Catchment Evaporation and Runoff Using MODIS Leaf Area Index and the Penman-Monteith Equation." *Water Resources Research* 44 (10). DOI: 10.1029/2007WR006563

Zhang, Y., R. Leuning, F. H. S. Chiew, E. Wang, L. Zhang, C. Liu, F. Sun, M. C. Peel, Y. Shen, and M. Jung. 2012. "Decadal Trends in Evaporation from Global Energy and Water Balances." *Journal of Hydrometeorology* 13 (February): 379–91.

Zhou, L., and G. Zhou. 2009. "Measurement and Modelling of Evapotranspiration over a Reed (*Phragmites australis*) Marsh in Northeast China." *Journal of Hydrology* 372 (1-4): 41–47. doi:10.1016/j.jhydrol.2009.03.033.

Zhu, W., Q. Yu, Y. Q. Tian, B. L. Becker, T. Zheng, and H. J. Carrick. 2014. "An Assessment of Remote Sensing Algorithms for Colored Dissolved Organic Matter in Complex Freshwater Environments." *Remote Sensing of Environment* 140 (January): 766–78. doi:10.1016/j.rse.2013.10.015.

Zreda, M., W. J. Shuttleworth, X. Zeng, C. Zweck, D. Desilets, T. Franz, and R. Rosolem. 2012. "COSMOS: The COsmic-Ray Soil Moisture Observing System." *Hydrology and Earth System Sciences* 16 (11): 4079–99.

Zwieback, S., K. Scipal, W. Dorigo, and W. Wagner. 2012. "Structural and Statistical Properties of the Collocation Technique for Error Characterization." *Nonlinear Processes in Geophysics* 19 (1): 69–80.

CHAPTER 7

Assessing the Characteristics of Required and Available Earth Observation Data

INTRODUCTION

For many potential applications, Earth observation (EO) data products will be immediately and obviously useful for improving water resources management (WRM) and water monitoring. Examples include using evapotranspiration (ET) to assess crop water use in irrigated regions, chlorophyll estimation to monitor water quality in water bodies that provide domestic water supply, and satellite rainfall to estimate the amount and duration of rainfall in ungauged regions.

In these examples, as in many others, careful consideration of the spatial resolution, temporal frequency, data latency, and longevity of the satellite systems is needed to select the most appropriate EO product from the often wide range of products available, taking into account the specific WRM problem to be addressed. Furthermore, there are as many, if not more, WRM issues where the application

of EO technologies and techniques is either not suitable or less apparent and needs to be augmented with hydrologic modeling or field-based metering to be useful.

This chapter provides guidelines to help project leaders to decide whether Earth observations may be useful and, if so, what the most suitable data sources to consider would be. For each water resources application area, issues related to accuracy, availability, maturity, complexity, and reliability are briefly discussed. The chapter aims to provide a simple framework to help decision makers to determine, for a given WRM issue, how EO products might best be employed to generate the required information and how to select the EO data products with the most appropriate characteristics or specifications. The focus lies on what questions to ask once it has been concluded that exploring EO options for the WRM problem at hand is worthwhile.

EO-based solutions are not always applicable. For this reason, the chapter begins by providing some precursor questions meant to clarify whether EO data products could potentially be useful. If it is decided that they could be useful, certain questions must be asked regarding the data characteristics. The chapter begins by summarizing these questions and

Figure 7.1
Guidelines for Determining Whether to Use EO Products

Note: EO = Earth observation; WRM = water resources management.

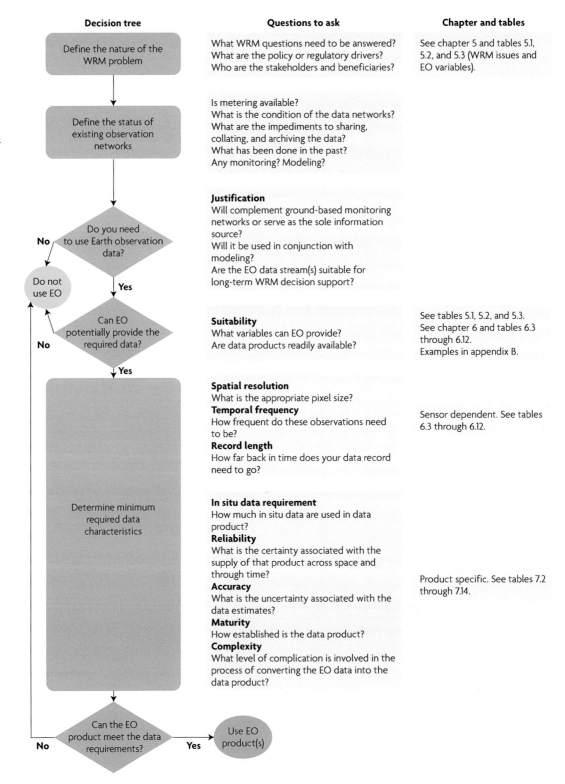

Decision tree	Questions to ask	Chapter and tables
Define the nature of the WRM problem	What WRM questions need to be answered? What are the policy or regulatory drivers? Who are the stakeholders and beneficiaries?	See chapter 5 and tables 5.1, 5.2, and 5.3 (WRM issues and EO variables).
Define the status of existing observation networks	Is metering available? What is the condition of the data networks? What are the impediments to sharing, collating, and archiving the data? What has been done in the past? Any monitoring? Modeling?	
Do you need to use Earth observation data? — No → Do not use EO / Yes	**Justification** Will complement ground-based monitoring networks or serve as the sole information source? Will it be used in conjunction with modeling? Are the EO data stream(s) suitable for long-term WRM decision support?	
Can EO potentially provide the required data? — No / Yes	**Suitability** What variables can EO provide? Are data products readily available?	See tables 5.1, 5.2, and 5.3. See chapter 6 and tables 6.3 through 6.12. Examples in appendix B.
Determine minimum required data characteristics	**Spatial resolution** What is the appropriate pixel size? **Temporal frequency** How frequent do these observations need to be? **Record length** How far back in time does your data record need to go?	Sensor dependent. See tables 6.3 through 6.12.
	In situ data requirement How much in situ data are used in data product? **Reliability** What is the certainty associated with the supply of that product across space and through time? **Accuracy** What is the uncertainty associated with the data estimates? **Maturity** How established is the data product? **Complexity** What level of complication is involved in the process of converting the EO data into the data product?	Product specific. See tables 7.2 through 7.14.
Can the EO product meet the data requirements? — No / Yes → Use EO product(s)		

then putting them in the context of their suitability for WRM decision support. It then summarizes the suitability of the EO data products described in chapter 6, guided by the questions outlined in this chapter. The information contained in this chapter and the key questions to ask are summarized in the flowchart presented in figure 7.1.

ESTABLISHING THE ROLE OF EARTH OBSERVATION TO SUPPORT WRM DECISION MAKING

What Questions Need to Be Answered?

Earth observation cannot provide an appropriate solution for all WRM problems. For this reason, box 7.1 poses some questions that can be asked to determine the nature of the WRM problem under investigation and the sources of information essential to the overall decision-making process. Points 1 and 2 of box 7.1 are discussed in greater detail in the following paragraphs. The questions listed under point 3 are related not to Earth observation but to institutional goals and capability; though important, they are not addressed in this publication.

Nature of the WRM Problem

It is important to begin by asking, what WRM questions need to be answered? Outlining the specific set of WRM questions is critical to establishing the scope of the investigation, including the geographic extent, amount of investment (What can be feasibly achieved?), and expectations for monitoring and reporting programs beyond a project of fixed duration. Government policy and regulatory drivers related to the broad WRM issues to be addressed probably exist, perhaps in response to an environmental crisis. The higher-level WRM statements and policy will need to be translated to very specific information and reporting requirements. The characteristics of key stakeholders and their information requirements and communication options may

---

BOX 7.1

Guiding Questions to Aid in the Decision Whether to Use Earth Observation for Water Resources Management

1. *Nature of the problem*
    - What WRM questions need to be answered?
    - What are the policy or regulatory drivers of these questions?
    - Who are the stakeholders and beneficiaries of a solution to the WRM problem?

2. *Existing data and observation networks*
    - What metering is currently available?
    - What is the condition of the data networks?
    - Are there any impediments to sharing, collating, and archiving the data (such as transboundary issues)?
    - What, if anything, has been done in the past to address the issues at hand?
        - Any monitoring? Modeling?
    - Can Earth observation fill an information gap?
        - Will it complement field-monitoring networks or serve as the sole source of information?
        - Will it be used in conjunction with modeling?
        - Are the EO data stream(s) suitable for long-term WRM decision support?

3. *Sustaining and maintaining WRM decision support and monitoring programs*
    - Is there capability to adopt a solution in the short and longer term?
    - What key national organizations and international experts could be potential partners regarding Earth observation?
    - What is the local capability to adopt new techniques and technologies?
        - What computing infrastructure, if any, is needed? Is it available, and who owns it?
        - To what degree will local expertise require training in new techniques and technologies?
    - What level of national versus international resourcing will be required?

---

place another constraint on the solutions that are feasible. For example, if the goal is to respond rapidly to an impending natural disaster, this will eliminate some of the EO products with greater latency.

Existing Data and Observation Networks

It is important to assess any existing (past or current) field observation networks and data. Sometimes a better solution may be to install a network of field-based sensors, upgrade existing networks, or rehabilitate former gauging networks. Of course, such a solution has important implications that need to be considered, for example, regarding spatial coverage and cost-efficiency (for example, capital costs, ongoing maintenance, and data management and processing). Alternatively, the current network might be appropriate in principle, but sharing measurements across organizational or jurisdictional boundaries—within or between nations—may be challenging. Conducting a thorough analysis of the status and access to existing observation networks and data is a valuable first step toward identifying any requirements for Earth observation to fill data gaps (see chapter 4 for additional information).

Although there are exceptions, EO data products are usually not directly suitable for addressing WRM problems unless augmented with additional data. Field measurements, where and when they are available, are critical in the development of any EO data product and in the assessment of accuracy and uncertainty (often called "validation," the subject of the chapters in part III). They are also highly valuable for correcting (or "calibrating") the product in regional applications or for enhancing the resolution (for example, through statistical downscaling).

Even more valuable, but also more complicated, is to use EO data along with field data and hydrologic computer models and with knowledge of the errors in each of these to constrain the hydrologic estimation or prediction (see chapters 4 and 11 for additional information). Such a model-data fusion approach makes the EO data more directly relevant and valuable to the WRM variables of interest.

Finally, the prospects for ongoing data collection and access need to be considered if they are to form a component of an operational data production system. This includes aspects such as the mission lifetime of the satellite, the options in case of mission failure, any redundancy in data streams through other sensors, service-level agreements, and ongoing provision of a stable data product with known and unchanging (or perhaps improved) characteristics. Of course, these aspects only need to be considered if "live" information systems are to be developed, for instance, for long-term decision-making support for water resources management and consistent monitoring over time.

DESCRIBING THE CHARACTERISTICS OF EO DATA PRODUCTS

To identify which data products might be suitable for a given application, numerous data characteristics can be assessed that relate to spatial and temporal attributes, accuracy, and reliability. Eight core data characteristics are useful for establishing the suitability of data for a predetermined task: spatial resolution, frequency and timing, record length, field data requirements, data product reliability, data product accuracy, data product maturity, and data product complexity (table 7.1). Three of these characteristics are sensor specific in that they depend on the satellite sensor from which they are derived, whereas the

Table 7.1 Major Characteristics of Data Products and Their Type of Dependence

DATA PRODUCT CHARACTERISTIC	DEPENDENCE
Spatial resolution	Sensor specific
Temporal frequency	Sensor specific
Record length	Sensor specific
Field data requirements	Product specific
Reliability	Product specific
Accuracy	Product specific
Maturity	Product specific
Complexity	Product specific

five other characteristics are product specific in that they depend more on how the data product was generated than on their sensor source. These eight characteristics are defined in this section.

Spatial Resolution

Sometimes called the spatial frequency or image resolution, the spatial resolution of EO data refers to the pixel size of the image. Spatial resolution of data determines the precision with which the spatial variation of the observed phenomenon can be captured. A relatively large pixel size will capture less spatial variation than a relatively small pixel size.

When a pixel straddles two (or more) distinct ground features (such as a water body and adjacent vegetation), the pixel captures a mixture of the signals from both features and is referred to as a "mixel." Mixels make image interpretation more difficult, and the larger the pixel size the more mixels the data are likely to contain.

Temporal Resolution

The temporal resolution of data (or the temporal frequency) refers to how often a sensor makes observations of a given location. In the case of polar-orbiting satellites, frequency is related to overpass frequency and is typically measured in days. The frequency of geostationary satellites is much higher, being measured in minutes to hours. Relatively high-frequency observations are able to capture the dynamics in fast-changing processes better than relatively low-frequency observations.

For some applications, the time of observation can be important to ensure that the observations occur at the same time each day or at specific times of the day, such as at noon.

Record Length

The record length refers to how long the record of data is. This is typically a function of the period of operation of the satellite and so is determined by the mission launch and end dates. Often, however, satellite sensors acquire data long past their mission end dates (for example, Landsat-5). Generally speaking, the longer the record length, the older the satellite and its associated technology. Thus there is usually a trade-off between record length and other data attributes, such as accuracy, spatial resolution, and number of spectral bands.

Field Data Requirements

Some EO data products are generated solely from satellite observations, and some are generated from a combination of satellite and field-based observations. The latter have much higher input data requirements and so are more dependent on the availability of suitable field data. They are also generally more complex to generate and can become limited to the specific locations and times that the field data represent:

- *Low* field-based (data) requirement products do not use field data or use it only for validation purposes.

- *Medium* field-based (data) requirement products need field data to calibrate the EO data or use a moderate amount of field data to derive the final EO product itself (such as when river gauge data are combined with satellite-derived flood extent data to estimate flood volumes).

- *High* field-based (data) requirement products incorporate multiple sources of field data (for example, most ET and soil moisture data products), sometimes in complex data assimilation systems.

Reliability

Data product reliability refers to the certainty of supply of that product across space and through time. The greater the spatial coverage, the more frequently the product is updated; the greater the number of options for sourcing the product, the higher the reliability of the product.

- *Low* reliability describes a product that is tailor-made for a specific time, region, or application or is generated by only one organization.

- *Medium* reliability describes a product that typically has wide (global) coverage and is frequently updated but comes from only one source organization.

- *High* reliability describes a product with global coverage that is frequently updated and can be sourced from multiple independent organizations.

Accuracy

The accuracy of data products is an estimation of the uncertainty associated with the data estimates. Accuracy can be described in absolute terms (that is, in physical units such as millimeters per year) or in relative terms (usually as a percentage). For example, if an estimate of evaporation of 200 millimeters per year has an error of 10 percent (therefore, an accuracy of 90 percent), the real value could be as low as 180 or as high as 220 millimeters per year.

Rarely will the accuracy of an EO data product be as high as that of an equivalent field measurement. Despite a generally lower accuracy, EO products can still be an important data source, as EO imagery can provide information with greater spatial extent, spatial density, or temporal frequency than most field-based (point-based) observation networks. For this reason, the combination of EO and field data generally provides the best information outcomes. Part III provides additional information about validation of EO estimates of precipitation, evapotranspiration, soil moisture, snow cover and snow water equivalent, surface water levels and streamflows, and streamflow outputs from models using EO inputs.

Maturity

Product maturity relates to how established the data product is. A well-established, or mature, product is generally founded on well-established science and can be gauged by its level of validation, acceptance, and adoption:

- *Low* maturity indicates that the product is still in an experimental stage.

- *Medium* maturity indicates that the product is developmental in that the underlying science is mature but the product's conversion to being operational is still in progress.

- *High* maturity refers to a proven—widely tested and adopted—operational product.

Complexity

Data product complexity describes the level of complication involved in converting the EO-processed data into the data product. Complexity is a function of, for example, the number of methodological steps involved, the number and type of input data sources, the level of mathematics involved, the volume of data to be processed, and the technical expertise required:

- *Low* complexity indicates no function or a very simple function for converting processed satellite data into the data product, requiring basic technical expertise.

- *Medium* complexity indicates a moderately complex method.

- *High* complexity indicates a highly complex method for generating the data product, requiring advanced technical or computational expertise.

DETERMINING THE CHARACTERISTICS OF MINIMUM REQUIRED EO DATA

By analyzing the information required to address a specific issue at hand, it should be possible to translate these requirements into minimum required data characteristics or specifications that can be used to assess the

Table 7.2 Guiding Questions for Determining the Minimum Requirements of EO Data Products

CHARACTERISTIC	GUIDING QUESTIONS
Justification	Do you need to use EO data?
Suitability	Can EO provide the required data products?
Spatial resolution	What is the appropriate pixel size?
Temporal frequency	How frequent do these observations need to be?
Record length	How far back in time does your data record need to go?
Reliability	Do you need guaranteed continuation of data supply into the future?
Accuracy	What degree of accuracy is needed in the data products?
Maturity	Do you want to use only data products that are commonly used?

Note: EO = Earth observation.

Screening for Adequacy of Field Observations

- Are the data well described—that is, is it clear what was measured, how, where, and when?
- Are the right variables measured?
- Are the data of sufficient spatial density across your area of interest?
- Do the data cover the period of interest?
- Are the measurements frequent enough?
- Are the measurements available throughout the time period, without important gaps?
- Are the data of known and suitable accuracy?
- Are the data guaranteed to be free from bias and manipulation?
- Are the data available in digital form and in an interpretable format?
- Are the data publicly available or is it clear they will be made available by their custodian?
- Do the data have to continue being collected into the future?

suitability of EO products. This section describes those minimum requirements. Table 7.2 presents a list of questions for determining the requirements.

Sometimes the answer to a question might not be obvious. For instance, there may be open questions about the overall approach to the WRM issue at hand or there may be a potential degree of circularity between what EO data are available and what the required characteristics are. Under such circumstances, consultation with an EO area expert is likely to be beneficial.

Justification: Do You Need to Use EO Data?

When field observations are accessible and sufficiently informative, it may well be possible to answer WRM questions directly, without using EO data. Relevant questions to consider are listed in box 7.2.

If the answer to any of these questions is negative, it may be worth exploring the potential usefulness of EO data products, either by themselves or, more typically, in conjunction with field observations and computer models.

Chapter 5, especially tables 5.1–5.3, discusses the water-related issues for which Earth observation may be useful, and chapter 6 provides information about each of the EO application areas relevant to water resources management and about existing and future EO systems (tables 6.3–6.12).

Suitability: Can EO Provide the Required Information?

Not all variables and processes can be measured with Earth observation, whether directly or through inference using a model. For this reason, a key question to ask is whether the required data or information products can be generated from remote sensing at all. Table 6.2 in chapter 6 provides an overview of the most commonly derived products suitable for WRM applications.

If the required data product is not readily available, it may still be possible to derive such a product from existing processed data, but this is likely to require engaging EO expertise. In that case, it would need to be determined if and how a desired data product might be derived from processed data. Determining suitability requires a deeper understanding of the characteristics of individual satellite sensors and the relationship between the observation and the variable of interest. Consultation with an EO expert should quickly settle whether there is any such prospect.

Spatial Resolution: What Is the Appropriate Pixel Size?

Spatial resolution is an important and almost universal characteristic of EO data. In each application it will be necessary to consider the minimal distances over which the phenomenon of interest (precipitation, soil moisture, or water quality) varies or distance over which any variations in the phenomenon would become significant for the purpose at hand. As a rule of thumb, the "pixel size" (the characteristic length of one image pixel as measured on the Earth's surface) should be no more than a quarter of the length over which the phenomenon varies and preferably finer. For example, if the phenomenon of interest is total crop evaporation from fields that are typically about 600 x 600 meters in size, the pixel size of the ET product should be no larger than 150 meters. Alternatively, if the variations in evaporation within that field are of interest, a resolution on the order of 10 meters might be required.

Tables 5.2 and 5.3 in chapter 5 provide details on the spatial resolution of the main EO data products suited to water resources management. The pixel size listed generally reflects the smallest pixel size of the sensor from which the data are derived.

Some practitioners may be inclined to use the highest resolution, but the cost of doing so can sometimes be very high and the value added may not be worth the cost. This caveat also applies to temporal frequency.

Temporal Resolution: How Frequent Do the Observations Need to Be?

The temporal resolution needs to suit the nature of the question asked—for example,

Over what time scales does the phenomenon of interest vary, or how long does it take for the phenomenon to vary significantly when considering the intended purpose? As a bare minimum, satellite observations should be available at least at the same frequency as the variation in the phenomenon of interest. For short-lived events, the exact timing of observation is also likely to be important. If the dynamics of a process or event are important, a frequency substantially less than the duration of the event will be necessary.

For instance, seasonal flooding may last for a month. However, if you are interested in peak flood extent and that peak only lasts a day, a single daily satellite measurement will suffice to capture it, but the timing of the measurement will be critical and may be difficult to achieve. Alternatively, if the advance and recession of the flood are of interest, regular (weekly or even daily) measurements will be required. Another example is an algal bloom in a lake that lasts a few days and can only be detected by a satellite sensor that has high frequency or that can be pointed at an area of interest and therefore target a specific area. The latter, of course, requires that there be sufficient time between knowledge of the event and acquisition of the imagery, and it usually comes at a cost. Conversely, if the seasonal pattern of algal levels across a year is of interest, as few as four images may be sufficient.

The satellite data product tables in chapter 6 (tables 6.3 through 6.12) provide details on the revisit times of the main EO data products suited to water resources management.

Record Length: How Far Back Does the Data Record Need to Go?

Analysis of changes (trends or shifts) in the behavior of a system will require a record that is sufficiently long to establish such changes with confidence. Similarly, accurate estimation of the mean and variance of a particular variable will require a sufficiently long record for calculation. The question as to what length of record is sufficient for these purposes cannot be answered, but some record length is required. As a general rule, a minimum of 15 years of observations is often required before trends in natural phenomena can be analyzed properly (see chapter 4 and table 4A.1 in annex 4A, available online at https://openknowledge.worldbank.org/handle/10986/22952, for additional information); the World Meteorological Organization defines "climate" as pertaining to a period of at least 30 years.

Alternatively, the application may provide near-real-time information and therefore perhaps only the most recent period (for example, a day or month) is of interest, although often such information will need to be considered in a historical context.

Finally, the particular application may only need data for a very specific period of interest, such as the 2013 growing season, one drought-flood cycle, or a water year. This reduces the demands on record length.

The satellite data product tables in chapter 6 (tables 6.3 through 6.12) describe the record lengths (launch and end dates, if applicable) of the main EO data products suited to water resources management.

Accuracy: How Good Do the Data Have to Be?

What is the acceptable tolerance of error in the data product for the purpose at hand? There are many possible ways in which to express accuracy. These will depend on the characteristics and intended use of the data product. Examples are given in box 7.3.

Conventional ways of validating EO data typically focus on the first two aspects—precisely the standard type of information that generally is provided. However, it can be very challenging to obtain accurate information on other aspects, sometimes even from experts on the particular data source.

Reliability: Is Continued Supply of Data into the Future Essential?

This is an important question to answer. Is assurance required that the EO data source

---

---

will remain available into the future with little or no interruptions? Or are the data required for a one-off, project-based study, with no follow-on monitoring being anticipated? This will determine whether it is possible to use only data derived from stable, likely long-term satellite missions with a track record of reliability or whether it is possible to include data from short-term or experimental missions (the majority of EO satellites even today). It may be important to ascertain whether there is a long-term plan to ensure that satellite sensors and the data stream will be available into the future. This is particularly important when deciding whether to invest in the infrastructure required for operational satellite imagery and geographic information system processing, perhaps including information validation programs and Web-based data services or other forms of information products.

However, officially available information about mission continuity should only be used as general guidance: a current continuation policy may be changed in future, whereas a mission that currently has no official prospect of continuation may be replaced by a comparable sensor with identical, similar, or even better characteristics in future. Arguably the most reliable test of the risk to investment is redundancy: if several missions make the same or quite similar observations, the associated risks are usually correspondingly lower.

The satellite data product tables in chapter 6 (tables 6.3 through 6.12) provide some details on mission reliability for the main EO data products used in water resources management.

Maturity: Can Data Products Be Limited to Well-Established Products?

Maturity refers to the degree to which an EO data product has been evaluated by the research or management community. With maturity comes a better understanding of the accuracy and suitability of the product for specific purposes and some pedigree and acceptance where its use has been successful.

Restricting the type of data products used to those that are well established and in common use reduces the risk of nondelivery and disappointment. Operational products—those that are readily available and have been widely adopted across the WRM community—are generally restricted to mature products, or conversely, maturity comes with increased adoption across the community.

However, interested parties may be willing to use emerging (experimental or developmental) products because they provide information that is otherwise not available and be willing to accept some degree of uncertainty related to product accuracy, suitability, and future availability. In such cases, undertaking a pilot or case study may be worth considering before attempting to implement an operational data service. If this is done in communication with the research and management community, such projects in themselves can rapidly achieve greater maturity and acceptance.

Complexity: What Data Management and Analysis Capacity Is Available?

Prior to pursuing an EO-based solution, it is probably beneficial to establish who will be responsible for running the WRM decision support or monitoring program and to evaluate their mandate, resources, and capabilities. Ongoing "live" monitoring systems will be more demanding to maintain than an unchangeable decision-support system. Knowing which government department or agency is ultimately likely to be responsible for maintaining any ongoing monitoring program and reporting the information helps to assess the available capacity and preparedness to adopt EO-based solutions.

An EO solution may also require input from other national or international agencies (through the provision of observations or data products). Identifying and securing such key partnerships up-front may be critical to success. To evaluate the resources available and required, the following aspects of information technology may be worth considering:

- Infrastructure for acquiring the data (via the Internet)

- Storage of the data and backup facilities

- Implementation and maintenance of the WRM system

Obviously, these infrastructure aspects also have implications for the human resources required to maintain and use them. In addition, area expertise will be required on an ongoing basis to interpret and report the information. Training may be needed, as well as ongoing user support in the transition from the research (or development) environment to the operational implementation of the solution. These aspects all depend on the complexity of the solution.

DETERMINING THE GENERALIZED CHARACTERISTICS OF EO DATA PRODUCTS

Now that the core characteristics have been suggested for describing the suitability of EO data products for water resources management and guidelines have been provided for determining what data characteristics are required for the application at hand, this section outlines the characteristics of available EO data products. Following the same format as table 5.2 in chapter 5 and the discussion in chapter 6, where EO-derived data products are summarized in eight broad types of information, this section contains eight tables presenting the characteristics, respectively, of precipitation, evapotranspiration, soil moisture, vegetation and vegetation cover types, groundwater, surface water, snow, and water quality data products.

Some of these core characteristics are related directly to the satellite sensor from which the data are derived and are discussed in chapter 5. These sensor-specific characteristics are spatial resolution, frequency, and record length. Assessments of the remaining five characteristics are summarized in the tables below, while accuracy is discussed in part III.

Beyond the constraints of the sensor observations used, the characteristics of derived data products also depend on the choices made in the process of generating the data product. A wide range of options may be available for any given type of data product, which may represent decisions about, for example, the trade-off between resolution and accuracy (averaging over larger areas or longer periods helps to increase the signal-to-noise ratio) or the ability to process, manage, and download the product (Internet speeds quickly become a bottleneck in using EO data). Therefore, some broad generalizations are made in the following tables. For more precise assessments, the documentation of individual products will need to be referred to, and product experts may need to be consulted.

Precipitation

Table 6.3 in chapter 6 provides an overview of the range and characteristics of precipitation products derived from EO data and their relation to alternative sources of precipitation data. The accuracy of the different products varies with the season. Table 7.3 provides

Table 7.3 Field Data Requirements and Characteristics of EO-Based Precipitation Products

PRODUCT	FIELD DATA REQUIREMENTS	RELIABILITY	ACCURACY	MATURITY	COMPLEXITY	COMMENTS ON LIMITATIONS
Rain gauge analysis	High	Low	Bias between ±0.2 millimeter day^{-1} (that is, as high as 60% for some regions); considered to be benchmark; accuracy decreases away from gauge location	High	Medium	Global gauge analyzes coarse spatial resolution; daily to monthly estimates; local or continental analyses typically about 1–10 kilometers; accuracy decreases with distance from gauge location
Radar rainfall	High	Low	Bias between ±0.5 millimeter day^{-1} (30–40% accuracy); subhourly rain rates; coverage limited, and estimates uncertain at distance from radar	High	Medium	Beam blockage (topography effects) hampers quality of estimate; higher resolution (in space and time) compared to satellite products, but patchy coverage for large-area applications
TIR, geostationary	Low	High	Bias between ±2 millimeters day^{-1} (often greater than 100% error), best at estimating small convective rainfall systems	High	High	Based on weak relationship between cloud top temperatures and rain rate; generally considered poorer-quality estimate than PMW; low latency (that is, real-time products possible)

(Continued)

Table 7.3 (Continued)

PRODUCT	FIELD DATA REQUIREMENTS	RELIABILITY	ACCURACY	MATURITY	COMPLEXITY	COMMENTS ON LIMITATIONS
PMW, polar orbiting	Low	High	Bias between ±1.5 millimeters day^{-1} (about 100% error); better than models at estimating convective rainfall systems over warmer months; patchy coverage	High	High	High-quality retrievals, but much coarser resolution than TIR; difficulty in capturing orographic or light rainfall; requires multiple PMW platforms for more complete coverage and needs to be calibrated with in-orbit precipitation radar
Merged TIR-PMW	Medium	Medium	Bias between ±1 millimeter day^{-1}; better at estimating convective rainfall systems over warmer months; global coverage	High	High	Coarse resolution but greater coverage than PMW alone; subdaily and near-real-time estimation possible
Merge TIR-PMW gauge	High	High	Bias reduced to between ±0.75 millimeter day^{-1} on average (often less than 100% error); performance as with merged TIR-PMW; long latency	High	High	Coarse resolution; could be downscaled further with additional gauge data or analyses; greater data latency
Model reanalysis	Low	High	Bias between ±1 millimeter day^{-1}; better than PMW at estimating stratiform rainfall systems typical of cooler months	High	High	Coarse spatial resolution
Merged model, satellite and gauge analysis	High	Medium	Bias between ±0.5 millimeter day^{-1} (often less than 100% error); coarse resolution	High	High	Coarse spatial resolution; requires access to multiple data from multiple agencies

Note: EO = Earth observation; TIR = thermal infrared; PMW = passive microwave.

summary estimates of the bias (the average difference between product and gauge observations), taken from International Precipitation Working Group (IPWG) validation pages.[1]

The values reported on the IPWG validation pages and in table 7.3 are regional averages. At the aggregate level, the errors can sometimes be of the same magnitude as the rainfall value itself or much higher (even greater than 100 percent relative error). The quality of satellite (and indeed of numerical weather prediction and gauge-based rainfall) estimates varies with geographic location, and it is recommended that persons interested in satellite precipitation products consult the IPWG websites or the literature (Ebert, Janowiak, and Kidd 2007; Sapiano et al. 2010) for

more detailed, quantitative analyses, including the categorical statistics (probability of detection, false alarm ratio). Chapter 9 discusses the validation of precipitation estimates derived from remote sensing (RS).

Evapotranspiration

For an overview of the generation of actual ET-related data products from EO data, satellite sensors suitable for generating such products, and sensor-specific data characteristics, see chapter 6, specifically table 6.4. In chapter 6, three broad classes of actual ET estimation approaches are defined that make use of remote sensing: empirical, PM (Penman-Monteith) leaf area index (LAI), and resistance energy balance model. Empirical methods seek to define statistical relationships between commonly observed EO data or products, usually either vegetation indexes or surface temperature. The PM LAI approach uses the Penman-Monteith "combination equation" and EO-based vegetation characteristics (usually LAI) to model surface conductance. Energy balance approaches mostly use EO-based land surface temperature to estimate sensible heat flux, which can then be used along with an estimate of the available energy to approximate latent heat flux.

Obviously, the metrics described in table 7.4 will depend on the specifics of the algorithms and characteristics of the data sets used. An attempt is made here to summarize actual ET products that are operationally available at either global or continental scale on a monthly or shorter time step, which usually relates to about 5-kilometer or finer spatial resolution.

For some specifics about reliability, accuracy, maturity, and complexity, see the references in the section on evapotranspiration in chapter 6. Chapter 9 discusses the validation of RS-derived ET estimates.

Soil Moisture

For an overview of the range of soil moisture products generated from EO data, the data characteristics, and their use, see chapter 6 and table 6.6. Metrics of interest are given in table 7.5. The absolute accuracy of satellite soil moisture products is very rarely (if ever) of interest. For example, preprocessing of the data eliminates systematic differences between model estimates and observations prior to assimilation. The soil moisture estimates derived from Earth observation only represent the first centimeters of the surface. Moreover, most applications (for example, in drought monitoring) require knowledge of soil

Table 7.4 Field Data Requirements and Characteristics of EO-Based Evapotranspiration Products

PRODUCT	FIELD DATA REQUIREMENTS	RELIABILITY	ACCURACY	MATURITY	COMPLEXITY	COMMENTS ON LIMITATIONS
Empirical	High	Medium	Usually better than 1 millimeter per day; most reliable when and where the actual ET is dominated by the EO metric from which the statistical relationship was defined; for example, an empirical relationship between actual ET and a moisture index would work best under water-limited conditions	Medium	Low	Limited ability to be improved via better process understanding; usually requires field calibration, which may only be regionally applicable
PM LAI	Medium	High	Usually better than 1 millimeter per day; generally reliable for places and times when transpiration is the main source of actual ET; has been implemented operationally over the globe	High	Medium	Limitations when ET is not dominated by transpiration (that is, open water or soil evaporation); accurate estimation of spatially and temporally varying conductance is difficult
Resistance energy balance model	Medium	High	Usually better than 1 millimeter per day; generally reliable for estimating instantaneous flux and thus eminently suited for use with geostationary data	High	High	Usually requires scaling instantaneous estimates to daily or longer time steps; may suffer from over-parameterization

Note: EO = Earth observation; ET = evapotranspiration; PM LAI = Penman-Monteith leaf area index.

Table 7.5 Field Data Requirements and Characteristics of EO-Based Soil Moisture Products

PRODUCT	FIELD DATA REQUIREMENTS	RELIABILITY	ACCURACY	MATURITY	COMPLEXITY	COMMENTS ON LIMITATIONS
Active	Low	Medium	Higher spatial resolution, hampered by noise; accuracy affected in areas of highly variable terrain	High	Medium	Higher spatial resolution than PMW but can be significantly noisier; terrain effects
PMW	Low	High	Generally considered more accurate than data from active systems; poor performance over areas of dense vegetation	High	High	Low spatial resolution; affected by dense vegetation and biased in the vicinity of coast or open-water bodies
Combined active–PMW	Low	Medium	Merged data, either through joint assimilation or statistical combination, better than individual products alone; well-known complementarity of the two sources	Medium	High	Requires multiple sensors; SMAP is only mission (planned) where a satellite will have both active and PMW sensors on one platform
Assimilated into land surface models	Low	Medium	Assimilating surface model products into land surface models has been shown to improve root-zone moisture estimation by 30–80%	Low	High	Only way to get root-zone moisture; however, it is still experimental (SMAP provides root-zone moisture product by assimilating satellite surface models into land surface models)

Note: EO = Earth observation; PMW = passive microwave; SMAP = Soil Moisture Active Passive.

moisture relative to some threshold or historical frequency. Therefore, correlation is a better standard metric for evaluating soil moisture products. For the products listed in table 6.6, values range from 0.6 to 0.9, depending on the product and where it is evaluated. Chapter 9 discusses the validation of RS-derived soil moisture estimates.

Vegetation and Vegetation Cover

For an overview of the generation of vegetation and vegetation cover–related data products from EO data, satellite sensors suitable for generating such products, and sensor-specific data characteristics, see chapter 6 and table 6.7. There are four vegetation-related products, as

Table 7.6 Field Data Requirements and Characteristics of EO-Based Vegetation and Vegetation Cover Products

PRODUCT	FIELD DATA REQUIREMENTS	RELIABILITY	ACCURACY	MATURITY	COMPLEXITY	COMMENTS ON LIMITATIONS
Albedo	Low (validation only)	High	5–10%	Medium	Low	
NDVI	Low (validation only)	High	Usually 5–10%	Medium	Low	Relationship to real-world values is sensor specific
LAI	Low (validation only)	High	Decreases as LAI increases; cannot detect change above values around 10	Medium	Medium	Performs best over low-density canopies (that is, LAI lower than 3–4)
fPAR	Low (validation only)	High	5–10%	Medium	Low	

Note: EO = Earth observation; NDVI = normalized difference vegetation index; LAI = leaf area index; fPAR = fraction of absorbed photosynthetically active radiation.

shown in table 7.6: albedo, the normalized difference vegetation index (NDVI), the leaf area index, and the fraction of photosynthetically active radiation absorbed by green leaves (fPAR).

A fifth product is vegetation cover, which is a qualitative classification of vegetation based on broad structural, climatic, or functional characteristics. Because vegetation cover data are so varied in what they represent and how they are derived, they are not included in table 7.6.

Groundwater

For an overview of the generation of groundwater-related data products from EO data and satellite sensors suitable for generating such products, see chapter 6 and table 6.9. The main EO approaches for estimating groundwater are through satellite gravity field mapping (gravimetry) and radar interferometry. The former measures changes in the regional gravity field, while the latter measures changes in land surface elevation (table 7.7). For some specifics

about reliability, accuracy, maturity, and complexity, see the references cited in the section on groundwater in chapter 6.

Surface Water

For an overview of the generation of surface water–related data products from EO data, the satellite sensors suitable for generating such products, and the sensor-specific data characteristics, see chapter 6 and table 6.10. In table 7.8, both reservoir area and flood extent refer to the delimitation of the area covered with standing water, although they differ in size and temporal dynamics: reservoir area can range from a few square meters (as in the case of small ponds) to large lakes of several thousands of square kilometers and generally change in area and volume relatively slowly in time. In general terms, floods are more dynamic in time than reservoirs and can change in area and volume in a matter of hours or days. Chapter 9 discusses the validation of RS-derived surface water estimates.

Table 7.7 Field Data Requirements and Characteristics of EO-Based Groundwater Products

PRODUCT	FIELD DATA REQUIREMENTS	RELIABILITY	ACCURACY	MATURITY	COMPLEXITY	COMMENTS ON LIMITATIONS
Gravity field	Low	Medium-low (GRACE is operating seven years beyond its intended lifetime; a follow-on mission is planned for 2017)	Suitable for very large areas; nominal precision is 1 gravity value	Medium	High	Spatial resolution for obtaining a reliable signal (about 400 kilometers) is limited to very large basins; may not be suitable in areas of tectonic rebound
Surface height	High	Low (no product per se, requires interpretation for each instance)	Varying accuracy depending on interpreter's skill and understanding of regional geology, groundwater systems, and surface conditions	Medium	High	Requires the relationship between vertical surface movement and groundwater storage to be quantified; changes in vertical surface movement are limited to regional interpretation, requiring a specialist

Note: EO = Earth observation; GRACE = Gravity Recovery and Climate Experiment.

Table 7.8 Field Data Requirements and Characteristics of EO-Based Surface Water Products

INDICATOR	FIELD DATA REQUIREMENTS	RELIABILITY	ACCURACY	MATURITY	COMPLEXITY	COMMENTS ON LIMITATIONS
Reservoir area	Low (validation only)	Medium	High (kappa greater than 90%) in classifications	High	Medium	No global, continuously updated product
Flood extent	Low (mapping flooded areas) to medium (estimating river discharge)	Medium	High (kappa greater than 90%) in most situations; kappa 50–90% possible when water is obscured by vegetation (flooded forests)	High	Medium	One global product; flooded area limited by cloud cover; optical methods give poor results in flooded forests
Water level	Low (validation only)	High	Altimetry accuracy dependent on sensor and size of water body; can be from about 10 centimeters to 50 centimeters[a]	High	Low	Limited to large reservoirs only

Note: EO = Earth observation.

a. A good pragmatic source of information about the accuracy of altimetry data can be found at http://www.pecad.fas.usda.gov/cropexplorer/global_reservoir/validation.htm.

Snow

For an overview of the generation of snow-related data products from EO data, satellite sensors suitable for generating such products, and sensor-specific data characteristics, refer to chapter 6 and table 6.11. Metrics related to snow cover, snow water equivalent, and snow moisture are given in table 7.9. Chapter 9 discusses the validation of RS-derived estimates of snow cover and snow water equivalents.

Water Quality

The six water quality variables that can be determined directly from EO data (see chapter 6) are listed again in box 7.4 for easy reference.

The additional criteria that can be used to determine whether EO is appropriate for a particular water quality application are summarized in this section. The information is presented in tables 7.10–7.12 covering empirical, semi-empirical, and physics-based inversion methods, respectively.

Table 7.10 presents empirical methods (where a statistical relationship is established between the spectral bands used and the field-based measurement of the variable, without necessarily being a causal relationship). This

Table 7.9 Field Data Requirements and Characteristics of EO-Based Snow Products

PRODUCT	FIELD DATA REQUIREMENTS	RELIABILITY	ACCURACY	MATURITY	COMPLEXITY	COMMENTS ON LIMITATIONS
Snow extent or fraction of snow cover	Low	Medium	10–20% error	Relatively mature	Medium	Affected by cloud cover
Snow water equivalent	Medium	Medium	20–30% error in flat areas; very large in mountainous areas	Mature for flat areas; low for mountainous areas	Medium for flat areas; complex for mountainous areas	Terrain is a major determinant of product quality; also affected by prior knowledge of snow properties such as density, particle size, and shape
Snow moisture	High	Low	Low	Very low	Complex	

Note: EO = Earth observation.

Table 7.10 Field Data Requirements and Characteristics of EO-Based Water Quality Products: Empirical Methods

PRODUCT	FIELD DATA REQUIREMENTS	RELIABILITY	ACCURACY	MATURITY	COMPLEXITY	COMMENTS ON LIMITATIONS
CHL	High	Medium	50–70%	High	Low	Empirical methods are only valid for field-based ranges; are not transportable to other water bodies; may provide spurious results; simultaneous acquisition of the in situ measurement during overpass of satellite is an absolute requirement to establish the empirical relationship
CYP	High	Medium	40–60%	Medium	Medium	Same as previous
CDOM	High	Low	40–60%	Low	High	Same as previous
TSM	High	High	80%	High	Low	Same as previous
K_d	High	High	80%	Medium	Medium	Same as previous
Turb/SD	High	High	70–80%	Medium	Low	Same as previous

Source: Matthews 2011.

Note: EO = Earth observation; CHL = chlorophyll; CYP = cyanobacterial pigments; CDOM = colored dissolved organic matter; TSM = total suspended matter; K_d = vertical attenuation of light coefficient; Turb/SD = turbidity/Secchi disk transparency.

BOX 7.4

Water Quality Variables Directly Determined by Earth Observation

Directly assessed:

- Chlorophyll
- Cyanobacterial pigments
- Colored dissolved organic matter
- Total suspended matter

Indirectly assessed:

- Vertical attenuation of light coefficient
- Turbidity/Secchi disk transparency

---

method is the least suitable for automation across large areas unless accompanied by a significant, ongoing field measurement activity across most water bodies present.

Table 7.11 refers to *semi-empirical methods* (where a causal relationship *is* established between the spectral bands used and the variable assessed). This method is less prone to providing spurious results, although results may have significantly higher errors outside the field-based range. This method has

medium suitability for automation across large areas.

Table 7.12 refers to physics-based inversion methods (also known as *semi-analytical inversion methods*): all variables are assessed simultaneously in one spectral inversion. This method provides physics-based consistency of results and is most suitable for automation across large areas.

Chapter 6 lists the water quality variables that EO can provide, and table 6.12 provides an inventory of EO satellites with their capabilities and suitability.

Whether it is possible to process the EO data to retrieve quantitative water quality information will depend on the availability and quality of field data with which to calibrate the relationships. The quality will depend on whether the field data cover all variables of concern (see chapter 6) and whether these coincide closely with the times of satellite overpasses.

Without any field data, empirical methods (where an empirical relationship is established between field data and EO image pixel values) will not work for quantitative assessments. However, it may be possible to apply

Table 7.11 Field Data Requirements and Characteristics of EO-Based Water Quality Products: Semi-Empirical Methods

PRODUCT	FIELD DATA REQUIREMENTS	RELIABILITY	ACCURACY	MATURITY	COMPLEXITY	COMMENTS ON LIMITATIONS
CHL	Medium	High	60–80%	High	Low	Semi-empirical methods may be extrapolated beyond field-based ranges, although nonlinear effects do occur; may be transportable to other similar water bodies; reduced requirement for field measurement simultaneous with satellite overpass; requires good atmospheric and water surface glint correction for time series assessments
CYP	Medium	Medium	50–70%	Medium	Medium	Same as previous
CDOM	Medium	Medium	50–70%	Medium	High	In waters with high organic particulate matter and high algal contents, the CDOM absorption signal is masked
TSM	Medium	High	80%	High	Low	Same as CHL and CYP
K_d	Medium	High	80%	Medium	Medium	Same as previous
Turb/SD	Medium	High	70–80%	Medium	Medium	Same as previous

Sources: Matthews 2011; Odermatt et al. 2012.

Note: EO = Earth observation; CHL = chlorophyll; CYP = cyanobacterial pigments; CDOM = colored dissolved organic matter; TSM = total suspended matter; K_d = vertical attenuation of light coefficient; Turb/SD = Turbidity/Secchi disk transparency.

Table 7.12 Field Data Requirements and Characteristics of EO-Based Water Quality Products: Physics-Based Inversion Methods

PRODUCT	FIELD DATA REQUIREMENTS	RELIABILITY	ACCURACY	MATURITY	COMPLEXITY	COMMENTS ON LIMITATIONS
CHL	Low	High	60–80%	Medium	High	High complexity: requires good atmospheric and water surface glint correction
CYP	Low	Medium	55–75%	Low	High	Same as previous
CDOM	Low	Medium	70%	Medium	High	Same as previous
TSM	Low	High	80%	Medium	High	Same as previous
K_d	Low	High	85%	Medium	High	Same as previous
Turb/SD	Low	High	80%	Medium	High	Same as previous

Source: Odermatt et al. 2012.

Note: EO = Earth observation; CHL = chlorophyll; CYP = cyanobacterial pigments; CDOM = colored dissolved organic matter; TSM = total suspended matter; K_d = vertical attenuation of light coefficient; Turb/SD = turbidity/Secchi disk transparency.

spectral band indexes derived from the literature to indicate relative measures of water quality. An alternative is to apply physics-based inversion techniques, which will require a high level of expertise but can be automated more easily in the long run. The parameterization of the physics-based inversion model will need to be based on expert assessment of the types of water present and the parameterizations available globally. Some generic approaches to assessing water quality are becoming available from the National Aeronautics and Space Agency (NASA) and the European Space Agency (ESA), for the coarse spatial resolution MODIS (Moderate Resolution Imaging Spectrometer) and MERIS (Medium Resolution Imaging Spectrometer) sensors.[2]

If appropriate field data are available in some or all of the water bodies of interest, it may be possible to develop and apply empirical methods and extrapolate these relationships to other nearby water bodies for which field data do not exist. It is essential that the range of field measurements (concentrations of suspended matter, chlorophyll, and others) be sufficiently large to be representative; it is not useful to apply empirical algorithms of clear glacier-fed lakes to turbid downstream rivers or lakes prone to algal blooms, for example.

With physics-based inversion methods, it may be possible to refine the parameterization of the waters that do have field data and to extrapolate these values downstream or to nearby water bodies. However, although physics-based methods are less prone to error than empirical relationships, they do need a suitable parameterization of initial values.

With access to a sufficient quantity of relevant field data for the water bodies of concern, the question of whether to use Earth observation becomes more relevant: Are the field data sufficient (regarding time range, frequency, spatial representativeness, timeliness) to inform water quality management decision making on their own? The following questions should be asked at this stage: How far back do the field data archives go with respect to the EO archives (see table 6.12)? Are all of the variables required available in the field data or not? Can Earth observation provide the extra variables that are required? Are real-time data products required?

WORKED EXAMPLES

To illustrate how the decision process might proceed in practice, this section describes two fictional case studies.

Improving Lake Water Quality
You are project manager with responsibility for developing a program that will help to improve the water quality of a large lake so that it may once again be in the condition to (a) provide water suitable for drinking (untreated for livestock but treated for human consumption), (b) support a local, small-scale freshwater fishing industry, (c) maintain biodiversity, and (d) allow recreational use. The lake has recently degraded from a mesotrophic system to a hypertrophic system prone to algal blooms. The lake displays potentially harmful algal blooms in spring, summer, and fall, which are probably caused by eutrophication as a result of direct and diffuse sources of agricultural and horticultural use of land around the lake as well as diffuse and point sources of untreated, primary sewage water. Field measurements of electrical conductivity and alkalinity or acidity are the only recently available water quality data. Anecdotal evidence suggests that the lake has transitioned from a clear productive lake 10 years ago to a turbid, algal bloom–dominated lake today.

At this stage, the first questions to ask are as follows: Do you want to do EO-based retrospective assessment of your water system to understand its evolution through time or do you need EO measurements now to inform you of the water quality situation today and into the future? Table 7.13 lists a further set of appropriate questions for informing the decision about whether to proceed on the basis of EO data.

This example illustrates how the information contained in the tables in chapters 5 and 6 may be used together with the guiding questions presented in this chapter to determine the most suitable EO sensor and method for assessing the development of water quality over the last 10 years for a lake undergoing environmental change.

Two real-world examples in the research literature provide some in-depth information on how MODIS and MERIS were used to assess similar conditions in lakes in China (Hu et al. 2010) and South Africa (Matthews, Stewart, and Lisl 2012), respectively.

Table 7.13 Guiding Questions for Determining the Characteristics of Required EO Data Products: Water Quality Example

GUIDING QUESTIONS	CHARACTERISTIC	QUALIFIED ANSWER
Do you need to use EO data?	Justification	Yes, if there is no other source of information on water quality going back 10 years. Information from EO data is needed as it is the only archival information of a (semi) quantitative nature available.
Can EO provide the required data products?	Suitability	Yes, retrospective information on chlorophyll, cyanophycocyanin, suspended matter, turbidity, Secchi disk transparency, and vertical attenuation coefficient of light through time and space is key to understanding what aquatic ecosystem processes occurred in the last 10 years. However, each satellite sensor will differ in terms of ability to differentiate water quality variables based on its spectral resolution (see table 6.12).
What is the appropriate pixel size?	Spatial resolution	Given that the lake is 40 x 8 kilometers, lies in the subtropics (with a wet cloudy season often obscuring the lake and a dry season with clear sky conditions) and a minimum period of interest of the last 10 years, a study of tables 5.1, 5.2, and 6.12 shows that the MODIS, MERIS, and Landsat sensor image data are the appropriate ones to use.
How frequent do these observations need to be?	Temporal frequency	Coarser-scale MODIS and MERIS data offer a higher temporal frequency of coverage. However, under cloud-free conditions, Landsat may offer sufficient frequency.
How far back in time does your data record need to go?	Record length	The length of the archive available and the period of interest will determine the suitability of each satellite sensor.
Do you need guaranteed continuation of data supply into the future?	Reliability	Use tables 5.1, 5.2, and 6.12 to identify the sensor systems with continuing future data supply.
What degree of accuracy is needed in the data products?	Accuracy	The capability to measure all water quality variables in table 6.12 increases from Landsat to MODIS to MERIS on the basis of their spectral characteristics. The accuracy will generally be highest for MERIS.
Do you want to use only data products that are commonly used?	Maturity	EO algorithms for water quality products are summarized in tables 7.10–7.12. Progressing from empirical methods (requiring a sufficient number of simultaneous field measurements synchronous with a satellite overpass) to semi-empirical measurements, to semi-analytical methods, reliability and accuracy increase, but complexity also increases, while maturity decreases. The relevant question for this specific case study is: Do you need qualitative assessment of change or do you need the most reliable concentration estimates?
		In this case, a qualitative assessment of the satellite archive where the transition in time and space can be mapped from a mesotrophic, clear lake to a hypertrophic, algal bloom–dominated lake over a span of about 10 years does not require accurate water quality retrievals but does require frequent images with the capability to see when cyanobacteria start dominating the system. This leads to the conclusion that you should focus on the MERIS archive, using off-the-shelf products available through the BEAM software package.

Note: EO = Earth observation.

Achieving More Sustainable Basin Water Management

The second hypothetical example is a river basin where irrigated agriculture is practiced regularly. Water is diverted from the river and also used from groundwater to irrigate crops. Natural vegetation, particularly wetlands, suffer from reduced water supply, especially in drier than average years. A new project intends to improve the long-term sustainability of both the rural communities that depend on crops and the environment by ensuring an adequate flow of water.

The main question that needs to be answered is how much water is taken from surface water and groundwater. Additional questions include how much water is used by crops, how much is lost in transportation to crops (through inefficiencies in canals), what is the variation of water use between years (particularly wet and dry years), how does water use vary across the region, how much water is used by each type of crop, and who uses the water. Ideally, this information should be available for the previous 15–20 years in order to characterize the spatial and temporal variability in water use.

What is the status of the information networks? In this hypothetical example, the information available from river gauges and diversion points is very poor. In addition, it is suspected that a large amount of water is taken from the rivers and pumped from the ground illegally. Precipitation and other meteorological data are also scarce. To inform whether to proceed on the basis of EO data, table 7.14 lists additional pertinent questions.

Table 7.14 Guiding Questions for Determining the Required EO Data Product Characteristics: Efficiency of Agricultural Water Use Example

GUIDING QUESTIONS	CHARACTERISTIC	QUALIFIED ANSWER
Do you need to use EO data?	Justification	EO is an appropriate tool for estimating crop extent and water use, which complements the existing, field-based information (or replaces it when such information is not available).
Can EO provide the required data? The required products?	Suitability	Yes, retrospective information on evapotranspiration, rainfall, and soil moisture can be obtained or generated.
What is the appropriate pixel size?	Spatial resolution	The required cell size depends on the size of the actual crop paddocks. It is assumed that images of tens of meters resolution are sufficient, such as Landsat TM/ETM or similar. Data of coarser resolution, such as MODIS, can be of use as well, as it can provide a higher temporal repeatability. Data from these two satellites can be used to estimate evapotranspiration. RS estimates of precipitation and soil moisture can complement the information available for the project, albeit at coarser resolution.
How frequent do these observations need to be?	Temporal frequency	The ET estimates should ideally include as many observations during the crop-growing cycle as possible. In practice, this will be limited by the data available. If using Landsat or similar sensor (to provide the highest spatial resolution possible), data are available every 16 days, but cloud cover (depending on location and season) will determine how often a useful observation is available. Coarse spatial resolution data such as MODIS can provide more frequent information (as it passes daily). A data blending technique could be used.
How far back in time does your data record need to go?	Record length	It is worth doing a retrospective analysis of water use in the last years to understand the interannual variability and trends in water use. How far back in time depends on the particular circumstances of the region under study and on the availability of data (both field based and from satellite) in the past. Data from the Landsat TM sensor are available from 1986–87 onward, so potentially almost 30 years of continuous observations at 30-meter resolution are available.
Do you need guaranteed continuation of data supply into the future?	Reliability	Yes, if the project intends to maintain a system that can provide information on water use in the area into the future. If it is a one-off study looking at the present and past, continuation of data supply is not needed.
What degree of accuracy is needed in the data products?	Accuracy	The accuracy of ET estimates from EO is equal to or better than 1 millimeter per day. This accuracy is generally adequate for assessing water balance in actively growing crops.
Do you want to use only data products that are commonly used?	Maturity	There is currently no operational ET product at high spatial resolution (tens of meters). Some research agency may need to develop it for the study area.

Note: EO = Earth observation; ET = evapotranspiration; RS = remote sensing.

NOTES

1. For the validation pages, see http://www.isac.cnr .it/~ipwg/.
2. For NASA, see oceancolor.gsfc.nasa.gov; for ESA's BEAM software, see www.brockmann-consult. de/cms/web/beam/.

REFERENCES

Ebert, E. E., J. E. Janowiak, and C. Kidd. 2007. "Comparison of Near-Real-Time Precipitation Estimates from Satellite Observations and Numerical Models." *Bulletin of the American Meteorological Society* 88 (1): 47–64.

Hu, C., Z. Lee, R. Ma, K. Yu, D. Li, and S. Shang. 2010. "Moderate Resolution Imaging Spectroradiometer (MODIS) Observations of Cyanobacteria Blooms in Taihu Lake, China." *Journal of Geophysical Research* 115(C4): C04002. doi:10.1029/2009JC005511.

Matthews, M. W. 2011. "A Current Review of Empirical Procedures of Remote Sensing in Inland and Near-Coastal Transitional Waters." *International Journal of Remote Sensing* 32 (21): 6855–99.

Matthews, M. W., B. Stewart, and R. Lisl. 2012. "An Algorithm for Detecting Trophic Status (Chlorophyll-A), Cyanobacterial-Dominance, Surface Scums, and Floating Vegetation in Inland and Coastal Waters." *Remote Sensing of Environment* 124 (September): 637–52.

Odermatt, D., A. Gitelson, V. E. Brando, and M. Schaepman. 2012. "Review of Constituent Retrieval in Optically Deep and Complex Waters from Satellite Imagery." *Remote Sensing of Environment* 118 (3): 116–26.

Sapiano, M. R. P., J. E. Hanoiak, W. Shi, R. W. Higgins, and V. B. S. Silva. 2010. "Regional Evaluation through Independent Precipitation Measurements: USA." In *Satellite Rainfall Applications for Surface Hydrology*, edited by M. Gebremichael and F. Hossain, 169–204. Dordrecht: Springer Science+Business Media.

PART III

Validation of Remote Sensing–Estimated Hydrometeorological Variables

Eleonora M. C. Demaria and Aleix Serrat-Capdevila

OVERVIEW

Satellite-estimated hydrometeorological variables are increasingly available at spatial and temporal scales suitable for different research and operational applications in the fields of agriculture, hydrology, meteorology, and water quality and supply, among others. In parallel, an increase in computational power has allowed the development of a broad range of scientific and operational applications that help with understanding the climate on Earth, forecasting weather and hydrologic events, and improving natural resources management. The continuous growth and improvement in the quality of the available remote sensing (RS) measurements provide scientists with an unprecedented capability to observe and evaluate different components of the water cycle at spatial scales ranging from local to global.

Satellite missions routinely measure or estimate—more or less accurately—precipitation, soil moisture, evapotranspiration, water levels (in large rivers, lakes, estuaries, and oceans), changes in aquifer mass (levels), topography (subsidence), temperature, snow cover, snow water equivalent, and many water quality parameters such as chlorophyll, cyanobacterial indicators, colored dissolved organic matter, and suspended matter. In addition, land surface and hydrologic models are used to assimilate satellite estimates to simulate river flows, crops, landslides, and vector-borne diseases, to name just a few (Fernández-Prieto et al. 2012; Guilloteau et al. 2014; Hong and Adler 2008; Serrat-Capdevila, Valdes, and Stakhiv 2013).

Current and planned satellite missions are of great interest to natural resources managers in data-poor countries who can use RS estimates for their short- and long-term planning when a lack of ground networks undermines the feasibility and quality of natural resources evaluations and forecasting.

However, validity or "ground truth" of RS products is one of the main characteristics to be taken into account when considering their potential use. Satellite estimations are prone to several sources of uncertainty, which can significantly affect the quality of the variables to be forecasted. The three main sources of uncertainty in satellite estimations are retrieval errors, sampling errors, and inadequate ground observations (figure III.1). Uncertainties may also arise from the need for model calibration, different spatial scales, and bias correction of the estimated values prior to being used for water resources applications.

Sampling errors result from discontinuities in space and time between two consecutive satellite passages. In the case of precipitation estimates, a satellite takes snapshots of the cloud fields (reflectivity) at specified times throughout the day. Numerical algorithms are subsequently used to extrapolate those measurements in space and time to obtain daily totals. Retrieval errors stem from sources such as noise in the instrument measurements, improper calibration of the sensor, the sensor's inability to delineate rainy and dry areas, errors in the transfer of information between the satellite and the ground, and errors in the algorithms used, for instance, to convert brightness temperatures and radar signatures into amounts of precipitation (Demaria et al. 2014). Additionally, coarse ground networks make the calibration of satellite estimates difficult or even impossible in many regions around the world.

Part III is organized as follows. Chapter 8 discusses the main challenges of using ground observations to validate RS estimates of hydrologic variables, and describes the methodological approach used to evaluate the reliability of RS products at different spatiotemporal scales. Chapter 9 evaluates the performance of RS products for measuring meteorological variables, and chapter 10 focuses on the use of remotely sensed variables in combination with hydrologic or hydrodynamic models for estimating streamflow. Chapter 11 provides a synthesis of the main take-home messages.

REFERENCES

Demaria, E. M. C., B. Nijssen, J. B. Valdés, D. A. Rodriguez, and F. Su. 2014. "Satellite Precipitation in Southeastern South America: How Do Sampling Errors Impact High Flow Simulations?" *International Journal of River Basin Management* 12 (1): 1–13.

Fernández-Prieto, D., P. van Oevelen, Z. Su, and W. Wagner. 2012. "Advances in Earth Observation for Water Cycle Science." *Hydrology and Earth System Sciences* 16 (2): 543–49.

Guilloteau, C., M. Gosset, C. Vignolles, M. Alcoba, Y. M. Touree, and J. Lacaux. 2014. "Impacts of Satellite-Based Rainfall Products on Predicting Spatial Patterns of Rift Valley Fever Vectors." *Journal of Hydrometeorology* 15 (4): 1624–35.

Hong, Y., and R. F. Adler. 2008. "Predicting Global Landslide Spatiotemporal Distribution: Integrating Landslide Susceptibility Zoning Techniques and Real-Time Satellite Rainfall Estimates." *International Journal of Sediment Research* 23 (3): 249–57.

Serrat-Capdevila, A., J. B. Valdes, and E. Z. Stakhiv. 2013. "Water Management Applications for Satellite Precipitation Products: Synthesis and Recommendations." *Journal of the American Water Resources Association* 50 (2): 509–25.

Figure III.1 Main Sources of Uncertainty in Satellite-Estimated Hydrologic Variables

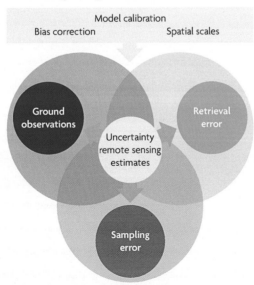

CHAPTER 8

Challenges of Remote Sensing Validation

INTRODUCTION

An important challenge is how to reconcile remote sensing (RS) estimates with ground measurements, as they can be observations of a very different nature. For example, rain gauge measurements represent the rainfall in a few square centimeters—with a time interval or aggregation that varies from seconds to daily and a spatial characterization limited by the number of rain gauges—and are often not available in real time (especially in developing-country settings). Satellite rainfall estimates are indirect measures (from infrared, passive microwave, or radar sensors), often having a spatial resolution[1] ranging from 0.04° to 0.25°—with a precipitation value representative of an area 16 and 625 square kilometers, respectively—and time steps ranging from half an hour to three hours or a day. The different spatial footprints of the reference data sets pose the most difficulties in evaluating and validating RS estimates. For this reason, the best representation of "ground truth" is an assimilation of both types of data: (a) direct point observations of rainfall that makes it to the ground surface and (b) radar and satellite estimates that provide the spatial distribution of the rainfall.

Thus validation efforts rely on reference data sets consisting of ground observations, radar or other satellite data, or a combination of observation types to measure and characterize the errors in satellite estimates. In regions where the density of ground observations is high (mostly in the United States and some European countries), gridded precipitation products from interpolated ground observation data are available, frequently at daily and monthly aggregations. However, in the absence of ground measurements of certain variables, RS data can also be evaluated against model-generated data, bearing in mind that model-generated data may contain significantly more errors than ground observations. This is the case of values for evapotranspiration or soil moisture content that have been estimated with hydrologic land surface models. In these cases, the hydrologic model has been calibrated and validated for the region using available or proxy observations, but the errors contained in the output data may be significant and need to be acknowledged. The use of model data (as a substitute for observations) for evaluation and validation purposes was not considered in this exercise.

In a validation effort, different types of errors may be considered. For example, RS estimates of precipitation may contain three types of errors: missed events (no detection of events), false alarms (detection of rainfall not recorded on the ground), and errors in the rain rate magnitude of correctly detected rainfall events. However, the errors from ground measurement networks should also be considered, and reference data sets need to be benchmarked (Anagnostou et al. 2010). The true errors in satellite estimates are significantly lower when the errors in ground networks and the covariance between errors in the two types of observations are acknowledged (Ali, Lebel, and Amani 2005). For each type of hydrometeorological variable considered, similar caveats apply to errors and limitations of both remote and in situ observations. All of these errors and potential limitations need to be accounted for in the evaluation and use of RS estimates.

METHODOLOGICAL APPROACH

The review of validation efforts of remote sensing (RS) estimates of key hydrometeorological variables proved challenging. The publications included and reviewed in this part use a wide range of metrics and approaches in their validation efforts for each case study's location. Special attention was given to articles published in peer-reviewed scientific journals, which are indexed based on the impact of the cited research on the field of study.

For the present review, 205 articles were initially selected from the scientific literature published in the last 11 years (2003–14). To facilitate comparisons, 94 articles were culled

from the initial selection, based on two criteria: (a) articles that used only ground observations for the validation process and (b) articles that used similar metrics to measure the errors in satellite estimates. This culling yielded the following selection: 24 articles about precipitation, 19 articles about evapotranspiration (ET), 17 articles about soil moisture, 19 articles about snow water equivalent and snow depth, and 15 articles about surface water levels and streamflows.

The uncertainty of the satellite estimates was grouped, when possible, by (a) temporal scale, ranging from daily to annual, (b) spatial scale, from point or cell to basin, and (c) variability on a global scale. A tabular summary of reliability indicators—the root mean squared error (RMSE), the bias, and the correlation coefficient (CC)—is presented for each key hydrologic variable. As pointed out, this review covered only scientific studies that used ground observations for the validation process. Additionally, it included as many worldwide validation sites as possible to obtain the geographic variability of the uncertainty.

To unify the results and make meaningful recommendations, the bibliographic analysis focused on the magnitude-of-error indicators: RMSE, bias, and CC. These are usually defined as follows:[2]

$$\text{RMSE} = \sqrt{\frac{1}{n} \sum_{t=1}^{n} (S_t - O_t)^2} \qquad (8.1)$$

$$\text{Bias} = S_t - O_t, \qquad (8.2)$$

$$CC = \frac{n\sum S_t O_t - \left(\sum S_t\right)\left(\sum O_t\right)}{\sqrt{n\left(\sum O_t^2\right) - \left(\sum O_t\right)^2} \sqrt{n\left(\sum S_t^2\right) - \left(\sum S_t\right)^2}} \qquad (8.3)$$

where S_t denotes satellite estimations and O_t denotes ground observations. Bias can also be expressed as a percentage of the observed value.

Chapter 10 gives (a) an overarching view of validation efforts to date for each key variable, (b) some indications regarding the context in which these were carried out, and (c) a sense of the range of findings. Only the variables most relevant to hydrologic applications and water resources management were included: precipitation, evapotranspiration, soil moisture, snow cover and snow water equivalent, water surface levels, and streamflow simulations using satellite-estimated precipitation.

The review of streamflow simulation applications in chapter 11 had to deal with the fact that most publications had used different hydrologic modeling approaches—lumped versus distributed models, different forcing variables and approaches for model calibration, raw versus bias-corrected satellite estimates, and different model specificities—as well as varied geographic locations, including flat or mountainous terrain and diverse weather regimes. Thiemig et al. (2014) provide a good framework for the evaluation of RS applications for modeling streamflow.

Groundwater estimations were not included in the review because of their limitations (described in the section on groundwater in chapter 6). The Gravity Recovery and Climate Experiment (GRACE) mission developed by the National Aeronautics and Space Administration and the German Aerospace Center can measure changes in the Earth's mass at a monthly time step and at spatial scales of about 250–300 kilometers, which yield spatial and temporal resolutions too coarse for planning and management purposes. However, aquifer-level measurements are sparse, and validation efforts require the use of hydrologic models as ground truth (Wahr, Swenson, and Velicogna 2006). Despite their limitations, satellite estimations have been used successfully to analyze long-term trends in changes in groundwater levels on a regional or continental scale (Famiglietti et al. 2011; Feng et al. 2013; Frappart, Seoane, and Ramillien 2013).

NOTES

1. National Aeronautics and Space Administration (NASA) missions that produce data parameters with a coarse spatial resolution typically report the resolution in geographic degrees or fractions of degrees. The size of a degree (or fraction of a degree) depends on how close the measured area is to the equator and the poles. The spatial area of a 1° x 1° square (that is, 1° of latitude x 1° of longitude) gets smaller the closer you get to the poles.

2. RMSE measures the differences between (sample or population) values predicted by a model or estimator and the values actually observed. The bias (of an estimator) is the difference between the estimator's expected value and the actual value of the parameter being estimated. CC represents the degree of linear dependence of two variables and always lies between −1 and +1.

REFERENCES

Ali, A., T. Lebel, and A. Amani. 2005. "Rainfall Estimation in the Sahel. Part I: Error Function." *Journal of Applied Meteorology* 44 (11): 1691–706.

Anagnostou, E. N., V. Maggioni, E. I. Nikolopoulos, T. Meskele, F. Hossain, and A. Papadopoulos. 2010. "Benchmarking High-Resolution Global Satellite Rainfall Products to Radar and Rain-Gauge Rainfall Estimates." *IEEE Transactions on Geoscience and Remote Sensing* 48 (4): 1667–83.

Famiglietti, J. S., M. Lo, S. L. Ho, J. Bethune, K. J. Anderson, T. H. Syed, S. C. Swenson, C. R. de Linage, and M. Rodell. 2011. "Satellites Measure Recent Rates of Groundwater Depletion in California's Central Valley." *Geophysical Research Letters* 38 (3). doi: 10.1029/2010GL046442.

Feng, W., M. Zhong, J. M. Lemoine, R. Biancale, H. T. Hsu, and J. Xia. 2013. "Evaluation of Groundwater Depletion in North China Using the Gravity Recovery and Climate Experiment (GRACE) Data and Ground-Based Measurements." *Water Resources Research* 49 (4): 2110–18.

Frappart, F., L. Seoane, and G. Ramillien. 2013. "Validation of GRACE-Derived Terrestrial Water Storage from a Regional Approach over South America." *Remote Sensing of Environment* 137 (October): 69–83.

Thiemig, V., R. Rojas, M. Zambrano-Bigiarini, V. Levizzani, and A. DeRoo. 2014. "Validation of Satellite-Based Precipitation Products over Sparsely Gauged African River Basins." *Journal of Hydrometeorology* 13 (6): 1760–83.

Wahr, J., S. Swenson, and I. Velicogna. 2006. "Accuracy of GRACE Mass Estimates." *Geophysical Research Letters* 33 (6). doi: 10.1029/2005GL025305.

CHAPTER 9

Validation of Remote Sensing Data

PRECIPITATION

Precipitation is the input variable most commonly found in hydrologic applications and processes related to the water cycle. Historically, the main source of precipitation data has been observations from ground gauge networks and in some places, if available, from precipitation radars. However, well-functioning ground networks are limited to the industrial countries and are extremely sparse in the underdeveloped parts of the globe. Moreover, network densities are relatively low over thinly populated, high-latitude areas. Satellite-based precipitation estimates are naturally of most interest in those parts of the world where ground observation networks are sparse. This is even more true if the population density in those areas is relatively high (and thus highly vulnerable to hydrologic extremes), entailing relatively high water needs and use.

Various precipitation products already exist that are either based exclusively on (visible, infrared, or passive microwave) satellite retrieval (Hsu et al. 1997; Huffman et al. 2001) or based on blended methods that use multi-satellites and multi-sensors (Huffman et al. 1997, 2007). This section evaluates the accuracy of satellite-based precipitation estimates based on the following products:

- Two products from the National Aeronautics and Space Administration (NASA): Tropical Rainfall Measuring Mission (TRMM) and Multisatellite Precipitation Analysis (TMPA) real-time product (TMPA 3B42RT) and TMPA 3B42

- One product from the Climate Prediction Center: the Climate Prediction Center MORPHing technique (CMORPH)

- One product from the University of California, Irvine: Precipitation Estimation from Remotely Sensed Information Using Artificial Neural Networks (PERSIANN)

- One product from the Japan Science and Technology Agency (JAXA): Global Satellite Mapping of Precipitation (GSMaP).

Table 9A.1 in annex 9A (available online at https://openknowledge.worldbank.org/handle/10986/22952) presents key aspects of the satellite products used in the validation process of the scientific literature reviewed. For each journal article reviewed, the table gives the geographic location of the validation site, the temporal scale (that is, daily, monthly, annual, or seasonal), and the magnitude of the root mean squared error (RMSE), bias, and correlation coefficient (CC).

Orographic Effects on Estimated Precipitation

In mountainous areas, satellite sensors have trouble capturing orographic precipitation and the effects of rain shadow. In addition, as ground networks are sparse or nonexistent in such areas, sensor calibration and validation are difficult. In the western Black Sea region of Turkey, where the complex topography is a major factor in the genesis of precipitation, studies have found that the volume of monthly precipitation is 50 percent less (within a 50-kilometer range) on the leeward (drier) side of the mountain range than on the windward (wetter) side, due to the rain shadow effect (Derin and Yilmaz 2014). On average, satellite products tend to underestimate observations on the windward side of mountains by –18 percent (negative bias) during the warm and dry season and by as much as –53 percent during the cold and humid season. Satellites tend to overestimate precipitation observations, with the exception of CMORPH estimates, on the leeward side, on average, by +2 percent during the warm season and by +25 percent during the cold season.[1] Since warm orographic processes cannot always be detected by passive microwave or infrared sensors (Dinku et al. 2007), biases in daily products range from –9.5 (warm season) to –51.8 percent (cold season) on the windward side and from +7.25 percent (warm season) to +38.3 percent (cold season) on the leeward side.

Extreme Precipitation Events

In data-poor regions where intense storms are responsible for substantial economic losses, large numbers of displaced people, and a flood-related death toll, satellite estimations of precipitation would be very valuable for the study and monitoring of such destructive meteorological phenomena. However, based on three-hour satellite estimations, Mei et al. (2014) find that warm-season extreme precipitation values (that is, those above the 90th percentile) are poorly correlated with ground observations—correlation values ranging from 0 for CMORPH to 0.51 for TMPA 3B42RT v7. During the cold season, the correlation is even weaker, with an average value of 0.16. The RMSE values range from 0.38 to 0.98 millimeter during the warm season and from 0.54 to 0.86 millimeter during the cold season.

TMPA 3B42 systematically underestimates the magnitude of tropical cyclones in Australia by –15 percent for rainfall intensities in the range of 50–75 millimeters per day and by –40 percent for intensities higher than 200 millimeters per day (Chen et al. 2013). Similarly, for tropical cyclones in the southeastern United States, TMPA products 3B42 and 3B42RT show biases in the ±25 and ±50 percent range of observations, respectively (Habib, Henschke, and Adler 2009).[2] In southeastern South America, where the most intense precipitation on Earth has been documented (Zipser et al. 2006), satellite products fail to capture the magnitude of average precipitation of meso-scale convective systems—thunderstorm systems with a spatial range of 100 kilometers or more. In the case of "pure" satellite products, the CMORPH estimate biases range from –70 to +60 millimeters per day, while the PERSIANN estimate biases range from –55 to +25 millimeters per day. Even the TMPA 3B42 rainfall estimates show biases in the range of –60 to +50 millimeters per day. This is surprising since this satellite product is routinely bias-corrected using ground observations. This suggests that, at least in certain regions of the world, this post-processing correction does not necessarily offer much of an improvement over the uncorrected data sets (Demaria et al. 2011).

Seasonal Precipitation

In Australia, infrared–passive microwave satellite products such as TMPA 3B42RT, CMOPRH, and PERSIANN have performed better in the tropics during the summer months (December–January), when rain is mostly of a convective nature, than in midlatitudes, where the accuracy of satellite sensors deteriorates slightly. Since several validation studies have been performed at the seasonal level, figure 9.1 shows the correlation coefficient between infrared–passive microwave satellite products and ground observations for the summer and winter, respectively, based on a subset of the summary data provided in table 9A.1 in annex 9.A (available online). Three-hourly, daily, monthly, and annual validation correlation coefficients are not included in the plot.

During summertime, correlation coefficients range from 0.35 to 0.85, with a median value of 0.65 (figure 9.1, green column).[3] In the winter months, they deteriorate slightly (most likely because of the nonconvective nature of winter

storms), with values ranging from 0.19 to 0.72 and a median value of 0.32 (figure 9.1, blue column). Winter storms, which are characterized by warm top clouds with insufficient ice for satellite sensors to detect precipitation, are responsible for satellite misses and an increase in the number of false alarms. For more intense precipitation (higher than 20 millimeters per day), satellite products show biases during the summer, especially in the mid-latitude regions, because they cannot observe the rapid temporal evolution of most convective storms (Ebert, Janowiak, and Kidd 2007).

Summary

The findings for the validation of precipitation products are as follows:

- In regions of complex topography, such as mountainous regions, satellite products tend to underestimate precipitation on the windward side of the mountain (−18 and −53 percent during the warm-dry and cold-wet season, respectively) and to overestimate precipitation on the leeward side (+2 and +25 percent during the warm-dry and cold-wet season, respectively).

- Satellite products have trouble estimating extreme precipitation events such as tropical and subtropical storms, with biases of ±25 and ±50 percent for the TMPA products 3B42 and 3B42RT, respectively.

- Satellite sensors are better at capturing convective, summer precipitation in the tropics and midlatitudes (CC ranges from 0.35 to 0.85, with a median of 0.65) than winter precipitation (CC ranges from 0.19 to 0.72, with a median of 0.32), which is usually of a nonconvective nature.

EVAPOTRANSPIRATION

Evapotranspiration (ET)—through evaporation from the soil, rainfall intercepted by plants, and plant transpiration—is a key component of

Figure 9.1 Correlation Coefficients between Observed and Satellite-Estimated Precipitation

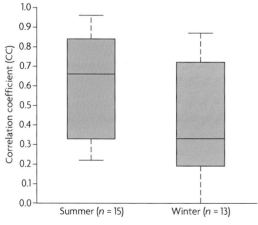

Note: The satellite products used include CMORPH, PERSIANN, GPROF 6.0, RFE 2.0, and TMPA 3B42 (both v6 and v7). *n* = sample size. The black horizontal line in both columns represents the median value.

the coupling between the atmosphere and the Earth surface. In most ET estimation methods, the driving parameter is net radiation, and the vapor pressure deficit is used to calculate water vapor transfer. In recent years, several ET data sets have been developed based on in situ ground data or satellite retrievals. Satellite imagery, increasingly available at fine spatial and temporal resolutions, has generated information that has allowed the development of ET estimation schemes. While satellite remote sensing provides reasonable estimates of different land surface fluxes, it does not measure evapotranspiration directly. Instead, the scientific community relies on retrieval algorithms to integrate those fluxes and simulate evapotranspiration's variability.

Several methods, of different degrees of complexity, have been developed using schemes that balance empirical and physically based components. The simplest method (direct method) uses thermal infrared to infer temperature in the atmosphere, which is then used along with ground temperature measurements to estimate ET rates. These methods are sensitive to cloud conditions and to errors in the ground- and satellite-measured temperature values. Deterministic methods use soil-vegetation-atmosphere transfer (SVAT) models, which can potentially be linked to climate and hydrologic models, but require accurate RS estimates of evapotranspiration and the estimation of several model parameters. SVAT models and RS data can be combined into more complex data assimilation processes (Courault, Seguin, and Olioso 2005).

As is the case of most hydrometeorological variables estimated with satellites, the lack of ground reference data is one of the main culprits of the estimates' uncertainty (Wang and Dickinson 2012). To mitigate the impact of the lack of observations, an international initiative was launched in the previous decade to evaluate and compare existing land ET products.[4] The project aims to create a global, multiyear benchmark data set of evapotranspiration at different spatial scales (Jiménez, Prigent, and Aires 2009; Jiménez et al. 2011; Mueller et al. 2011, 2013).

Validation of Remotely Sensed ET Estimates

Table 9A.2 in annex 9A (available online) presents a comparative summary of different ET estimates. In general, satellite products derived on a monthly time scale have stronger agreement with ground observations than those derived on a daily basis. Moreover, estimates show better agreements in humid (subtropical) than in arid and semiarid regions, as shown for the African continent, where ET products systematically overestimate reference values (Trambauer et al. 2014). However, the uncertainty band ranges from −30 percent underestimation to +20 percent overestimation, most likely as a result of model deficiencies—more specifically, the failure to account fully for changes in soil moisture resulting from plant transpiration and forest rainfall interception (Miralles et al. 2011). The RMSE ranges from 0.26 millimeter to 3 millimeters per day, with an average value of 0.94 millimeter per day and a standard deviation of 0.73 millimeter per day. Comparisons with ground observations (flux

Figure 9.2 Correlation Coefficients between Observed and Satellite-Estimated Evapotranspiration

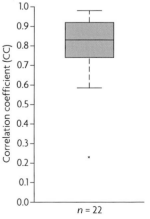

Note: n = sample size. The black horizontal line in the column represents the median value.

towers) worldwide suggest a robust linear correlation (median value of CC = 0.83) between satellite-estimated ET and ground observations (figure 9.2), despite the large biases.[5]

Summary

The findings for the validation of evapotranspiration products are as follows:

- Satellite observations can estimate the main drivers of evapotranspiration (temperature, latent heat, sensible heat) on a global scale and thus can be very valuable in meeting the need for global ET estimates.

- However, large discrepancies in the estimates indicate that land evapotranspiration is, and will remain, one of the most uncertain components of the water balance, with biases ranging from −30 to +10 percent and average RMSE values of 0.94 millimeter per day (±0.73).

SOIL MOISTURE

Soil moisture—water stored in the soil—controls the partitioning of available energy into sensible and latent heat fluxes and influences the evolution of weather and hydrologic processes in a basin. In recent decades, soil moisture has routinely been estimated with several satellite sensors (Dorigo et al. 2010). However, the lack of soil moisture observations that can be used for validation remains a fundamental problem. To address this issue, an international network has been created to support efforts aimed at establishing and maintaining a global in situ soil moisture database, which is essential for the scientific community to be able to validate and improve global satellite observations.[6] Typically, existing and planned ground-based soil moisture networks cover areas ranging from 100 square kilometers to 10 million square kilometers. However, because of the spatial variability of observed soil moisture, coarser networks often lack the resolution required to validate satellite products and introduce significant sampling uncertainty (Crow et al. 2012).

The theoretical basis for using remote sensors to measure soil moisture content is based on the contrast between the dielectric properties of the dry soil material and the water. Water has a large dielectric constant (of about 80); when this is added to the dry soil matrix (dielectric constant of about 4), the soil's dielectric constant rises significantly and the emission and scattering properties of the soil change (de Jeu et al. 2008). The validation of RS soil moisture is challenging due to the disparity between the spatial scales of the satellite and those of in situ observations. Conventional soil moisture observations provide point measurements, while satellite observations provide estimates covering a much larger spatial area (Su et al., 2011 and 2013). Moreover, soil moisture has a relatively large spatial and temporal variability, related to the presence or absence of vegetation coverage. Soil emissions tend to be attenuated by the vegetation canopy, resulting in decreased sensitivity of sensors to variations in soil moisture. Extremely dry soils, such as are found in desert regions, can also introduce uncertainty in the sensors' measurements because of higher backscatter (de Jeu et al. 2008). Examples of soil moisture sensors aboard different satellites are provided in table 6.6 in chapter 6.

Validation of Remotely Sensed Soil Moisture Estimates

Table 9A.3 of annex 9A (available online) shows the results of validation efforts using satellite-estimated soil moisture and ground observations from intensive field campaigns and existing networks in Australia, France, Italy, Spain, and the United States as well as in Asia and West Africa. The RMSE values[7] range from 0.01 to 0.36 cubic meter of water per cubic meter of soil (m^3/m^3) and have a mean value of 0.11 (±0.09) m^3/m^3. However, most RMSE values are small (figure 9.3, panel a), as 69 percent of the studies evaluated have RMSE

Figure 9.3 Errors in RS Estimations of Soil Moisture

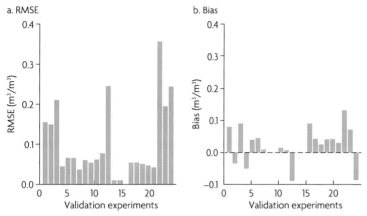

Note: The x-axis shows individual satellite products. For the validation exercise, only 17 scientific studies were considered. Since all of the satellite products from each study were included in the analysis, n = 22; RMSE = root mean squared error.

correlation coefficients larger than 0.7 and 40 percent of the sites have correlation coefficients larger than 0.6. Figure 9.4 shows the distribution of the correlation coefficients grouped by type of sensor (passive, active, and combined). While the correlation coefficients of the active sensors show slightly less dispersion than those of the passive sensors, both types of sensors have similar mean CC values, indicating that, for the studies included in this report, both methods are comparably effective at retrieving soil moisture data from space. Su et al. (2011, 2013) provide additional examples of RS soil moisture validations, focusing on the Tibetan Plateau.

values less than 0.15 m³/m³. Satellite estimates tend to overestimate the value of observations, as shown by the mean positive bias of 0.04 (±0.05) m³/m³. As is the case with the RMSE, biases range from –0.09 to 0.13 m³/m³, with 82 percent of the validation sites showing positive values (figure 9.3, panel b).

The correlation coefficients between observations and RS estimates range from 0.11 to 0.96. Despite a mean CC value of 0.58 (±0.19), around 15 percent of the validated sites have

Summary

The findings for the validation of soil moisture are as follows:

- Satellite estimates are only representative of the top 5 centimeters of the soil layer, which can limit their applicability.

- Lack of ground observations limits satellite-derived estimate validation to a few locations and to special field campaigns.

- The soil moisture satellite products analyzed yielded a mean RMSE of 0.11 (±0.09) m³/m³ and a mean positive bias of 0.04 (±0.05) m³/m³.

- RS estimations of soil moisture are promising, considering the mean correlation coefficient of 0.58 (±0.19).

Figure 9.4 Correlation Coefficients between Observed and Satellite-Estimated Soil Moisture, by Type of Sensor

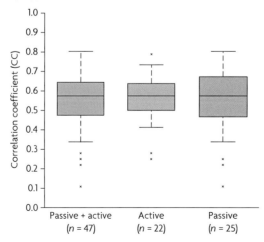

Note: n = sample size. The black horizontal line represents the median value of the corresponding sample.

SNOW COVER AND SNOW WATER EQUIVALENT

Accurate information on snow in the wintertime is an important component of spring and summer soil moisture predictions. The actual values of these parameters, in turn, have an impact on precipitation patterns, hydrologic extremes (floods and droughts), wildlife dynamics, and water supply. Natural ecosystems rely heavily on spring streamflows for important transitional stages in their life cycle. Despite their importance for natural resources management, in situ snow measurements are sparse, and given the high spatial variability in snow distribution, remote sensing constitutes an invaluable source of global spatially distributed snow estimates.

Uncertainty in RS-derived snow estimates, in addition to sampling and retrieval errors, results from snow reflectance, forest transmissivity, forest reflectance (of an opaque canopy), and snow-free ground reflectance for different classes of land cover (Dong, Walker, and Houser 2005). In addition, cloud cover has a large impact on the overall accuracy of satellite-derived snow cover estimates. For example, Maurer et al. (2003) report that the accuracy of the MODIS daily snow cover mapping algorithm under clear sky conditions is more than 80 percent. To reduce the impact of cloud cover on snow, cloud masks are routinely developed to identify the areas where land products should be retrieved based on the amount of cloud obstruction (Hall et al. 2002).

Validation studies indicate that satellite sensors have higher accuracy in plains areas, with little or no forest cover, than in forested areas in the northern latitudes. The forest cover masks the emission of microwaves by snow. As is the case of precipitation estimates, complex topography significantly affects the quality of snow data retrieval.

Unlike the satellite-derived estimates discussed above, satellite sensors can estimate snow cover and snow water equivalent in two ways: (a) as binary estimates (that is, snow or no snow), where the sensor only detects the presence or absence of snow on the ground (but cannot estimate depth of snow or snow water equivalent), and (b) as fractional estimates of snow-covered area, based on mixing different satellite spectral bands.

Satellite estimates available in a "binary" format are MOD10A1 and MYD10A1 Binary, both derived from the MODIS on board the Aqua and Terra satellites. An example of a fractional product is the MYD10A1 Fractional (Rittger, Painter, and Dozier 2013), which has the advantage that its estimates of snow depth can be directly compared with ground observations. In contrast, binary estimates are validated using a so-called contingency matrix (also called a confusion matrix), which counts the number of coincidences between satellite and ground measurements of "snow" and "no snow." The National Oceanic and Atmospheric Administration's Advanced Very High Resolution Radiometer (AVHRR) and the U.S. Air Force Defense Special Sensor Microwave Imager (SSM/I) also offer fractional satellite products.

Validation of Remotely Sensed Snow Cover and Snow Water Equivalent Estimates

Table 9A.4 of annex 9A (available online) summarizes the errors recorded in satellite-estimated snow cover and snow water equivalent for different satellite products. In densely forested areas of Canada, the uncertainty of satellite products ranges from −25 to +10 percent (Foster et al. 2005). In these areas, a dense forest canopy diminishes the ability of the satellite to determine the amount of snow underneath it.

Despite the lack of agreement on the magnitude and sign of the errors, the linear correlation between ground observations and satellite estimations for the 15 studies included in this analysis has a median value of 0.53 (±0.22) (figure 9.5, panel a). The RMSE ranges from 13 to 75 millimeters, with a mean value of 32.3 millimeters (±20.2). A mean negative bias of −4.4 millimeters indicates that satellites underestimate observations. However, the bias shows a high variability and has a standard deviation of 26.7 millimeters.[8]

By contrast, snow cover products compare favorably with ground observations, thanks to improvements in spatial and temporal resolution and in cloud mapping. Figure 9.5, panel b, shows that the median agreement value, or

Figure 9.5 Correlation Coefficients and Snow Mapping Agreement between Observed and Satellite-Estimated Snow Water Equivalent and Snow Cover

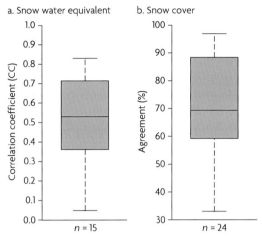

a. Snow water equivalent   b. Snow cover

Note: n = sample size. The horizontal black lines in both columns represent mean values.

accuracy, of estimated snow cover is 70 percent (sample size = 24). The standard deviation of estimated snow cover for the products reviewed is 23.3 percent, indicating that binary satellite products are quite effective at determining whether there is snow on the ground.

Summary

The findings for the validation of snow cover and snow water equivalent are as follows:

- The uncertainty in satellite estimates of snow water equivalent and snow depth is still high for the available products. The RMSE between observed and satellite-estimated snow water equivalent has a mean value of 32.3 millimeters (±20.2). Satellite estimates tend to underestimate observations by −4.4 millimeters, on average. Moreover, the bias has a relatively high variability and a standard deviation of 26.7 millimeters.

- Satellites can successfully estimate ground snow cover, as reflected by the 70 percent (±23) agreement of satellite products with ground observations.

- Since the largest snow accumulations occur at higher elevations, sparsely distributed snow stations contribute significantly to the uncertainty.

- The high accuracy of satellite sensors in detecting the presence of snow on the ground is partially due to improvements in cloud mapping techniques. Ongoing efforts to combine satellite estimates with ground observations have the potential to reduce the uncertainty in future products.

SURFACE WATER LEVELS AND STREAMFLOWS

Since stream gauges are distributed sparsely around the globe, using remote sensing to characterize river flow is extremely useful in river basins with extensive flood plains, in wetlands, and in braided rivers, where multiple river channels make it prohibitive to install several gauging stations. Satellite estimates of surface water levels are also useful for flood forecasting, especially in transboundary river basins, where the hydrologic information generated from upstream areas in the basin is not shared with the downstream partners (Biancamaria, Hossain, and Lettenmaier 2011). In regions where ground-based data are difficult to obtain due to funding shortages or political unrest, satellite data may be available in near real time for implementation in flood forecasting models (Coe and Birkett 2004).

Satellite sensors can estimate surface water levels in rivers and wetlands by using the high reflectivity of water. Therefore, unless the microwave pulses emitted by water bodies are intercepted by vegetation, small changes in water-level depths can be measured with centimeter-scale accuracy (Alsdorf and Lettenmaier 2003). The Ocean Topography Experiment (TOPEX)/Poseidon mission and the Japanese Earth Resources Satellite 1 (JERS-1) synthetic aperture radar (SAR) mission carry onboard radar altimeters designed to operate over water and ice surfaces. An altimeter radar continuously emits microwave pulses toward the surface of the Earth, and the time that passes between the pulse emission and the echo reception is used to estimate the height of the topographic surface (Birkett 1998; Hess et al. 2003).

Streamflows cannot be measured from space. Instead, satellite sensors can measure water levels, channel width, channel slope, and flow velocity, among others, and models or statistical relationships between these variables can then be used to estimate channel flows (Bjerklie et al. 2003). In addition, infrequent satellite overpasses, limited sampling frequency (determined by the distance between measurements along the satellite orbit), and incomplete spatial coverage make estimations uncertain. One of the main constraints is the need to use hydraulic models (or statistical correlations) (a) to route water levels along the river channel to compare gauge-height observations with satellite measurements in virtual stations (points where the satellite altimeter measurements are taken), as these rarely coincide with the location of a gauging station, and (b) to propagate water levels downstream to forecast flows for the areas of interest.

Validation of Remotely Sensed Surface Water Level Estimates

The most widely used satellites for estimating streamflow are the TOPEX/Poseidon mission developed by NASA and the French Space Agency, the JERS-1 SAR developed by JAXA, GRACE developed by NASA and the German Aerospace Center, and Envisat (no longer operational) developed by the European Space Agency.

Changes in the water level of lakes and wetlands can be estimated by remote sensing with relatively high reliability (see table 9A.5 of annex 9A, available online), as evidenced by a median correlation coefficient of 0.96 (±0.24). The error in lake water levels is 0.28 (±0.45) meter on average and can range from 0.04 meter

to 1.5 meters. The results suggest that the accuracy of the estimates is larger during periods with high water levels: 2 percent RMSE[9] for Lake Chad in Africa and 15-centimeter RMSE for wetland flooding in the Amazon River basin. During the rest of the year, the errors are as high as 10 percent in Lake Chad and –2.2 meters in the Amazonian wetlands (Birkett 2000; Hess et al. 2003).

Recent work by Hossain et al. (2014) has demonstrated the feasibility of implementing a five-day lead time water-level forecast system in the Brahmaputra River basin using Jason-2 estimates. Altimetry measurements to forecast stages used to force a hydrodynamic model inside Bangladesh yield forecast results with RMSE values ranging from 0.2 (± 0.2) meters for the monsoon season and 0.7 (± 0.4) meters for the dry season, when compared with a posterior "nowcasting" using observed stages. These results strongly suggest that in large rivers, water-level altimetry measurements can be used as inputs for hydrodynamic flow propagation models and thus can be especially useful in transboundary settings.

Despite the successful implementation of the system in Bangladesh, table 9A.5 shows that satellite estimates of river water levels have RMSEs ranging from 0.27 meter to 1.1 meters, which can be considered poor when compared with ground-based gauge measurements. However, these values do allow comparison of the interannual and seasonal variability of water heights across the basin (Birkett et al. 2002).

Summary

The findings for validation of surface water and streamflow are as follows:

- The uncertainty in satellite estimates of water surface is still high for the available products. The RMSE in lake water levels is 0.22 (±0.45) meter, on average, with greater accuracy during periods with high water levels.

- Infrequent satellite overpasses and incomplete spatial coverage mean that hydrodynamic models have to be used to propagate estimated river water levels from the satellite virtual stations to locations of interest downstream.

ANNEX 9A. SUMMARY OF SCIENTIFIC LITERATURE ON SATELLITE PRODUCTS INCLUDED IN VALIDATION

Annex 9A is available online at https://open knowledge.worldbank.org/handle/10986 /22952.

NOTES

1. These average values are based on the paper by Derin and Yilmaz (2014) and are not shown in table 9A.1 in annex 9A (available online).
2. These real-time products are described in table 6.3 in chapter 6.
3. The values shown were taken from table 9A.2 in annex 9A (available online). The winter and summer values were analyzed (and are shown) separately to highlight the seasonal differences in the correlation coefficient.
4. For information on this initiative, see http://www .iac.ethz.ch/groups/seneviratne/research/Land Flux-EVAL.
5. The RMSE values expressed in millimeters per day do not say much about the performance of the RS estimates. For that reason, the figures in this section only highlight the correlation coefficient.
6. For information on the network and efforts to create a soil moisture database, see http://ismn .geo.tuwien.ac.at/ismn/.
7. In this context, only RMSE values with m^3/m^3 units are considered.
8. Many of the reviewed journal articles provide a range of values, and the means of those ranges were used to arrive at these figures. The underlying values are not shown in the tables of annex 9A.
9. While the RMSE is usually expressed in the unit of the dependent variable, it can also be expressed as a percentage.

REFERENCES

Alsdorf, D. E., and D. P. Lettenmaier. 2003. "Tracking Fresh Water from Space." *Science* 301 (5639): 1491–94.

Biancamaria, S., F. Hossain, and D. P. Lettenmaier. 2011. "Forecasting Transboundary River Water Elevations from Space." *Geophysical Research Letters* 38 (11): art. 4.

Birkett, C. M. 1998. "Contribution of the TOPEX NASA Radar Altimeter to the Global Monitoring of Large Rivers and Wetlands." *Water Resources Research* 34 (5): 1223–39.

———. 2000. "Synergistic Remote Sensing of Lake Chad: Variability of Basin Inundation." *Remote Sensing of Environment* 72 (2): 218–36.

Birkett, C. M., L. A. K. Mertes, T. Dunne, M. H. Costa, and M. J. Jasinski. 2002. "Surface Water Dynamics in the Amazon Basin: Application of Satellite Radar Altimetry." *Journal of Geophysical Research: Atmospheres* 107 (D20): 8059.

Bjerklie, D. M., S. L. Dingman, C. J. Vorosmarty, C. H. Bolster, and R. G. Congalton. 2003. "Evaluating the Potential for Measuring River Discharge from Space." *Journal of Hydrology* 278 (1-4): 17–38.

Chen, Y., E. E. Ebert, K. J. E. Walsh, and N. E. Davidson. 2013. "Evaluation of TMPA 3B42 Daily Precipitation Estimates of Tropical Cyclone Rainfall over Australia." *Journal of Geophysical Research: Atmospheres* 118 (21): 11966–78.

Coe, M. T., and C. M. Birkett. 2004. "Calculation of River Discharge and Prediction of Lake Height from Satellite Radar Altimetry: Example for the Lake Chad Basin." *Water Resources Research* 40 (1): 27–33.

Courault, D., B. Seguin, and A. Olioso. 2005. "Review on Estimation of Evapotranspiration from Remote Sensing Data: From Empirical to Numerical Modeling Approaches." *Irrigation and Drainage Systems* 19 (3): 223–49.

Crow, W. T., A. A. Berg, M. H. Cosh, A. Loew, B. P. Mohanty, R. Panciera, P. de Rosnay, D. Ryu, and J. P. Walker. 2012. "Upscaling Sparse Ground-Based Soil Moisture Observations for the Validation of Coarse-Resolution Satellite Soil Moisture Products." *Reviews of Geophysics* 50 (2): RG2002.

de Jeu, R. A. M., W. Wagner, T. R. H. Holmes, A. J. Dolman, N. C. van de Giesen, and J. Friesen. 2008. "Global Soil Moisture Patterns Observed by Space Borne Microwave Radiometers and Scatterometers." *Surveys in Geophysics* 29 (4): 399–420.

Demaria, E. M. C., D. A. Rodríguez, E. E. Ebert, P. Salio, F. Su, and J. B. Valdes. 2011. "Evaluation of Mesoscale Convective Systems in South America Using Multiple Satellite Products and an Object-Based

Approach." *Journal of Geophysical Research: Atmospheres* 116 (D8). doi: 10.1029/2010JD015157.

Derin, Y., and K. K. Yilmaz. 2014. "Evaluation of Multiple Satellite-Based Precipitation Products over Complex Topography." *Journal of Hydrometeorology* 15 (4): 1498–516.

Dinku, T., P. Ceccato, E. Grover-Kopec, M. Lemma, S. J. Connor, and C. F. Ropelewski. 2007. "Validation of Satellite Rainfall Products over East Africa's Complex Topography." *International Journal of Remote Sensing* 28 (7): 1503–26.

Dong, J. R., J. P. Walker, and P. R. Houser. 2005. "Factors Affecting Remotely Sensed Snow Water Equivalent Uncertainty." *Remote Sensing of Environment* 97 (1): 68–82.

Dorigo, W. A., K. Scipal, R. M. Parinussa, Y. Y. Liu, W. Wagner, R. A. M. de Jeu, and V. Naeimi. 2010. "Error Characterisation of Global Active and Passive Microwave Soil Moisture Datasets." *Hydrology and Earth System Sciences* 14 (12): 2605–16.

Ebert, E. E., J. E. Janowiak, and C. Kidd. 2007. "Comparison of Near-Real-Time Precipitation Estimates from Satellite Observations and Numerical Models." *Bulletin of the American Meteorological Society* 88 (1): 47–64.

Foster, J. L., C. J. Sun, J. P. Walker, R. Kelly, A. Chang, J. R. Dong, and H. Powell. 2005. "Quantifying the Uncertainty in Passive Microwave Snow Water Equivalent Observations." *Remote Sensing of Environment* 94 (2): 187–203.

Habib, E., A. Henschke, and R. F. Adler. 2009. "Evaluation of TMPA Satellite-Based Research and Real-Time Rainfall Estimates during Six Tropical-Related Heavy Rainfall Events over Louisiana, USA." *Atmospheric Research* 94 (3): 373–88.

Hall, D. K., G. A. Riggs, V. V. Salomonson, N. E. DiGirolamo, and K. J. Bayr. 2002. "MODIS Snow-Cover Products." *Remote Sensing of Environment* 83 (1-2): 181–94.

Hess, L. L., J. M. Melack, E. Novo, C. C. F. Barbosa, and M. Gastil. 2003. "Dual-Season Mapping of Wetland Inundation and Vegetation for the Central Amazon Basin." *Remote Sensing of Environment* 87 (4): 404–28.

Hossain, F., A. H. Siddique-E-Akbor, L. C. Mazumder, S. M. ShahNewaz, S. Biancamaria, H. Lee, and C. K. Shum. 2014. "Proof of Concept of an Altimeter-Based River Forecasting System for Transboundary Flow Inside Bangladesh." *IEEE Journal of Selected Topics in Applied Earth Observations and Remote Sensing* 7 (2): 587–601.

Hsu, K. L., X. G. Gao, S. Sorooshian, and H. V. Gupta. 1997. "Precipitation Estimation from Remotely Sensed Information Using Artificial Neural Networks." *Journal of Applied Meteorology* 36 (9): 1176–90.

Huffman, G. J., R. F. Adler, P. Arkin, A. Chang, R. Ferraro, A. Gruber, J. Janowiak, A. McNab, B. Rudolf, and U. Schneider. 1997. "The Global Precipitation Climatology Project (GPCP) Combined Precipitation Dataset." *Bulletin of the American Meteorological Society* 78 (1): 5–20.

Huffman, G. J., R. F. Adler, D. T. Bolvin, G. Gu, E. J. Nelkin, K. P. Bowman, Y. Hong, E. F. Stocker, and D. B. Wolff. 2007. "The TRMM Multisatellite Precipitation Analysis (TMPA): Quasi-Global, Multiyear, Combined-Sensor Precipitation Estimates at Fine Scales." *Journal of Hydrometeorology* 8 (1): 38–55.

Huffman, G. J., R. F. Adler, M. M. Morrissey, D. T. Bolvin, S. Curtis, R. Joyce, B. McGavock, and J. Susskind. 2001. "Global Precipitation at One-Degree Daily Resolution from Multisatellite Observations." *Journal of Hydrometeorology* 2 (1): 36–50.

Jiménez, C., C. Prigent, and F. Aires. 2009. "Toward an Estimation of Global Land Surface Heat Fluxes from Multisatellite Observations." *Journal of Geophysical Research: Atmospheres* 114 (D6). doi: 10.1029/2008JD011392.

Jiménez, C., C. Prigent, B. Mueller, S. I. Seneviratne, M. F. McCabe, E. F. Wood, W. B. Rossow, G. Balsamo, A. K. Betts, P. A. Dirmeyer, J. B. Fisher, M. Jung, M. Kanamitsu, R. H. Reichle, M. Reichstein, M. Rodell, J. Sheffield, K. Tu, and K. Wan. 2011. "Global Intercomparison of 12 Land Surface Heat Flux Estimates." *Journal of Geophysical Research: Atmospheres* 116 (D2). doi: 10.1029/2010JD014545.

Maurer, E. P., J. D. Rhoads, R. O. Dubayah, and D. P. Lettenmaier. 2003. "Evaluation of the Snow-Covered Area Data Product from MODIS." *Hydrological Processes* 17 (1): 59–71.

Mei, Y., E. N. Anagnostou, E. I. Nikolopoulos, and M. Borga. 2014. "Error Analysis of Satellite Precipitation Products in Mountainous Basins." *Journal of Hydrometeorology* 15 (5): 1778–93.

Miralles, D. G., R. A. M. de Jeu, J. H. Gash, T. R. H. Holmes, and A. J. Dolman. 2011. "Magnitude and Variability of Land Evaporation and Its Components at the Global Scale." *Hydrology and Earth System Sciences* 15 (March): 967–81.

Mueller, B., M. Hirschi, C. Jimenez, P. Ciais, P. A. Dirmeyer, A. J. Dolman, J. B. Fisher, M. Jung, F. Ludwig, F. Maignan, D. G. Miralles, M. F. McCabe, M. Reichstein, J. Sheffield, K. Wang, E. F. Wood, Y. Zhang, and S. I. Seneviratn. 2013. "Benchmark Products for Land Evapotranspiration: Landflux-EVAL Multi-Data Set Synthesis." *Hydrology and Earth System Sciences* 17 (10): 3707–20.

Mueller, B., S. I. Seneviratne, C. Jimenez, T. Corti, M. Hirschi, G. Balsamo, P. Ciais, P. Dirmeyer, J. B. Fisher, Z. Guo, M. Jung, F. Maignan, M. F. McCabe, R. Reichle, M. Reichstein, M. Rodell, J. Sheffield, A. J. Teuling, K. Wang, and E. F. Wood. 2011. "Evaluation of Global Observations-Based Evapotranspiration Datasets and IPCC AR4 Simulations." *Geophysical Research Letters* 38 (6). doi: 10.1029/2010GL046230.

Rittger, K., T. H. Painter, and J. Dozier. 2013. "Assessment of Methods for Mapping Snow Cover from MODIS." *Advances in Water Resources* 51 (January): 367–80.

Su, Z., P. de Rosnay, J. Wen, L. Wang, and Y. Zeng. 2013. "Evaluation of ECMWF's Soil Moisture Analyses Using Observations on the Tibetan Plateau." *Journal of Geophysical Research: Atmospheres* 118 (11): 5304–18.

Su, Z., J. Wen, L. Dente, R. van der Velde, L. Wang, Y. Ma, K. Yang, and Z. Hu. 2011. "The Tibetan Plateau Observatory of Plateau Scale Soil Moisture and Soil Temperature (Tibet-Obs) for Quantifying Uncertainties in Coarse Resolution Satellite and Model Products." *Hydrology and Earth System Sciences* 15: 2303–16.

Trambauer, P., E. Dutra, S. Maskey, M. Werner, F. Pappenberger, L. P. H. van Beek, and S. Uhlenbrook. 2014. "Comparison of Different Evaporation Estimates over the African Continent." *Hydrology and Earth System Sciences* 18 (1): 193–212.

Wang, K., and R. E. Dickinson. 2012. "A Review of Global Terrestrial Evapotranspiration: Observation, Modeling, Climatology, and Climatic Variability." *Reviews of Geophysics* 50 (2). doi: 10.1029/2011RG000373.

Zipser, E. J., D. J. Cecil, C. Liu, S. W. Nesbitt, and D. P. Yorty. 2006. "Where Are the Most Intense Thunderstorms on Earth?" *Bulletin of the American Meteorological Society* 87 (8): 1057–71.

Validation of Streamflow Outputs from Models Using RS Inputs

INTRODUCTION

In recent decades, remote sensing (RS)–derived precipitation data have become increasingly available at temporal and spatial scales that are useful for hydrologic purposes such as streamflow monitoring and forecasting, drought forecasting, and water resources management (WRM). While chapter 10 reviews error evaluation and validation efforts of specific satellite products, this chapter focuses on the evaluation of errors in streamflow estimates obtained using remotely sensed variables, such as precipitation and water surface elevation, in combination with hydrologic or hydrodynamic models.

Due to the highly nonlinear responses in the hydrologic cycle, errors in RS-derived precipitation estimates can be amplified in some fluxes (evapotranspiration, streamflows) and dampened in others. Methods to improve the performance of satellite-driven simulated streamflows include (a) bias correction (removing biases) of satellite estimates prior to running a hydrologic model and (b) recalibration of hydrologic models using satellite rainfall inputs. Calibration of hydrologic models accounts for many factors beyond parameter values, such as structural model inadequacies, availability of spatial and temporal input, and errors in input data. Thus in order to obtain optimal simulation results, it is necessary to calibrate hydrologic models with the bias-corrected RS estimates that will be used to run such models for monitoring or predictive purposes (Serrat-Capdevila et al. 2013).

This chapter reviews the errors in streamflow estimates obtained from two approaches: (a) rainfall-runoff modeling using satellite rainfall estimates and other meteorological variables and (b) water-level altimeter measurements and hydrodynamic models.

A synthesis of the results reported in the literature is presented in table 9A.6 (in annex 9A, available online at https://openknowledge.worldbank.org/handle/10986/22952), When evaluating the performance of streamflow simulations, three main errors have to be analyzed: the bias (errors in the mean), differences in variability (errors in representation of the observed variability), and correlation errors (errors in the timing of simulated responses or events). These errors can be mathematically expressed in several metrics (which vary across the literature). In order to gain an understanding of the sources and nature of errors in hydrologic simulations, Gupta et al. (2009) decompose the mean squared error into three terms: the error in mean, the error in variance, and the error in correlation:

$$MSE = 2\sigma_s\sigma_o - 1 - \gamma + (\sigma_s - \sigma_o)^2 + (\mu_s - \mu_o)^2, \tag{10.1}$$

where μ_s is the mean of the satellite estimates; μ_o is the mean of the ground observations; σ_s is the standard deviation of the satellite estimates; σ_0 is the standard deviation of the ground observations; and γ is the correlation coefficient (CC) between satellite data and the reference observed data.

In a study of three satellite precipitation products (SPPs) over the African continent, Serrat-Capdevila et al. (2016) show how bias correction of satellite precipitation can correct errors in the mean and variance terms of precipitation, but not in the correlation term.

STREAMFLOW SIMULATIONS USING RAINFALL-RUNOFF MODELING

Tobin and Bennett (2014) use the Tropical Rainfall Measuring Mission (TRMM) Multisatellite Precipitation Analysis (TMPA) 3B42 (research product, nonreal time) and the Climate Prediction Center MORPHing technique (CMORPH) to force simulations in 10 basins in Australia, Brazil, and the Republic of Korea, ranging in size from 32 to 6,500 square kilometers. They compare statistics at monthly, 10-day, and daily intervals. They report that performance statistics are worse for daily simulations using satellite products than for simulations using rain gauges, except in a few cases, where both types of simulations sometimes perform equally well. They also find that the magnitude of errors increases as basins get smaller.

Gourley et al. (2011) evaluate streamflow simulations using real-time rain gauges, a denser Micronet gauge network, radar (unadjusted and stage IV, that is, gauge adjusted), Precipitation Estimation from Remotely Sensed Information Using Artificial Neural Networks-Cloud Classification System (PERSIANN-CCS), and Tropical Rainfall Measuring Mission-real time (TRMM-RT) (figures 10.1–10.3). They argue that recalibration based on potentially biased satellite data would "yield better simulations for the wrong reasons" and that it is better to calibrate the model using ground observations of rainfall data. This argument can be reversed easily to defend the use of satellite data rather than ground data for the purpose of calibration, as a model in principle always tends to produce better results when run with the same forcing data as were used in its calibration. In addition, how many rain gauges are needed to represent the truth accurately over the entire basin? As calibration addresses a range of issues and attempts to compensate for errors in the input data (present in either satellite or ground observations), for optimal performance, hydrologic models are ideally calibrated with the type of forcing data they will be using in simulations (Serrat-Capdevila et al. 2014). The framework proposed by Thiemig et al. (2013) demonstrates this argument and is the one to use.

PERSIANN-CCS yields streamflows with a very small fractional bias (figure 10.1, panel b), but a root mean squared error (RMSE) comparable to that of TRMM-RT (figure 10.2, panels c and d). The relatively small fractional bias could

Figure 10.1 Fractional Bias of Streamflow Simulations Forced by Rainfall Algorithms

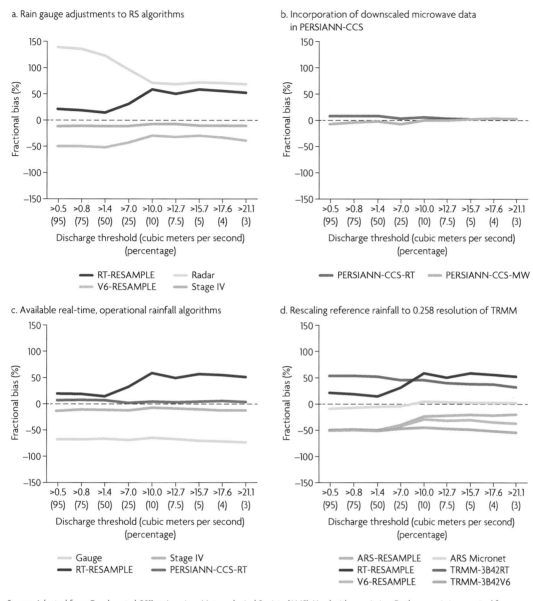

a. Rain gauge adjustments to RS algorithms

b. Incorporation of downscaled microwave data in PERSIANN-CCS

c. Available real-time, operational rainfall algorithms

d. Rescaling reference rainfall to 0.258 resolution of TRMM

Source: Adapted from Gourley et al. 2011. © American Meteorological Society (AMS). Used with permission. Further permission required for reuse.

Note: The rainfall algorithms used are indicated in the legend for each panel. Scores are plotted as a function of flow exceedance threshold.

be the result of many errors (including false alarms and missed events) that compensate each other when aggregated. Thus it can be accompanied by a high RMSE, which still indicates poor performance.

The improved performance, in terms of Micronet-relative efficiency (MRE)—that is improvements over using Micronet—for TMPA 3B42RT was achieved by recalibrating the model at the resolution of TMPA (0.25°

and three hours), but still using rain gauge values as calibration forcing. As a result, the MRE improved to –10 from an MRE of –30 and –40, depending on the magnitude of discharge (no improvement was seen in the RMSE or in the bias). The MRE of PERSIANN-CCS ranged from –17 to –25, performing better than the original runs with 3B42RT (before model recalibration at 0.25° and three-hour resolution).

Figure 10.2 RMSE of Streamflow Simulations Forced by Rainfall Algorithms

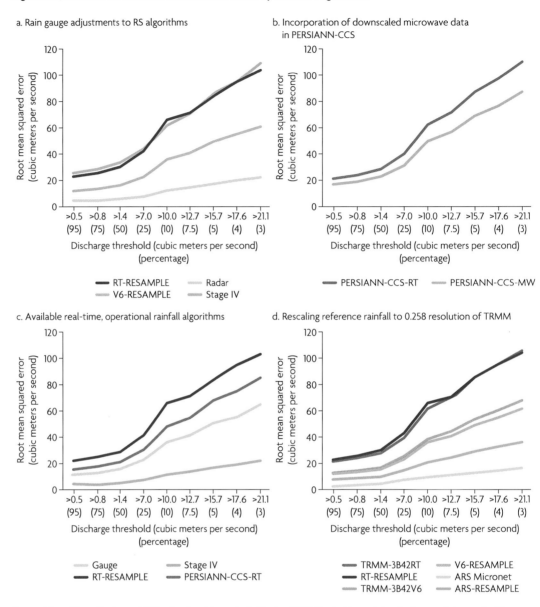

Source: Adapted from Gourley et al. 2011. © American Meteorological Society (AMS). Used with permission. Further permission required for reuse.

Note: The rainfall algorithms used are indicated in the legend for each panel. Scores are plotted as a function of flow exceedance threshold. RMSE = root mean squared error.

Hossain and Anagnostou (2004) examine the impact of passive microwave rainfall retrieval frequency and sampling errors on flood prediction uncertainty in a medium-size basin in northern Italy using a semi-distributed hydrologic model. Regarding temporal sampling frequencies, they find that three-hour rainfall retrievals yield similar flood prediction uncertainties as do hourly inputs, but the six-hour rainfall retrievals amplify the runoff prediction error by a factor of three. Extending these results to short-duration, extreme flood-producing storms is one goal of the Gourley et al. (2011) study. Sangati and Borga (2009) find that spatial rainfall aggregation has a significant effect on simulations of peak discharge for extreme flooding events.

Gourley et al. (2011) also show that seasonal performance and statistics are not representative of extreme events: all satellite products

Figure 10.3 Relative Efficiency of Streamflow Simulations Forced by Rainfall Algorithms

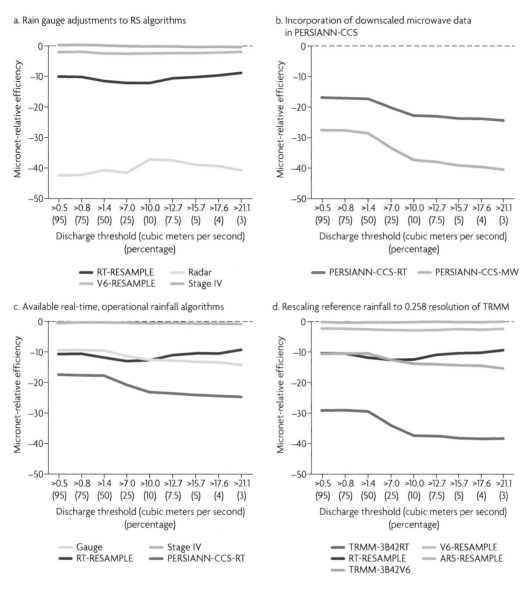

a. Rain gauge adjustments to RS algorithms

b. Incorporation of downscaled microwave data in PERSIANN-CCS

c. Available real-time, operational rainfall algorithms

d. Rescaling reference rainfall to 0.258 resolution of TRMM

Source: Adapted from Gourley et al. 2011. © American Meteorological Society (AMS). Used with permission. Further permission required for reuse.

Note: The rainfall algorithms used are indicated in the legend for each panel. Scores are plotted as a function of flow exceedance threshold.

perform very poorly for a 500-year extreme event. The ranking of simulation performance from the seasonal analysis actually reverses for the extreme event. They do not address why recalibrating the model—by aggregating the reference data set to the resolution of the satellite product—improves the simulations. This is likely due to the averaging of errors and parameters in the coarser resolution of the satellite product.

Thiemig et al. (2013) evaluate simulations in two African basins (Volta and Baro-Akobo) and four sub-basins with various SPPs using the Kling-Gupta efficiency (KGE), an error metric that combines three components—bias, variability, and correlation (Kling, Fuchs, and Paulin 2012)—as follows:

$$KGE = 1 - \sqrt{(r-1)^r + (\beta-1)^2 + (\gamma-1)^2}$$

(10.2)

$$\beta = \frac{\mu_s}{\mu_o} \qquad (10.3)$$

$$\gamma = \frac{CV_s}{CV_o} \frac{\sigma_s/\mu_s}{\sigma_o/\mu_o}, \qquad (10.4)$$

where μ_s is the mean of the satellite estimates; μ_o is the mean of the ground observations, σ_s is the standard deviation of the satellite estimates; σ_o is the standard deviation of the ground observations; r is the linear correlation (Pearson product-moment) coefficient between satellite data and the reference observed data; β the bias ratio; and γ is the variability ratio between the coefficients of variation, CV.

They use a structured approach to benchmark improvements in the simulation's performance in those two basins:

1. Calibrating the hydrologic model with interpolated rain gauge data

2. Running SPP simulations with reference (gauge) calibration for each satellite product (to determine the intrinsic value of raw SPPs)

3. Running simulations with SPP-specific calibration (to determine the value of recalibration and raw SPPs)

4. Running simulations (with reference calibration parameters) for bias-corrected SPPs

5. Running simulations with bias-corrected SPP-specific calibration (to determine the combined benefits of bias-correction and SPP-specific recalibration).

In the lowlands, performance is good or intermediate for African Rainfall Estimation Algorithm Version 2 (RFE2) and TRMM, but poor for CMORPH and PERSIANN. In the mountainous basin, CMORPH performs better. Most of the poor and very poor performance can be attributed to bias and variability (errors in mass balance and shape of distributions).

CMORPH and PERSIANN clearly benefit strongly from both bias correction and model recalibration, and these processes correct mainly the bias term. In other words, CMORPH and PERSIANN contain significant biases that can be corrected. Bias correction is more effective than recalibration (which is unable to correct mass balance) at correcting products with large biases and yielding improved simulations. For products without large biases, model recalibration yields more significant improvements than bias correction, an intuitive result. Finally, as recommended by Serrat-Capdevila et al. (2013), the combined use of bias correction and recalibration of hydrologic models with bias-corrected SPP data yields the best possible performance.

In a flow-forecasting system for the Yellow River—a Sino-Dutch cooperation project—Rosema et al. (2008) use RS data (from hourly visual and thermal infrared bands) for river basin management, including energy and water balance, drought monitoring, and flow and flood forecasting. This large project has custom-made satellite precipitation retrievals and modeling as well as a forecasting system. The means employed for this project probably go beyond the resources of most similar studies. The water resources forecasting system (flow forecasting) yields correlations of 0.8 to 0.94 for the sub-basins, with Nash-Sutcliffe efficiency (NSE) coefficients of 0.77 to 0.84.[1]

BOX 10.1

Validation of Streamflow Simulations Using Rainfall-Runoff Modeling

- The performance of hydrologic applications using RS data can be highly variable, depending on basin size, geography, topography, and storm systems.

- Hydrologic simulations will generally yield better results if RS inputs are bias corrected (if they contain biases) and if the hydrologic models are recalibrated with the same type of input data that will be used in these models for predictive purposes.

Their high-water forecasting system (flood forecasting) yields correlations of 0.75 to 0.80 (slightly lower than for flow forecasting) and NSEs of 0.71 to 0.79 (see table 9A.6, available online).

Box 10.1 summarizes the findings for validating streamflow simulations using rainfall-runoff modeling.

STREAMFLOW SIMULATIONS BASED ON REMOTELY SENSED WATER LEVELS UPSTREAM

Flood-prone developing countries usually lack the in situ hydrologic data necessary to implement flood forecasting systems. In the case of transboundary basins, downstream countries are usually "blind" to what is happening in the upper part of the basin, because of the lack of international cooperation and scarcity of ground observation networks.

For instance, presently there is no mechanism for the Bangladeshi government to receive timely information on upstream conditions of the Ganges-Brahmaputra basin. Stream measurements at the borders where the rivers enter the country only allow the Bangladeshi government to forecast water levels downstream with a lead time of two to three days at most. Recent work by Hossain, Siddique-E-Akbor, Mazumder et al. (2014) and by Hossain, Siddique-E-Akbor, Yigzaw et al. (2014) has demonstrated the feasibility of implementing an 8- to 10-day ahead water-level forecast system in the Brahmaputra River basin using Jason-2 estimates. Measurements of river surface levels upstream in India and a hydrodynamic model (the Hydrologic Engineering Centers River Analysis System, HEC-Ras) are used to predict how the observed water levels upstream will propagate to areas downstream. In operational forecasts during the high-flow season of August 2012, a five-day water-level forecast system had average errors ranging from −0.4 to 0.4 meter, with

BOX 10.2

Validation of Streamflow Simulations Using Remotely Sensed Water Levels Upstream

Estimating water levels in large river basins using altimeters is a more direct way to monitor stage height and streamflow (and make predictions downstream) than using only basin-wide rainfall-runoff models, which can be particularly complex in the case of very large basins.

An operational forecast system based on satellite surface water altimetry to drive flow propagation models has extended forecast lead times in Bangladesh from 3 days to 8 or 10 days, with an RMSE of 0.7 meter at the India-Bangladesh border.

RMSE values ranging from 0.2 to 0.7 meter at selected river stations (Hossain, Siddique-E-Akbor, Mazumder et al. 2014). Currently, a forecast system with lead times of 8 to 10 days has shown an RMSE of 0.7 meter at the India-Bangladesh border (Hossain, Siddique-E-Akbor, Yigzaw et al. 2014). These results indicate that countries with large transboundary rivers could implement operational forecast systems with currently available and planned altimeter missions to manage water risks in flood-prone regions. The authors argue that satellite radar altimetry is probably more valuable in large rivers than rainfall-runoff simulations using satellite precipitation estimates to anticipate the occurrence of high-water conditions in the basin (see box 10.2).

NOTE

1. The Nash-Sutcliffe coefficient of efficiency is used to assess the performance of hydrologic models in replicating observed streamflows and is defined as follows:

$$E = 1 - \frac{\sum_{t=1}^{T}(Q_o^t - Q_m^t)^2}{\sum_{t=1}^{T}(Q_o^t - \overline{Q}_o)^2},$$

where $\overline{Q}_o$ is the mean of observed discharge, Q_m is modeled discharge, and Q_o^t is observed discharge at time t.

REFERENCES

Gourley, J. J., Y. Hong, Z. L. Flamig, J. Wang, H. Vergara, and E. N. Anagnostou. 2011. "Hydrologic Evaluation of Rainfall Estimates from Radar, Satellite, Gauge, and Combinations on Ft. Cobb Basin, Oklahoma." *Journal of Hydrometeorology* 12 (5): 973–88.

Gupta, H. V., H. Kling, K. K. Yilmaz, and G. F. Martinez. 2009. "Decomposition of the Mean Squared Error and NSE Performance Criteria: Implications for Improving Hydrological Modeling." *Journal of Hydrology* 377 (1-2): 80–91.

Hossain, F., and E. N. Anagnostou. 2004. "Assessment of Current Passive-Microwave- and Infrared-Based Satellite Rainfall Remote Sensing for Flood Prediction." *Journal of Geophysical Research: Atmospheres* 109 (D7). Republished with an errata in 2005.

Hossain, F., A. H. Siddique-E-Akbor, L. C. Mazumder, S. M. ShahNewaz, S. Biancamaria, H. Lee, and C. K. Shum. 2014. "Proof of Concept of an Altimeter-Based River Forecasting System for Transboundary Flow Inside Bangladesh." *IEEE Journal of Selected Topics in Applied Earth Observations and Remote Sensing* 7 (2): 587–601.

Hossain, F., A. H. M. Siddique-E-Akbor, W. Yigzaw, S. Shah-Newaz, M. Hossain, L. C. Mazumder, T. Ahmed, C. K. Shum, H. Lee, S. Biancamaria, F. J. Turk, and A. Limaye. 2014. "Crossing the Valley of Death: Lessons Learned from Implementing an Operational Satellite-Based Flood Forecasting System." *Bulletin of the American Meteorological Society* 95 (8): 1201–07.

Kling, H., M. Fuchs, and M. Paulin. 2012. "Runoff Conditions in the Upper Danube Basin under an Ensemble of Climate Change Scenarios." *Journal of Hydrology* 424-425 (March 6): 264–77.

Rosema, A., M. De Weirdt, S. Foppes, R. Venneker, S. Maskey, Y. Gu, W. Zhao, C. Wang, X. Liu, S. Rao, D. Dai, Y. Zhang, L. Wen, D. Chen, Y. Di, S. Qiu, Q. Wang, L. Zhang, J. Liu, L. Liu, L. Xie, R. Zhang, J. Yang, Y. Zhang, M. Luo, B. Hou, L. Zhao, L. Zhu, X. Chen, T. Yang, H. Shang, S. Ren, F. Sun, Y. Sun, F. Zheng, Y. Xue, Z. Yuan, H. Pang, C. Lu, G. Liu, X. Guo, D. Du, X. He, X. Tu, W. Sun, B. Bink, and X. Wu. 2008. *Satellite Monitoring and Flow Forecasting System for the Yellow River Basin.* Sino-Dutch Cooperation Project ORET 02/09-CN00069 Scientific Final Report. Delft, the Netherlands: EARS Earth Environment Monitoring BV, December.

Sangati, M., and M. Borga. 2009. "Influence of Rainfall Spatial Resolution on Flash Flood Modelling." *Natural Hazards and Earth System Sciences* 9 (2): 575–84. doi:10.5194/nhess-9-575-2009.

Serrat-Capdevila, A., J. B. Valdes, and E. Z. Stakhiv. 2014. "Water Management Applications for Satellite Precipitation Products: Synthesis and Recommendations." *Journal of the American Water Resources Association* 50 (2): 509–25. doi: 10.1111/jawr.12140.

Serrat-Capdevila, A., M. Merino, J. B. Valdes, and M. Durcik. 2016. "Evaluation of the Performance of Three Satellite Precipitation Products over Africa." University of Arizona, submitted to *Atmospheric Research.*

Thiemig, V., R. Rojas, M. Zambrano-Bigiarini, and A. De Roo. 2013. "Hydrological Evaluation of Satellite-Based Rainfall Estimates over the Volta and Baro-Akobo Basin." *Journal of Hydrology* 499 (August): 324–38.

Tobin, K. J., and M. E. Bennett. 2014. "Satellite Precipitation Products and Hydrologic Applications." *Water International* 39 (3): 360–80.

CHAPTER 11

The Bottom Line

On the basis of the literature review of the state-of-the-art of remote sensing (RS) for hydrologic simulations, several tentative conclusions may be drawn regarding the use of Earth observation (EO) to support water management applications:

- Satellite estimations are prone to several sources of uncertainty, which can significantly affect the quality of the variables to be forecast.

- To inform natural resources managers about the usefulness of RS products for their decision-making processes, it is imperative to evaluate the reliability of those products at different spatiotemporal scales.

- RS data in case studies and applications should always be used with ground data when available and with some level of validation.

- Hydrologic simulations generally yield better results if RS inputs have been bias corrected (if they contain biases) and the hydrologic models have been recalibrated with the same type of input data that will be used in these models for predictive purposes.

- Accuracy and performance vary depending on climate, topography, the variable estimated, time aggregation, and basin size. The tables presented in annex 9A (available online at https://openknowledge.worldbank.org/handle/10986/22952) give a good idea of the most suitable RS products for hydrologic applications, the contexts in which they can be most useful, and when more caution is warranted in the face of greater uncertainties.

Finally, satellite estimations are overall well correlated with ground observations (figure 11.1)—showing median correlation coefficient (CC) values of 0.55 (±0.25) for precipitation, 0.83 (±0.17) for evapotranspiration, 0.58 (±0.19) for soil moisture, and 0.53 (±0.21) for snow water equivalent.[1] Precipitation shows a broad range of CC values, which can be attributed to differences in the validation sites (which include mountain and plain locations distributed across the globe). Evapotranspiration and soil moisture validation efforts are limited to fewer validation sites and to field experiments, which can partly explain the better linear relationship between satellite-derived products and observations. Despite the strong correlation found for ET estimates, biases in the range of −30 to +10 percent (relative to observed values) have been reported in the literature (see the section on evapotranspiration in chapter 10). Similarly, for soil moisture, mean root mean squared estimate values of 0.11 (±0.09) cubic meter by cubic meter and a mean positive bias of 0.04 (±0.05) cubic meter by cubic meter have been calculated (see the section on soil moisture in chapter 9), indicating that, despite strong correlations, the uncertainty of satellite estimates is still large. Snow water equivalent estimates also show a large variability, with bias values ranging from −20 to +20 percent (see the section on snow water equivalent in chapter 9).

Figure 11.1 Correlation Coefficients between Ground Observations and Satellite Estimates

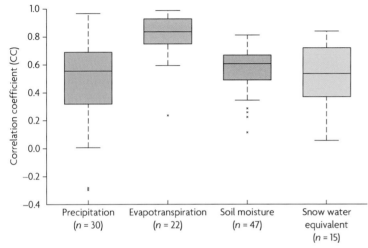

Note: n = sample size. The black horizontal line represents the median value.

NOTE

1. Error margins given in parentheses refer to standard deviation values. These cannot be extracted from the corresponding tables but were computed separately.

PART IV

Concluding Remarks

WATER AND DEVELOPMENT

Good water resources management (WRM) and planning are essential to sustain economic and human development as well as to maintain the health of the socioecological systems of which humans are a part. Especially in developing nations, water supply and sanitation and a healthy environment form the basis of successful poverty reduction strategies. With that ultimate goal in mind and to face other global water resources challenges, contributions are needed to bridge the gap between existing technologies and operational applications in support of the planning, design, operation, and management of water resources.

POTENTIAL OF REMOTE SENSING

There is great potential for space-based Earth observation (EO) to enhance the capability to monitor the Earth's vital water resources, especially in data-sparse regions of the globe. Despite this potential, EO data products are currently underused in WRM. One key reason for this appears to be the lack of familiarity among the WRM community with available EO products and the ways in which they can be used to address WRM issues. This publication reviews the state of the art in the use of remote sensing (RS) for water resources applications, guided by the general scope and requirements of the World Bank's Water Global Practice.

Important topics like water supply for rural or urban water users, sanitation and hygiene, agricultural water management, WRM and environmental services, and hydropower can be informed by eight variables that may contribute to and modify water resources management. These variables are precipitation, evapotranspiration, soil moisture, vegetation and vegetation cover, groundwater, surface water, snow and ice, and water quality. An understanding of these eight biophysical parameters as well as of the theoretical basis for their estimation through Earth observation is important. Equally important is to have a list of current and near-future sensors that can provide such information, indicates their suitability for water resources management, and, where appropriate, describes existing data products that are produced on a regular basis.

CHALLENGES

Given the dynamic nature of Earth observation, it is no less important to have a way to keep this list up to date. The number of EO applications is growing as rapidly as the number of new, space-based technology, satellite missions, and data products. In addition, EO sensors are becoming more sophisticated, more sensitive, and more agile (as illustrated by on-demand programming for image acquisition from commercial, high-resolution sensors). The algorithms that translate top-of-atmosphere EO data to ground-level information are evolving rapidly.

Field measurement systems are also becoming more sophisticated as new information technology, telemetry, and sensing solutions are developed. Moreover, methods to integrate observations and models through model-data fusion are being developed rapidly. While this bodes well for the usefulness of Earth observation for water resources management, it also means that some of the information in this publication will become outdated over the next few years. The reader may therefore still need to seek advice from area experts on the most recent developments and solutions.

Numerous reports and publications on hydrologic applications of remote sensing focus on the tools (products and models), but few publications focus on the needs of the practitioners and the characteristics of the decisions that such tools could be informing. Hence there is a great gap in the adoption of such tools by practitioners. To some extent, this is normal, as it is difficult to incorporate new, uncertain information into a decision process, especially if neither the uncertainty nor the reliability of the source is well quantified. While scientists and providers can work toward including uncertainty and reliability estimates, practitioners in developing regions can work toward characterizing in detail the climate- and water-sensitive decisions in their planning and management.

A WORD OF CAUTION

Despite its limitations, the literature review presented in this publication reflects the state of the art of remote sensing for hydrological purposes. On that basis, several statements can be made regarding the use of Earth observation to support water management applications:

- It is imperative to evaluate the validity of RS data products at different spatiotemporal scales if they are to be of use for decision making.

- Validity and performance vary depending on climate, topography, the variable being estimated, time aggregation, and basin size. It is good to know the contexts in which RS data can be most useful and when to be particularly alert to greater uncertainties than usual.

- Satellite estimations are generally well correlated with ground observations. Despite these strong correlations, however, the uncertainty of some satellite estimates may still be large (but that may also be the case of ground measurements).

MAKING DECISIONS

The decision whether to use Earth observation to address a spatiotemporal information requirement should be based on criteria regarding the accuracy, availability, maturity, complexity, and reliability as well as the validity of required data. The suitability of using Earth observation for addressing a WRM need will also depend on whether it is the only source of data (in which case, the suitability of Earth observation is clear); whether EO information augments existing, but sparse, in situ information (in which case Earth observation will still be a critical source of information, providing the spatiotemporal framework for maximizing the value of existing information); whether other relevant data exist; and whether Earth observation is needed mainly for its spatiotemporal aspects (in which case Earth observation will only add value if its relevance, coverage, and accuracy significantly improve the information derived from in situ data).

A WORD OF HOPE

Some organizations like the World Bank have funded or supported projects using EO information. Through their water resources projects, these organizations could potentially be among the world's largest adopters of remote sensing in water resources management. They may want to consider whether a coordinated approach to remote sensing for WRM applications could increase the effectiveness and efficiencies in executing their projects. For example, if multiple projects involve similar applications, EO data sources, and EO techniques, it may be possible to use available resources more efficiently by developing a single data infrastructure (for example, for an entire region or transboundary basin). Similarly, if the same data are required repeatedly in projects or if monitoring applications are considered, it may be worthwhile to develop a centralized data infrastructure that keeps such data sets up to date. Some of the options could be to establish in-house EO capabilities or to partner with institutions or consortia that have regional or global outreach.

A phased approach—where several specific EO applications are chosen in an area of frequent WRM activity and are developed in a generic manner that may subsequently be replicated elsewhere—is a possible pathway to widespread uptake and implementation. Such judicious planning of demonstration projects, involving areas with a clear need for EO-derived information across relevant WRM application areas, possibly together with other relevant agencies, could create synergy while rapidly strengthening this area of activity.

From the satellite-sensor point of view, much coordination takes place via the Committee on Earth Observing Systems, whereas the Group on Earth Observations plays a global coordinating role for the end users of this information. Other agencies with a need for EO-derived information at multiple resolutions having global coverage are, for example, the United Nations Environmental Programme, the World Health Organization, and the Food and Agriculture Organization; coordination with these organizations could be highly effective.

DOWNSCALING TO THE LOCAL CONTEXT

Given these considerations and the information gathered for this publication, the following are suggested for helping developing-country practitioners to bridge the gap between scientific-academic and real-world uses of RS technology:

1. Technical support for mainstreaming the knowledge on how to make the best possible use of remote sensing as a tool for the water sector in particular.

2. Technical orientation and definition of clear procedures and criteria to assess the usability of RS products for decision making and planning conditioned by uncertainty (error estimates), accuracy (characterization of errors), precision (spatial and temporal resolution), timeliness, and validity of the data. This could include the quality and quantity of data generated to fill the information gaps, whether the information gathered has been validated or calibrated, the resolution used, or the level to which remote sensing has significantly influenced project performance.

3. Knowledge about errors and uncertainty. If products are used as inputs for modeling applications, it is important to know how errors are propagated or

compounded through model calculations and what uncertainty is contained in the output variables.

4. Technical orientation on reliability assessments of applications, including EO estimates. Given a specific application designed to model or predict a variable, reliability evaluations should be performed to see in how many simulated historical events the observations fell within the uncertainty bounds of the application's predictions. Such a reliability assessment would allow for improved characterization of the application's limitations.

5. A good characterization of the planning and decision processes to be informed by RS data and applications. If new developments bring about new decision-making processes, these processes should likewise be well characterized. Starting from a comprehensive, basin-wide development plan, identify the specific management and planning decisions to be made and then characterize the climate- or water-sensitive decisions that RS products could inform and what the benefits of such information would be. The following questions may be relevant for that purpose:

   • What are the climate- or water-sensitive management decisions that client country ministries, departments, and agencies are confronted with in their water management and planning cycles?

   • What degree of accuracy and precision is required in each of these decisions, and how much uncertainty can be tolerated?

   • What are the consequences of a mistake caused by faulty data and what kind and degree of failure can be tolerated?

   • What improvements in the hydrometeorological information being used—or what new information—would make the greatest positive difference?

   • What changes in decision making (decision thresholds and decision process) would result if such new information were available?

   • What changes in the institutional framework would be needed to obtain and be able to use this new information and to make these changes in decision making?

6. Financial support windows for specialized technical assistance to individual projects or groups of projects. This support could include financial support for the development of specific applications that could benefit many projects in the same or similar regions.

7. Financial and institutional support for data repositories and RS data libraries of different products with potentially built-in applications, for easy use by project teams.

8. Practical guidelines—such as those offered in this publication—from the user's point of view. These guidelines would include when in situ measurements and RS applications would be more operationally advantageous and when value would be added by using one as a complement to the other (RS as complementary to in situ measurements or vice versa), taking into account their relevance, availability, level of detail, and the accuracy required as well as developing countries' capabilities.

9. Financing mechanisms for in-country capacity building to improve decision making and better characterize decisions. This would help to identify the value of

potential data and their relevance for a specific decision-making activity.

OUTLOOK

A good understanding of the answers to these questions can inform the design of special tools for specific purposes. As new information becomes available, it may give new insights into how to apply this information in practice within a specific management and planning setting. Thus communication between scientists, researchers, and practitioners should be a two-way street.

The World Bank and other development banks, United Nations agencies such as the World Meteorological Organization, and other international entities could play a role in closing the gap between science application efforts and operational decision-making needs. In addition, they could promote and facilitate data sharing, capacity-building strategies, and the co-production of knowledge by scholars and practitioners.

This publication provides a guide to WRM professionals considering the use of Earth observation. Essential questions are provided that must be answered to help to navigate and evaluate the abundance of EO-based options and data products, including the likely validity of water resource variables estimated though Earth observation. The focus is on appropriate questions to ask once it has been concluded that exploring EO options for the WRM problem at hand is worthwhile. A flowchart presented in chapter 7 offers a "road map" for this purpose (figure 7.1).

It is hoped that the information collected in this publication will contribute to a greater and more judicious use of EO data in global WRM issues, thereby helping to alleviate poverty, promote sustainable growth, and increase the efficient use of the world's water resources.

Examples of Earth Observation Applications in World Bank Projects

P050647	UTTAR PRADESH WATER SECTOR RESTRUCTURING
P122770	UTTAR PRADESH WATER SECTOR RESTRUCTURING PHASE 2 (POTENTIAL USE OF REMOTE SENSING)
PROJECT DETAILS	
Team task leaders	Winston Yu, Anju Gaur
Contact	Winston Yu, Anju Gaur
Status	**P050647** (2001–11; closed) **P126703** (2012–20; active)
Description/objectives	**P050647:** To set up an enabling institutional and policy framework for water sector reform in Uttar Pradesh State for integrated water resources management and to initiate irrigation and drainage subsector reforms to increase and sustain water and agricultural productivity in the state. **P122770:** To strengthen the institutional and policy framework for integrated water resources management for the entire state and to increase agricultural and water productivity by supporting farmers in targeted irrigation areas.
Project component related to remote sensing	In past projects, evaluating project performance has been weak, and some level of monitoring and evaluation has been required, leading to the need to adjust the project design during implementation. Funds were provided to recruit third-party expertise for the monitoring and evaluation of each component of the project (P050647). As a result, benchmarking, remote sensing, geographic information system (GIS), and participatory monitoring and evaluation were carried out for different components of the project. Baseline data collected during preparation and implementation of each specific intervention were used to assess project impact through the collection and analysis of similar information at specific points in time during the project period and, eventually, in other project areas.
Use of remote sensing	These projects use remote sensing (RS) tools to establish a strong monitoring and evaluation system in order to assess project progress and impact. The use of remote sensing in P050647 was intended to produce a geospatial evaluation tool to assess the progress and impact of agricultural and water projects supported by the World Bank in India. In this case, a selected pilot study was carried out in the Jaunpur Branch System to serve as a benchmark for other project areas.
Window/initiative	Not applicable

REMOTE SENSING INFORMATION	
Input (data type, source, resolution, etc.)	1. *Landsat data.* Images for the study area were identified and acquired through the Landsat Program website to complement overall project objectives of distributing a multitemporal, multispectral, and multiresolution range of imagery appropriate for irrigation impact analysis. Due to cloud cover in the region, additional sensor data sets—Landsat Thematic Mapper (TM), Landsat Enhanced Thematic Mapper Plus (ETM+), and Global Land Surveys (GLS)—were used to fill the scanline gaps. 2. *MODIS (Moderate Resolution Imaging Spectroradiometer) data.* Daily global imagery provided spatial resolutions of 250-meter (red and NIR1) and 500-meter (blue, green, NIR2, SWIR1, and SWIR2). The MDOO9A1 data sets in 2000 to 2010 were acquired from the U.S. Geological Survey's Earth Resources Observation Systems Data Center website. The following three indexes were calculated for each MODIS eight-day composite: (1) normalized differential vegetation index (NDVI), (2) enhanced vegetation index (EVI), and (3) land surface water index (LSWI) using surface reflectance values from the blue, green, red, NIR1, and SWIR bands.
Model (source, variables, selection criteria)	*MODIS time-series analysis.* The vegetation phenological analyses were calculated using the seasonal dynamics of the three indexes—EVI, NDVI, and LSWI—from 2000 to 2010. The analysis included cropping intensity (number of crops per unit area in a year), length of growing season, and beginning and ending of the growing season. For identifying multiple cropping cycles in an image pixel, the temporal profile of the indexes was analyzed by applying a computational algorithm to all of the individual pixels for delineating the number of cropping cycles in a year. *Mapping multiple cropping areas.* Multiple cropping areas were assessed for a regular calendar year (January–December). Given the nature of the cropping season in India and monsoon patterns, the cropping calendar was remapped from July to June for 11 years starting in 2000–01 at 500-meter spatial resolution. *Annual vegetation anomalies.* Annual vegetation anomalies were calculated by subtracting the annual mean NDVI from the long-term mean (2000–10). The main objective was to see the dynamics of cropland vegetation at annual intervals compared to the long-term average. *Land use/land cover change analysis.* Advanced Wide Field Sensor (AwiFS) based on land use maps was used to quantify the change in land use that occurred between 2004–05 and 2008–09. The change in area was further analyzed at head reach, middle reach, and tail ends to see changes at each distribution. *Crop intensity.* Crop intensity was estimated before and after project implementation as follows: cropping intensity = (gross cropped area / net sown area) x 100. Higher cropping intensity means that a higher portion of the net area is being cropped more than once during one agricultural calendar year. This also implies higher productivity per unit of arable land during one agricultural calendar year. *Dynamics of the crop phenology.* Satellite images were used from the MODIS sensor. For each eight-day composite image, the EVI and LSWI were calculated using surface reflectance values from the blue, red, near infrared (NIR, 841–875 nanometers), and shortwave infrared (SWIR, 1,628–1,652 nanometers) bands. The MODO9A1 files include quality control flags to account for various image artifacts (for example: clouds, cloud shadow). In addition, blue band reflectance was used to eliminate further contaminated observations (such as clouds, aerosols). Annual maximum values of EVI were selected for pixels from all of the remaining good observations in a year, and the dates for annual maximum EVI and LSWI were recorded. The study used seasonal maximum values of EVI and LSWI (magnitude) and date of seasonal maximum vegetation index (timing) as a measure for crop phenology.
Output (results: maps, indexes, etc.)	• Mapping of multiple cropping areas (single, double, and triple) for 2004–05 and 2008–09 • Mapping of annual vegetation anomalies from the long-term mean (2000–10) and spatial distribution of vegetation dynamics • Analysis of land use and land cover change • Identification of differences in crop intensity between 2004–05 and 2008–09.
Collaboration	A partnership was formed between the Uttar Pradesh Irrigation Department and the Remote Sensing Agency in Uttar Pradesh.

Outcome relevant to the objective of the component	Potential for using remote sensing from the activity described above:
	• RS-based analysis indicates that project intervention improved the vegetation health and distribution across the basin, which is a good indicator of increased productivity.
	• The methodology was overseen by a Bank team and proven useful to the client.
	• A partnership was formed between the Uttar Pradesh Irrigation Department and the Remote Sensing Agency in Uttar Pradesh.
	• This work led to an actual component in a new operation that will use this methodology.
	• The approach developed in this pilot study, though data intensive, is efficient with respect to the amount of fieldwork that would be required to do similar analysis.
	• Such a methodology can be replicated easily in other operations.
	• As in this case, RS methodologies can be an effective approach (especially when using free RS data) to monitoring agricultural performance in large geographic areas and potentially be mainstreamed into monitoring and evaluation approaches for irrigation projects.

P114949	ZAMBIA WATER RESOURCES DEVELOPMENT
P117617	SHIRE RIVER BASIN DEVELOPMENT PROJECT
P104446	MALAWI DISASTER RISK REDUCTION AND RECOVERY PROJECT
P102459	ZAMBIA IRRIGATION DEVELOPMENT AND SUPPORT PROJECT
PROJECT DETAILS	
Team task leaders	Marcus Wishart, Pieter Waalewijn, Kremena M. Ionkova, Indira Ekanayake
Contact	Marcus Wishart, Pieter Waalewijn, Kremena M. Ionkova, Indira Ekanayake, Nagaraja Harshadeep
Status	**P114949** (2013–18; active)
	P117617 (2012–18; active)
	P104446 (2007–10; closed)
	P102459 (2010–18; active)
Description/objectives	**P114949:** To support the implementation of an integrated framework for development and management of water resources in Zambia.
	P117617: To generate sustainable social, economic, and environmental benefits by effectively and collaboratively planning, developing, and managing the Shire River basin's natural resources.
	P104446: To increase yields per hectare and volume of products marketed by smallholders benefiting from investments in irrigation in selected sites served by the project.
	P102459: To increase yields per hectare and volume of products marketed by smallholders benefiting from investments in irrigation in selected sites served by the project.
Project component related to remote sensing	These projects use Earth observation (EO) tools to map small water bodies in Zambia, assess water quality in Lake Malawi, and assess erosion patterns in some areas in the Shire River basin of Malawi.
	Satellite Earth observation has added value to the task of making inventories of small water bodies, which are often sources of irrigation water for rural communities in Zambia. The network of ground measurements and inventories of these water bodies are often incomplete, sparse, or difficult to maintain. Conversely, the use of EO tools allowed the mapping of small reservoirs, which made more efficient use of existing ground measurements. This component focused on rural communities that will benefit from improved small-scale water resources infrastructure and basin planning.
	In Lake Malawi and nearby lakes Malombe and Chilwa, the existing ground data for assessing water quality are limited and inadequate. For example, it is critical to assess the sediment loads in these lakes and rivers accurately since high sediment loads have caused problems for hydroelectric power stations in the past. However, based on existing ground measurements, it is difficult to assess the hydrologic status of the basin. On the contrary, information derived from Earth observation can supplement ground measurements to improve watershed management in some catchments of the lake.

	Soil erosion has been a major concern in Malawi due to population growth, deforestation, and development of new settlements. EO information provides accurate and up-to-date information on land use and changes in land use in order to optimize planning for water resource investments, flood mitigation, and watershed management in selected catchments of the Shire basin. The experience of these projects shows that EO information and modern satellite products can be used to find innovative approaches to prioritize investments.
Use of remote sensing	• Identification, mapping, and cataloguing of small-scale water bodies, reservoirs, and lake extensions based on SAR (synthetic aperture radar) data, including their evolution over time • Production of Lake Malawi water quality products, including lake surface temperature measurements as well as historical water-level records • Estimation of soil loss and erosion using very high-resolution optical data (SPOT5) from 2005 to 2010.
Window/initiative	EOWorld, TigerNET
REMOTE SENSING INFORMATION	
Input (data type, source, resolution, etc.)	*Small reservoir mapping (Zambia).* Landsat, Advanced Synthetic Aperture Radar (ASAR) imagery. *Monitoring of Lake Malawi.* Envisat- Medium Resolution Imaging Spectrometer (MERIS) data were used to evaluate key water quality parameters, including chlorophyll-a as a proxy for biomass, total suspended matter concentrations and Kd (attenuation coefficient) as a proxy for turbidity and transparency, and colored dissolved organic matter as a proxy for the presence of humic substances. *Shire River basin.* The estimation of soil loss and erosion within Malawi's Shire River basin was based on SPOT5 acquisitions from 2005 to 2010 and covered 10,798 square kilometers in 17 land use classes.
Model (source, variables, selection criteria)	Lake Malawi water quality: BEAM (Basin Economic Allocation Model); WISP (Water Information System Platform)
Output (results: maps, indexes)	• Identification and mapping of small reservoirs and assessment of relevant storage evolution over time • Land cover and land use maps and deforestation rates • Erosion maps • Water quality maps.
Collaboration	European Space Agency, Netherlands Geomatics and Earth Observation B.V. (Netherlands), Technical University of Delft (Netherlands), Water Insight (Netherlands)
Outcome relevant to the objective of the component	EO information was used to assist the prioritization of investments, the monitoring of lakes and basins, basin planning for water resource investments, flood mitigation and risk reduction, and watershed management in selected catchments.

Examples of Water Information Product Generation Systems

INTRODUCTION

The main text highlights the data needed to address the most pressing water issues in the developing world and explains where and how Earth observation (EO) can help to provide this information. This appendix lists and briefly describes some water information systems that are notable examples of the integration of ground observations, EO data, and models. This is a subjective selection, not a comprehensive list of all existing systems.

FLOOD WARNING AND MONITORING SYSTEMS

Dartmouth Flood Observatory

The Dartmouth Flood Observatory provides historical and near-real-time monitoring of large flood events worldwide.[1] The service uses Moderate Resolution Imaging Spectrometer (MODIS) 250-meter data to map surface water areas and compare them with historical imagery to detect flood occurrence. The Dartmouth Flood Observatory also uses time series of passive microwave daily observations at selected locations to estimate river discharge (River Watch). In each of these locations, an empirical linear model has been fitted between observed discharge and the passive microwave signal, providing an estimate of discharge in near real time when floods occur. The service allows users to access historical events.

Using the same algorithms as those developed by the Dartmouth Flood Observatory, the National Aeronautics and Space Administration (NASA) has implemented a near-real-time service called Global MODIS Flood Mapping.[2] This service allows users to download rasters of surface water and flood water in several formats (figure B.1).

Figure B.1 Map Showing Surface Water Extent in a Flood Event in Bolivia in March 2014 and Discharge Estimate from Passive Microwave

a. Surface water extent

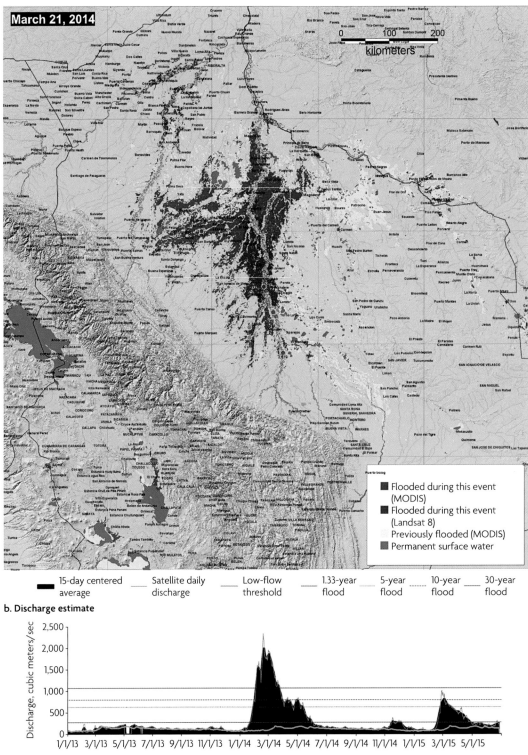

b. Discharge estimate

Global Flood and Landslide Monitoring

The Global Flood and Landslide Monitoring web service uses the Tropical Rainfall Measuring Mission (TRMM) Multisatellite Precipitation Analysis (TMPA) sensor to monitor rainfall accumulation across the globe, excluding high-latitude regions (figure B.2).[3] It

Figure B.2 Example Outputs from the Global Flood and Landslide Monitoring System

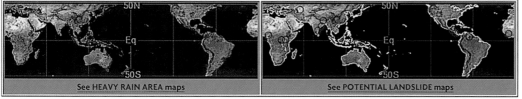

Click on the maps below for **regional displays** with more information

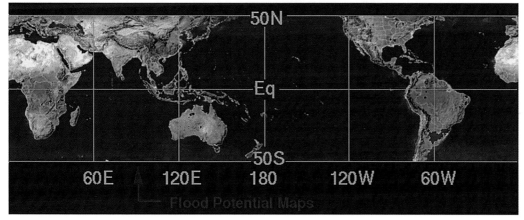

Source: Goddard Space Flight Center, National Aeronautics and Space Administration (NASA). http://trmm.gsfc.nasa.gov/publications_dir/ potential_flood_hydro.html.

uses the satellite observations for estimating flood risk (Hong et al. 2007; Wang et al. 2011) and potential landslide sites (Hong, Adler, and Huffman 2006, 2007).

SOIL MOISTURE AND DROUGHT MONITORING SYSTEMS

U.S. Drought Monitor

The U.S. Drought Monitor provides a weekly map of drought conditions across the United States and is produced jointly by the National Oceanic and Atmospheric Administration

(NOAA), the U.S. Department of Agriculture (USDA), the National Drought Mitigation Center (NDMC), and the University of Nebraska, Lincoln.[4] The system uses climatic, hydrologic, and soil condition observations from more than 350 contributors around the United States and expert opinions from 11 climatologists to produce the weekly drought condition map. This evaluation product is qualitative (and to some extent subjective), not quantitative. Several external data sources that use Earth observation are also tapped to determine drought intensity:

- *Vegetation drought response index*, produced by the NDMC and the U.S. Geological

Survey, combines data on the average percentage of seasonal greenness and start of season anomaly from the Advanced Very High Resolution Radiometer (AVHRR) normalized difference vegetation index (NDVI) with other biophysical and climate data (Brown et al. 2008; Gu et al. 2008)

- *Evaporative stress index*, produced by the U.S. Department of Agriculture, is retrieved via the energy balance using remotely sensed land surface temperature time-change signals and data from the geostationary operational environmental satellites (GOES)

- *Vegetation health index*, produced globally by NOAA, is calculated by combining a scaled NDVI (vegetation condition index) with a scaled brightness temperature index (temperature condition index), both derived from AVHRR

- *NDVI greenness maps*, produced for the Wildland Fire Assessment System, are derived from AVHRR

- *Precipitation analysis*, by the National Weather Service, is produced by merging rainfall radar and gauge data

- Groundwater and soil-moisture data from the Gravity Recovery and Climate Experiment (GRACE), produced by NASA, are assimilated into a land surface model.

The dominance of AVHRR observations may be evident and can be explained by the long time series required to distinguish drought conditions of different severity.

European Drought Observatory

The European Drought Observatory uses meteorological data and vegetation indexes obtained from remote sensing to provide continuous drought assessments over Europe.[5] Three indexes are combined:

- The standardized precipitation index, which measures the rainfall anomaly from observations

- Soil moisture anomaly, which is obtained from modeling

- The fraction of photosynthetically active radiation absorbed by vegetation, obtained from the Medium Resolution Imaging Spectrometer (MERIS) sensor.

Australian Water Availability Project

The Australian Water Availability Project (AWAP) monitors the state and trend of the terrestrial water balance of the Australian continent. The system uses the Waterdyn25M model (Raupach et al. 2009), which includes remotely sensed fraction of absorbed photosynetically active radiation to estimate vegetation cover and surface temperature, aimed at improving the estimation of evapotranspiration fluxes. The AWAP system provides weekly and monthly estimates of all the water balance components, including soil moisture in two soil layers, transpiration, runoff, and deep drainage. These estimates are operationally available from 2007 onward; historical model runs have been produced for 1900–2011 to generate continental estimates of the water balance components. The Australian Bureau of Agricultural and Resource Economics and Sciences uses the AWAP system to report weekly on soil moisture conditions across the country (figure B.3).

IRRIGATION WATER USE AND CROP GROWTH MONITORING SYSTEMS

FieldLook

Fieldlook, a system run by the eLEAF Company in the Netherlands, provides satellite-derived information to farmers.[6] Weekly estimates of biomass production, carbon dioxide intake, leaf area index, and vegetation index are provided to subscribers, mostly in the Netherlands, but also in some Eastern European countries. Key to the system is the ET Tool, which is an adaptation of model evapotranspiration across large areas based on the

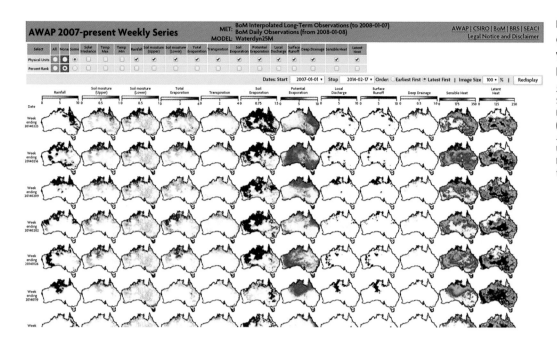

Figure B.3 Example Output of Selected Variables Generated by the AWAP System

Source: Commonwealth Scientific and Industrial Research Organisation (CSIRO). http://www.eoc .csiro.au/awap/. © CSIRO. Used with permission. Further permission required for reuse.

Surface Energy Balance Algorithm for Land (SEBAL) model.

Irrigateway

irriGATEWAY, a system run by the Commonwealth Scientific and Industrial Research Organisation (CSIRO), aims to improve decision making for agricultural water resources management.[7] Among the tools run by the system, most relevant in this context are the crop coefficient (K_c) maps for irrigation districts (see figure B.4), which are generated using NDVI calculated from Landsat imagery. Actual evapotranspiration estimates are generated for selected irrigation areas, and the ratio of actual to potential evapotranspiration is calculated to provide K_c. The data for individual paddocks are extracted and sent automatically via text messages to farmers who have subscribed to the service. These farmers, in turn, use the information to refine the irrigation volumes and benchmark their water use against that of other irrigators who subscribe to the service. Water providers can also use the system as an auditing tool.

Crop Explorer and GeoGLAM: Crop Monitor

The Crop Explorer system is run by the U.S. Department of Agriculture and provides a global assessment and seasonal forecasts of crop growth and production.[8] The website allows zooming into continents and regions and displays several observed or modeled variables—including rainfall and soil moisture—obtained from the World Meteorological Organization and the U.S. Air Force Weather Agency. It also provides vegetation indexes and anomalies from the vegetation (Satellite for Earth Observation, SPOT) and MODIS sensors. Crop Explorer also provides interactive access to graphs and maps of reservoirs and lake levels from the Jason-2 and Envisat sensors.[9]

The system provides an interactive map that allows users to select a lake or reservoir and displays the time-series data from either sensor showing height variation. Users also have the option of downloading the data in ASCII format.

The GeoGLAM Crop Monitor is a joint initiative involving NASA and the Goddard Space Flight Center, the U.S. Department of Agriculture and the Foreign Agricultural Service,

Figure B.4 Example Output of a Crop-Coefficient (K_c) Map Produced by irriGATEWAY

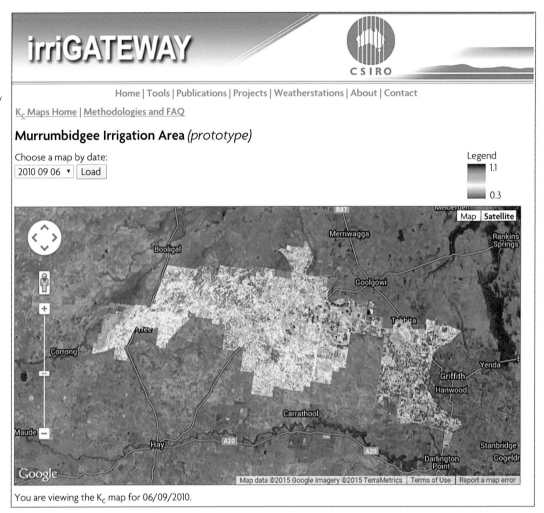

Science Systems and Applications, Inc., and the University of Maryland.[10] It uses MODIS NDVI data to monitor croplands globally and provides detailed maps at 250-meter resolution of vegetation index anomalies. Users can select a point or polygon and obtain time-series data of NDVI from 2000 until the present.

CropWatch

CropWatch, China's global crop monitoring system, uses EO data combined with selected field data to determine key crop production indicators, including crop acreage, yield and production, crop condition, cropping intensity, crop-planting proportion, total food availability, and status and severity of droughts. Results are combined to analyze the balance between supply and demand for various food crops and, if needed, provide early warning against possible

food shortages. CropWatch estimates crop area and yields and also assesses drought and crop conditions.

SNOW EXTENT

NOAA's National Snow Analysis

Several U.S agencies produce a variety of satellite-derived snow products that range from regional to global in scale and from daily to monthly in frequency:

- The NOAA National Environmental Satellite Data and Information Service Northern Hemisphere snow extent maps

- The National Snow and Ice Data Centre (NSIDC) Northern Hemisphere EASE-Grid Weekly Snow Cover and Sea Ice Extent product

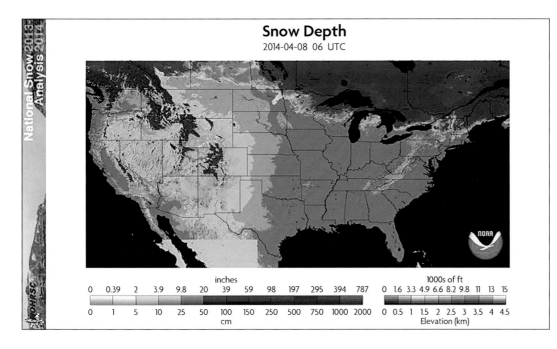

Snow Depth
2014-04-08 06 UTC

inches

| 0 | 0.39 | 2 | 3.9 | 9.8 | 20 | 39 | 59 | 98 | 197 | 295 | 394 | 787 |

| 0 | 1 | 5 | 10 | 25 | 50 | 100 | 150 | 250 | 500 | 750 | 1000 | 2000 |
cm

1000s of ft

| 0 | 1.6 | 3.3 | 4.9 | 6.6 | 8.2 | 9.8 | 11 | 13 | 15 |

| 0 | 0.5 | 1 | 1.5 | 2 | 2.5 | 3 | 3.5 | 4 | 4.5 |
Elevation (km)

Figure B.5 Snow Depth for the Continental United States on April 8, 2014

Source: National Operational Hydrologic Remote Sensing Center. http://www.nohrsc.noaa.gov/nsa/.

- The NSIDC Near-Real-Time SSM/I EASE-Grid Daily Global Ice Concentration and Snow Extent product

- The U.S. National Operational Hydrologic Remote Sensing Center's (NOHRSC) National Snow Analysis.[11]

These products are made specifically for application to hydrologic analyses (figure B.5). The analyses provide daily, operational monitoring of snow across the United States, including snow depth, snow water equivalent, and snow melt.[12]

Products provide information on the physical properties of snow by combining satellite-, airborne-, and field-based observations with snow models. Satellite imagery comes from both geostationary (GOES) and polar-orbiting operational environmental satellites (POES) operated by both NOAA and the European Organisation for the Exploitation of Meteorological Satellites (EUMETSAT). The POES instruments include the optical AVHRR, thermal High Resolution Infrared Radiation Sounder (HIRS/3), and microwave sensors from the Advanced Microwave Sounding Unit and Mitsubishi Heavy Industries. The GOES

instruments include the optical imager and thermal sounder.

MODIS Snow Data Product

NASA produces the MODIS suite of global snow products, composed of products covering a range of spatial resolutions (from 500 meters to 0.25°) and temporal resolutions (daily, eight-day, and monthly). Snow cover is described as fractional cover; snow albedo is also available. Together these are designated as the MOD10 data product. MOD10 data are derived from the visible and infrared channels on MODIS and use the normalized difference snow index (NDSI), which compares the differences in reflectance between green and mid-infrared wavelengths (Hall et al. 2002).

GlobSnow

The European Space Agency (ESA) funded GlobSnow-1, which produced hemispheric, long-term, daily, weekly, and monthly records of snow cover and snow water equivalent. This task is now being continued through the GlobSnow-2 Project. The snow cover data are based on optical data from Envisat's Advanced Along Track Scanning Thermal Radiometer

(AASTR) and European Remote Sensing Satellite (ERS-2) sensors, while the snow water equivalent record is based on the time series of measurements by two different space-borne passive microwave sensors (the Scanning Multichannel Microwave Radiometer [SMMR] and the Special Sensor Microwave Imager [SSM/I]). The snow water equivalent product combines satellite-based passive microwave measurements with weather station data through a data assimilation scheme.

China Meteorological Administration

The China Meteorological Administration operationally monitors the snow cover of China and the Northern Hemisphere.[13] Monitoring is done using a combination of optical and microwave data from the geostationary and polar-orbiting satellites Fengyun-2D (FY-2D), Fengyun-2E (FY-2E), and Fengyun-3B (FY-3B). These products have been favorably compared against the MODIS snow products (Yang et al. 2014).

Central Asia Snow Melt Forecasting

Snowmelt is a critical water resource for many of the arid countries in Central Asia. Having suitable capacity to predict snowmelt is therefore important for water and food security in this region. The Regional Centre for Hydrology in Central Asia, a Swiss-backed initiative, is tasked with (among other things) forecasting snowmelt across the five member countries (Kazakhstan, the Kyrgyz Republic, Tajikistan, Turkmenistan, and Uzbekistan).[14] Forecasts are produced by combining satellite imagery (AVHRR), expert opinion, ground observations, and modeling.

WATER RESOURCES MONITORING SYSTEMS

According to Van Dijk and Renzullo (2011), "Few satellite data are used in only a handful of operational surface water resources monitoring systems. There appears to be little evidence that the information they provide has found wide uptake in water management." Van Dijk and Renzullo (2011) define "spatial water resources monitoring systems" as software that integrates observations into models to produce spatial estimates of current (and past) water resources distribution. A few examples of such systems are given below.

North American and GLOBAL Land Data Assimilation Systems

The North American Land Data Assimilation Systems (NLDAS) combines data from multiple sources within models to produce gridded maps of land surface states and fluxes.[15] Among the states and fluxes reported, and of interest for regional hydrology, are soil moisture, streamflow, runoff, and evapotranspiration. The modeling framework behind the NLDAS system includes the Mosaic, Noah, Sacramento, and VIC models (Xia, Mitchell, Ek, Cosgrove et al. 2012; Xia, Mitchell, Ek, Sheffield et al. 2012). The NLDAS uses remotely sensed information of downward shortwave radiation from the GOES-8 satellite and the Climate Prediction Center's MORPHing technique (CMORPH) for estimating precipitation. The NLDAS Drought Monitor provides estimates of soil moisture, snow water equivalent, total runoff, streamflow, evapotranspiration, and precipitation for the continental United States. It also provides forecasts of these variables of up to six months. Using an approach similar to NLDAS, a global version (GLDAS) has been developed.[16]

Satellite observations are used in GLDAS directly and indirectly. In particular, the meteorological forcing data are derived from "a combination of NOAA/GDAS atmospheric analysis fields, spatially and temporally disaggregated NOAA Climate Prediction Center Merged Analysis of Precipitation (CMAP) fields, and observation-based radiation fields derived using the method of the Air Force Weather Agency's AGRicultural METeorological modeling system."

Australian Water Resources Assessment System

The Australian Water Resources Assessment System (AWRA) uses a series of coupled landscape, groundwater, and river models to provide consistent water information for Australia.[17] The Australian Bureau of Meteorology uses the AWRA system, along with other data sources, to produce the Australian Water Resources Assessment and annual National Water Account.

The AWRA provides consistent water information on climatic conditions and landscape characteristics, patterns and variability in water availability over time, surface water and groundwater status, floods, streamflow salinity and inflows to wetlands, and urban and agricultural water use. Previous AWRA reports such as the 2012 assessment (BoM 2013) used a grid-based landscape model, AWRA-L (Van Dijk 2010; Van Dijk and Warren 2010) to produce information on the landscape water balance (figure B.6). More recently, this has been coupled with a continental groundwater model (AWRA-G) and a river water accounting model (AWRA-R), which will be used in future reports.

Asia-Pacific Water Monitor

The Asia-Pacific Water Monitor, an experimental water balance monitoring system developed by CSIRO and Australian National University, provides near-real-time water balance estimates for the Asia-Pacific region and interprets these in a historical context.[18] Maps show precipitation, streamflow, catchment water storage, and actual and potential evapotranspiration. Information is presented as actual values, deciles, anomalies, and percentage of average and is available for daily totals and 30-day averages.

The Asia-Pacific Water Monitor is based on a water balance model that is updated daily using weather data derived from a mix of field and satellite measurements and weather forecasts. The model used in the monitor is the World-Wide Water Resources Assessment (W3RA) model. It shares a common heritage with the Australian Water Resources Assessment Landscape (AWRA-L) model but is applicable to a wider range of conditions. Processes such as evapotranspiration, soil and groundwater movement, and streamflow are represented for two vegetation classes in each 1° grid cell (forest and nonforest cover). The climate data that are fed into the model are a combination of several sources, which are blended to obtain the best estimates of past and current conditions. The model is forced by "ERA-Interim" weather forecast model reanalysis data from the European Centre for Medium-Range Weather Forecasts. For low latitudes, these are combined with near-real-time TRMM multisensor precipitation analysis data (TMPA 3B42 RT) (Huffman et al. 2007) to improve estimates of convective rainfall (Peña-Arancibia et al. 2013).

WATER RESOURCES ASSESSMENT AND SCENARIO STUDIES

Murray-Darling Basin Sustainable Yields Project

In 2007 and 2008, CSIRO led a consortium to assess the likely impacts of climate change on the surface water and groundwater resources of the Murray-Darling basin. This region covers 1 million square kilometers and supplies at least 40 percent of Australia's agricultural production. The Murray-Darling Basin Sustainable Yields Project delivered the most comprehensive and complex whole-of-basin water assessment ever undertaken in Australia and was probably the world's first regarding the scale of assessment.

The project, funded by the Australian National Water Commission, reported on water availability and water use under historical and likely future climates, together with a consideration of possible changes in farm dams and forestry. It brought together nearly 200 people from more than 15 organizations and assembled a complex, computer-based model of the basin's

Figure B.6 Example Summary Output from AWRA for 2012 in the Murray-Darling Basin

Source: Reproduced from BoM 2013. © Bureau of Meteorology. Used with permission. Further permission required for reuse.

Landscape water flows			
	Region average	Difference from 1911–2012 long-term annual mean	Decile ranking with respect to the 1911–2012 record
Rainfall	651 mm	+40%	10th—very much above average
Evapotranspiration	559 mm	+29%	10th—very much above average
Landscape water yield	65 mm	+110%	10th—very much above average

Streamflow (at selected gauges)	
Annual total flow:	Predominantly above average flow throughout the region and numerous stream gauges in the upper Darling River with very much above average flow
Salinity:	Annual median electrical conductivity predominantly below 1,000 µS/cm throughout the region
Flooding:	Major floods in the upper Darling River and in the Lachlan and Murrumbidgee rivers

Surface water storage (comprising about 88% of the region's total capacity of all major storages)

Total accessible capacity	30 June 2012		30 June 2011		Change	
	accessible volume	% of total capacity	accessible volume	% of total capacity	accessible volume	% of total capacity
30,192 GL	25,230 GL	84%	22,006 GL	73%	+3,224 GL	+9%

Wetlands inflow patterns (for selected wetlands)	
Currawinya Lakes and Paroo River wetlands:	Very much above average flows in the normally wettest month of February and above average flows in December and March
Gwydir wetlands:	Very much above average flows in November, December, and February
Macquarie Marshes:	Very much above average flows in March and April
Barmah–Millewa Forest:	Very much above average flows in March, above average flows in July and August

Groundwater (in selected aquifers)	
Levels:	Predominantly rising groundwater levels in the northern aquifers, variable to stable groundwater level trends in the southern aquifers
Salinity:	Nonsaline groundwater (< 3,000 mg/L) in most aquifers in the uphill areas, mostly saline (≥ 3,000 mg/L) in the downhill basin aquifers

Urban water use (Canberra)

Total sourced in 2011–12	Total sourced in 2010–11	Change	Restrictions
44 GL	41 GL	+3 GL (+7%)	Permanent Water Conservation Measures

Annual mean soil moisture (model estimates)	
Spatial patterns:	Predominantly very much above average throughout the region, with some areas of above average in the south and east of the region
Temporal patterns in regional average:	Consistently very much above average during the year

water resources. This was achieved by linking 40 existing and new models of surface and groundwater supplies and extractions across the basin's 18 individual regions.

The project found that water resources development has profoundly affected the Murray-Darling basin: it has changed the flooding regimes that support nationally and internationally important floodplain wetland systems, reduced the total water flow at the Murray mouth by 61 percent, and caused the river to cease flowing through the Murray mouth

40 percent of the time, compared with 1 percent of the time before water resources had started being developed. It also found that the impacts of climate change by 2030 are uncertain. However, surface water availability across the entire basin is more likely to decline than increase.

The project intensively used rainfall-runoff models, together with past climate observations and future climate scenarios. It also used EO information to draw up a set of river water balance accounts (Kirby et al. 2008). These accounts were used to evaluate the uncertainty in preexisting river hydrology models that were used in the scenario studies (Van Dijk et al. 2008). The EO information used included the following:

- Irrigated cropping areas, derived by combining NDVI patterns with agricultural statistics (BRS 2006)

- Dynamic data on the extent of permanent and semi-permanent surface water areas

- Estimates of evapotranspiration from open water, irrigated land, wetlands, and dryland (Guerschman et al. 2008, 2009).

Satellite observations were also involved in determining forest cover and changes in forest cover (Furby 2002), which served as input for the scenario modeling.

National Atlas of Groundwater-Dependent Ecosystems

One of the issues of concern in groundwater management is how to avoid damage to groundwater-dependent ecosystems. The National Atlas of Groundwater-Dependent Ecosystems presents the current knowledge of groundwater-dependent ecosystems across Australia and was developed to improve understanding of these ecosystems and facilitate how they are considered in water resources management. The atlas displays ecological and hydrogeological information on ecosystems that are known to depend on groundwater and ecosystems that potentially use groundwater.

It is a tool to assist the consideration of ecosystem groundwater requirements in natural resources management, including water planning and environmental impact assessment. The atlas was funded by the Australian government and developed by a consortium of private and public organizations; it is hosted by the Bureau of Meteorology.[19]

Development of the atlas used a wide range of data, field surveys, observations, and academic and management expertise and required an extensive geographic information system framework to integrate these different sources of information. MODIS and Landsat observations played a critical role in the project, particularly for the many regions where detailed field observations were not available.

Specifically, the accuracy of 250-meter resolution MODIS-derived estimates of evapotranspiration (Guerschman et al. 2009) was enhanced using GRACE observations, and the seasonal patterns of evapotranspiration were combined with rainfall information to identify areas likely to be reliant on external water inputs other than rainfall. The resulting information was combined with inundation mapping (Guerschman et al. 2011) to identify surface water–fed ecosystems (Barron et al. 2014). Furthermore, spatial classification of seasonal Landsat NDVI and wetness patterns were used to enhance mapping spatially in a subset of regions (figure B.7).

Water Quality, Potential Harmful Algal Blooms, and Aquaculture

Several programs combine field data, models, and EO data in a data-data fusion—that is, neither a model-data fusion nor a model-data assimilation—to gain more insight into the phenomena observed or to predict potentially harmful algal blooms. The European Union and ESA Copernicus Programme's website provides a substantial overview of what is possible in the near future for EO-based information services and provides scoping information for current and near-future applications.[20]

Figure B.7 Example View from the Atlas of Groundwater-Dependent Ecosystems, Hosted by the Bureau of Meteorology

Source: © Bureau of Meteorology. Used with permission. Further permission required for reuse.

Note: The likely presence of groundwater-dependent ecosystems is shown in dark colors around Mont Gambier, a karst region on the border between Victoria and South Australia.

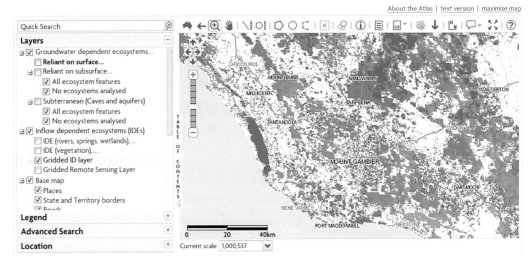

Marine Water Quality and Forecasting

The Copernicus Programme of the European Union and the ESA has been funding the MyOcean Programme since 2009. MyOcean (2009–12) and now MyOcean2 (2012–14) are committed to developing and running a European service based on a worldwide capacity for ocean monitoring and forecasting, using observations data, modeling, and assimilation systems.[21] MyOcean offers reliable and easy access to valuable core information about the ocean. The service is intended to serve any user requesting generic information on the ocean, but especially downstream service providers, who use the information as input for their value added services to end users. The interactive catalogue allows users to select products according to the following:

- *Seven geographic areas:* Global–Ocean, Arctic Ocean, Baltic Sea, Atlantic-European Northwest Shelf–Ocean, Atlantic-European Southwest Shelf–Ocean, Mediterranean Sea, and Black Sea

- *Parameters and variables:* ocean temperature, ocean salinity, ocean currents, sea ice, sea level, winds, ocean optics, ocean chemistry, ocean biology, and ocean chlorophyll

- *Product type:* forecast, near-real-time, multiyear, time-invariant products (either from observations or modeling).

The Australian eReefs Marine Water Quality Dashboard

Using the latest technologies to collate field-based and EO-derived information and new and integrated modeling, eReefs has started producing powerful visualization, communication, and reporting tools.[22] The Marine Water Quality Dashboard provides access to archival and real-time data on ocean color and sea surface temperature for the entire Great Barrier Reef.[23] It provides reef information akin to that provided by the Bureau of Meteorology for weather. This information could benefit government agencies, reef managers, policy makers, researchers, industry, and local communities.

The eReefs Project delivers the following:

- Expanded and improved monitoring data

- Measurement technologies and data delivery tools (for example, mobile and Internet tools)

- A suite of new and integrated models across paddock, catchment, estuary, reef lagoon, and ocean

- A framework to explore the impact of multiple factors such as temperature, nutrients, turbidity, and acidity, and to communicate this information to those who will be affected by it

- An interactive visual picture of the reef and its component parts, accessible to all

- Citizen science initiatives to engage the broader community on the health of the reef

- Targeted communication products to allow the public to interact with the reef—contributing monitoring information and learning about the reef.

Inland Water Quality

In 2005, the local management authority of the largest freshwater lake in the Netherlands, Lake IJssel, asked the Institute for Environmental Studies (Vrije Universiteit) to demonstrate the status of operational spatial monitoring and modeling. The results are summarized in an atlas of Lake IJssel (IJsselmeer). The atlas contains water quality products from SeaWiFS for the year 2003. For the summer, it provides fortnightly median maps for chlorophyll-a; for the winter period, it contains monthly median maps. These data are compared to field data and model simulation results. The capacities of MERIS on monitoring chlorophyll-a are also illustrated in the special maps section.

A major objective of the Water Framework Directive is to establish an integrated, spatially explicit monitoring and management system for all waters. Information such as that presented in this atlas could support monitoring and management of Lake IJssel. In addition, this set of measurements and model results for 2003, an unusually sunny, hot, and dry year, is ideal for investigating the relation between climate change (meteorological conditions, input by the IJssel River) and water quality in Lake IJssel.

Harmful Algal Blooms

The experimental Lake Erie Harmful Algal Bloom Bulletin was developed to provide a weekly forecast for microcystis blooms in western Lake Erie.[24] Many different species of single-celled organisms live in the Great Lakes, including algae. When certain conditions are present, such as high levels of nutrients or light, these organisms can reproduce rapidly to produce a dense population of algae, called a bloom. Some of these blooms are harmless, but when the blooming organisms contain toxins, other noxious chemicals, or pathogens, they become harmful. Harmful algal blooms can cause the death of nearby fish, foul up nearby coastlines, and produce harmful conditions for aquatic life as well as humans.

If a harmful bloom is detected, scientists will issue a forecast bulletin. The bulletin depicts the current location and future movement of harmful algal blooms and categorizes the intensity on a weekly basis. This research project aims to determine the factors controlling microcystin production and develop methods for determining cyanobacteria blooms from satellite imagery. Imagery is currently available, but it is not yet able to discriminate toxic microcystis blooms from other algal blooms within the images. The combined field data and satellite image data produced from the initial efforts are critical first steps in the characterization of bloom dynamics and the development of future bloom forecasting tools.

The Applied Simulations and Integrated Modelling for the Understanding of Toxic and Harmful Algal Blooms (ASIMUTH) aims to develop forecasting capabilities to warn of impending hazardous blooms in five European countries.[25] Through the ASIMUTH project, scientists and industry from five countries along Europe's Atlantic Margin have formed a network to produce the first realistic advisory and forecasting capability as a downstream service to the European aquaculture industry. The early warning of severe blooms will allow fish and shellfish farmers to adapt their culture and harvesting practices in time, so as to reduce potential losses.

ASIMUTH is the first step toward developing short-term hazardous algal bloom alert systems for Atlantic Europe. This will be achieved using information on the most current marine conditions (weather, water characteristics, toxicity, harmful algal presence), combined with local numerical predictions. ASIMUTH will use geospatial products from the MyOcean project to initiate the models developed during the project. Experts from each country will evaluate data from the monitoring programs, satellite images, and model output to produce bulletins to inform the public and the aquaculture sector. The bulletins produced will present the current state of hazardous algal blooms in each area and the likelihood of a toxic or harmful event of target species in the following week.

Aquaculture

Smartshell is a real-time, online tool that provides information on the water quality of coastal areas, aimed at the aquaculture sector.[26] It uses maps of chlorophyll and sediment concentrations as well as transparency derived from satellite data and ancillary data such as wind force and direction data, water depth, and temperature. If required, frequent and flexible field measurements can be done with the Water Insight Spectrometer with three radiometers (WISP-3) handheld water quality

scanner. These data also serve as input for growth models. Currently, Smartshell provides three basic services: (a) site selection, (b) real-time monitoring, and (c) production monitoring and projection.

NOTES

1. For information on the Dartmouth Flood Observatory, see http://floodobservatory.colorado.edu/.

2. For information on Global MODIS Flood Mapping, see http://oas.gsfc.nasa.gov/floodmap/.

3. For information on Global Flood and Landslide Monitoring, see http://trmm.gsfc.nasa.gov/publications_dir/potential_flood_hydro.html.

4. For information on the Drought Monitor, see http://droughtmonitor.unl.edu/.

5. For information on the European Drought Observatory, see http://edo.jrc.ec.europa.eu/.

6. For information on Fieldlook, see http://www.mijnakker.nl/.

7. For information on irriGATEWAY, see http://www.irrigateway.net/.

8. For information on Crop Explorer, see http://www.pecad.fas.usda.gov/cropexplorer/.

9. For information on the interactive graphs and maps, see http://www.pecad.fas.usda.gov/cropexplorer/global_reservoir/.

10. For information on GeoGLAM Crop Monitor, see http://www.geoglam-crop-monitor.org/.

11. For information on the NOHRSC National Snow Analysis, see http://www.nohrsc.noaa.gov/nsa/.

12. For information on the National Operational Hydrologic Remote Sensing Center, see http://www.nohrsc.noaa.gov/nsa/.

13. For information on the China Meteorological Administration, see http://cmdp.ncc.cma.gov.cn/Monitoring/en_snow_ice.php.

14. For information on the Regional Centre for Hydrology in Central Asia, see http://www.rch-aralsea.ch/index.html.

15. For information on the NLDAS, see http://ldas.gsfc.nasa.gov/nldas.

16. For information on the GLDAS, see http://ldas.gsfc.nasa.gov/gldas/.

17. For information on the AWRA, see http://www.bom.gov.au/water/awra.

18. For information on the Asia-Pacific Water Monitor, see http://eos.csiro.au/apwm.

19. For information on the atlas, see http://www.bom.gov.au/water/groundwater/gde/.

20. For an overview of the Copernicus Programme, see http://gmesdata.esa.int/web/gsc/core_services/downstream_services.

21. For information on MyOcean, see http://www.myocean.eu/web/26-catalogue-of-services.php.

22. For information on eReefs, see http://www.bom.gov.au/environment/eReefs_Infosheet.pdf.

23. For the Marine Water Quality Dashboard, see http://www.bom.gov.au/marinewaterquality/.

24. For information on the Lake Erie Harmful Algal Bloom Bulletin, see http://www.glerl.noaa.gov/res/Centers/HABS/lake_erie_hab/lake_erie_hab.html.

25. For information on ASIMUTH, see http://www.asimuth.eu/en-ie/Pages/default.aspx.

26. For information on Smartshell, see www.smartshellservices.com.

REFERENCES

Barron, O. V, I. Emelyanova, T. G. Van Niel, D. Pollock, and G. Hodgson. 2014. "Mapping Groundwater-Dependent Ecosystems Using Remote Sensing Measures of Vegetation and Moisture Dynamics." *Hydrological Processes* 28 (2): 372–85. doi:10.1002/hyp.9609.

BoM (Bureau of Meteorology). 2013. "Australian Water Resources Assessment 2012." Australian Bureau of Meteorology, Melbourne.

Brakenridge, G. R., D. Slayback, A. J. Kettner, F. Policelli, T. De Groeve, and S. Cohen. 2014. "Rapid Response Mapping and Measurement of the 2014 Flooding in Bolivia." Dartmouth Flood Observatory, University of Colorado, Boulder, CO, USA (http://floodobservatory.colorado.edu/RapidResponse/2014Bolivia4117/2014Bolivia.html).

Brown, J. F., B. D. Wardlow, T. Tadesse, M. J. Hayes, and B. C. Reed. 2008. "The Vegetation Drought Response Index (VegDRI): A New Integrated Approach for Monitoring Drought Stress in Vegetation." *GIScience & Remote Sensing* 45 (1): 16–46. doi:10.2747/1548-1603.45.1.16.

BRS (Bureau of Rural Sciences). 2006. *1992/93, 1993/94, 1996/97, 1998/99, 2000/01 and 2001/02 Land Use of Australia,* Version 3. Bureau of Rural Sciences, Canberra.

Furby, S. 2002. "Land Cover Change: Specification for Remote Sensing Analysis." Australian Greenhouse Office, Canberra.

Gu, Y., E. Hunt, B. Wardlow, J. B. Basara, J. F. Brown, and J. P. Verdin. 2008. "Evaluation of MODIS NDVI and NDWI for Vegetation Drought Monitoring Using Oklahoma Mesonet Soil Moisture Data." *Geophysical Research Letters* 35 (22): L22401. doi:10.1029/2008GL035772.

Guerschman, J., A. Van Dijk, T. McVicar, T. Van Niel, L. Li, Y. Liu, and J. Peña-Arancibia. 2008. *Water Balance Estimates from Satellite Observations over the Murray-Darling Basin.* Report to the Australian Government from the CSIRO Murray-Darling Basin Sustainable Yields Project. Canberra: Commonwealth Scientific and Industrial Research Organisation.

Guerschman, J. P., A. I. J. M. Van Dijk, G. Mattersdorf, J. Beringer, L. B. Hutley, R. Leuning, R. C. Pipunic, and B. S. Sherman. 2009. "Scaling of Potential Evapotranspiration with MODIS Data Reproduces Flux Observations and Catchment Water Balance Observations across Australia." *Journal of Hydrology* 369 (1-2): 107–19.

Guerschman, J. P., G. Warren, G. Byrne, L. Lymburner, N. Mueller, and A. I. J. M. Van Dijk. 2011. *MODIS-Based Standing Water Detection for Flood and Large Reservoir Mapping: Algorithm Development and Applications for the Australian Continent.* Canberra: Commonwealth Scientific and Industrial Research Organisation.

Hall, D. K., G. A. Riggs, V. V. Salomonson, N. E. DiGirolamo, and K. J. Bayr. 2002. "MODIS Snow-Cover Products." *Remote Sensing of Environment* 83 (1-2): 181–94.

Hong, Y., R. F. Adler, F. Hossain, S. Curtis, and G. J. Huffman. 2007. "A First Approach to Global Runoff Simulation Using Satellite Rainfall Estimation." *Water Resources Research* 43 (8): W08502.

Hong, Y., R. Adler, and G. J. Huffman. 2006. "Evaluation of the Potential of NASA Multi-Satellite Precipitation Analysis in Global Landslide Hazard Assessment." *Geophysical Research Letters* 33 (22): L22402. doi:10.1029/2006GL028010.

———. 2007. "Use of Satellite Remote Sensing Data in the Mapping of Global Landslide Susceptibility." *Natural Hazards* 43 (2): 245–56. doi:10.1007/s11069-006-9104-z.

Huffman, G. J., R. F. Adler, D. T. Bolvin, G. Gu, E. J. Nelkin, K. P. Bowman, Y. Hong, E. F. Stocker, and D. B. Wolff. 2007. "The TRMM Multisatellite Precipitation Analysis (TMPA): Quasi-Global, Multiyear, Combined-Sensor Precipitation Estimates at Fine Scales." *Journal of Hydrometeorology* 8 (1): 38–55.

Kirby, J. M., A. I. J. M. Van-Dijk, J. Mainuddin, J. L. Peña-Arancibia, Y. Liu, S. Marvanek, and L. T. Li. 2008. *River Water Balance Accounts across the Murray-Darling Basin, 1990–2006.* A report to the Australian Government from the CSIRO Murray-Darling Basin Sustainable Yields Project. Canberra: Commonwealth Scientific and Industrial Research Organisation.

Peña-Arancibia, J. L., A. I. J. M. Van Dijk, L. J. Renzullo, and M. Mulligan. 2013. "Evaluation of

Precipitation Estimation Accuracy in Reanalyses, Satellite Products, and an Ensemble Method for Regions in Australia and South and East Asia." *Journal of Hydrometeorology* 14 (4): 1323–33.

Raupach, M. R., P. R. Briggs, V. Haverd, E. A. King, M. Paget, and C. M. Trudinger. 2009. *Australian Water Availability Project (AWAP): CSIRO Marine and Atmospheric Research Component: Final Report for Phase 3.* Canberra: Bureau of Meteorology and Commonwealth Scientific and Industrial Research Organisation.

Van Dijk, A. I. J. M. 2010. *The Australian Water Resources Assessment System.* Technical Report 3. Landscape Model (version 5.0) Technical Description. Water for a Healthy Country National Research Flagship. Canberra: Commonwealth Scientific and Industrial Research Organisation.

Van Dijk, A. I. J. M., J. M. Kirby, Z. Paydar, G. Podger, M. Mainuddin, S. Marvanek, and J. Pena-Arancibia. 2008. *Uncertainty in River Modelling across the Murray-Darling Basin.* Report to the Australian Government from the CSIRO Murray-Darling Basin Sustainable Yields Project. Canberra: Commonwealth Scientific and Industrial Research Organisation.

Van Dijk, A. I. J. M., and L. J. Renzullo. 2011. "Water Resource Monitoring Systems and the Role of Satellite Observations." *Hydrology and Earth System Sciences* 15 (January): 39–55.

Van Dijk, A. I. J. M., and G. Warren. 2010. *The Australian Water Resources Assessment System.* Technical Report 4. Landscape Model (version 0.5) Evaluation against Observations. Canberra: Commonwealth Scientific and Industrial Research Organisation.

Wang, J., Y. Hong, L. Li, J. J. Gourley, S. I. Khan, K. K. Yilmaz, R. F. Adler, F. S. Policelli, S. Habib, D. Irwin, A. S. Limaye, T. Korme, and L. Okello. 2011. "The Coupled Routing and Excess Storage (CREST) Distributed Hydrological Model." *Hydrological Sciences Journal* 56 (1): 84–98.

Xia, Y., K. Mitchell, M. Ek, B. Cosgrove, J. Sheffield, L. Luo, C. Alonge, H. Wei, J. Meng, B. Livneh, Q. Duan, and D. Lohmann. 2012. "Continental-Scale Water and Energy Flux Analysis and Validation for North American Land Data Assimilation System Project Phase 2 (NLDAS-2): 2. Validation of Model-Simulated Streamflow." *Journal of Geophysical Research: Atmospheres* 117 (D3): 3110.

Xia, Y., K. Mitchell, M. Ek, J. Sheffield, B. Cosgrove, E. Wood, L. Luo, C. Alonge, H. Wei, J. Meng, B. Livneh, D. Lettenmaier, V. Koren, Q. Duan, K. Mo, Y. Fan, and D. Mocko. 2012. "Continental-Scale Water and Energy Flux Analysis and Validation for the North American Land Data Assimilation System Project Phase 2 (NLDAS-2): 1. Intercomparison and Application of Model Products." *Journal of Geophysical Research: Atmospheres* 117 (D3): 3109.

Yang, J., L. Jiang, J. Shi, S. Wu, R. Sun, and H. Yang. 2014. "Monitoring Snow Cover Using Chinese Meteorological Satellite Data over China." *Remote Sensing of Environment* 143 (March 5): 192–203.

Index